RELIGIOUS WRITER'S MARKET-PLACE

The definitive sourcebook— wholly revised and updated

by William H. Gentz

Running Press
Philadelphia, Pennsylvania

9 8 7 6 5 4 3 2 1

Digit on the right indicates the number of this printing.

Library of Congress Cataloging in Publishing Data:
Main entry under title:
Religious writer's marketplace.
 Bibliography: p.
 Includes index.
 1. Religious literature—Publication and distribution—United States—Directories. 2. Religious literature—Publication and distribution—Canada—Directories. 3. Religious newspapers and periodicals—United States—Directories. 4. Religious newspapers and periodicals—Canada—Directories. 5. Religious literature—Authorship—Handbooks, manuals, etc. I. Gentz, William H., 1918-
Z479.R44 1985   070.5'0973   84-27691

ISBN: 0-89471-305-1

Cover design by Toby Schmidt.
Typography: Garth by rci, Philadelphia, PA.
Printed by Port City Press, Baltimore, MD.

This book can be ordered by mail from the publisher. Please include $1.50 for postage. **But try your bookstore first.** Running Press Book Publishers, 125 South 22nd Street, Philadelphia, Pennsylvania 19103.

◄CONTENTS◄

◄AN INVITATION► TO READERS

We have made every effort to make this new edition of *Religious Writer's Marketplace* as accurate and up-to-date as possible—even going so far as to make changes and additions in the last galley proofs being sent to the printer.

Inevitably, however, periodicals—and even publishers—come and go. Editors frequently change positions. Local writers' groups dissolve, and new ones are constantly being founded. And in addition, more and more resources and other guides are becoming available to religious writers. And so, to keep ourselves abreast in all of these many areas, we at Running Press welcome your assistance.

As we continue to update material in preparation for the next edition of *Religious Writer's Marketplace,* we will deeply appreciate receiving your corrections, additions, and suggestions. Please write Department E, Running Press, 125 South 22nd Street, Philadelphia, PA 19103.

◄ACKNOWLEDGMENTS◄

We are indebted to hundreds of editors, publishers, and editorial staff members who have contributed information about the religious periodicals and publishers of books listed in this volume, as well as the incidental information included in several sections.

Special acknowledgment should be made to the following, who made major contributions to the book: Lionel Koppman, who designed the questionnaire and supervised the writing of the entries in Chapter Four; Cecil Murphey, who wrote the helpful foreword; Sally Stuart, who shared with us her lists of markets for religious writing and collected the information on the more than one hundred writers' groups in Chapter Six, and Geri Hess Mitsch for the writing of Chapter Seven.

We also want to thank the following who contributed material in their special fields of expertise: Barbara Uittenbogaard on writing for the local church, Patti Garr on marketing religious poetry, Larry Neagle on creating cartoons, K. Maynard Head on writing for newspapers and syndicates, E. Jane Mall on self-publishing, Norman Rohrer for the foreword to Chapter Six, and Birdie Etchison and Marian Brincken Forschler for their items from *Christian Writer's Newsletter* republished here.

In addition, we are grateful to the staff of Running Press for sponsoring this second edition of this book, carefully studying the questionnaires, writing the entries, editing the manuscript and proofs, and distributing the book to religious writers everywhere.

–W.H.G.

◄*I CORINTHIANS 13*◄
FOR WRITERS

Though I've taken ten years of English and six writing courses, attended every writer's conference within 200 miles, and know fifty writers and twelve editors, if I have not love, my writing will be hollow and shallow.

Though I write five hours a day, study *Writer's Market* endlessly, and sell eighty percent of what I write, if I have not love, I am nothing.

Though I tithe my sales, donate book reviews to my church newsletter, host a critique group regularly, praise my fellow writers' work, study the Bible and books on writing diligently, and pray for God's guidance over my pen—if I have not love, it doesn't mean a thing.

Love doesn't get jealous when another writer sells to *Guideposts.*

Love doesn't show off a $3,500 check from *Reader's Digest* for a sale to "Drama In Real Life."

Love is not rude to those who only talk about writing and are too slothful to work or polish their skills.

Love is gracious when the editor loses your manuscript.

Love is not happy when a fellow writer's book fails to sell.

Love keeps on loving editors through rejections and soiled manuscripts.

Love isn't thwarted by interruptions of writing schedules, writer's block, or harsh criticism.

Love doesn't get so busy writing that there isn't time for God, family, and friends.

Love never fails. Whether you have knowledge of article forms and strong verbs, you'll forget to use them. Whether your manuscripts are long or short, some will be rejected. Whether you need payment or not, you won't get as much as you deserve. But love is never forgotten, and needs no recompense.

And now abide faith, hope, and love—these three; but the greatest of these is genuine love that keeps on loving God, family, editors, other writers, and himself because of the miracles God performs in us.

–Marian Brincken Forschler
Renton, Washington

◢FOREWORD◣

Early in my writing career, I learned that writers have two basic choices in writing for publication. They can write what they want, give it the slant they wish, and make it as long or as short as they desire. Once their manuscript is completed, they then have to discover a publisher who seems right for it.

The second approach reverses the process. Writers study a particular publisher, then attempt to tailor their writing to that company's guidelines.

I won't debate the issue of which approach is right or better, because I have gone both ways. But now that I am publishing just about everything that I write, I can look back in amusement at my early marketing mistakes. At the age of 24, I wrote a religious book that probably never should have been printed (it wasn't). But at least I sent the manuscript to a publisher of religious books.

Almost a decade later, when I had learned a little about writing and mailed off an article, the editor sent me a check within two weeks. My next article, to a different magazine, also sold, along with my third and fourth pieces. But then I received several rejections before I sold anything else.

After two years of writing, I finally learned a few lessons. First, my lack of selling had little to do with my technique, style, or ability. I simply didn't understand how to market my manuscripts. Once I realized the problem, I worked at solving it and eventually I learned how to sell my writing and receive those nice checks in the mail. So can you! I don't think there are any real secrets to successful marketing. It's largely a matter of putting energy and time into obeying one of the first rules that professional writers tell students: *Know Your Market*.

In the beginning I learned to sell more by intuition than by analytical thinking. I read widely, asked questions, prayed about my writing, and kept sending out the manila envelopes with SASE's. But after I had sold at least a dozen articles, as well as my first book, I realized that I had figured out how to market my writing! I had consciously analyzed what I had done so that my material sold.

Over the years, I've asked editors about the kinds of submissions they get—especially the ones they reject. While publishers have dozens of reasons for not accepting an article, one thing I hear often goes like this: "They have no idea what kind of magazine we put out."

I suspect that most nonselling writers have no idea what it means to "know their markets." Most professionals emphasize knowledge of the markets, and rightly so—then we wonder if the newcomers bothered to listen. Or perhaps many writers prefer to take the lazy path and won't put the effort into finding the answer. Another possibility is that many of us who sell regularly may not know why we sell and, therefore, we don't know how to explain marketing to others.

For years I have used the annual *Writer's Market,* which offers immense help in learning about new markets for my materials. Later I discovered the *Religious Writer's Marketplace,* which proved even more helpful because I specialize in the religious-inspirational market.

Hearing of the new edition delighted me for several reasons. First, because *Religious Writer's Marketplace* provides the best information on the religious markets. In using it, I discovered that it listed magazines I couldn't find in other publications. For example, I opened the 1984 edition of *Writer's Market* and under "G" they gave me four magazines. In *Religious Writer's Marketplace,* I found seven. Under "P" *Religious Writer's Marketplace* scored fifteen to the other listing of eight.

Second, *Religious Writer's Marketplace* gives more detailed information about the magazines and book publishers listed. Since the author specializes in this field, I would expect more detailed information—and I get it.

Third, as a writer in the religious-inspirational field, I realized that, like two computers that interface, we spoke the same language. *Writer's Market* appeals to a broad spectrum of writers. While avoiding jargon, entries in *Religious Writer's Marketplace* use the language of the religious world. By itself, this book can't possibly tell writers everything they need to know about a specific publication or publisher. But it does give enough information so that I know if I want to investigate further.

When I purchased the first edition of *Religious Writer's Marketplace,* I read through the entire section "Writing for Religious Periodicals," and coded entries so that I would not have to reread every blurb later. Also I have drawn a large X over half a dozen entries because I find my theology incompatible with theirs and choose not to consider that market. In the margins of my book I note publishers with a distinctive denominational perspective.

How else can *Religious Writer's Marketplace* help writers? I frequently flip through it, pausing to read entries I previously overlooked, sometimes even underlining items. For instance, I am now a full-time writer, and if a magazine pays in copies only, I choose not to send them anything. If I find two possible markets, but one pays two cents a word and the other offers five cents, you know my decision on that one! Occasionally I'll find a publication listed that either I've never heard of or one I've not seriously considered before.

When Bill Gentz asked me to write this foreword, he said, "You're a person who studies markets and has had success with your writing because of it." I've never had any inside information or developed secret strategies that others can't also develop. Some people won't pay much attention to the suggestions here because marketing demands work and patience. It's not always easy to know where to send manuscripts. But as any selling writer can tell you, it's worth making the effort. It's that putting in of extra effort and trying just a little harder that makes a writer a professional.

—Cecil Murphey
Decatur, Georgia

◂A NOTE ON ALPHABETIZING▸

In all of the listings in this book, we follow strict letter-by-letter alphabetization for the names of publishers and periodicals—with one exception: When the name of a publisher is that of a person, we follow the rule used by *Literary Market Place* and other reference guides in alphabetizing by last name—as if the entry were a name in the telephone directory. For example, you'll find Thomas Nelson Publishers under *N*, David C. Cook Publishing Company under *C*, and John Knox Press under *K*. When in doubt, consult the indices at the back of this book.

·ONE·

How to Use This Book

Like its predecessor, this second edition of *Religious Writer's Marketplace* is a book about markets, about *where* religious writing can be published. It is not a guidebook about the *how* of religious writing, although a careful reading of the material in this book will give you much information about how to find help in improving your writing technique. And, of course, there is much information throughout the book on how to market your writing.

Neither is this a book about the *why* of religious writing. Perhaps more than in any other field of writing, religious authors need to be inspired to their task. They need to feel compelled to write, to tell the story, to relay the truths about God's world as they see them. The inspiration to do that comes primarily from sources other than books of this kind. Writers who study this book carefully will be inspired by the sheer numbers of opportunities that lie before them, but the motivation to write must come from other sources of inspiration.

This book, then, attempts primarily to answer the *where* in the writer's life. Where can markets for publishing be found? Where can one get extra help in writing? Where can one write for aid in the process?

Every writer, the religious author no less, wants to be published. There is not much point in putting words on paper (except perhaps for the therapy involved) unless someone reads those words in print in a book, magazine, journal or newspaper. This book is the answer to the need among the increasing numbers of religious writers for up-to-date and detailed information, all in one place, about the markets that exist.

There is little doubt that religious writing is a burgeoning field. There are evidences of this everywhere! The sheer numbers of religious books being produced each year and the numbers of religious periodicals in print are staggering. *Religious Books and Serials in Print,* published by Bowker (New York, NY) contains information on all religious publications in print in the United States and Canada. That volume uses more than a thousand pages, each with four columns of very fine print, just to list all of the books and periodicals by title, author, and subject.

To gather information for this book's first edition, questionnaires were sent to more than 1,000 outlets for religious writing. Since the publication of that book, I have kept month-by-month records of changes of information, new publishers, and publications being established and others going out of business. For this second edition, new questionnaires with requests for new and up-to-date information were again sent to these same publishers. In addition some 300 new sources were contacted. The expanded information received is contained in this edition.

The challenge lies ahead in finding herein the markets you want. Let's look briefly at what the book contains and how best to find and make use of the information you need.

The major portion of this book—Chapters Two, Three, and Four—is devoted to publishers and publications with which you will want to become acquainted. Note, first, the construction of the entries. Most (except for the very brief ones) are made up of three paragraphs:

> **1.** *The first paragraph* gives you the important statistical information about the entry: The name and address and phone number (where available) of the periodical or publisher, the name of the chief editor and others to whom manuscripts can be sent and the name of the sponsoring group or church, if this information is vital. Then, there is a brief characterization of the publisher or publication, the circulation in the case of a periodical, the number of books per year in the case of a book publisher.
>
> **2.** *The second paragraph* brings you more detailed information about the publisher or publication. It tells you something of the audience that it aims at, the publisher's purpose, the theological position, the age group of the readers, and the kind of material being sought. In many cases, there are lists of successful titles or well-received articles. These, too, will give you a clue about the publisher or publication. Wherever we quote a publisher or editor directly, quotation marks surround those sentences or phrases.
>
> **3.** *The third paragraph* gives you the all-important information about the mechanics of submitting material to each particular publisher. How long is the average article or book? Does the publisher want queries first or only finished manuscripts? Are sample copies or author's guidelines available? What other special instructions does the publisher have for authors? Is there any payment for submissions? How much and how soon? In the case of book publishers, some indication of the percentage of royalties and the amount of advances is given wherever possible. How soon does the publisher report on submissions?

Just browsing through these entries will give you many ideas about where and how to send the material you are writing. But I suggest that you begin by studying the indexes in the back of the book, where you will find publishers and periodicals listed according to the characteristics of their publishing or their denominational affiliations. There is also a listing of the entries according to the kinds of material the publishers accept. If you are a poet, for example, you will find it much easier to look up "poetry" in the index than to go through the pages of entries looking for poetry publishers. The indexes of this book will be your best friend each time you consult the lists for a particular need. Use them!

In the planning stages of the first edition of this book, we decided to list Jewish markets separately in Chapter Four. Since the needs, the kinds of materials sought, and the terminology used are usually different from those in the entries for the Christian market, a separate questionnaire was sent for both editions to Jewish periodicals and publishers of Judaica. Lionel Koppman, director of public information for the Jewish Welfare Board (JWB) and an author of several books, devised the questionnaire and supervised the writing of the entries in the Jewish chapter.

Increasingly, many publishers, primarily concerned with publishing for the Christian market, are adding books of Jewish interest to their lists. In these cases we have entered their names in both sections.

Some of the information submitted by publishers is not included here—namely the basics that every writer should know about how to submit material to a publisher. Yet these concerns are mentioned so often in writers' guidelines that all indications are that many writers either are unaware of them or ignore them. Such directions as "be sure to include SASE (self-addressed, stamped envelope) or your manuscript will not be returned," are repeated often. Again this is not primarily a book about the "how" of religious writing; that you should learn from other volumes or from studying the guidelines provided by publishers. We suggest you also reread the excellent foreword by Cecil Murphey, a successful, full-time freelance writer who has some good advice on procedures of marketing.

Once you have made yourself familiar with what is contained in the entries and learned how to use the indexes to find your way through them, you will also want to get acquainted with the many other suggestions offered to writers in Chapters Five, Six, and Seven. In Chapter Five you will find a number of ideas for branching out into other fields of writing. This chapter is also greatly expanded in this second edition. Not all of religious writing is contained in books and periodicals. There are dozens of other opportunities in greeting cards, curriculum, music, radio and T.V., as well as in writing for nonprofit religious organizations and your own church or synagogue. In addition, this chapter suggests some of the hundreds of regional religious periodicals that are close to your home and for whom you may well want to write. We list names and addresses of those under the supervision of four denominations who have the most extensive network, but we urge you to seek other opportunities or make some for yourself.

In Chapter Six you will find information you can use that will be of great help to you in your writing. Listed are opportunities for gaining new skills, broadening your concepts, and finding new markets through local and regional writers' groups, writers' conferences, newsletters, correspondence courses, cassette training programs, and a host of books—all prepared for the religious writer. Again, the number of these opportunities has greatly expanded in the years since the first edition of this book. For example, the number of writers' groups has multiplied more than five times! Here are many opportunities to read, study, and improve as you write as well as to compare notes with others on where to find markets for your writing.

In Chapter Seven you will find some good direction on how to go about the "business" of marketing—keeping files, keeping the manuscripts circulating, etc., so that you make the most of the opportunities that are out there.

In all, there are more than 1,500 names and addresses in this book—publishers, publications, agencies, conferences, workshops, newsletters—all waiting to be used by you as you pursue your intention to become a *well-published* religious writer.

·TWO·
Writing for Religious Periodicals

In this chapter you will find listed periodicals that publish Christian religious material. These include magazines (weekly, semi-monthly, monthly, or bimonthly), journals (mostly quarterlies), yearbooks, newspapers, newsletters, take-home story papers, and other types of periodicals whose formats are difficult to categorize.

Among these, there is a great variety, from general magazines whose circulation is more than a million, down to those published for specialized markets of only a few hundred. Some magazines listed here pay little, and still others pay their contributors nothing. Because many religious writers want to be published but are not overly anxious about payment, we have included the names of every periodical that returned our widely distributed questionnaire.

There is variety, too, in the audiences for whom these periodicals are published. Some are broad and general, others limited and very specialized. Some are for adults only; some are for children, young readers, or senior citizens; and many are for a general readership that includes all of these. In each of the entries, you will find information about who their readers are.

We have also tried to indicate the theological emphasis of each periodical, as given by the editor. Some are Roman Catholic, some appeal only to Evangelicals, some to liberals, some to mainline Protestants, some to all Christians. Certain periodicals are published by denominational houses primarily for their own church members. Others, published by independent houses, cross denominational lines. A few publications also cross faith lines and are intended for both Christian and Jewish readers. In such cases, we have listed the publication in Chapter Four, "Writing for the Jewish Market," as well.

Publications are listed here in strictly alphabetical order, by title. You may want to page through the chapter and get an overall view of the many kinds of markets there are for your writing. But if you have some specific kind of article or a specific market in mind, you will want to consult the indexes in the back of this book, where you will find publications listed under both their sponsorship and major emphasis, as well as under the kinds of materials they print—fiction, poetry, photos, etc.

For writers eager to discover the correct markets for their material, probably the most useful advice we can give is to request sample copies of publications and author's guidelines. Studied carefully, these will help immeasurably in determining where you should send which kind of writing. Most writers who are serious about their craft keep a file or notebook for this information and consult it frequently. For some suggestions on these procedures, consult Chapter Seven.

In submitting material to periodicals, remember that they are dated and often contain material that is seasonal in nature. Keep this in mind and also remember that periodicals are planned well ahead of time. You should submit seasonal material from six months to a year in advance of the season in which it is to be used.

Some periodicals have very specific objectives or want their contributors to know their stated purposes. In these instances, we have quoted directly either from the guidelines or from questionnaires filled out by the periodical staff member, and we have put quotation marks around such material.

Many other requests made by editors of periodicals are not repeated in the individual listings. These are the kinds of things that any writer ought to know, or are common practice among publishers. The following list of directions is a composite of the instructions given on most author's guidelines:

- Use a good grade of bond paper, 8½ by 11 inches.
- Type all manuscripts, double-spaced, on one side of the paper only.
- Leave at least a one-inch margin on all sides.
- If you must make corrections on a typewritten manuscript, make them in ordinary lead pencil—not ink.
- Be consistent in your use of punctuation, capitalization, and other rules of style and grammar.
- Follow the standard style rules as far as possible. Consult a good style book, such as the *Chicago Manual of Style* or *Words Into Type*.
- Be accurate and complete in citations, bibliographies, and permissions lists.
- Check all quotations against the original (including Bible quotations) at the manuscript stage.
- In a brief covering letter, give a few facts about yourself and your qualifications for writing the manuscript.
- Enclose a SASE (self-addressed, stamped envelope) for return of the manuscript if it is not used, and when requesting materials (e.g., free copies, author's guidelines) to be sent to you.

As stated previously in this book, serious writers of religious material will do everything possible to be professional—not only in the way they write, but also in the way they submit written material to the editor or publisher. You will also want to study the new copyright law or read articles in books or newsletters that inform you of what rights you have over your material. Then be as careful as possible to follow the directions given by the editor, and check everything before sending it on to be read and evaluated for publication.

Birdie Etchison, a freelance writer from Portland, Oregon, wrote a humorous (yet serious) analysis for the *Christian Writers Newsletter* of the things to avoid in submitting material to magazines. We quote from it here, with her permission. In her article entitled, ''I Can't Believe I Did It!'' this writer warns us:

I can't believe I sent out my manuscript without pages 4 and 5, but I found them on top of my ''in and out'' file when I got home from the Post Office. *HINT: Make a quick last-minute check of page numbers.*

I can't believe I sent the same story twice within a year to the same editor. A foul-up in my bookkeeping was responsible. *HINT: Keep a cross-file of titles, subjects, and editors.*

I can't believe I sent that story out with a word missing on page 2. I remember whiting out the mistake, but forgetting to make the correction. *HINT: Have some other person check your manuscript for errors.*

I can't believe I sent out a manuscript with a rejection slip from another editor enclosed. Someone had a good chuckle! *HINT: Doublecheck everything.*

Of course no reader (or writer) of this book would make such foolish mistakes. Or would we? Or have we? In spite of human failings and unwitting errors, editors are anxious to hear from freelance writers. In fact, they depend on you to provide them with the material they need. Read on and get acquainted with the many editors and publishers of periodicals who are waiting to hear from you.

ACCENT ON YOUTH, United Methodist Publishing House, 201 Eighth Avenue South, Nashville, TN 37202. (615) 749–6225. A magazine published monthly (except September) for young teens in the United Methodist Church.
□*Accent On Youth* seeks to communicate to youth in early adolescence in ways that help them discover meanings in today's changing world that are consistent with Christian values. Areas of concern include self-guidance, health, science and the natural world, biblical and theological issues—especially activities carried on by early teen church and nonchurch groups; unique forms of church ministries; seasonal features, worship. Also uses mood pieces, teen activities, photo features and cartoons.
　　Articles should be 800 to 1,200 words; short stories 1,500 to 2,000 words. Free sample copies and writer's guidelines available. Photographs should be 8″ by 10″ black-and-white glossies or color transparencies. Puzzles should be slanted to ages 12 through 14; should have large, perfectly formed capital letters, preferably drawn in India ink. Wants unfinished puzzle as well as answer grid for reproduction. Pays on acceptance: 3¢ per word, and up. Reports in 2 to 3 months.

ACTION (formerly *Discovery*), 999 College Avenue, Winona Lake, IN 46590. (219) 267–7161. Vera Bethel, Editor. An 8-page weekly digest take-home paper for evangelical children published by the Free Methodist Church with a national distribution of 35,000.
□*Action* ordinarily publishes puzzles on Bible themes and fiction about activities a typical 5th-grader would engage in, showing action, crises, and decision-making appropriate to the age level—not too heroic, in other words. Also interested in nonfiction, poetry, and photos and illustrations with articles.
　　Articles should be 300 to 800 words, 1,000 to 1,500 for fiction. Sample copy and author's guidelines available. Pays on acceptance: 2¢ per word for stories, 25¢ per line for poetry. Reports in 4 weeks.

ACTION INFORMATION, c/o the Alban Institute, Inc., Mount St. Alban, Washington, DC 20016. (202) 244–7320. Founded 1976. Celia A. Hahn, Director of Publications. A bimonthly journal.
□*Action Information* prints articles designed to help, support, and guide pastors of various denominations. Well-received articles: "Ten Models of Ordained Ministry" by Margaret Fletcher, "The Minister's Wife—Does She Have Religious Liberty?" by Ann Raymond, "The Vulnerability of Clergy" by Roy Oswald.
　　Sample copies available for $2.50 each. Query letters desirable. Reports in 4 weeks.

ADVANCE, 1445 Boonville Avenue, Springfield, MO 65802. (417) 862–2781, extension 1462. Gwen Jones, Editor. A 40-page monthly professional magazine published by the Assemblies of God.
□*Advance* is published for a clerical audience, most of whom are associated with the Assemblies of God Church and "interested in articles slanted to ministers on preaching, doctrine, practice, etc.; sermon outlines (not sermons); and how-to-do-it features." Serves as a vehicle of communication between national headquarters department and the local churches, consolidating in one unit promotional and program materials, posters, church administration aids, and ministerial helps. Much of the material is departmentally written or assigned. A limited amount of freelance material accepted,

especially fresh and creative sermon ideas, outlines, and how-to suggestions.

Articles should be 800 to 1,000 words. Sample copy and author's guidelines available. Pays 3¢ per word, on acceptance. Reports within 1 week.

ADVENT CHRISTIAN WITNESS, P.O. Box 23152, Charlotte, NC 28212. (704) 545–6161. Founded 1952. Robert J. Mayer, Editor-in-Chief. A 32-page monthly magazine sponsored by Advent Christian General Conference, with a circulation of 5,000 throughout the U.S. and the eastern Canadian provinces.

□*Advent Christian Witness* seeks "human interest, Christian discipleship, and contemporary issues," and prints fiction, articles, interviews, Bible study, some theology, and photos and illustrations. Well-received articles: "Oh, God, Don't Let Her Die," a Christian pastor's struggle with the complications of his daughter's birth; and a series of four articles on the Charismatic movement. Readers are adults, both clergy and lay members of the Advent Christians.

Articles should be between 500 and 700 words. "We are always looking for good photo essays, and for articles showing how God is working through circumstances and situations in people's lives." Author's guidelines and sample copies available. Will consider reprints. "For freelance contributions we normally pay $10 for 200 to 500 words, $20 for 500 to 700 words, and $25 thereafter, on acceptance." Reports in 4 weeks.

AGAIN, Conciliar Press, P.O. Box 106, Mt. Hermon, CA 95041. (408) 338–3644. Founded 1977. Weldon M. Hardenbrook, Editor. A 36-page quarterly magazine sponsored by the Evangelical Orthodox Church, P.O. Box 1325, Goleta, CA 93116. National circulation of 3,000.

□*AGAIN* prints articles, poetry, interviews, photos and illustrations, church history, theology, and a "challenge to return to orthodox faith. Our goal is to produce the finest, concise publication that calls people back to Orthodoxy. Endeavor to keep that in mind as you write." Well-received articles: "Infant Baptism: Myth or Reality?"; "What's in a Name?"; "Grief," in two parts. Readers are children, youth, and adults, both clergy and lay members.

Articles should be between 1,500 and 2,000 words, "written on a popular but not simplistic Christian faith as it is expressed in the 20th century. Must seek to balance historic orthodoxy with a proper evangelical spirit." Sample copy and concise guidelines available. Particularly interested in "personal experiences of those who have returned to the historic sacramental Orthodox faith." Query letters required; will consider reprints. Pays per article, on publication. Reports in 4 weeks.

AGLOW MAGAZINE, P.O. Box I, Lynnwood, WA 98046–1557. (206) 775–7282. Gwen Weising, Editor. A 24-page bimonthly magazine published by Aglow Publications, a ministry of Women's Aglow Fellowship International, with an international distribution of 40,000.

□*Aglow* is for Christian women and looks for first-person articles written for women and by women of all ages. Articles should be either a testimony of, or a teaching about, Jesus as Savior, as Baptizer in the Holy Spirit, as Healer, or as Strengthener. Also accepts as-told-to articles.

Articles should be 1,000 to 2,000 words. Sample copy and author's guidelines available. Pays on acceptance; complimentary copies of the published work are sent to authors. Reports in 3 to 5 weeks.

ALIVE! FOR YOUNG TEENS, Box 179, St. Louis, MO 63166. (314) 371–6900. Jerry O'Malley and Michael Dixon, Editors. A 32-page monthly magazine sponsored by the Christian Board of Publication, Christian Church (Disciples), with a national distribution of 14,000.

□*Alive!* is for 12- to 15-year-olds in several mainline Protestant denominations. Materials should deal with concerns and situations peculiar to this age group: interesting youth, church youth groups, projects, and activities. Prints fiction, essays, photo features, poetry, cartoons, puzzles, riddles, tongue-twisters, and daffy definitions. "In all areas, we give special consideration to submissions of usable quality from 12- to 15-year-olds. Those in this age range should include their ages with their submissions."

Articles should be 800 to 1,000 words; fiction, up to 1,200 words. Photo features use 6 to 10 photos and brief copy of interest to junior high youth. Submit photos in batches. Poetry should be no longer than 20 lines. Query letters desirable; some material staff-assigned. Sample copies are $1.00 to cover postage and handling; author's guidelines available. Pays, on publication, usually 3¢ per word; up to $10 each for photos, 25¢ per line for poetry; $8 for cartoons. Payment on puzzles, riddles, etc. varies according to material, up to $10. Reports on submissions within 1 month, usually sooner.

ALIVE NOW, 1908 Grand Avenue, Nashville, TN 37202. (615) 327-2700. Mary Ruth Coffman, Editor. A 64-page magazine published 6 times a year by The Upper Room, United Methodist Church, with a national distribution of 60,000.
□*Alive Now* looks for thought-provoking material for devotional reflection that fits into a thematic approach planned for each issue. Particularly needs material on family and interpersonal relationships, and on applying biblical perspective to everyday life. Reading audience consists of youth, general lay adults, of mixed mainline Protestant denominations. Publishes short fiction, nonfiction, poetry, humor, devotional thought pieces, parables, and photos.

Articles should be short, poetic in general, 100 to 250 words. Sample copy and author's guidelines available. Pays $5 to $30 per article, on publication. Reports in 4 to 8 weeks, on the average.

THE ALLIANCE TEACHER, 3825 Hartzdale Drive, Camp Hill, PA 17011. Founded 1955. Anne D. Gallaher, Editor. A 16-page quarterly magazine sponsored by the Christian and Missionary Alliance, Box C, Nyack, NY 10960. National circulation of 3,000.
□*The Alliance Teacher* prints "how-to articles from Sunday School teachers and workshop articles to sustain their enthusiasm and achievement." Also prints profiles, interviews, photos and illustrations. Well-received articles: "Child Abuse: The Church's Concern," "Teaching the Single-Parent Child," "How to Develop a Handicapped Ministry." Readers are adults, both clergy and lay members of all Protestant denominations.

Articles generally run 1,000 to 1,500 words. Guidelines and sample copy available. Particularly interested in "articles dealing with current trends in society and how they are affecting the Sunday School." Query letters desirable; will consider reprints. Pays $15.00 remuneration for each article, on publication. Reports in 2 weeks.

THE ALLIANCE WITNESS, P.O. Box C, Nyack, NY 10960. (914) 353-0750. Maurice R. Irvin, Editor; Doug Wicks, Managing Editor. The official biweekly organ of the Christian and Missionary Alliance churches, with an international distribution of 54,000.
□*The Alliance Witness'*s writers "are people who have a message to communicate and who know that acceptance by us assures them of a wide and appreciative audience." Query letters welcome. By policy, does not pay for manuscripts submitted voluntarily, "though they get our careful, prayerful consideration."

THE A.M.E. CHRISTIAN RECORDER, 500 Eighth Avenue South, Nashville, TN 37203, or P.O. Box 24730, Nashville, TN 37202. (615) 256-8548. Rev. Robert H. Reid, Jr., Editor. An 8-page biweekly newspaper, the official publication of the African Methodist Episcopal Church, with a national distribution.
□*The A.M.E. Christian Recorder* is interested in news of the church world generally, but especially as it applies to blacks and the A.M.E. Church. Most interested in material dealing with human concerns as related to the Christian faith. Written for adults—both clergy and laity. Welcomes photos illustrating the articles.

Sample copies available. Does not pay for material used.

THE A.M.E. CHURCH REVIEW, 468 Lincoln Drive N.W., Atlanta, GA 30318. (404) 794–4991. William D. Johnson, Editor-Manager. An 80- to 100-page quarterly magazine with a national distribution.
□*The A.M.E. Church Review* is published for an audience of youth and adults, but mostly clergy, of a black mainline Protestant denomination. Uses nonfiction, poetry, stories of people, and photos and illustrations. Special interest in material about Africa, South America, Hawaii, and the Caribbean.
   Articles should be 1,500 to 2,000 words. Query letters welcome. Sample copy and author's guidelines available. Pays on acceptance: by the word to a maximum of $20. Reports in 1 or 2 months.

AMERICA, 106 West 56th Street, New York, NY 10019. (212) 581–4640. George N. Hunt, S.J., Editor. A 24- to 32-page weekly magazine, sponsored by the Jesuit Order, with a national distribution of 40,000.
□*America* is published for an adult, general lay reader audience of primarily Roman Catholics with a "liberal" approach to the problems of society and the church. Material should "develop an original analysis or interpretation with strong attention to ethical and religious values, or current events and ideas." Articles are nonfiction. Uses some poetry. Well-received subjects that demonstrate the areas of concern: how to pray, Indochinese refugees, American bishops in Central America, the spirituality of John Paul II. Runs frequent reviews, primarily of scholarly books, and semi-annual book issues.
   Articles should be 1,500 to 2,000 words (occasionally longer) and deal with the concerns of the magazine. Query letters not required. Sample copies and author's guidelines available. Material should be carefully researched and opinions documented. Pays on acceptance: $50 to $100 for articles, $7.50 to $25 for poems. Reports in 2 to 4 weeks.

ANGLICAN THEOLOGICAL REVIEW, 600 Haven Street, Evanston, IL 60201. (312) 328–9300. Rev. W. Taylor Stevenson, Editor. A 120-page quarterly journal with a national distribution and an international circulation of about 150.
□*Anglican Theological Review* is published primarily for an adult audience of scholars and clergy of a mixed, but mainly liberal, mainline Protestant background. Articles are all nonfiction and deal with theological topics. "We consider articles in general areas of speculative and applied theology as well as some historical theology and other theological disciplines. We will review all manuscripts submitted to us which conform to our commitment to recover the Christian tradition."
   Articles should be 5 to 30 pages, depending on the topic covered. Free samples are available on request. No payment for material used. Reports in 2 months.

ASPIRE MAGAZINE, 1819 East 14th Avenue, Denver, CO 80218. (303) 322–7730. Jeanne Pomranka, Editor. A 64-page monthly magazine, published by the Divine Science Federation International, with a national distribution of 1,200.
□*Aspire* is published for youth and adults, both clergy and laity, with a metaphysical background and interest. "An organ of Divine Science teaching, based on ancient truths and wisdom, but also including the newest discoveries in Truth. Readers are primarily New Thought students. We do not want 'churchiness' but material on man's relationship to God and his fellow man: eternal spiritual truth." Uses very little poetry.
   Articles should average 600 words; limit is 1,200. Sample copy and author's guidelines available on request; enclose 42¢ in stamps. Pays approximately 1¢ per word, on publication. Reports in 2 weeks.

THE ASSOCIATED REFORMED PRESBYTERIAN, One Cleveland Street, Greenville, SC 29601. Founded 1839. Ben Johnston, Editor. A 40-page monthly magazine, sponsored by the Associated Reformed Presbyterian Church. Circulation: 5,933; 95% in the southeastern U.S.
□*The Associated Reformed Presbyterian* prints fiction, nonfiction, humor, devotions, in-

terviews, photos and illustrations, theology, Bible study, and "news of interest to our denomination." Well-received were "Focus" issues of the magazine, on abortion, grief, prayer, pornography, and senior citizenhood. Readers include youth, adults, and senior citizens, both clergy and general lay readers.

Rarely uses freelance material; most articles are on assignment. Sample copy available. "We have an annual contest for writers of children's fiction; entries sought from January through March." Write for contest rules. Currently looking for a cartoonist with an appreciation of Reformed theology, to initiate a monthly cartoon or comic strip. Articles should be 500 to 1,500 words. Pays $20 to $50 per article, on acceptance. Query letter desirable; will consider reprints. Reports in 4 weeks.

AT EASE, 1445 Boonville Avenue, Springfield, MO 65802. (417) 862–2781. Lemuel D. McElyea, Editor. A 4-page bimonthly publication distributed free to military personnel by the Assemblies of God.
☐*At Ease* places a strong emphasis on evangelism and Christian development. Includes reports of Christian projects related to servicemen and articles to inform them of Assemblies of God ministries.

Freelance needs are for devotional articles of up to 400 words. If writer is unknown to Editor, a letter of introduction is appreciated. Author's guidelines available. Payment is usually 2¢ per word for first or all rights.

ATHLETES IN ACTION, Publications Department, Campus Crusade for Christ, Arrowhead Springs, CA 92414. (714) 886–5224, extension 332. John Carvalho, Editor. A 48-page quarterly magazine published by Campus Crusade for Christ.
☐*Athletes in Action* is published for an audience of evangelical youth and adults and a large general public interested in athletics. Most interested in stories of athletes, humor on athletic topics, and any other material dealing with athletics and evangelical interests. Wants "inspiring personality features that show the faith of well-known Christian athletes and stories on controversial issues in sports that invite a Christian response." All material must be written in a sportswriting style, lively but avoiding clichés, sensitive to both the evangelical community and the general public as well. Well-received articles: "Violence in Sports," "What Makes Tom Landry Smile?," "The Stainless Steelers."

Articles should be 1,300 to 1,700 words. Since articles must be in tune with special editorial needs, query letters are absolutely necessary. Most articles are initiated by the staff; better to write and give qualifications for writing and then be assigned a topic by the magazine. Sample copies available. Pays 10¢ per word, on publication.

BAPTIST LEADER, c/o American Baptist Educational Ministries, P.O. Box 851, Valley Forge, PA 19442–0851. (215) 768–2153. Linda Isham, Editor. Distribution: 14,000.
☐*Baptist Leader* focuses on practical how-to articles for the local church-school teachers and administrators.

Articles should be 1,200 to 1,600 words (or 2 printed pages), occasionally longer if topic requires it. Author's guidelines available. Manuscript should be typed, 50 characters per line (including space and punctuation), 25 lines to a page (four pages thusly typed equal one printed page). Send photographs whenever possible and allow space for their inclusion in the article.

THE BAPTIST WORLD, 1628 Sixteenth Street N.W., Washington, DC 20009. (202) 265–5027. Reinhold J. Kerstan, Editor. An 8-page quarterly circulated in 143 countries by the Baptist World Alliance.
☐*Baptist World* is published for an audience of scholars, clergy, and general lay readers. All material is either staff-written or written on assignment.

BIBLE ADVOCATE, P.O. Box 33677, Denver, CO 80233. (303) 452–7973. Jerry Griffin, Editor; F. P. Walter, Associate Editor. A 28-page monthly magazine published by the

General Conference of the Church of God (Seventh-Day), with an international circulation.

□*Bible Advocate* prints articles in the following categories: doctrinal, practical/ethical, contemporary, seasonal, devotional/inspirational, and consecrative. "Personal-interest stories are attractive to us." Audience is Protestant and evangelical, generally adult lay readers.

Articles should be 800 to 2,000 words; also uses series of articles. Query letters desired but not required. Sample copy available. Generally does not compensate monetarily for articles; does purchase photographic work. Reports in 30 days.

THE BIBLE NEWSLETTER, 1716 Spruce Street, Philadelphia, PA 19103. (215) 546–3696. Founded 1981. J. Randall Petersen, Managing Editor. An 8-page monthly newsletter sponsored by Evangelical Ministries, Inc. National circulation of 6,000.

□*The Bible Newsletter* prints devotions, Bible study, puzzles, and word studies as well as articles, "nothing more than 1,200 words." Well-received articles have been on archeology, nuclear war (and our fear of it), trends in biblical criticism, Bible curriculum for disabled children, Bible reading and prayer in public schools. Readers are general lay adults of an evangelical slant.

Material should "relate the Bible to today's world and to everyday life, with new insights into Scripture passages." Sample copy and writer's guidelines available. Particularly interested in puzzles, archeology field reports, and first-hand accounts of home Bible studies. Query letters desirable; no reprints. Pays $50 for a one-page (1,000-word) article, $20 to $30 for partial-page pieces, on publication. Reports in 3 weeks.

BIBLICAL ARCHEOLOGIST, 1053 LSA Building, University of Michigan, Ann Arbor, MI 48109. (313) 764–4475. David Noel Freedman, Editor. A 64-page quarterly journal published by the American Schools of Oriental Research, 126 Inman Street, Cambridge, MA 02139 with a national and overseas distribution of 9,500.

□*Biblical Archeologist* is the foremost journal in the field of biblical archeology, designed to illuminate biblical backgrounds, customs, and people in the light of the most recent archeological research. Seeks to "provide the general reader with an accurate, scholarly, yet easily understandable account of archeological discoveries and their bearing on the biblical heritage." Aimed at an audience of adult scholars, clergy, and general lay readers of all denominational backgrounds. Heavily illustrated with photos, drawings, and maps.

Articles are generally 20 typewritten pages with a 50-50 division between text and illustrative material. Samples of the journal and guidelines are available upon request. The sponsoring organization supports archeological institutes all over the Mediterranean basin, thus has a direct pipeline to the field where archeology is most active. Many articles are staff-written. Ordinarily no payment for materials used.

BOOKSTORE JOURNAL, P.O. Box 200, Colorado Springs, CO 80901. (303) 576–7880. Cherie Rayburn, Editor. A 175-page (on the average) magazine published monthly (10 times a year) by the Christian Booksellers Association, with an international distribution of 7,500.

□*Bookstore Journal* is designed "to help Christian booksellers have a more effective ministry by improving their management and marketing skills." Major articles are about financial management, retail business procedures, and selling/marketing to consumers. Feature articles on Christian bookstores and suppliers and book reviews also appear regularly. Occasional articles about authors, artists, and their products; consumer-slanted articles seldom used. Readers fall into three categories: Christian booksellers, publishers or suppliers, and sales representatives. All material should be aimed at one or more of these groups.

Most articles assigned to people with expertise in business or bookstore management. Freelance writers used occasionally for reporting on industry events or for special assignments. Art and illustration ideas welcome, but final decision is made by the editors. Articles should average 1,200 words. Outlines acceptable, but completed manuscripts preferred. Sample copy and author's guidelines available. Payment on publication averages $100 per printed page; freelance assignments paid on a project basis. Reports in 40 days.

BREAD, 6401 The Paseo, Kansas City, MO 64132. (816) 333-7000. Gary Sivewright, Editor. A 34-page monthly youth magazine of the Church of the Nazarene, with a national distribution of 25,000.
☐*Bread* seeks articles that help a teenager apply basic biblical truth to everyday life; articles written in a way that shows that the writer understands how a teen thinks and feels. Particularly needs articles dealing with building positive dating relationships, "understanding who God is and how He is enough, developing a personal ministry, maintaining an effective prayer life." Prints fiction, nonfiction, stories of people, humor, and photos and illustrations. Well-received articles: "Overcoming Shyness," "Taking Care of Your Words," "Getting Along With Your Parents."
    Articles should be 1,200 to 1,500 words. Prefers to see complete manuscripts. Sample copy and author's guidelines available with SASE. Pays 3½¢ per word, on acceptance. Reports in 6 to 8 weeks.

THE BRETHREN EVANGELIST, 524 College Avenue, Ashland, OH 44805. (419) 289-2611. Richard C. Winfield, Editor. A 28-page monthly magazine published by The Brethren Publishing Company of The Brethren Church with a national distribution of 3,500.
☐*The Brethren Evangelist* seeks "to help our readers become effective disciples of Jesus Christ and responsible, active participants in the life, thought, and ministry of The Brethren Church." Prints articles dealing with all aspects of Christian life; for example, marriage, family, prayer, the devotional life, theology, Bible study, the church and its programs. Also likes articles about people and their victories in the Christian life.
    Articles should be 1,000 to 1,200 words; limit is 1,500 words. Query letters desirable but not required. Free samples and writer's packet available. Pays on publication approximately 2¢ per word. No set time on reporting on submissions; depends on press of other work.

BRIGADE LEADER, Box 150, Wheaton, IL 60189. (312) 665-0630. David R. Leigh, Editor; Sharon Long, Assistant Editor. A 32-page quarterly magazine of the Christian Service Brigade.
☐*Brigade Leader* "helps Christian men meet the needs of boys through Christian Service Brigade programs and in personal contact with boys; helps, inspires, and instructs the Christian man in every area of his life in order to be a better model of Christian manhood." Prints nonfiction and family-oriented stories, particularly ones dealing with father-son relations. Well-received articles: "Endurance in Leadership," "The Brigade Leader as Counselor," "Maximizing Your Evangelistic Potential." Readers are adults, clergy, and general lay readers of evangelical Protestant denominations.
    Articles average 1,200 words. Query letters only. Sample copies available for $1.50 each. Pays upon publication: $40 to $125 per article. Reports in 1 to 6 weeks.

CALL TO PRAYER, Box WGM, 3783 State Road 18E, Marion, IN 46952. (317) 664-7331. David B. Kellogg, Administrative Editor; Thomas H. Hermiz, Editor. A 16-page newspaper published 10 times a year with a national distribution of 40,000.
☐*Call to Prayer* is a national evangelical missionary newspaper that publishes articles from their missionaries only. No payment.

CAMPUS LIFE MAGAZINE, 465 Gundersen Drive, Carol Stream, IL 60187. (312) 260-6200. Gregg Lewis, Editor. A monthly magazine with a national distribution of 164,000.
☐*Campus Life* is for a readership in college and high school. "Though our readership is largely Christian, the magazine reflects the interests of all kids—music, bicycling,

photography, cars, and sports. The magazine is *not* overtly religious; the indirect style is intended to create a safety zone with our readers and to reflect our philosophy that God is interested in all of life. Therefore, we publish message stories side by side with general interest, humor, etc. The best manuscript for a freelancer to try to sell us would be a well-written first-person story (fiction or nonfiction) focusing on a common struggle young people face in any area of life—intellectual, emotional, social, physical, or spiritual. Most manuscripts that miss fail in quality of style. Since our style is distinctive, it is one of the biggest criteria in buying an article. Interested writers must therefore study *Campus Life* to get an understanding of our audience and style. Don't submit unless you have *at least* read the magazine."

Articles should be 500 to 3,000 words. Query or submit complete manuscript. Sample copy $2.00; guidelines free. Pays $100 to $250, on acceptance. Pays $50 for 8" by 10" black-and-white glossy photos, $90 minimum for color transparencies, $250 for cover photo. Buys one-time rights. Reports in 2 months.

CANADIAN CHURCHMAN, 600 Jarvis Street, Room 232, Toronto, Ontario M4Y 2J6, Canada. (416) 924–9192. Jerrold F. Hames, Editor. A 24- to 32-page monthly tabloid; published by the General Synod of the Anglican Church of Canada, with a distribution, mostly inside Canada, of 267,000.
□*Canadian Churchman* is aimed at adults—clergy, laity, mostly Anglicans, leaning toward a liberal, mainline Protestant tradition. Articles should be nonfiction, dealing with news and feature material about the church and its people or events of interest to them. Stories of people—mainly church people—desirable. Does not use poetry. Welcomes photos or illustrations.

Articles should be 600 to 1,500 words, but most articles are assigned. Query letters desirable, as very little unsolicited material is accepted. Sample copies available upon request. Also distributes calendars.

CATHEDRAL AGE, Mount St. Alban, Washington, DC 20016. (202) 537–6247. Nancy S. Montgomery, Editor. A 32-page magazine, published quarterly, for 22,000 subscribers.
□*Cathedral Age,* under the aegis of the National Cathedral (Episcopal) in Washington, is designed to tell the stories of cathedrals all over the world. Welcomes news and feature articles about what is happening to and in cathedrals and their programs. Audience aimed at is mostly mainline Protestant, some youth but largely adults, including scholars, clergy, and laity of all denominations.

Freelance submissions on the subject of cathedrals and their programs are welcome. Query letters essential. Sample copy available on request. Articles should be aimed at a mixed and varied audience; photos desirable. Pays $25 to $50 per article, on publication. Reports on material "immediately."

CATHOLIC BIBLICAL QUARTERLY, Catholic University of America, Washington, DC 20064. (202) 635–5519. Rev. John P. Meier, Editor. A 200-page quarterly journal sponsored by the Catholic Biblical Association, with a national distribution of 4,000.
□*Catholic Biblical Quarterly* is published for adult scholars of a mixed, but mostly Catholic, background. Articles are all of a scholarly nature in the field of biblical theology and related disciplines.

Articles should be between 10 and 20 printed pages. Author's guidelines available on request. The sole compensation for material used is 50 offprints of the article. Reports "within some months."

CATHOLIC DIGEST, P.O. Box 64090, St. Paul, MN 55164. Henry Lexau, Editor. A 144-page monthly digest, published by the College of St. Thomas, St. Paul, MN 55105, with a national distribution of 640,000.
□*Catholic Digest* is published for adult Roman Catholics, mostly laity. Interested in nonfiction articles, stories of people, and humor. Needs warm humor, close-to-home religion, and everyday, true-to-life narratives of real people.

Articles should be 1,000 to 6,000 words. Payment varies: most often $100 for reprints, $200 for originals; pays for articles on acceptance, for fillers on publication. Reports in 1 day to 2 weeks.

CATHOLIC LIBRARY WORLD, 461 West Lancaster Avenue, Haverford, PA 19041. (215) 649-5251. John T. Corrigan, CFX, Editor. A 48-page monthly (10 times a year) magazine, published by the Catholic Library Association for 4,000 subscribers.
□*Catholic Library World* is published for adults involved in libraries in Catholic seminaries, colleges, parochial schools, and parishes. Prints material on all important subject areas and on all methods and techniques for "putting knowledge to work." Seeks information on developing areas of librarianship, and the information sciences and technologies. Informative papers on the administration, organization, and operation of libraries and information centers are solicited. Welcomes biographies and book reviews.
Material can be in the form of full-length articles, brief reports and communications, or letters to the editor. Photos and artwork welcome. Articles should be 1,500 to 2,000 words. Query letters are requested. Free samples and author's guidelines available. Ordinarily no payment for material used. Reports in 6 weeks.

CATHOLIC LIFE, 35750 Moravian Drive, Fraser, MI 48026. (313) 791-2100. Robert C. Bayer, Editor. A 32-page monthly (except July and August) magazine, published by the P.I.M.E. Missionaries, with a national distribution of 19,800.
□*Catholic Life* focuses on missionary topics involving the operations of the Catholic Church in India, Burma, Bangladesh, the Philippines, equatorial Brazil, Hong Kong, Japan, and Africa. Factual articles or personality profiles are the standard. Always in the market for good missionary articles on a variety of subjects within the missionary framework. Well-received articles: "They Look for Love," about Asian children; "Krishna," about a leprosy victim and his rehabilitation; "Sri Lanka: The Resplendent Land."
Articles should be 800 to 1,200 words. Query letters desirable. Author's guidelines available. Pays on publication: 4¢ per published word, $2 for each black-and-white photo submitted that is used to illustrate article. Usually reports in 2 weeks.

CATHOLIC NEW TIMES, 80 Sackville Street, Toronto, Ontario M5A 3E5, Canada. (416) 361-0761. Mary Jo Leddy and Grant Jahnke, Co-Editors. A 20-page biweekly newspaper.
□*Catholic New Times* is published for an adult, liberal Catholic audience, largely laity. "Looking for news features featuring the laity in the church, social issues, and other areas of renewal, such as the ecumenical efforts and developing theology." Carries national news from all of Canada; uses photos.
Articles should be 250 to 1,000 words. Query letters desirable. Sample copy available. No payment offered for material used. Reports within 2 weeks.

CATHOLIC TWIN CIRCLE, 6404 Wilshire Boulevard, Suite 900, Los Angeles, CA 90048. Mary Louise Frawley, Editor. A 20- to 24-page weekly magazine with a national circulation of 65,000.
□*Catholic Twin Circle* is a weekly Catholic feature tabloid that carries "family-oriented, uplifting, and informative articles, including interviews with Catholic celebrities and people doing something for their church. We also encourage how-to articles, economic advice, medical information, and human-interest stories." Well-received articles: stories on saints and on Mary, profiles of influential Catholics. Readers are Roman Catholic lay adults.
Articles should be under 1,000 words. Writer's guidelines available; for sample copy, send 9" by 12" SASE. Particularly interested in "material of interest to young adult Catholics raising families today—inspirational, practical, etc." Query letters not required; will consider reprints. "Please check the background of 'Catholic' personalities. Has a star been in sexually-explicit films; does he/she live with someone without being

married?" *Catholic Twin Circle* assumes no responsibility for unsolicited manuscripts, and all submissions must be accompanied by a SASE. Pays 8¢ per published word on original material, 3¢ to 5¢ for reprints. Reports in 8 weeks.

CHARISMA, 190 North Westmonte Drive, Altamonte Springs, FL 32714. (305) 869–5005. Stephen Strang, Editor and Publisher. A magazine of 150 pages or more published 12 times a year with a national distribution of 150,000.
□*Charisma* is an evangelical, Charismatic magazine aimed at a general adult lay audience, using stories that characterize life in the Spirit, covering home, family, church. Also likes Christian adventure stories in which there was a problem and God's intervention made a clear difference. Needs include Christian adventure stories about missionaries, touching first-person inspirational articles of God's intervention in specific situations, articles about significant Christians. Also needs ghost-written anecdotal teaching pieces from top Charismatic leaders' sermons or lectures. No fiction or poetry.
   Articles should be 1,200 to 5,000 words. Query letters mandatory. Unsolicited manuscripts returned unread. "Writers who do not familiarize themselves with our magazine waste their time and ours." Pays $150 to $400 per article, on publication.

THE CHRISTIAN ADVENTURER, P.O. Box 850, Joplin, MO 64802. (417) 624–7050. Rosemarie Foreman, Editor. An 8-page weekly take-home paper sponsored by the Pentecostal Church of God, with a national distribution of 3,500.
□*The Christian Adventurer* ordinarily prints manuscripts with a clear Christian message, seldom uses stories lacking one. Does not use material that violates the Holiness-Fundamentalist taboos. Edits material to fit the particular needs of the Pentecostal Church of God. Does not use articles or stories that include dancing, drinking, smoking, or mixed swimming, except in rare instances when these are used in a negative way with no hint of approbation. Avoids articles and stories that make use of television, most sports of a professional nature, and the use of makeup and the wearing of shorts or slacks for women. Interested in fiction, nonfiction, stories of people, humor, and devotionals. Readers are youth and adults.
   Articles should be 1,500 to 1,800 words. Sample copies available for 50¢ each. Pays 1½¢ per word, on publication. Reports within 2 weeks.

CHRISTIAN BOOKSELLER, 396 East St. Charles, Wheaton, IL 60187. (312) 653–4200. Karen Ball, Editor. A monthly trade journal slanted to booksellers, published by Christian Life, Inc., with a distribution of 10,500.
□*Christian Bookseller* serves religious bookstores, general bookstores with religious departments, Christian camps, bookstores, libraries, and other outlets of church and Sunday School supplies. Subjects needed are reports of bookstores using unique methods of merchandising and promotion; administrative and personnel how-to for bookstores; stories of trends and developments in religious publishing and religious music; success stories of publishers and stores. Subscribers are adults, mostly laity, of evangelical opinions, from mixed denominations.
   Articles should be 1,500 to 2,000 words and on the subjects described above. Photos desirable if appropriate to illustrate article. Query letters desirable. Sample issues $2 each, author's guidelines free. Pays $60 to $150 per article, on publication. Reports in 2 to 3 weeks.

CHRISTIAN BUSINESSLIFE DIGEST, 3108 West Lake Street, Minneapolis, MN 55416. (612) 926–0353. Founded 1984. Terry White, Editor. A 24-page bimonthly magazine with a national circulation that is "just beginning."
□*Christian BusinessLife Digest* is "designed to help inspire, inform, equip, and encourage Christian business and professional people. The editorial mix is a combination of material digested from other publications and a few pieces of original material." Also prints profiles and interviews, but relatively few graphics and photographs. Subscribers

include men and women in business, managers who use the magazine to focus employees on moral and ethical issues, and "Christians who use it as a tool for Christian witness to non-Christian employees, clients, and customers."

Articles should be 1,200 words maximum. Sample copies and guidelines available. "High priority is placed on specific application of Scripture to problem-solving. Our doctrinal and theological stance is presented in the statement of faith of the National Association of Evangelicals, available on request." Query letters desirable on features; send manuscripts on shorter items; will consider reprints. Pays $120 for lead articles, otherwise 5¢ per published word. Pays on publication. Reports in 4 weeks.

THE CHRISTIAN CENTURY, 407 South Dearborn Street, Chicago, IL 60605. (312) 427-5380. James M. Wall, Editor. A 32-page weekly magazine of news and opinion about the Christian Church and the world, with a national distribution of 37,000.
□*The Christian Century* is aimed at an audience of clergy and informed laity of mixed Protestant denominations, mainline or liberal, with strong interests in ecumenical affairs. Appeals to a theologically well-versed audience. Many articles are assigned and are part of a series, such as "Religion in the '80s" or "How My Mind Has Changed," or "The Denominations Today." Priority given to newsworthy articles on current topics. Uses some poetry, few illustrations. Runs several book reviews and criticism reports in each issue. Many writers are well-known, but freelance contributions are welcome.

Articles should be 2,500 words. Query letters "helpful." Guidelines and sample copies available on request. Photos should be black-and-white. Payment is per article, on publication. Reports in 4 to 6 weeks.

THE CHRISTIAN CHALLENGE, P.O. Box 2624, Victoria, TX 77901. (512) 578-1501. Dorothy A. Faber, Editor. A 24-page monthly magazine published by the Foundation for Christian Theology, with a national and regional circulation throughout the Anglican community.
□*The Christian Challenge* is published for scholars, clergy, and general adult lay readers, evangelicals, and traditionalists. Articles espouse and uphold the Christian traditionalist and universal positions and teachings. Interested in nonfiction, stories of people, humor, theological writings, church news and issues, as well as photos and illustrations.

Articles should be 500 to 10,000 words; average is 5,000 words. Sample copy and author's guidelines available. No payment; all articles are sent as contributions by their authors. Reports within 1 month.

CHRISTIAN COMPUTING MAGAZINE, 72 Valley Hill Road, Stockbridge, GA 30281. (404) 474-0007. Founded 1984. Dr. Nancy White Kelly, Editor. A 36-page bimonthly magazine with national and worldwide circulation of 10,000.
□*Christian Computing Magazine* is nondenominational and wants "to inform and inspire Christians around the world to use computers in the work of our Lord. We like to have articles that address any aspect of computing in a Christian environment." Well-received articles: "A Complete Guide to Church Computer Systems," "Christian Colleges in the Computer Age," "A Computerized, Living Christmas Tree," "Starting a High School Computer Program." Also prints profiles, interviews, humor, fillers, photos and illustrations. "Though the majority of our subscribers are clergy and missionaries, we strive to appeal to laity as well."

Articles should be 1,500 words, varying according to subject matter. Sample copies $3.00; writer's guidelines free. "We don't need generalized articles relating that computers can help churches. Our readers already assume this." Particularly interested in profiles of successful Christians using computers in their ministries, stories of missionaries using computers in the field. Pictures are definitely a plus. Query letters desirable; will consider reprints. Pays 3¢ per word and up, on acceptance. Reports in 3 weeks.

THE CHRISTIAN COURIER, 915 West Wisconsin Avenue, Suite 214, Milwaukee, WI 53233. (414) 271-6500. John M. Fisco, Jr., Publisher; Rita Bertolas, Editor. A 12- to 16-page monthly newspaper published for a large Midwest audience.
□*The Christian Courier* is interested in short articles on Christian subjects—nonfiction, with photos—written for a lay audience from all Protestant denominations. Stories of people are important.
Sample copy available on request. Also distributes calendars and records.

CHRISTIAN EDUCATORS JOURNAL, c/o Lorna Van Gilst, Managing Editor; 639 Ridge, Ripon, CA 95366. (209) 599-2265. A 32-page journal published quarterly with 3,500 subscribers.
□*Christian Educators Journal* is interested in "theoretical and practical articles for Christian school teachers on all levels, from kindergarten through college and in all disciplines." Material is aimed at these teachers, mostly in the Reformed Protestant tradition. Poetry also acceptable. Submit articles and poetry to Managing Editor; book reviews accepted by Book Review Editor Don Oppewal, Calvin College, Grand Rapids, MI 49506.
Articles should be 1,200 to 1,500 words. Query letters desirable but not necessary. Free sample copy and author's guidelines available on request. Pays on publication: $15 for articles, $10 for poems and book reviews. Reports in 4 to 6 weeks.

CHRISTIAN HERALD, 40 Overlook Drive, Chappaqua, NY 10514. (914) 769-9000. David Kucharsky, Editor. A 60- to 104-page magazine, published 11 times a year, with a national distribution of 200,000.
□*Christian Herald* is an evangelical family magazine about Christian faith in everyday life, "designed to exalt Jesus Christ as Savior and Lord and to make disciples for him. It promotes the teachings of the Bible as the Word of God written." Articles used are evangelically-oriented, well-focused, geared to young families. Particular needs include humor—providing that it doesn't ridicule individuals or institutions. Also considers nonfiction, poetry, stories of people, and photos and illustrations. Well-received articles: "Whatever Happened to the Family That Prayed Together?," "Kids *Vs.* Drugs: How to Handle Burnout," "Five Mistakes the Newly-Married Make."
Articles should be 1,500 to 2,000 words; maximum 3,500. Query letters desirable, as very few unsolicited manuscripts are accepted. Sample copy $2.00 from the *Christian Herald* circulation office; author's guidelines available. Normally pays on acceptance: $100 to $200 for full-length article; $35 to $100 for shorter feature; $5 and up for poetry; $50 to $150 for illustrations; $15 to $50 for black-and-white photos; $25 to $75 for color photos. Better writers and artists get larger amounts. Reports in 6 to 8 weeks.

CHRISTIAN HOME, 1908 Grand Avenue, Box 189, Nashville, TN 37202. (615) 327-2700. David I. Bradley, Editor. A 64-page quarterly magazine published by The Upper Room, with a national distribution of 60,000.
□*Christian Home* seeks "to encourage Christian marriage and family life by providing information, moral support, study materials, and devotional resources. Interested in fiction, nonfiction, stories of people, and materials related to family and marriage." Well-received articles: "Binding Family Through Traditions," "Celebrate Family," "Sharing Values." Readers are adults, usually couples.
Articles should be around 1,400 words, 160 lines typed, 68 characters per line. Query letters required. Sample copies given free "occasionally"; author's guidelines available. Pays $50 to $65 per article, on acceptance.

CHRISTIAN HOME AND SCHOOL, 3350 East Paris Avenue S.E., P.O. Box 8709, Grand Rapids, MI 49508. (616) 957-1070. Gordon L. Bordewyk, Ph.D., Editor; Kimberley D. Paxton, Assistant Editor. A 32-page magazine published 8 times a year by Christian Schools International, with an international distribution of 13,500.
□*Christian Home and School* is designed for parents in the United States and Canada

who support Christian education. Features news, profiles, reviews, and special articles that confront current issues affecting the Christian family, such as divorce, alcoholism, sex education, preschools, computer education, television, and working mothers. No short stories or poems accepted.

Most articles are assigned by the editorial staff, but some freelance writing is accepted. Writers should submit a proposal letter outlining their ideas for articles, along with copies of previously published material. Buys first rights only. Pays on publication: $70, depending on length. Would also consider printing excerpts of a book just published or about to be published.

CHRISTIANITY AND CRISIS, 537 West 121st Street, New York, NY 10027. (212) 662-5907. Wayne H. Cowan, Editor. A 16-page journal published 22 times a year with a national distribution of 19,000.
□Christianity and Crisis addresses a highly-educated, well-informed audience. Most subscribers are Christians; some are Jewish or nonreligious. The magazine describes itself as "heir to the Social Gospel and the Christian Realism of Reinhold Niebuhr, C&C's principal founder." Left of center in both politics and theology, nonpacifist but favors disarmament and far stronger forms of international governance, along with reform of the international economic order. As an independent religious journal, it discusses church politics from a detached and sometimes critical perspective. Carries no "devotional" material, but welcomes solid contemplative reflections.

Articles should be 1,000 to 3,000 words, but some run longer. Query letters desirable. Sample copy and author's guidelines available. Writers should avoid technical jargon and footnotes and other scholarly apparatus. Pays an honorarium of $25 to $150, on publication. Reports in 3 weeks.

CHRISTIANITY TODAY, 465 Gundersen Drive, Carol Stream, IL 60188. (312) 260-6200. Dr. V. Gilbert Beers, Editor. Published 18 times a year, with a national distribution of 180,000.
□Christianity Today emphasizes orthodox, evangelical religion. Readers are clergy and lay adults of mixed denominational backgrounds. Primarily a thought magazine with theological, ethical, historical, and informational (not merely inspirational) articles.

Typical article is 2,000 words. Query letters only. Unsolicited manuscripts not accepted. Pays $50 to $200, on acceptance.

THE CHRISTIAN LEADER, Box L, Hillsboro, KS 67063. (316) 947-3966. Wally Kroeker, Editor. A 24-page biweekly magazine published by the Mennonite Brethren Publishing House, with a national distribution of 8,900.
□The Christian Leader publishes material primarily by and for members of the Mennonite Brethren Church; readers are general adult lay readers of evangelical Protestant denominations. Aims to examine the mission of the church and open windows to greater understanding of how Christ's gospel relates to the lives of believers today.

Interested in nonfiction articles of 1,200 to 1,500 words and photos and illustrations. Query letters preferred. Free sample available on request. Pays approximately 2¢ per word, on publication. Reports within 2 weeks.

CHRISTIAN LEADERSHIP, P.O. Box 2458, Anderson, IN 46018-2458. (317) 642-0256. Founded 1946. Donald A. Courtney, Editor. A 20-page monthly (except July and August) magazine sponsored by the Board of Christian Education of the Church of God. National circulation of 4,200.
□Christian Leadership is "published for leaders in all phases of the Church of God's ministries through local congregations." Prints how-to articles for clergy and church workers "for all age levels and program areas." Well-received articles: "Does Time Work for You or Against You?," "The Happy Sunday School Teacher," "Growing Leaders in the Small Church," "Characteristics of a Caring Family," "Sharing Your Personal Beliefs with Youth."

Articles should be 1,000 to 2,000 words, "but shorter articles of 700 to 900 words are also desired." Guidelines and sample copy available. Reprints will be considered. Pays 50¢ per column inch for a usual total of $12 to $25. Reports in 6 weeks.

THE CHRISTIAN LIBRARIAN, Prairie Bible Institute, Three Hills, Alberta TOM 2A0, Canada. (403) 443–5511. Ron Jordahl, Editor. A 24-page quarterly professional journal with a circulation in both the United States and Canada, published by the Christian Librarian's Fellowship.

□*The Christian Librarian* is designed for professional librarians with an evangelical emphasis. Looking for "articles on all aspects of library science and materials treating the application of Christian faith to the profession." Especially interested in articles on current issues, such as the future of the card catalog, censorship, copyright. Premium on stories about librarians.

Articles should be 1,000 to 5,000 words. Query letters desirable. Sample copy and author's guidelines available. No payment for material used. Reports in 2 weeks.

CHRISTIAN LIFE MAGAZINE, 396 East St. Charles Road, Wheaton, IL 60188. (312) 653–4200. Robert Walker, Editor; Jan Franzen, Executive Editor. A 76- to 90-page monthly magazine with a national distribution of 100,000.

□*Christian Life* is intended for a general evangelical reading audience. Articles may be of several types: 1) trend articles—what's happening in the Christian world—should include evidence of the subject's significance; 2) inspirational articles, showing the success of persons, ideas, events, and organizations in encouraging the reader to become involved in similar Christian pursuits; 3) adventure articles, told in the first person, recounting dramatic events in which the Lord has intervened; 4) personality profiles on what believers are doing and thinking; 5) general features on a wide variety of subjects. Also uses some fiction, which must be of "high quality."

Most articles should be 1,000 to 3,000 words. Query letters are encouraged, especially for longer articles. Sample copy and extensive author's guidelines available. Pays on publication: from $50 for shorter pieces to $175 for major features. Reports in 2 weeks.

CHRISTIAN LIVING, 850 North Grove Avenue, Elgin, IL 60120. (312) 741–2400. Anne E. Dinnan, Associate Editor. A 4-page weekly Sunday School take-home paper, published by David C. Cook Publishing, with a national distribution of 125,000.

□*Christian Living* seeks "writers who can communicate effectively with senior-high teens through its class-and-home paper. Particularly interested in features in the following general areas: well-researched contemporary, interesting articles for senior-high students; features on teens working in their communities and churches, doing special service projects; articles on teens doing unusual things that may serve as idea-starters for readers; or on young people who have unusual experiences or accomplishments that would be an encouragement to others."

Articles should be approximately 1,200 words. Query letters required on any idea. Sample copies and author's guidelines available. Pays on acceptance: usually 3¢ to 5¢ per word ($20 to $100, depending on the story). Additional payment is made for any photographs used. Reports in 1 month.

CHRISTIAN MEDICAL SOCIETY JOURNAL, 124 Garden Lane, Decatur, GA 30030. Founded 1947. Sidney S. Macaulay, Th.M., Editor. A 32-page quarterly journal with a national circulation of 6,000.

□*Christian Medical Society Journal* focuses on "the application of Christian faith to problems in the lives and practices of medical and dental professionals. Emphasis is on priorities as well as on ethical issues." Prints articles, interviews, profiles, poetry, devotions, Bible study, theology, and a feature, "Faith At Work in Medicine." Well-received articles: "When the Doctor Plays God," "Type A Behavior: Spiritual Disease," "Balance in a Christian Doctor's Life," "Can Marriage and Medicine Co-Exist?" Readers are youth and adults, including scholars, clergy, and lay readers of all Protestant denominations.

Articles range from 1,500 to 2,500 words. Sample copies and guidelines available.

Particularly interested in biblical studies and "Christian wisdom throwing valid and fresh light on medical/ethical issues." Query letters desirable; will consider reprints. Pays $50 per article, sometimes $75. Reports in 4 weeks.

THE CHRISTIAN MINISTRY, 407 South Dearborn Street, Chicago, IL 60605. (312) 427–5380. Alfred P. Klauser, Editor. A 40-page bimonthly magazine sponsored by the Christian Century Foundation, with a national distribution of 14,000.
□*The Christian Ministry* discusses any topics that are relevant to the Christian ministry today—both practical and theoretical. Intended as a professional journal for the clergy, it does not use photos or illustrations. Readers are clergy of all denominations, mostly those with a decided ecumenical leaning.

Articles should be 2,000 to 2,500 words. Most major articles are done on assignment, so query letters are required. Sample copies available. Payment is on publication and varies according to subject, author, and need. Reports in 1 week.

CHRISTIAN SCHOLAR'S REVIEW, 255 Grapevine Road, Wenham, MA 01984. Dr. Clifton Orlebeke, Editor. A 96-page quarterly with a national distribution.
□*Christian Scholar's Review* is aimed at evangelical scholars and clergy. Welcomes "articles of high standards of original scholarship and of general interest dealing with all aspects of Christian thought and the interrelationship of Christian thought with all areas of scholarly interest. Normally, articles should reflect a Christian perspective. However, articles of general interest to the Christian community or of such a character as to promote communication between Christians and non-Christians may be included as well." The journal is about one-half articles and one-half book reviews.

Typical articles run 15 to 25 manuscript pages (5,000 to 10,000 words). Query letters desirable. Free sample copy and author's guidelines available. Articles should be sent to Dr. Clifton Orlebeke, Editor, Calvin College, Grand Rapids, MI 49506; book reviews to Russell Bishop, Gordon College, 255 Grapevine Road, Wenham, MA 01984. There is normally no payment for material used; authors receive 25 copies of the journal in which their articles appear.

CHRISTIAN SINGLE, 127 Ninth Avenue, North, Nashville, TN 37234. Founded 1979. Cliff Allbritton, Editor. A 52-page monthly magazine, sponsored by the Southern Baptist Convention, with an international paid circulation of 105,000.
□*Christian Single* prints "Good clean humor (funny happenings which you as a Christian single have experienced or funny stories about single life); articles on hobbies, sports, recreation, or any leisure-time activity; personal experiences of the realities of widowhood, divorce, or the never-married life; and on caring for others, relating, and sharing. Assignments are made to those who have particular expertise in fields relating to Christian singularity and who possess writing skill." Also prints devotions, photos, and illustrations. Readers are adults of all denominations.

Articles should be a maximum of 200 33-character lines (500 to 600 words preferred; top is 1,000 to 1,200 words). Sample copies and guidelines available. Particularly interested in "variety rather than repetition." Query letters desirable, along with previous writing sample and personal background; no reprints. Pays 4¢ per word, on acceptance; average article pays between $20 and $50. Reports in 6 weeks.

CHRISTIAN STANDARD, 8121 Hamilton Avenue, Cincinnati, OH 45231. (513) 931–4050. Sam E. Stone, Editor. A 24-page weekly magazine serving Christian Church/ Church of Christ, with a national circulation of 70,000.
□*Christian Standard* prints essays, comment, news, and inspirational material devoted to "the restoration of New Testament Christianity, its doctrines, its ordinances, and its fruits." Designed to appeal to and to develop a thoughtful, well-indoctrinated, and consecrated membership among undenominational Christian churches. Heart of its ministry is its essay features. Constantly seeking good essays on doctrinal, practical, and inspirational themes representing undenominational Christianity to church leaders. Particularly needs articles on the family and the forces that threaten it, personal

growth, and applying biblical truth to modern life. Glossy black-and-white photos used for cover and inside.

Articles should be 1,000 to 2,000 words; 1,200 to 1,500 preferred. Sample copies and author's guidelines available. Pays 1¢ to 3¢ per word, on publication. Reports in 2 to 4 weeks.

THE CHRISTIAN WRITER, P.O. Box 5650, Lakeland, FL 33807. (813) 644–3548. Founded 1982. Thomas A. Noton, Editor. A 48-page monthly newspaper with a national circulation of 15,000.

□*The Christian Writer* "wants articles that give practical help to writers. Specific how-to articles are our mainstay. Profiles on productive authors are used occasionally." Well-received articles: "Women in Writing," "Writing Poetry,""Inspirational Romance," "Writing For Children" (all themes that are highlighted throughout the year). Readers are adults of all denominations, and include some academics.

Fillers are under 800 words; articles from 1,000 to 2,400 words. Sample copies and guidelines available. Query letters desirable; no reprints. Pays $10 to $150, depending on length. Reports in 6 weeks.

CHRISTOPHER NEWS NOTES, 12 East 48th Street, New York, NY 10017. (212) 759–4050. Joseph R. Thomas, Editor. An 8-page journal, published 7 times a year, by the Christophers Organization, with a national distribution of 700,000.

□*Christopher News Notes* is published for a widespread and diverse audience. Although its sponsors are Roman Catholic, it reaches into all groups, appealing to both clergy and lay adults. Articles, limited to nonfiction, should be motivational and fit into the philosophy and purpose of the Christophers. Uses "material that will inspire and move people to bring about constructive institutional, governmental, and social change."

Sample copy available. No longer accepting outside manuscripts.

THE CHURCH ADVOCATE, P.O. Box 926, Findlay, OH 45840. (419) 424–1961. Linda M. Draper, Editor. A 40-page monthly magazine of the Churches of God General Conference, with a national distribution of 8,000.

□*The Church Advocate* exists "to encourage an informed people to be the Church." Prints nonfiction, stories of people, photos and illustrations. Well-received article: "The Role of the Pastor in Christian Education." Audience includes children, youth, adults and senior citizens, clergy and laity of the Church of God denomination.

Articles should be 1,000 to 2,500 words, 3 to 3½ pages, 72 typed characters per line. Free sample copies available on a limited basis. Pays $10 per printed page on publication; reports on submissions on payment. Also distributes calendars, appointment calendars, and tapes.

CHURCH AND STATE, 8120 Fenton Street, Silver Spring, MD 20910. (301) 589–3707. Joseph Conn, Managing Editor. A 24-page monthly magazine, the official publication of Americans United for Separation of Church and State, with a national distribution of 50,000.

□*Church and State* deals mainly with religious liberty and church-state relations issues, such as tax aids for religious institutions, religion in the public schools, government meddling with religion. Uses only nonfiction material. Readers are adults—scholars, clergy, and laity of evangelical, liberal, and mainline Protestant leanings from mixed denominations.

Articles should be 500 to 3,000 words. Query letters desirable. Free sample copies and author's guidelines available. Pays from $25 to $500, on acceptance. Reports in 3 weeks.

CHURCH AND SYNAGOGUE LIBRARIES, P.O. Box 1130, Bryn Mawr, PA 19010. (215) 853–2870. William H. Gentz, Editor; Bernard Deitrick, Book Review Editor. A 16-page bimonthly publication of the Church and Synagogue Library Association, with a national distribution of 2,600.

☐*Church and Synagogue Libraries* is interested in feature articles, news, and fillers concerning the work of local libraries in churches and synagogues throughout the world. Also carries news of the sponsoring association as well as other library groups, particularly those associated with religious organizations. Especially interested in how-to articles and success stories of congregational libraries and librarians. Also uses photos and book reviews.

Articles should be 500 to 750 words. Fillers can be a paragraph or two, news items of varying lengths. Query letters welcome. Sample copies available. No cash payment for material used. Reports in 1 month.

CHURCH EDUCATOR, 765 Penarth Avenue, Walnut, CA 91789. (714) 594–2060. Founded 1976. Robert Davidson, Editor. A 30-page monthly magazine with a national distribution of 6,000.
☐*Church Educator* focuses on "how-to articles dealing with Christian education, such as program ideas for senior high youth, crafts projects for elementary children, adult study class ideas, etc." Well-received articles: "How to Use Biblical Criticism in Teaching," "Effective Role Play," "Using Summer Time Creatively," "No Place to Pay," "The Value of Forgiveness," "Intentional Time and the Family." Readers are adults, generally mainline Protestant clergy.

Articles should be 500 to 1,500 words. Sample copies available. Particularly interested in youth programs. Query letters desirable; will consider reprints. Pays 3¢ per word, on publication. Reports in 12 weeks.

THE CHURCH HERALD, 1324 Lake Drive S.E., Grand Rapids, MI 49506. (616) 458–5156. John Stapert, Editor. A 32-page bimonthly magazine, the official publication of the Reformed Church in America, with a national distribution of 59,000.
☐*The Church Herald* is aimed at a diverse audience of Christians of all ages—evangelical and mainline Protestants. Most are members of the Reformed Church in America. Interested in all subjects that concern the church and its members today; Christianity and culture, government and politics, forms of worship, ethics, business relationships, parenthood, moral issues in society, Christian education, etc. Uses mostly nonfiction, but interested in fiction written from a Christian perspective. Publishes one poem, of not more than 30 lines, in each issue.

Articles should be 400 to 1,500 words. Prefers complete manuscripts rather than queries, except on doctrinal and biblical subjects. Pays an average of 3¢ per word or $10 per manuscript page, on acceptance. Reports in 3 to 4 weeks.

THE CHURCHMAN, 1074 23rd Avenue North, St. Petersburg, FL 33704. (813) 894–0097. Edna Ruth Johnson, Editor. A 24-page newspaper published 9 times a year by The Churchman Associates, with a national distribution of 10,000.
☐*The Churchman* is published for a mixed audience of adults and youth from all denominations. Claims a "humanistic" approach to its news and feature articles, which are aimed at mainline and liberal Protestants. Uses some poetry, but no fiction or photos. Emphasis on current events and news.

Articles should be 500 to 1,000 words. Sample copy available. No payment for material used. Reports in 1 week.

CHURCH MEDIA LIBRARY MAGAZINE, 127 Ninth Avenue, North, Nashville, TN 37234. (615) 251–2752. Floyd B. Simpson, Editor. A 50-page quarterly journal published by the Sunday School Board of the Southern Baptist Convention, with a national distribution of 17,000.
☐*Church Media Library Magazine* is published "to assist churches in the establishment and development of a media library and to encourage the growth of that library in the quality of its materials and services in support of all the ministries of the local church." Welcomes any material pertaining to this general purpose. Uses many how-to articles but also material that deals with the philosophy and spiritual ministry of the church media library. Published mainly for use in Southern Baptist churches, but has

subscribers in churches of other denominations as well.

Articles should be 600 to 1,200 words, typed 40 characters per line, 25 lines per page. Query letters desirable. Sample copy and author's guidelines available upon request. Pays 4½¢ per word, on acceptance. Reports in 2 weeks.

THE CHURCH MUSICIAN, 127 Ninth Avenue, North, Nashville, TN 37234. (615) 251–2961. William M. Anderson, Jr., Editor. A 52-page monthly magazine published by the Southern Baptist Convention, with a national distribution of 20,000.
□*The Church Musician* is for church music leaders—music directors (full-time, part-time, volunteer), pastors, pianists, organists, graded choir coordinators, and members of planning groups. Uses stories of people.

Articles should be approximately 1,000 words, although longer and shorter manuscripts will be accepted. Query letters desirable, but not required. Free samples sent on request. Pays on acceptance: approximately 4¢ per word (about $24 per printed page). Reports in 2 months.

CHURCH OF GOD EVANGEL, 922-1080 Montgomery Avenue, Cleveland, TN 37311. (615) 476–4512. O. W. Polen, D.D., Editor. A 32-page biweekly magazine, published by the Church of God, with an international distribution of 50,000.
□*Church of God Evangel* is interested in human-interest stories with an inspirational slant, nonfiction, poetry, photos and illustrations. Well-received articles have been on how to deal with worry, fear, resentment, suffering; special Easter, Mother's Day, Father's Day, Pentecost Sunday, Labor Day, Thanksgiving, and Christmas themes.

Articles should be 500 words. Query letters welcomed, but not required. Sample copies and author's guidelines available on request. Pays 2¢ per word, on acceptance. Reports usually within 2 weeks.

CHURCH RECREATION MAGAZINE, MSN 166, 127 Ninth Avenue, North, Nashville, TN 37234. (615) 251–2733. Sharon Wegman, Assistant Editor. A 50-page quarterly magazine sponsored by the Church Recreation Department, Southern Baptist Sunday School Board.
□*Church Recreation* is produced to stimulate and guide churches and denominational leaders in the effective use of recreation in all church programs. Material directed toward professional staff leaders in churches as well as lay persons with leadership responsibilities in the area of recreation. Must "communicate to readers how churches can effectively use recreation to tell people about Jesus Christ, strengthen fellowship between believers, and complete the God-directed cycle of work, worship, and play." Prints nonfiction, testimonial articles about suggested recreation activities (camping, drama, socials, senior citizen trips, parties, retreats) that are instructional and how-to in nature.

Articles should be 500 to 2,000 words; average is 1,000 words. Most material is solicited from previously published authors. Do not query; send complete article. Author's guidelines available. Pays 4¢ per word within 6 months of notice of acceptance. Reports within 6 months.

CHURCH TEACHERS, 7214 East Granada Road, Scottsdale, AZ 85257. (602) 949–1003. Locke E. Bowman, Jr., Editor. A 40-page magazine published 5 times a year for teachers in the church by National Teacher Education Program, with a national distribution of 15,000.
□*Church Teachers* is interested in articles written by practicing church teachers and addressed to others who teach. Reading audience is adult, made up of both clergy and laity in mainline Protestant, Roman Catholic, and Orthodox churches. Looking for "thoughtful evaluations of teaching episodes that were successful in church classes—with preschoolers, youth, children, and adults." Prefers "clear descriptions of what the teacher did and why . . . and how it turned out." Special need for more material on adult and youth education. Also looking for very short pieces (one or two paragraphs) describing a workable technique. Does *not* want object lessons or

children's sermons. Successful articles: "How We Celebrated Pentecost in Our Church School," "Youth and Adults Study Together," "Ways to Improve Adult Education at the Church."

Major articles should be 750 to 2,000 words, averaging about 1,250 words. No query letters; prefers finished manuscripts. Sample copies available. Pays $35 per page, 60 to 90 days after publication. Reports in 10 days.

THE CHURCH WOMAN, Room 812, 475 Riverside Drive, New York, NY 10115. (212) 870-2344. Margaret Schiffert, Editor. A quarterly magazine published by Church Women United, with a national distribution of 10,000.
□*The Church Woman* is the magazine of Church Women United, an ecumenical organization of Protestant, Roman Catholic, Orthodox, and other Christian women. Prints articles, interviews, Bible studies and meditations highlighting women's and peace and justice issues.

Query letters desirable. Sample copy and author's guidelines available upon request. Payment in copies only.

THE CIRCUIT RIDER, 201 Eighth Avenue, South, Nashville, TN 37202. (615) 749-6488. J. Richard Peck, Editor. A 24-page monthly magazine published by the United Methodist Publishing House, with a national distribution of 48,000.
□*The Circuit Rider* is a professional magazine for United Methodist clergy. Articles should be of interest to this group, their work, their concerns. Well-received articles have been on preaching, counseling, bio-ethics, funerals, weddings, church administration. Photos welcome.

Articles should be 800 to 1,600 words. No queries; send complete articles. Pays $35 to $100 per article, on acceptance. Reports in 30 days.

CLARION, THE CANADIAN REFORMED MAGAZINE, 9210-132 A Street, Surrey, British Columbia, V3V 7E1, Canada. (604) 581-2290. J. Geertsema and W. Pouwelse, Editors. A 24-page biweekly magazine with a national distribution of 1,700.
□*Clarion* is published for a mixed reading audience of all ages in the Reformed churches of Canada. Has its own circle of contributors and generally does not consider material from outside writers. Sample copy available from Premier Printing Ltd., 1249 Plessis Road, Winnipeg, Manitoba, R2C 3L9, Canada.

THE CLERGY JOURNAL, P.O. Box 1625, Austin, TX 78767. (512) 327-8501. Manfred Holck, Jr., Editor. A 44-page magazine for the clergy, published monthly except in June and December, with a national distribution of 20,000.
□*The Clergy Journal* is aimed at mainline Protestant clergy. Articles are nonfiction. Purpose is to provide sermons, sermon helps, and other how-to articles that assist clergy in administering their congregational programs more effectively and efficiently. Well-received articles included those on the fiscal structure of the church, how to pay your pastor, maximizing church contributions, and a sermon series on marriage.

Articles should be 1,000 to 1,500 words. Query letters are encouraged. Sample copy available for $2.50. Pays $25 to $35 per article, on publication. Reports in 3 weeks. Also distributes tapes, which are produced in-house.

CLUBHOUSE, Box 15, Berrien Springs, MI 49103. Founded 1951; name changed to *CLUBHOUSE* in 1982. Elaine Meseraull, Editor. A 32-page, 10-times-yearly magazine with 16,000 national subscribers.
□*CLUBHOUSE* is "a Christian magazine for children 9 through 13. Our primary goal is to let children who have little or no Christian influence in their lives know there is a God and that He loves kids. Our staff composes a central Bible story with accompanying puzzles and games for each issue. Other stories, puzzles, games, and recipes are usually supplied by freelance writers and are not religiously oriented in an overt way, though they do represent Christian principles of behavior." Also publishes humor and poetry.

Lead story should be 1,000 to 1,200 words; "Story Cubes," 600 to 800 words, can be broken up into 4 to 6 sections, each with its own illustration, in checkerboard layout; "Thinker Tales," 600 to 800 words, are parables in classic or modern style that teach Christian principles. "Stories should be programmed for 12- to 13-year-olds." For sample copy send SASE with 54¢ postage; SASE with 20¢ postage gets guidelines. Will consider reprints. Send material during April and May: "Since nearly all stories are selected in May, we compose a logical mix at that time from stories available. We receive about 2,500 a year and use about 50." Pays $25 to $35 for stories, $10 for cartoons and puzzles approximately 2 months after acceptance. Reports in 3 weeks.

CMBC CONTACT MAGAZINE, P.O. Box 2728, Glen Ellyn, IL 60137. (312) 653–4588. Phil Landrum, Director of Literature. A 20-page bimonthly magazine published by the Christian Business Men's Committee of U.S.A., with a national distribution of 15,000.
□*CMBC Contact Magazine* assigns all articles used. Sample copies available. Payment is according to the assignment.

CO-LABORER, P.O. Box 1088, Nashville, TN 37202. (615) 361–1010. Founded 1961. A 32-page quarterly sponsored by the Woman's National Auxiliary Convention (Free Will Baptist). National circulation of 18,000.
□*Co-Laborer* is "missionary-oriented and prefers material related to this theme," including profiles, poetry, devotions, Bible study, photos and illustrations, and programs for monthly meetings. Well-received articles: a series by missionaries on how prayer helped them on the mission field, profiles of some home mission workers, a poetry page introducing a poet and how she came to write poetry. Readers are lay adults, largely women and Free Will Baptists.
Articles should be 2 to 3 pages; programs 5 to 6 pages. No payment. Sample copy and writer's guidelines available. "Most of our material is gleaned from our annual creative arts contest, in which awards are given." Particularly interested in "interesting programs on missions for busy women." Will consider reprints. No report time given.

COLUMBAN MISSION, c/o the Columban Fathers, St. Columbans, NE 68056. (402) 291–1920. Rev. Richard Steinhilber, Editor. A 24- to 32-page monthly Roman Catholic magazine with a national distribution of 240,000.
□*Columban Mission* seldom uses freelance material unless writer has first-hand knowledge and expertise on countries of Latin America and Asia where Columban Fathers serve.
Uses nonfiction articles of 1,500 to 2,000 words. Query letters desirable. Free sample copy available. Pays on acceptance. Reports in 1 month. Also distributes calendars, which are produced in-house.

COLUMBIA, P.O. Drawer 1670, New Haven, CT 06507. (203) 772–2130, extension 263 or 264. Elmer Von Feldt, Editor. A 32-page monthly magazine of the Knights of Columbus, with a national distribution of 1,367,402.
□*Columbia* is read by a Roman Catholic adult audience, particularly members of the Knights of Columbus and their families. Prints factual articles that deal with current events, social problems, Catholic apostolic activities, programs and movements, education, rearing a family, patriotic endeavors, profiles of those who have triumphed against overwhelming handicaps, literature, science, ecumenism, arts, sports, and leisure. Glossy color photos or transparencies required for illustration.
Articles should be 2,500 to 3,000 words. Query letters desirable. Free sample copy and author's guidelines available on request. Pays $600 for articles, including photos. Humorous or satirical articles of 1,000 words should be directed to current religious, social, or cultural conditions; pays up to $200. For photo stories, pays $25 per photo used and 10¢ per word. (Same themes used as for factual articles.) Artists' color sketches for cover should use humorous or religious themes dealing with seasonal or current situations. Pays $1,000 for paintings accepted. Cartoons should be pungent, captionless humor; pays $25 per cartoon. Pays on acceptance. Reports in 4 weeks.

COMMONWEAL, 232 Madison Avenue, New York, NY 10016. (212) 683–2042. Peter Steinfels, Editor. A 32-page biweekly Roman Catholic magazine.

□*Commonweal* is published for adult clergy and general laity, primarily in the Roman Catholic Church. Uses nonfiction and poetry. Seeks "thoughtful and interpretive articles on present-day issues and developments in public affairs, religion, literature, and the arts."

Articles should be 1,200 to 3,000 words. Query letters desired. Sample copy available. Pays on acceptance. Reports in 2 or 3 weeks.

COMPANION OF ST. FRANCIS AND ST. ANTHONY, Box 535, Station F, Toronto, Ontario M4Y 2L8, Canada. (416) 924–6349. Phil Kelly, OFM Conv., Editor. A 32-page monthly magazine published by the Conventual Franciscans, with a national distribution of 8,000.

□*Companion of St. Francis and St. Anthony* is a Catholic family magazine that features material of human interest, trials of family, health hints, travelogues of shrines, stories on humanitarians. Interested in fiction, nonfiction, stories of people, family life, and problems of youth for a wide readership of adults, youth, senior citizens, clergy, and general lay readers. Live modern topics of human interest are best. Should be of fairly wide interest to Canadian readers; no U.S. content accepted. Immediate preference given to any manuscript accompanied by black-and-white photos.

Articles should be 1,000 to 1,250 words. Deadline for copy and pictures is 3 months preceding the month of issue. Fiction should be wholesome but not preachy. Author's guidelines available; send SASE with Canadian postage or payment for postage in coin or international reply coupons. Pays 6¢ per word on acceptance, $8.00 per photo. Reports in 3 weeks.

CONTEMPORARY CHRISTIAN MAGAZINE, P.O. Box 6300, Laguna Hills, CA 92654. (714) 951–9106. Founded 1978. Ted Ojarovsky, Editor. A 56-page monthly magazine with a national distribution of up to 100,000.

□*Contemporary Christian Magazine* prints feature articles, reviews, editorials, short news items, and cartoons, all reflecting a contemporary Christian perspective. Emphasized are personality profiles of dynamic Christians 18 to 34 years of age, human interest stories, and trend articles relating to Christians in this same age group. Well-received articles were interviews with Cristina DeLorean and Richard Roberts, features on the *Star Wars* series, and personality profiles of Steve Taylor and Bob Dylan. Readers are "baby boom" Christians, 20 to 40, 60% male, 40% female.

Record, book, and film reviews should be 600 words, feature articles 1,500 words. Sample copies and very detailed guidelines available. Particularly interested in "honest, bold, provocative journalism for Christians who want to think and act righteously." Query letters desirable; will consider reprints. Pays 8¢ per word, on publication. Reports in 6 weeks.

CONVICTION, 7704 24th Avenue N.W., Seattle, WA 98117. Founded 1966. Paul Zettersten, Editor. A 16-page monthly magazine sponsored by the Fellowship of Christian Assemblies, with a national distribution of 5,000.

□*Conviction* prints 1) missions articles; 2) upbeat, encouraging pieces; 3) articles with an evangelistic message; and 4) seasonal articles (Christmas, Thanksgiving, etc.). Also publishes profiles and interviews, devotions, theology, photos and illustrations. Well-received articles included a series on the 23rd Psalm, an article on divine healing, a piece offering advice to freshman college students, and reflections by a retiring minister. Readers are adults, both clergy and laity, of various evangelical and Pentecostal denominations.

Articles should be 800 to 1,200 words. "We are always seeking brief (800-word) articles that have a salvation message." Sample copy and author's guidelines available. No payment for materials used, but will consider reprints. Reports in 4 weeks.

COUNSELOR, Box 632, Glen Ellyn, IL 60138. (312) 668-6000. Grace Fox Anderson, Editor. A 4-page take-home paper for children 8 to 12, published quarterly by SP Publications, Inc., with a national distribution of 160,000.

□*Counselor* aims to "win juniors for Christ, inspire them to turn Bible knowledge into Christian living, and help them understand how God works in the world. Write clearly, but don't write down to the reader." No fiction accepted. Buys true experiences of children 10 to 14 years old and adults, in either the first or third person.

Stories should be 900 to 1,100 words. Also "wants photos of story subjects—black-and-white, color prints, or slides. Looking for good photo stories about one child or a group, ages 9 to 12, involved in some interesting Christian service project in the U.S. or other countries." Query first. Author's guidelines available. Buys first rights; pays on acceptance, up to 7¢ per word based on quality of material. Reports within 4 weeks.

THE COVENANT COMPANION, 5101 North Francisco Avenue, Chicago, IL 60625. (312) 784-3000. James R. Hawkinson, Editor. A 48-page monthly magazine, published by the Evangelical Covenant Church, with a national distribution of 26,500.

□*The Covenant Companion* prints "material with a Christian impact, growing out of the author's life experience, reflection, and/or reading, that illustrates the relevance of Jesus Christ to daily life at this time and place." Interested in nonfiction, stories of people, and humor. Particular needs include material slanted toward the Church year: seasonal material for Advent, Christmas, Epiphany, Lent, Easter, Pentecost, etc. Readers are a wide audience of children, youth, senior citizens, clergy, and general lay readers of evangelical and mainline Protestant denominations.

Articles submitted should be 110 to 120 lines, typed double-spaced, 70 characters per line. Sample copies available for $1.50. Payment is generally $10, $25, or $35, depending on the length of the article; reprints less. Pays in the month following publication.

CREATION SOCIAL SCIENCE AND HUMANITIES QUARTERLY, 1429 North Holyoke, Wichita, KS 67208. (316) 683-3610. Founded 1978. Paul D. Ackerman, Ph.D., Editor. A 32-page quarterly magazine sponsored by the Creation Social Science and Humanities Society, with a national (and some foreign) distribution of 1,000.

□The *Quarterly* prints "scholarly articles, well-researched and with references, but written with educated lay readers also in mind. Topics: psychology, sociology, economics, philosophy, history, art, literature—the whole range of the social sciences and humanities. Should be developed from an explicitly biblical Christian perspective, but not be 'denominational' in basic theology. We have readers in all branches of Christianity, including Catholic and Orthodox." Well-received articles: "Creation and Human Language," "The Restoration of the Divine Image Through Christ," "Does Man Have 'Natural Rights'?"

Articles should be from 5 to 20 typed, double-spaced pages; footnotes and bibliography in addition. Poems 1 to 2 pages. Book reviews 3 to 5 pages. Print-ready black-and-white art for cover and illustrations also welcome. Sample copies and guidelines available. "We could use more book reviews of both new publications and older books." Query letters desirable; will consider reprints. "We do not have finances to pay our authors; however, the author receives 6 free copies of the issue and a free 1-year subscription." Reports in 3 weeks.

CREATIVE YEARS [formerly *Writer's Opportunities*], 2490 S.W. 14th Drive, #40, Gainesville, FL 32608. (904) 373-7445. Founded 1980. Eloise Cozens-Henderson, Editor-Publisher. A 32-page bimonthly magazine with an international distribution of 2,000.

□*Creative Years* is "a Christian-oriented publication, though not a strictly religious magazine." Prints articles on health, travel, consumer problems, sewing and designing, puzzles, inspirational articles, fiction, and advice for writers. Well-received articles: "Preachin' Every Fourth Sunday," "Find a Friend," "Trust in the Lord Pays Off," "I Remember Grandma," "The Day the Sky Fell," "Conquest of Fear." Also prints poetry, profiles and interviews, nostalgia, recipes, crafts, devotions, and Bible study. "We would like to see sports stories or stories about old-time professionals like Babe Ruth and Ty Cobb." Readers are adults and senior citizens.

Articles should be 750 to 1,500 words. Query letters desirable. Sample copies and author's guidelines available. "We pay presently in copies of author's work; this is mostly by request of writers—especially new writers." Reports in 4 weeks.

CREATOR MAGAZINE, 25 Rolling Hills Drive, Wichita, KS 67212. (316) 722–8092. Founded 1978. Cyndi Sanders, Editor. A 68- to 94-page bimonthly magazine with a national distribution of 4,000.
☐*Creator Magazine* prints articles, profiles, interviews, humor, devotions, instructional materials, and photos and illustrations. Would-be contributors should request a sample copy and guidelines. Query letters desirable; will consider reprints. Pays $40 to $60 per article, or 3¢ to 5¢ per word, upon publication; "some special arrangements made." Reports in 8 weeks.

CROSS CURRENTS, 103 Van Houten Fields, West Nyack, NY 10994. Joseph Cuneen, Editor. A 128-page quarterly journal with a national distribution of 6,000.
☐*Cross Currents* seeks "to explore the implications of Christianity for our times," providing "critical analyses of contemporary issues from a religiously-informed stance." Aimed at an ecumenical adult audience of scholars, clergy, and educated laity. Articles limited to nonfiction. Articles solicited on such subjects as atomic power, Africanization of Christianity, feminism and Judaism, and Islam and social ethics.

Articles should be 2,500 to 7,000 words. Query letters helpful. Sample copy available. No payment for material used. Reports in 1 month.

CRUSADER MAGAZINE, Box 7244, Grand Rapids, MI 49510. (616) 241–5616. G. Richard Broene, Editor. A 24-page magazine published 7 times a year by the Calvinist Cadet Corps, with a distribution in the U.S. and Canada of 12,500.
☐*Crusader Magazine* is a Christian-oriented publication for boys aged 9 to 14 of several evangelical Protestant denominations. Prints material designed to appeal to the pre-adolescent boy. "Generally speaking, the boys are active, inquisitive, and imaginative. They imitate 'heroes' they see around them, and they love adventure. They are sociable and form gangs easily. Many of them make decisions for Christ that affect them the rest of their lives. Main material used is fast-moving, high-interest fiction." Prints stories of people, humor, craft and hobby articles, camping and sports articles, and nature articles; also jokes, riddles, and cartoons.

Articles should be approximately 1,500 words. Sample copies and author's guidelines available. Pays 2¢ to 5¢ per word, on acceptance. Reports in 3 weeks.

DADS ONLY/DADS & MOMS, P.O. Box 340, Julian, CA 92036. (714) 765–1815. Paul Lewis, Editor. A 12-page monthly newsletter with a national distribution of 25,000.
☐*Dads Only* reaches an audience of both clergy and general lay readers in evangelical and mainline Protestant denominations. *Dads & Moms* reaches secular, corporate employees. Interested in nonfiction, family (husband and wife) articles that are crisp, practical, and to the point with meaning. Well-received articles: "Dealing With Death," "Kids And Allowances," "Kids' Rights."

Articles should be 1,200 words for teaching values, 50 words for ideas; 600 to 700 words in "To Better Love Her" column. Query letters desirable. Sample copies available. Pays $35 to $50 per article, $10 per idea. Reports in 14 days. Also markets tapes, for which payment varies.

DAILY BLESSING, P.O. Box 2187, Tulsa, OK 74171. Oral Roberts and Billye Morris, Editors. A daily devotional booklet with a national distribution of 425,000.
☐*Daily Blessing* meditations are based on the blessing theme and should encompass a dynamic thought that is positive and uplifting in tone. Scriptural selection should have

devotional quality; Scripture and central idea of meditation should be appropriate to each other. A good meditation includes a life-situation story, human experience, anecdote or example. Story should illustrate the idea presented in the Scripture. Do not write in the first person; the only first-person devotionals are those written by Mr. Roberts.

Meditations should be 27 lines including title, typed 50 characters to a line. Sample copy and author's guidelines available. Payment depends upon amount of editorial work necessary to prepare the material for publication. Pays $5 to $15 on acceptance, usually within 30 to 90 days. Photo requirements: for covers, 4" by 5" color transparencies or 35 mm slides of seasonal scenic photos; payment $35 to $75. For black-and-white 8" by 10" glossies of seasonal, scenic and mood shots, usually pays $10.

DAILY MEDITATION, P.O. Box 2710, San Antonio, TX 78299. Ruth S. Paterson, Editor. A 96-page quarterly magazine with an international distribution.
□*Daily Meditation* prints material "with fresh approaches to Truth, practical applications of the teachings of Jesus, and general self-improvement." Readers are adult, general lay readers of mixed denominations.

Articles should be 450 to 1,500 words. Do not query; must see finished article. Sample copies and author's guidelines available upon receipt of 50¢. Pays ½¢ to 1½¢ per word, on acceptance. Reports in 60 to 90 days.

DAILY WORD, Unity Village, MO 64065. (816) 524–3550. Jeanne Allen, Editor. A monthly manual of daily readings and studies published by Unity School of Christianity, with a national distribution of 2,500,000.
□*Daily Word* uses short devotional articles to be read as daily meditations by the readers. Articles should be brief. May include poetry or quoted material for which source is given. Bible quotations should conform to the Revised Standard Version and references should be given. Appeals to an adult reading audience.

Prospective writers should read samples before submitting material. Sample copy and author's guidelines available. Pays $20 per page for articles, $1 per line for poetry, on acceptance. Reports in 4 weeks.

DASH, Box 150, Wheaton, IL 60189. (312) 665–0630. David R. Leigh, Editor; Sharon Long, Associate Editor. A 24-page magazine published 8 times a year by the Christian Service Brigade.
□*Dash* readers (ages 8 through 11) are active in their Christian Service Brigade "Stockade" groups run by their local churches. Addresses issues of concern to boys from a local perspective; provides entertaining reading; promotes involvement in Stockade and respect for its leaders; and presents a positive image of Christian manhood. Uses true stories, fiction, puzzles, and quizzes.

Articles average 1,200 words. Query letters only. Sample copies available for $1.50 each, plus SASE. Pays 5¢ to 10¢ per word, on publication. Reports in 1 to 6 weeks.

DAUGHTERS OF SARAH, 2716 West Cortland, Chicago, IL 60647. (312) 252–3344. Founded 1974. Reta Finger, Editorial Coordinator. A 32-page bimonthly magazine with a national distribution of 3,500.
□*Daughters of Sarah* is "a Christian feminist magazine with a biblical emphasis," and prints articles on biblical interpretation from a feminist perspective; on "our foremothers," meaning women's history; and on social issues from a feminist perspective. Also prints fiction, poetry, humor, Bible study, theology, photos, and illustrations. Well-received articles: "Ladders into Circles," about patriarchy *versus* mutuality; "The Biggest Invisible Problem in the World," about women and food production; and articles on women in prison. Subscribers "are largely women (and some men) who are concerned about women's full participation in the Body of Christ and of the relationship of mutual submission . . . a wide variety of religious backgrounds, from Catholic to mainline Protestant to evangelical, Anabaptist, and charismatic churches. Most are college-educated."

Articles vary from 750 to 2,000 words, from 4 to 8 typewritten, double-spaced pages; but can be shorter. Sample copies and guidelines available. Particularly interested in articles, stories, or poems on women and the health-care system, abortion—from all sides, healing, biblical, and historical articles. Query letters desirable; will consider reprints. "Include a brief description of yourself, including your credentials for this particular piece." Pays $15 per printed page, on publication. Reports in 6 to 8 weeks.

DECISION, 1300 Harmon Place, Minneapolis, MN 55403. (612) 338–0500. Roger C. Palms, Editor; Lori J. P. Sorensen, Assistant Editor and Director of the School of Christian Writing. A 44-page monthly magazine published by the Billy Graham Evangelistic Association, with a national distribution of over 2,000,000.
□Decision is directed to youth and adults in every walk of life. The purpose is "1) to set forth to every reader the Good News of salvation in Jesus Christ with such vividness and clarity that he or she will be drawn to make a commitment to Christ; 2) to encourage, teach, and strengthen Christians." Uses a positive, not a preachy, approach. Needs personal experience articles (How did God intervene in your life? How have you applied biblical principles to everyday living?); personal testimonies (A conversion testimony that conveys what Christ has done in your life); "Where Are They Now?" features (If you made a decision at a Billy Graham Crusade); teaching articles that relate to spiritual growth and doctrine; vignettes; and poetry (prefers free verse, but some rhymed poetry is accepted).
Articles should be 1,800 to 2,200 words for personal experience, personal testimony, and teaching articles; 600 to 800 words for "Where Are They Now?"; 200 to 800 words for vignettes; 4 to 24 lines for poetry. Sample copy and author's guidelines available. Pays on publication, according to length of article or poem. Reports within 6 weeks.

DIALOG: A JOURNAL OF THEOLOGY, 2375 Como Avenue, St. Paul, MN 55108. (612) 641–3456. Robert Jenson, Editor, Lutheran Theological Seminary, Gettysburg, PA 17325. An 80-page quarterly theological journal with an international distribution of 2,400.
□Dialog is aimed at a largely Lutheran audience of scholars, clergy, and some laity. Each issue has a theme, and all of the articles in that issue are related to that theme—e.g., Easter, the work of Christ, Church versus State, education, ethics, liturgy. Limited to nonfiction and theologically oriented subjects.
Articles should be 2,500 words or 10 to 16 pages of manuscript. Sample copies and a list of future themes can be obtained by writing Myles Stenshoel, Augsburg College, Minneapolis, MN 55414. For assigned material, pays $100 per article, on acceptance. Reports promptly on queries and submissions.

DIMENSIONS OF MINISTRY, 1312 Massachusetts Avenue N.W., Washington, D.C. 20005. (202) 659–6873. Elly Murphy, Editor. A 24-page bimonthly Roman Catholic magazine.
□Dimensions of Ministry is aimed at a general lay audience in the Roman Catholic churches. Uses nonfiction articles with photos, treating all phases of Catholic religious education—resources, programs, conferences, etc.
Almost all material is staff-written; uses very little from outside writers. Samples available on request.

THE DISCIPLE, Box 179, St. Louis, MO 63166. (314) 371–6900. James L. Merrell, Editor. A 62-page monthly magazine published by the Christian Board of Publication of the Christian (Disciples of Christ) Church, with a national distribution of 57,800.
□The Disciple welcomes unsolicited material of various kinds: inspirational, devotional, sermons, news of local Christian churches and their communities, articles related to the general concerns of the Church, poetry, photos, and cartoons. Particularly interested in seasonal and historical material. Aimed at an adult readership of clergy and laity, primarily members of the Christian Church.

Short devotional material and fillers should be 200 to 300 words; major articles, 700 to 900 words. Sample copies available. Query letters not necessary except on theological subjects. Pays on publication: $5 for filler material, $10 to $30 for longer articles. Reports in 3 to 6 weeks.

DISCIPLESHIP JOURNAL, P.O. Box 6000, Colorado Springs, CO 80934. Founded 1981. E. Calvin Beisner, Editor. A 48-page bimonthly magazine sponsored by The Navigators, with an international distribution of 75,000.

□*Discipleship Journal* prints articles that are "strongly Bible-centered, encouraging personal application of Scripture, emphasizing evangelism, discipling, or equipping; that challenge to broaden thinking and living of Christian faith; examples of excellence in form and content." Also publishes some devotions, Bible study, theology, and articles on ethics, apologetics, and the practical disciplines of devotion and discipling. Readers are clergy and lay adults of various Protestant denominations.

Feature articles (no more than one per issue) run 4,000 to 5,000 words; theme articles (5 to 7 per issue) 2,750 to 3,250 words; general-interest articles (4 to 6 per issue) 1,750 to 2,750 words; meditations 750 to 1,000 words. Well-received articles: "A Vessel of Grace"; "Contentment: The Cure to Coveting"; "The Ten Commandments as a Blueprint for Loving"; "Listening in the Great Silence," a meditative prayer. Sample copies available. "We rarely use testimony articles unless clearly illustrative of scriptural principles. All articles should address a mix of the following issues: the exaltation of God, the Lordship of Christ, the nature and functions of the church—local and universal, outreach, leadership for Christ's Church and for society, contemporary issues, and prayer." Query letters required for pieces over 1,500 words; will consider reprints. Pays when article is sent to printer: 10¢ a word for all rights; 7¢ per word for first rights; 2¢ per word for reprint rights. Reports in 6 weeks.

DISCOVERIES, 6401 The Paseo, Kansas City, MO 64131. (816) 333-7000. Libby Huffman, Editor. An 8-page weekly take-home paper published by the Children's Ministries of the Church of the Nazarene, with an international distribution of 100,000.

□*Discoveries* is written for children aged 8 through 12, grades 3 through 6, "to provide a leisure reading piece that will build Christian behavior and values and provide reinforcement of biblical concepts taught in the Sunday School curriculum." Stories are needed to correlate with curriculum themes: faith in God, obedience to God, putting God first, choosing to please God, accepting Jesus as Savior, finding God's will, choosing to do right, trusting God in hard times, prayer—trusting God to answer, importance of Bible memorization, appreciation of Bible as God's word to man, Christians working together, showing kindness to others, witnessing. Fiction should vividly portray definite Christian emphasis or character-building values, without being preachy. The setting, plot, and action should be realistic. Cartoons and humor should involve children.

Stories should be 800 to 1,000 words. Sample copies and author's guidelines available. Pays on acceptance: for prose, 5¢ per word for first rights, 2¢ per word for second rights (reprint); for 8" by 10" black-and-white glossy photos, $15 to $25; for illustrations (by assignment), $25 to $40. Reports in 2 weeks to 1 month.

EAST ASIA MILLIONS, 404 South Church Street, Robesonia, PA 19551. (215) 693-5881. Fay Goddard, Editor. A 24-page bimonthly magazine published by the Overseas Missionary Fellowship, with a national distribution of 16,000.

□*East Asia Millions* presents up-to-date material to readers from Overseas Missionary Fellowship missionaries working in southeast Asia. Covers hospitals, leprosy clinic work, tribal church planting, student work, literature and institutional work, camps and conferences, etc. Readers are youth and adults, general lay readers of mixed denominations.

No freelance material accepted. All articles are written by members of the Overseas Missionary Fellowship, which also distributes calendars, appointment calendars, and flash-card stories for children.

ECW NEWSLETTER, 1523 Silver Strand Circle, Palatine, IL 60074. (312) 351–0471. Founded 1983. Sandra J. Hovatter, Editor; Glory E. Borgeson, Executive Vice-President. A 4- to 6-page bimonthly newsletter sponsored by Executive Christian Women, with a national circulation of 100.

□*ECW Newsletter* seeks articles "that encourage Christian business women to be a light in the workplace God has sent them to." Publishes profiles, interviews, fillers, poetry, and articles to help readers and encourage them in their everyday lives. Well-received articles: "Evangelism in the Workplace"; "Freedom to Focus on Christ"; "Excellence in the Workplace."

Articles should be no more than 800 words. "We have a need for *good* articles. Many we've received haven't hit our target audience, haven't been doctrinally sound, or just haven't been good writing at all." Put total number of words of article at the top of the first page. Author's guidelines and sample copies available. No payment for material used, but authors receive 2 copies of the newsletter in which their material appears. Also interested in reprints.

EMPHASIS ON FAITH AND LIVING, 3901 South Wayne Avenue, Fort Wayne, IN 46807. (219) 456–4502. Michael Reynolds, Editor. A 24-page monthly magazine published by the Missionary Church for distribution in the U.S. and Canada.

□*Emphasis on Faith and Living* gives priority to articles describing personal experiences of people and their Christian lives. These articles should illustrate the love, power, and ministry of God in various circumstances. Articles promoting the cause of missions and the church are also welcome. Readers are evangelical adult laity.

Articles of 100 to 500 words are preferred. Longer articles will be considered. Some payment for material is offered. Reports in 1 month.

ENDURING WORD: ADULT TEACHER/STUDENT/DIGEST, 6401 The Paseo, Kansas City, MO 64131. (816) 333–7000, extension 436. John B. Nielson, Editorial Director. A quarterly magazine published by The Church of the Nazarene; teacher's edition is 96 pages, student's is 48 pages. Circulation is international: 25,000 to teachers, 190,000 to students.

□*Enduring Word* is for Sunday School teachers of young people and adults; using articles of interest to such teachers, or articles and poetry relevant to the Uniform Lessons. Material published includes teacher guidance, articles of inspiration, biblically based on related life stories, family life, and Bible characters.

Articles should be 1,000 to 1,200 words. Also uses photos and illustrations. Pays on acceptance: 3¢ per word for prose, 25¢ per line for poetry. Reports immediately.

ENGAGE/SOCIAL ACTION, 100 Maryland Avenue N.E., Washington DC 20002. (202) 488–5632. Lee Ranck, Editor. A 48- to 64-page magazine published monthly (11 times a year) by the United Methodist Board of Church and Society, with a national distribution of 5,000.

□*engage/social action* is published for adult clergy and laity of liberal or mainline Protestant churches who are interested in dealing with social issues in relation to their Christian faith. Interested in such issues as war and peace, race relations, economic and labor issues, ethnic concerns, women's rights, health and welfare. Limited to nonfiction material.

Articles should be 1,500 to 2,000 words. Query letters desirable. Sample copies and author's guidelines available. Pays $50 to $100 per article, on publication.

EPIPHANY JOURNAL, P.O. Box 14727, San Francisco, CA 94114. Founded 1980. Philip Tolbert, Editor. A 120-page quarterly journal with a national distribution of 2,000.

□*Epiphany Journal* prints "well-thought-out articles (not first-person accounts) that apply Christian principles to current cultural problems and that contain a discernible moment of 'epiphany'—when the Spirit brings forth an insight not seen before. The writer must struggle to be a channel for this realization and not simply repeat time-worn statements." Well-received articles: "A Christian Ethic of the Environment," "The

Marion Dimension," "Wolfram's *Parzival* as Christian Initiation," "Sleeping in Gethsemane." Also prints interviews, theology, and book reviews. Readers are scholars, clergy, and general lay members of all denominations.

Book reviews should be 1,500 to 2,000 words, researched articles 2,000 to 5,000 words. "Purchase a sample copy ($4.00 for authors) and familiarize yourself with our style, then send a query letter with a sample of your writing." Will consider reprints. Pay is on publication and varies according to type of article—$25 is average, top is $100. Reports in 8 weeks.

THE EPISCOPALIAN, 1930 Chestnut Street, Philadelphia, PA 19103. (215) 564–2010. Richard L. Crawford, Publisher; Judy Mathe Foley, Managing Editor. A 24-page monthly newspaper published for the Episcopal Church, with a national distribution of 285,000.
□*The Episcopalian* is looking for "action, nonfiction articles about people—preferably Episcopalians—whose Christian ministry makes a difference in the world, nation, and/or community." Especially interested in articles about Episcopalians exercising ministry in secular careers in the community or in the congregation. Readers are primarily adult laity. Uses photos; looking for pictures of cats, preferably in action, for regular "Episcocats" column.

Articles can vary in length according to need, but should not be more than 800 to 1,000 words. Query letters strongly recommended. Will send sample copy on receipt of two first-class stamps. Pays an honorarium on publication for articles and photos on a varied scale. Reports as soon as possible.

EPISCOPAL RECORDER, P.O. Box 152, Pipersville, PA 18966. (215) 364–0964. Bishop Howard D. Higgins, Editor. The official publication of the Reformed Episcopal Church, 25 South 43rd Street, Philadelphia, PA 19104, with a national distribution of 1,000.
□*Episcopal Recorder* is published for members of the Reformed Episcopal churches and deals with material of interest to the clergy and laity of those churches. The denomination considers itself the evangelical wing of the Episcopal Church.

ETERNITY, 1716 Spruce Street, Philadelphia, PA 19103. (215) 546–3696. William J. Petersen, Editor. A 56- to 68-page magazine published monthly by Evangelical Ministries, Inc., with a national distribution of 50,000.
□*Eternity* is interested in nonfiction, inspirational articles, stories of people, humor, some poetry, book reviews. Wants "articles slanted toward the mature Christian interested in Bible study and biblical emphasis on contemporary developments; carefully researched and skillfully written articles on matters of biblical knowledge, personal development, church issues, and ethical problems. Willing to deal with responsible treatment of controversial subjects." Interested in personality profiles (750 words) with photos. Writing should be popular rather than academic, concrete rather than abstract. Readers are evangelical adults, laity primarily.

Most articles assigned, but some freelance material accepted. Articles should be 250 to 3,500 words; average is 2,000. Query by letter, enclosing SASE. Sample copy and editorial guidelines available. Pays $50 to $150 for standard-length articles, on acceptance. Reports in 3 to 6 weeks.

EVANGEL, 999 College Avenue, Winona Lake, IN 46590. (219) 267–7161. Vera Bethel, Editor. An 8-page weekly digest published for evangelical youth by the Free Methodist Church, with a national distribution of 35,000.
□*Evangel* looks for interviews or personal-experience articles about how a person has coped with a crisis or tragedy—or how certain persons are making a unique contribution to the community in service areas; something that will challenge the reader to serve and not just absorb. Also uses fiction and poetry.

Fillers should be 300 to 500 words; 500 to 1,000 for articles, 1,200 to 1,500 for fiction. Sample copy and author's guidelines available. Pays on acceptance: 2¢ per word, 25¢ per line for poetry. Reports in 4 weeks.

THE EVANGELICAL BEACON, 1515 East 66th Street, Minneapolis, MN 55423. (612) 866-3343. George M. Keck, Editor. A 32-page semimonthly magazine published for the adults of the Evangelical Free Church of America (EFCA), with a national distribution of 40,000.

□*The Evangelical Beacon* publishes articles relating to the Evangelical Free Church as a whole, or to individual Evangelical Free Churches, or articles by or about individuals with some EFCA connection. Articles ordinarily used include interesting, biblically-based articles on current issues; articles on interesting people; personal testimonies; descriptions of Church outreach efforts; and inspirational devotionals. Must be helpful to readers, evangelical in outlook.

Articles purchased are usually 300 to 1,500 words in length. Shorter devotional articles, of 100 words, are sometimes purchased. Sample copies and author's guidelines available. Photos often enhance the salability of an article and are appreciated. Pays (subject to change without notice) 3¢ per word; extra payment for photos. Reports in 6 to 8 weeks.

EVANGELICAL VISITOR, Box 166, Nappanee, IN 46550. (219) 773-3164. Glen Pierce, Editor; Elwyn Hock, Publisher. A 32-page monthly magazine published by the Brethren in Christ Church, with a national distribution of 4,200.

□Readers are youth, adults, and senior citizens; general lay readers of evangelical Protestant denominations. Does not purchase many manuscripts.

EVANGELIZING TODAY'S CHILD, Box 348, Warrenton, MO 63383. (314) 456-4321. Elsie Lippy, Editor. A bimonthly training and resource magazine for Sunday School teachers, Christian education leaders, and children's workers in every phase of Christian ministry, with a national distribution of 35,000.

□*Evangelizing Today's Child* is a specialized magazine, each issue of which is built around a specific theme. Resource Center is primarily an idea bank for those who teach children the Word of God. Uses creative teaching tips, scripts, short stories for children that have a scriptural solution worked into the text, Bible puzzles, quizzes, drills (length of time for a child or class to complete each item should not exceed 10 minutes). Impact column presents the testimony of an effective Christian adult who was saved as a child under the age of 10 and was preferably from a non-Christian home.

Feature articles average 1,500 to 2,000 words; query in advance. Short stories should be 700 to 800 words; scripts 500 to 1,500 words. Buys full rights to most feature articles. Pays 5¢ to 7¢ per word. Payment for Resource Center items is $2.50 to $15, depending on originality, length, and practicality of ideas submitted. Impact column payment is 5¢ per word. Also markets videotapes. Pays within 90 days of acceptance.

FAITH AND FELLOWSHIP, Box 655, Fergus Falls, MN 56537. (218) 736-7357. Rev. David Rinden, Editor. A 16-page semi-monthly magazine published by the Church of the Lutheran Brethren for 4,000 subscribers.

□*Faith and Fellowship* is published for an adult audience, members of the Church of the Lutheran Brethren denomination, both clergy and laity. Submissions should be of interest to members of the denomination.

Material is limited to nonfiction and poetry and is supplied mostly by the magazine's own constituency. No payment for material used.

FAITH FOR THE FAMILY, Bob Jones University, Greenville, SC 29614. (803) 242-5100. Dr. Bob Jones, Editor; Robert Franklin, Managing Editor. A 32-page magazine published 10 times a year with an international distribution.

□*Faith for the Family* is designed to interest readers in the entire family, clergy, general laity of fundamentalist and mixed Protestant denominations, mostly Baptist. Uses for leads: exposés or subjects of high interest among Christians, practical and interesting articles that appeal to fundamentalists. Especially needs practical Christian nonfiction; also accepts general Christian fiction for children, teens, and adults. For various reasons, *cannot* consider fictionalized Bible stories, poetry, quizzes and puzzles, or articles dealing with diet, divorce, sports, games, or recreation. Strongly recommends that writers thoroughly familiarize themselves with the magazine and its positions before submitting material.

Articles should be 1,200 to 1,500 words normally; leads can be longer. Free sample copy and author's guidelines available. Pays on acceptance: 3¢ per word, rarely over $50 (though lead stories might pay more). Reports in 4 weeks.

FAMILY FESTIVALS, 160 East Virginia Street, #290, San Jose, CA 95112. (408) 286–8505. Founded 1981. Editor: Sam Mackintosh, 23 Madison Drive, Laurel Springs, NJ 08021. A 24-page bimonthly magazine with a national distribution of 10,000.
☐*Family Festivals* prints articles about the feasts and seasons of the year in both the Christian and civil calendars, family activities, stories, and ideas for passing on religious traditions to children. Well-received articles: Rites of passage for children and adolescents; ethnic food recipes associated with feasts and holidays; Easter, Christmas, and autumn celebrations for families. Readers are adults of all denominations.

Articles should be 1,000 to 1,300 words. Sample copies $2.75; guidelines available. "Authors should write from their own religious experience, offering examples of celebrations based on real-life situations. Do not offer theoretical or untried suggestions." For particular interests, write Editor. Query letters desirable, no reprints. Pays $10 to $30 per article, according to contract terms. Reports in 10 weeks.

FAMILY LIFE TODAY, P.O. Box 93670, Pasadena, CA 91109. (213) 794–4304. Phyllis E. Alsdurf, Editor. A 32-page monthly magazine published by Gospel Light Publications to help families develop a Christian lifestyle, with a national distribution of 32,000. *check*
☐*Family Life Today* uses practical articles on Christian family living, dealing with the specific problems and joys that families face. Does not want articles that give pat answers to difficult situations ("And they all lived happily ever after."). Instead, seeks ones that honestly show the struggles and triumphs of couples and families. Readers are conservative Christians with children; articles dealing with issues relevant to such families would be of interest. Needs more articles on marriage that deal with specific truths or lessons a couple has learned, more articles by men, fewer articles by mothers on parenting preschoolers or on how a marriage has been enriched, etc.

Articles should be no more than 1,500 words; shorter articles welcome and often preferred. Query letters not required. Sample copy and author's guidelines available. Pays on acceptance: 4¢ to 5¢ per word for first rights, 3¢ per word for reprints. Reports within 2 months.

FELLOWSHIP, Box 271, Nyack, NY 10960. (914) 358–4601. Richard A. Chartier, Editor. A 24- to 32-page magazine published monthly (sometimes bimonthly) by the Fellowship of Reconciliation, a peace organization.
☐*Fellowship* is looking for "fresh perspectives on the task of helping to build a world of peace and justice; information about pacifist/nonviolent life, action, and witness." Interested in any material in this general area written from a religious point of view. Readers are youth and adult clergy and laity, mostly of liberal or mainline Protestant denominations.

Articles should be 2,500 words for major submissions, or 800 to 1,000 words for reports on areas and problems related to peace movements and people. Query letters desirable. Sample copies available. No payment for material used; writers are given subscription to the magazine for themselves or a friend. Reports in 1 to 2 weeks.

FELLOWSHIP IN PRAYER, 20 Nassau Street, Room 230, Princeton, NJ 08540. (609) 924–0880. Founded 1949. Paul Griffith, Editor. A 16- to 20-page bimonthly magazine with a national audience of 2,000 subscribers.
☐*Fellowship In Prayer* is published for a general adult lay audience, mainly liberal Protestants. "We hope, with Divine Assistance, to foster a deeper spirit of understanding and fellowship among humankind, thereby helping to bridge the gaps caused by dif-

ferences in sex, creed, race, class, and culture." Looking for "serious explorations in high-quality writing of contemporary prayer and spiritual experience." Seeks fiction, nonfiction, poetry, stories of people—all related to first-person experiences of prayer. Also prints photos and illustrations, reflections and poetry.

Articles should be 1,000 to 2,000 words. No query letters. Sample copy available. Articles are accepted as donations for one-time use; authors receive 5 free copies of the issue and receive future issues at no charge. Reports as quickly as possible.

FIRM FOUNDATION, Box 17200, Pensacola, FL 32522. (904) 433-4258. William S. Cline, Editor; John G. Priola, Associate Editor. A 16-page weekly magazine published by the Firm Foundation Publishing House, Inc., with a national distribution of 15,000. □*Firm Foundation* caters primarily to interests of the Churches of Christ and has an adult lay readership of mixed evangelical denominations. Prints nonfiction articles and articles on biblical themes.

Article length is 1,200 words or less. Query letters not necessary. Sample copy of publication available. Articles are contributed by authors—no payment.

FLOODTIDE: MAGAZINE OF LITERATURE EVANGELISM, Box C, Fort Washington, PA 19034. (215) 542-1242. Deborah Meroff, Editor. A 24-page quarterly magazine, published by the Christian Literature Crusade, with an international subscription of 6,000. □*Floodtide* reports on news and developments of Christian literature around the world. Articles on the power and impact of print on the lives of individuals are welcome. Does not solicit articles—staff supplies material and obtains information from other sources. Publishes missionary items (missiological subjects) pertaining to literature distribution.

Free sample copy available.

FOCUS ON THE FAMILY Magazine, 41 East Foothill Boulevard, Arcadia, CA 91006. (818) 445-1579. Founded 1978. S. Rickly Christian, Editor; Scotty Sawyer, Associate Editor. A 16-page monthly magazine with a national distribution of 500,000. □*Focus on the Family* seeks how-to articles of practical help to family members, issue-oriented pieces, and emotional pieces; also prints profiles, interviews, fillers, photos, and illustrations. Well-received articles have been on voter registration, Francis Schaeffer, and problem pregnancies. Readers are general lay adults of various evangelical and mainline Protestant denominations.

Articles should be 1,000 to 1,500 words; sometimes longer for issue articles. Query letters desirable: "Would like to see query letters offering practical help to married couples and parents; issue-oriented articles of concern to families (abortion, pornography, over-35 pregnancies, etc.)." Sample copies available. Pays 10¢ per word, on acceptance. Reports in 4 weeks.

THE FORERUNNER, P.O. Box 1799, Gainesville, FL 32602. (904) 375-6000. Founded 1981. Robert T. Weiner, Editor. A 24-page evangelical charismatic monthly newspaper sponsored by the Maranatha Christian churches, with an international circulation of 7,000. □*The Forerunner* prints "news stories or testimonials which particularly relate to the university student and key world and national issues." Well-received articles: "Science and the Bible," Parts I, II, and III; "The Forge of Christian Character"; "Whatever Happened to the English Language?"; "The Election of Our Lifetime." Also prints interviews, fillers, photos, and illustrations.

No length limit on articles. Sample copy available on request. Will consider reprints. Does not pay. Reports in 2 weeks.

FOR PARENTS, 7052 West Lane, Eden, NY 14057. Founded 1977. Carolyn C. Shadle, Editor. An 8- to 10-page bimonthly newsletter (published 5 times a year) with an optional 2-page newssheet insert, *For Churches.* National distribution: 3,000. □*For Parents* prints inspirational, practical resources of interest to Christian parents, and church leaders who work with families. Well-received articles include the TV and Resources pages. Readers are adults and clergy of Roman Catholic and mainline Protestant denominations.

Short articles should be 100 words. Query letters required. Free sample copy and author's guidelines available. Pays on publication: $5 for short items 70 to 300 words, $25 for full-page articles. Reports in 4 weeks. Will consider reprints.

FOURSQUARE WORLD ADVANCE, 1100 Glendale Boulevard, Los Angeles, CA 90026. (213) 484-0105. Janice Pederson, Editor. A 16-page magazine issued 10 times a year by the International Church of the Foursquare Gospel, with a national distribution of 70,000.

□*Foursquare World Advance* is aimed at adults—clergy and laity, evangelicals, mostly members of the Foursquare Church. Most writers are also members of the denomination. Emphasizes people whose lives have demonstrated outstanding faith and service. Regular features contain news about Foursquare people and activities and Bible studies and other inspirational messages from the leadership of the church. Also uses photos.

Articles should be 2 to 5 manuscript pages and feature information about Foursquare people and activities. Query letters desirable. Sample copy available. Pays $10 to $25 for articles, on publication. Reports in 2 weeks.

FREEING THE SPIRIT, 1234 Massachusetts Avenue N.W., Washington D.C. 20005. (202) 347-4619. Ronald LaMarr Sharps, Editor. A 32- to 40-page quarterly magazine on black liturgy, published by the National Office for Black Catholics.

□*Freeing The Spirit* seeks to "provide a sense of history and direction to black Catholics as well as models for black Catholic worship and leadership in the church." Aimed at an audience of black adults—scholars, clergy, and laity, mostly Catholics, but some Protestants as well. Uses fiction, nonfiction, poetry, photos, and illustrations on general subjects of interest to the readers. Especially interested in liturgies, histories, prayers, drama concerning the black experience. Also needs articles that focus on ecumenical relations and describe pieces of special liturgies.

Articles should be 1,500 to 3,000 words. Longer articles can be serialized and paid for as separate items. Query letters desirable. Sample copy and author's guidelines available. Pays on publication: $35 for major articles, $25 for shorter pieces.

FREEWAY, Box 632, Glen Ellyn, IL 60138. (312) 668-6000. Cindy Atoji, Editor. A 4-page Sunday School take-home paper, published quarterly and distributed weekly by Scripture Press publications. National distribution: 70,000.

□*Freeway* needs true stories written in the first person, 1,000 words or less. Stories should show how God has worked in a specific area of a teen's life. Interview a teen and write about his experience "as told to you," or write a personal experience. No fictionalized stories based on true experiences. Clear photos, preferably black-and-white, should accompany the article. Also needs short true stories, 750 words or less, revolving around a central anecdote or theme. Incorporate detail, action, personal thoughts, emotion, humor, and Scripture into stories. "We do not need true stories dealing with accidents or illness; we do need true stories dealing with emotions and events of everyday life." Well-received articles: "How I Overcame Shyness," "Pimples Pickled My Social Life." Readers are conservative, evangelical teens, ages 14 through 21.

Prefers to see complete manuscript, not query letters. Free sample copy and author's guidelines available. For first rights, pays 4¢ to 7¢ per word, for second rights (reprint) 3¢ to 5¢ per word. Reports in 1 month.

FRIENDS JOURNAL, 1501 Cherry Street, Philadelphia, PA 19102. (215) 241-7277. Vinton Deming, Editor-Manager. A 32-page magazine, published 19 times a year in close association with Friends General Conference (Quakers), with a paid circulation of over 9,000 subscribers and an estimated readership of 27,000.

□*Friends Journal* is published for a liberal, spiritually-curious audience of both Friends and non-Friends. Interested in nonfiction, poetry, and humor "to combine spiritual insights and analysis with traditional Quaker social concerns: simplicity, peacemaking, native Americans, women's rights, prisons, international affairs, human rights, and much more. With a peace church orientation, the magazine tries to be both contemporary and historical. Has a continuing need for biblically-focused, socially relevant material.

Articles should be 8 to 10 manuscript pages. Shorter pieces welcome. Query letters desirable. Sample copy and author's guidelines available. No payment for material used. Acknowledges receipt of material immediately.

FUNDAMENTALIST JOURNAL, Lynchburg, VA 24514. Founded 1982. Deborah Huff, Editor. A 68-page monthly (11 issues per year) magazine sponsored by the *Old-Time Gospel Hour*, with 60,000 paid subscribers.
□*Fundamentalist Journal* prints "articles of general interest to a Fundamentalist Christian audience." Well-received articles: "An Alternative to Legalism"; "Are Divorce and Remarriage Ever Permissible?"; "Is Repentance Part of the Gospel?"; other subjects included abortion, Christian responsibility, and interviews. Also publishes profiles, humor, devotions, fillers, Bible study, theology, photos and illustrations, and "very little" fiction and poetry. Readers are adults and senior citizens, clergy and lay fundamentalists (mainly Baptist).

Articles should be a maximum of 2,500 words: 800 to 2,000 words preferred. Guidelines and sample copies available. Will consider reprints. Pays on publication: 10¢ per printed word, 5¢ per printed word for reprints. Reports in 13 weeks.

THE GEM, Box 926, Findlay, OH 45839. Founded 1866. Marilyn Rayle Kern, Editor of Curriculum. An 8-page weekly magazine sponsored by the Churches of God, General Conference, with a national distribution of 7,200.
□*The Gem* prints "stories and articles that will be relevant to a diversity of ages and life situations, true-to-life experiences of God's help, of healed relationships, and of growing maturity in faith. An unchurched person should be able to perceive persons portrayed and solutions to problems as being genuine." Well-received articles: "The Holy Week of Our Lives," "ABC's for Sleepless Nights," "A Different Victory," "An Unexpected Gift," "A Grass-Roots Grandma" (all P. R. Tedesco stories). Also publishes fiction, humor, and fillers. Readers are youth, adults, and senior citizens, both clergy and lay members of the Churches of God.

Fillers should be 50 to 300 words, short articles 400 to 950 words, feature stories 1,000 to 1,600 words. Guidelines and sample copy available "with long SASE." Particularly interested in humor that increases self-awareness and empathy, and "nonjudgmental encouragement of discernment in TV watching." Prefers complete manuscripts to query letters; will consider reprints. Pays $5 to $15 on publication, depending on length. Reports in 6 weeks, "for material to be returned. Those held for possible publication may be on file 6 months before use—longer if seasonal."

GLAD MAGAZINE, P.O. Box 11, St. Mary's OH 45885. Founded 1982. M. Taylor Overbey, Editor. A 32-page bimonthly newspaper sponsored by Word-Centered Productions, Inc., with an international distribution of 10,000.
□*Glad Magazine* prints "humorous Christian literature that teaches biblical principles." Well-received articles: "Leave it to Believer," "The Ism of God." Also publishes fiction, scripts, narratives, panel gags, comic strips, and Bible study. Readers are children, youth, and adults, both clergy and lay members of a variety of denominations.

Articles should be 300 to 400 words maximum. Guidelines and sample copies available. Query letters desirable, does not want reprints. Pays "approximately $10 per page," on acceptance. Reports in 6 weeks.

GOOD NEWS, Wilmore, KY 40390. (606) 858-4661. James V. Heidinger II, Editor. A 60-page magazine published 6 times a year, with a national distribution of 18,500.
□*Good News* is the official "voice" of the movement—it provides a form for scriptural Christianity within the Evangelical United Methodist Church. Proposes "to make an ef-

fective witness for Christ and historic Wesleyanism within the denomination, to uphold Scripture, to deal with vital issues, to inspire and encourage readers in the Christian life. " Looking for testimony articles (competition here is stiff), history pieces on United Methodist characters, occasional missionary pieces, articles on programs that have worked well in other churches that readers might want to emulate in their churches, etc. Does not want didactic material—looks for manuscripts with anecdotal, highly readable style. Good poetry, humor, and filler material are always needed. Fresh, well-written history pieces that relate to the United Metholist/Evangelical United Brethren heritage also welcome.

Articles should be 4 to 5 double-spaced, typed pages. Query letters not required, but are desirable. Sample copy of magazine available for $1.00; author's guidelines free. Pays on acceptance: 5¢ to 7¢ per word for normal-length manuscripts, $10 to $35 for short fillers and short poetry. Reports within about 2 months. Also publishes promotional pamphlets and sometimes accepts article reprints that inspire and encourage readers in the Christian life and which uphold Scripture.

GOOD NEWS BROADCASTER, Box 82808, Lincoln, NE 68501. (402) 474–4567. Norman A. Olson, Managing Editor. A 64-page monthly magazine (July/August issues combined) with a national distribution of 150,000.

□Good News Broadcaster, read by evangelical adults, wants nonfiction material that is biblical, at least in principle; which explains the Bible and how it is relevant to daily life. Strives "to present Christ as Savior to the lost and to promote the spiritual growth of believers."

Articles should be approximately 1,500 words. Query letters desirable. Free sample copy and author's guidelines available. Pays on acceptance: 3¢ per word for freelance articles, 4¢ per word for assigned articles, 2¢ per word for reprints. Reports within 1 month.

THE GOOD NEWSPAPER, Box 219214, Houston, TX 77218. Founded 1982. Edward Fudge, Editor. A 16-page biweekly newspaper with a national distribution of 5,000.

□The Good Newspaper prints "inspirational, practical articles of personal Christian living, articles on Christian homes, relationships, and attitudes." Also prints profiles and interviews. Readers are lay adults of various Protestant denominations.

Articles should be 400 to 800 words. Sample copy free with 9″ by 12″ SASE. Will consider reprints. No pay, but author gets byline and two free issues of the paper containing his or her contribution. No decision time given.

GOSPEL CALL, 232 North Lake Avenue, Suite 206, Pasadena, CA 91101. (213) 796–5425. Rev. Walter E. Zurfluh, Editor. A 16-page bimonthly magazine of the Eastern European Mission, with a national distribution of 3,500.

□Gospel Call publishes information and reports from Eastern European Mission missionaries and national workers in the field, in addition to other information gathered relating to fields of ministries in Europe. Readers are clergy and general lay adults of evangelical and other Protestant denominations.

Sample copies available. Rarely purchases material.

THE GOSPEL CARRIER, P.O. Box 850, Joplin, MO 64802. (417) 624–7050. Rosmarie Foreman, Editor. A 104-page quarterly magazine of the Pentecostal Church of God, with a national distribution of 3,500.

□The Gospel Carrier's articles are edited to meet the particular need of the Pentecostal Church of God and related churches served by this literature. Ordinarily uses manuscripts with a clear Christian message; does not use material that violates the "Holiness-Fundamentalist" taboos. For this reason, does not publish a type of article commonly used by the houses that publish for a wider readership. Prints fiction, nonfiction, stories of people, humor, and devotionals.

Articles should be 1,500 to 1,800 words. Query letters not required. Sample copy and author's guidelines available for 50¢. Pays on publication: 1½¢ per word for all manuscripts. Reports within 2 weeks.

THE GOSPEL MESSAGE, 10000 North Oak, Kansas City, MO 64155. (816) 734–8500. Abe Reddekopp, Editor. A 16-page magazine, published quarterly by the Gospel Missionary Union, with a national distribution.
☐*The Gospel Message* uses mission-oriented material to help inform, motivate, or stimulate Christians and local churches relative to world missions. Particular needs include articles on urban church planting and on "what God did in my life to make me more effective for him—in missions."
Articles should be 2½ to 3 or 5 to 6 double-spaced pages, with photos if available. Query letters desirable. Free sample copy available. No payment.

GUIDE, Review and Herald Publishing Association, 55 West Oak Ridge Drive, Hagerstown, MD 21740. Penny Estes Wheeler, Editor. A 32-page weekly magazine of the Seventh-Day Adventist Church, with a national distribution of 55,000.
☐*Guide* is geared for 10- through 15-year-olds. Uses one poem per issue, occasionally uses feature articles on outdoor activities, wildlife, or other subjects interesting to this age bracket. Mostly uses "true" stories that emphasize the positive aspects of Christian living (obedience, courage, unselfishness, etc.). Does not use made-up stories, but it is permissible to invent dialogue for the purpose of flow. Always needs true, character-building stories, especially about boys. Can always use "drama in real life" stories that show God's protection; and seasonal stories for Christmas, Thanksgiving, Valentine's Day, etc.
Articles should be 1,000 to 2,500 words; 1,800 words is average—prefers them not shorter than 1,000 words. Poems can be up to 16 lines. Query letters okay, but it's best to send manuscript. Author's guidelines free; sample copies free with 28¢ postage included with request. Pays on acceptance: 3¢ to 4¢ per word; $1 per line for poetry. Reports in 4 to 6 weeks, often sooner.

GUIDEPOSTS, 747 Third Avenue, New York, NY 10017. (212) 754–2200. Ruth Stafford Peale and Norman Vincent Peale, Editors-in-Chief and Publishers; Van Varner, Editor. A 48-page digest-sized monthly magazine with an international distribution of 4,300,000.
☐*Guideposts* publishes first-person experience inspirational stories of people and aims at a wide general (mostly Christian) audience. All stories are nonfiction, emphasize human interest heavily, and make one spiritual point. Guidelines observe the following: "Don't tell an entire life story. Focus on one specific point. Stick to the viewpoint of one person. Keep the reader's interest with the dominant person. Everything in the article should be tied to this one specific theme." Does *not* use essay or sermon material nor stories about deceased people. Uses third-person presentations in "Quiet People," one-page features (query in advance on this). Also uses short fillers with an anecdote or spiritual point. Especially interested in stories of celebrities and sports figures.
Average length of articles is 1,200 words. Query letters desirable. Pays, on acceptance, $10 to $25 for short features of 250 words; $25 to $100 for manuscripts of 250 to 750 words; $200 to $300 for full-length manuscripts of 750 to 1,500 words. Occasionally higher payments for subsequent sales. Reports in 4 weeks. Also distributes a Christmas card that is produced in-house.

HAPPY TIMES, Board of Parish Education, Concordia Publishing House, 3558 South Jefferson Avenue, St. Louis, MO 63118. (314) 664–7000. A story and activity monthly for pre-primary Christian children, with a national distribution of 65,000.
☐*Happy Times* prints material that strengthens and supports Christian home training by showing characters living with and growing in Christian principles, but is no longer accepting freelance submissions.

HEARTBEAT, P.O. Box 1088, 1134 Murfreesboro Road, Nashville, TN 37202. (615) 361–1010. Don Robirds, Editor. A bimonthly magazine, usually of 16 pages, published by the Department of Foreign Missions of the National Association of Free Will Baptists, with a national distribution of 30,000.

☐*Heartbeat* seeks "human-interest articles relating to life on the mission field. Wants stories that will challenge Christians to become more concerned and involved in world outreach. Needs articles that show God at work in the world—tangible, visible results!"

Articles should be approximately 1,000 words because number of pages is limited. Query letters desirable. Pays 3¢ per word, on publication. Reports within 1 month.

HERALD OF HOLINESS, 6401 The Paseo, Kansas City, MO 64131. (816) 333–7000. W. E. McCumber, Editor. A 36-page magazine published twice a month by the Church of the Nazarene, with an international distribution of 200,000.

☐*Herald of Holiness,* the official organ of the Church of the Nazarene, uses devotional, doctrinal, ethical, and inspirational articles as well as ones devoted to Christian home and family life. Articles should be written in un-technical language, with high human-interest quotient. Some short poetry is also used. "A very limited market. Biggest need is for well-written articles on doctrine and moral issues. Writers unacquainted with the denomination seldom hit the mark."

Articles generally are 800 to 1,200 words. Free sample copy and author's guidelines available. Pays, on acceptance, 3½¢ per word for prose, 25¢ per line for poetry. Reports within 1 month.

HICALL, 1445 Boonville Avenue, Springfield, MO 65802. (417) 862–2781. William P. Campbell, Youth Editor. An 8-page weekly magazine published by the Assemblies of God Church, with a national distribution of 160,000.

☐*HiCall* is a weekly Sunday take-home paper slanted to 15- to 17-year-olds of the Assemblies of God denomination. Material used includes fiction that presents believable characters working out their problems according to Bible principles, and articles emphasizing some phase of Christian living, presented in a down-to-earth manner. Particular needs are for holiday stories (Easter, Christmas, etc.). All special day material should be sent in one year in advance. Subjects recently well-received include family-teen relations, dating, campus action, and job situations.

Fillers should be 300 to 500 words, stories 900 to 1,800 words. Query letters not required. Free sample copy and author's guidelines available. Pays on acceptance: 2¢ to 3¢ per word. Reports in 2 weeks.

HIGH ADVENTURE, 1445 Boonville Avenue, Springfield, MO 65802. (417) 862–2781, extension 1497. Johnnie Barnes, Editor. A 16-page quarterly newspaper published for the Royal Rangers of the Assemblies of God Church, with a national youth distribution of 70,000.

☐*High Adventure* articles fall into the following categories: adventure stories, Western and pioneer adventure stories, nature study features, campcraft features, and special devotions. "Stories and articles should require very little editing. If article involves drawings, author should send in a rough layout."

Adventure stories should be about 1,200 words; nature study and campcraft articles should range between 500 and 600 words, depending on how many illustrations are used. Query letters desirable. Sample copies and author's guidelines available. "All articles are placed in our files. When the decision is made to use an article in a specific issue, a check is sent to the author." Pays about $20 per printed page, $1 for jokes, $3 to $5 for cartoons. Reports usually within 1 to 2 months.

HIS MAGAZINE, 5206 Main Street, Downers Grove, IL 60515. (313) 964–5700. David Neff, Editor. A 32-page magazine published 9 times a year by Inter-Varsity Christian Fellowship, 233 Langdon Street, Madison, WI 53703. International distribution about 26,000.

☐*His Magazine* is published mainly for college students, primarily for Christians attending secular colleges. Whenever possible, articles should be student-oriented rather than general. Uses college-related material on relationships, discipleship, evangelism, love/sex/marriage, college interests, personal testimonies, moral and international issues, and Bible exposition. Also prints fiction, poetry, stories of people, humor, and photos and illustrations. Particularly interested in articles on the Christian and military service and exploration of biblical passages.

Manuscripts range anywhere from 200 to 2,000 words; eight double-spaced, typed pages is usual maximum. Do not query; prefers to read entire manuscripts. Free sample copy and author's guidelines available. Pays $25 to $60 per article, on acceptance; less for poems (of which it does not accept many). Reports within 4 months.

HOME LIFE, 127 Ninth Avenue North, Nashville, TN 37234. (615) 251-2271. Reuben Herring, Editor; Mary Paschall Darby, Assistant Editor. A 68-page monthly magazine of the Sunday School Board of the Southern Baptist convention with a distribution, mainly in the South, of 785,000.
☐*Home Life* is for adult lay readers of the Southern Baptist Churches. Its purpose is to enrich family life. "Most of the manuscripts should have a family orientation. An important question to ask about a manuscript is, 'Will the article help our readers grow and develop in their family relationships?' " Top priority subjects are marriage enrichment articles, then articles on parenthood, family relationships, family vacations, concerns, and problems; family humor, and inspirational articles. Prefers manuscripts that grow out of life experiences or that describe life experiences in a realistic way. (Use essay approach with believable case studies.) Article possibilities include self-esteem and individuality in marriage, husband-wife communication, solving conflicts responsibly, changing roles of husbands and wives, finding time for each other, marriage and money management.

Articles should be 350 to 2,400 words. Query letters desirable, but not required. Free sample copy and author's guidelines available. Pays 4¢ per word, on acceptance. Also pays $12 to $20 for poems, $30 for cartoons; also uses fiction. Reports within 2 months.

HORIZON INTERNATIONAL MAGAZINE, P.O. Box 28429, San Diego, CA 92128. (619) 566-3404. Founded 1980. Jennie Gillespie, Editor. A 16-page bimonthly tabloid magazine with a national distribution of 35,000.
☐*Horizon International Magazine* is "looking for articles that carry a positive, not preachy, message based on solid biblical principles, to be used as a tool for evangelism—humorous articles, personal experiences, testimonies, interviews with interesting (not necessarily famous) people; inspirational, youth- , and family-oriented pieces; news and informational articles, in-depth contemporary social issue pieces, and some poetry. While most media reviews are done by the staff, we are open to being queried in this area." Also publishes fillers, and photos and illustrations. Readers are lay adults, 15 to 40 years old of various Protestant denominations.

Well-received articles: "New Music: The Power Sounds of the '80s," "Child Abuse," *Return of the Jedi* and *Gandhi* movie reviews, "Dungeons & Dragons," "Number One Enemy—A Courageous Chinese Family."

Articles should be 1,800 to 2,000 words for major themes or stories; 1,500 words for first-person stories; 500 to 1,000 words for inspirational pieces; 200 to 400 words for news and short items. Guidelines and sample copies available. Query letters desirable "for long, issue-oriented, or interview pieces;" will consider reprints. Pays $50 and up per article, on the average, on publication. Reports in 12 weeks.

THE HYMN, c/o The Hymn Society of America, National Headquarters, Texas Christian University, Fort Worth, TX 76129. (817) 921-7608. A 75-page quarterly magazine sponsored by the Hymn Society, with a national distribution of 3,200.
☐*The Hymn* is published for a mixed audience, mainly clergy and church musicians in mainline and evangelical Protestant as well as Roman Catholic churches. Interested in both scholarly and practical articles on the hymnody of the Christian church. Recent ar-

ticles, for example, dealt with inclusive language in hymnody, how to improve congregational singing, and the history of the publication of special types of hymns.

Articles should be 500 to 1,000 words. Free sample copy and author's guidelines available. No payment for material used. Reports immediately.

INDIAN LIFE, Intertribal Christian Communications, Box 3765, Station B, Winnipeg, Manitoba R2W 3R6, Canada. (204) 949–9452. Founded 1979. George McPeek, Editor. A 16-page bimonthly magazine with an international distribution throughout the U.S. and Canada of 12,000. Two-thirds of the circulation goes to hospitals, prisons, schools, and churches for bulk distribution.

☐*Indian Life* prints "legends and historical stories of Indians, positive true stories of individuals overcoming problems through faith in God, profiles on leading Indian figures who maintain a Christian testimony." Well-received articles: treatment and help for alcoholics, story about overcoming drugs, etc. Also publishes a very limited amount of fiction, fillers, photos and illustrations, interviews, and general Indian news. Readers are children, youth, and adults, both clergy and lay members (some Roman Catholic, mostly Protestant).

Main articles should run 1,000 to 1,200 words, news items 250 to 750 words. Sample copies and guidelines available. "*Indian Life* maintains a nondenominational stance. We aim at Grade 8 reading level, but articles should not talk down to the reader. Most of our writers are Indians, because they speak from within the culture. Manuscripts will be read, but queries are preferred." Use SASE with Canadian stamps or International reply coupon. Pays 2¢ to 4¢ per word, poetry and fillers by the line, on publication. Reports in 6 to 8 weeks.

INNOVATIONS FOR THE CHURCH LEADER, 850 North Grove, Elgin, IL 60120. Founded 1984. Marlene D. LeFever, Senior Editor. A 32-page magazine published 5 times a year by the David C. Cook Publishing Company, with a national distribution.

☐*Innovations* focuses on "profiles of church programs that show excellence and creativity and could be duplicated in other church situations, and interviews with significant church leaders." Well-received articles: "The Art of Nonpartisan Politics," "Sensory Worship Experience," "When They Want You to Be a Solomon," "ESL in the Church," "Success with Growth Groups." Readers are both clergy and lay adults of various denominations: evangelical, Roman Catholic, and mainline Protestant.

Interviews and profiles should be 1,500 to 1,800 words. Sample copy available. Particularly interested in how-to articles by church leaders on any aspect of ministry. Query letters desirable; does not want reprints. Pays $200 per printed page, on acceptance. Reports in 8 weeks.

IN SEASON, 324 East Fourth Street, Royal Oak, MI 48067. (313) 546–4510. F. Dean Leuking, Editor. A 4-page weekly publication with a national distribution of 1,600.

☐*In Season* is a sermon publication based on the 3-year lectionary now in use in several denominations. Each issue contains one sermon based on one of the texts for the Sunday in question, plus a summary of the teaching, a prayer, suggested hymn, and material on the author of the week. The sermons, while intended primarily for Lutheran use, are applicable to any denomination using the 3-year lectionary series. Readers are primarily clergy.

Query letters encouraged, since most writing is by assignment. Sample available. Pays by agreement with authors, on publication.

INTERACTION MAGAZINE, 1333 South Kirkwood Road, St. Louis, MO 63122-7295. Founded 1960. Martha Streufert Jander, Interim Editor. A bimonthly 12-page magazine and 11-times-a-year 8-page newsletter, sponsored by the Lutheran Church—Missouri Synod, with a national distribution of 17,000.

☐*Interaction* prints "practical helps for Sunday School teachers and other church workers in the areas of theology, education, teaching methods, and psychology." Well-received articles: "An Ascension Celebration," "Worship in the Sunday School,"

"Planning for Discipline," "Put Yourself into the Bible Story." Also prints filler-type items in the newsletter column, "Interchange": "These items should be about 200 words or less and written in the first-person—teaching techniques 'I' have tried and found successful." Readers are adult Lutheran Sunday School workers.

Articles should be 750 to 2,000 words, "the fewer for a one-page article, more for two pages. We buy only a few articles, poems only occasionally. We prefer a popular, readable style. Writers must be familiar with the theology and doctrines of the Lutheran Church—Missouri Synod." Sample copies and author's guidelines available. Query letters not required; will consider reprints. Pays on publication: $35 per article generally, but up to $50 "depending on the quality of the material"; pays $5 for fillers. Reports in 8 weeks.

INTERLIT, David C. Cook Foundation, Cook Square, Elgin, IL 60120. (312) 741-2400. Gladys J. Peterson, Editor. a 24-page quarterly magazine with a national and overseas distribution.
☐*Interlit* uses only articles dealing with communications, literature, literacy, leadership training, and the mass media. Most features are "This is how it ought to be done," or "This is how we did it." Practically all articles are assigned. Readers are missionaries, publishers, professors, students, lay persons, and others involved in the four specialized fields listed above; desired are articles that will encourage and help them in their work.

Length of articles ranges from 800 to 1,500 words. Query before sending articles or photographs. Free sample copy available. Pays on acceptance: $20 to $75 for 500 to 1,500 words. Reports in 2 weeks. Also distributes monographs; pay depends on length and on expertise of writer.

INTERNATIONAL CHRISTIAN COMMUNICATIONS, INC., 2002 Main Street, Niagara Falls, NY 14305. (716) 284-5194. Founded 1970. Rev. Ronald J. Marr, Publisher. A 36-page tabloid newspaper published 11 times a year, with a national distribution of 70,000.
☐*International Christian Communications, Inc.* seeks short articles on moral, social, spiritual concerns from a biblically conservative perspective, treated as news, comment, and analysis. Well-received articles were on religious freedom, anti-Communism, and pro-life. Readers are general lay adults of various evangelical Protestant denominations.

Articles should be "short in all categories." Query letters desirable. Sample copy and author's guidelines available. Usually no payment for material used, but special arrangements can be made, in which case payment is on publication. Reports in 5 weeks. Also considers reprints.

INTERNATIONAL PENTECOSTAL HOLINESS ADVOCATE, P.O. Box 12609, Oklahoma City, OK 73157. (405) 787-7115. Shirley Spencer, Editor. A 20-page monthly publication of the International Pentecostal Holiness Church, with a national distribution of 40,000.
☐The *Advocate* addresses itself to adults, mostly laity and members of Pentecostal Holiness churches. Uses nonfiction articles, stories of people, photos, and some brief sermons.

Articles should be 800 to 1,200 words. No payment for material used. Also distributes calendars featuring denominational events.

INTERPRETATION: A JOURNAL OF BIBLE AND THEOLOGY, 3401 Brook Road, Richmond, VA 23227. (804) 355-0671, extension 296. Paul J. Achtemeier, Editor. A 112-page quarterly journal, published by Union Theological Seminary in Virginia, with an international distribution of 12,000.
☐*Interpretation* publishes articles and essays of biblical and theological interpretation in the community of faith for adult scholars, clergy, and laity of all denominational backgrounds.

Solicits most material, but also accepts freelance submissions. Query letters not necessary. Reports in 1 month.

ISSUES AND ANSWERS, 1405 South Ivy Way, Denver, CO 80224. Founded 1978. Publishes both youth and adult editions. Youth editor: William C. Sack. Adult editor: Tim Hastings, Director of Publications, P.O. Box 608, Herrin, IL 62948. An 8-page monthly newspaper sponsored by Student Action for Christ, Inc., with a national distribution of 20,000.

□*Issues and Answers* prints articles "that present the Christian world view in all current events and people's interests: sports, theater, film, books, business and economics, government, education, psychology. Most articles are for high school students; some are just for adults." Well-received articles: film review of *Footloose* showing how it gave a good depiction of dating, interview with Olympic track star Carl Lewis. Also prints profiles, humor, and photos and illustrations. Readers are youth and adults of various denominations.

Articles should be 3 to 4 pages, typed, and double-spaced on 8½" by 11" paper. Sample copies and guidelines available. Particularly interested in writers who would like to contribute regularly in a field of their interest: Broadway, film, Washington, historical biography, pro sports. Query letters desirable; will consider reprints. Pays in complimentary copies of the publication. Reports in 5 to 6 weeks.

JED SHARE, 132 West 31st Street, New York, NY 10001. (212) 239–8700. Norma E. Koenig, Editor. A 32-page quarterly magazine published by JED (Joint Educational Development), a coalition of 12 mainline Protestant denominations.

□*JED Share* is aimed at church teachers and leaders in the denominations that sponsor its publication, along with curriculum planned for these churches. Articles should be concerned with church education or be of interest to church educators. Uses nonfiction only, and photos. Needs seasonal materials. Issues have focused on education in the '80s, the small church, the family, youth and the arts, and education for action.

Articles may be of different lengths, depending on needs. Contributors should study the magazine before submitting material. Pays on publication: $15 to $20 per printed page, $35 for a 2-page article, 15¢ to 20¢ per line for shorter items. Reports on material promptly, but may hold photocopies of articles for future use, if appropriate.

JOURNAL OF CHRISTIAN CAMPING, Christian Camping International, P.O. Box 646, Wheaton, IL 60189. (312) 690–8606. A bimonthly publication with a national distribution of 5,400.

□*The Journal of Christian Camping* serves the unique needs of youth-camp and Bible-conference leaders. Articles should concentrate on the new and innovative—things actually in use by one or more camping organizations. Subjects can cover the total area of residential, wilderness, travel, and day camping, as well as conferences. Considers such topics as running a business office, maintaining a healthy cash-flow, advertising and promoting, working with government regulations and inspectors, maintaining grounds and equipment, improving the physical appearance of a camp, planning new construction, purchasing new equipment, training counselors, programming to meet campers' needs, running a palatable food-service program, providing nutritional meals, and assuring camper health and safety.

Articles should be 600 to 3,000 words. Query first. Sample copy $2.00; free author's guidelines available. For articles, pays $25 to $150, on acceptance. Pays $7.50 for 5" by 7" or larger black-and-white prints. Send contact sheets or prints with accompanying query or manuscript. Also uses 35mm color transparencies. Reports in 4 weeks.

JOURNAL OF CHRISTIAN NURSING, 5206 Main Street, P.O. Box 1650, Downers Grove, IL 60515. Founded 1984. Ramona Cass, Editor. A 32-page quarterly sponsored by the Nurses' Christian Fellowship, 233 Langdon, Madison, WI 53703. National circulation of 7,000.

□*Journal of Christian Nursing* prints "articles by or for nurses to help them integrate faith and nursing. Perspectives and experiences of others like chaplains, doctors, patients, and patients' family members welcome." Well-received articles: "How to Assess Spiritual Needs of Children and Their Families," "My Child Has a Brain

Tumor," "Does Christianity Cause Mental Illness?," "When a Nurse Steals Narcotics," "My Baby or My Health—How Could I Decide?" Other features include profiles of nurses, humor, poetry, accompanying photos and illustrations. Readers are mainly nurses—that is, lay adults—who may be evangelical Protestant or Roman Catholic.

Articles should be 6 to 8 pages, typed, and double-spaced. Topics list, writers' guidelines, and sample copy available. Does not pay. Query letter desirable; will consider reprints. No report time given.

JOURNAL OF CHURCH MUSIC, 2900 Queen Lane, Philadelphia, PA 19129. (215) 848-6800, extension 251. Andrew K. Heller, Editor. A 32-page magazine published monthly (except July-August) by the Board of Publication of the Lutheran Church in America for 5,200 subscribers.

□*Journal of Church Music* provides resource material for the church musician—how-to's, literature, light research, and other music-related topics. Needs short, well-written articles geared toward the volunteer small-church musician who has little access to techniques and materials except through this publication. Welcomes historical and theoretical material as well as practical. Interested in both organ and choral techniques. Special need in the area of children's choirs. Occasional articles directed toward clergy and members of music committees. Both Protestant and Catholic subscribers.

Articles should be 1,500 to 3,000 words. Pays on acceptance: 2¢ per word. Acknowledges material immediately; reports in 1 to 6 months. Articles published become the property of the publisher on a work-for-hire basis, but permission for subsequent use by the author will not be unreasonably withheld.

JOURNAL OF ECUMENICAL STUDIES, Temple University (022–38) Philadelphia, PA 19122. (215) 787-7714. Dr. Leonard Swidler, Editor. A 160- to 240-page quarterly journal with an international distribution of 2,500.

□*Journal of Ecumenical Studies* publishes scholarly articles on ecumenical matters—that is, interreligious dialogue. These may be discussions between Protestants and Catholics, Jews and Christians, Hindus and Christians, Buddhists and Christians, Moslems and Christians and Jews, Christians and Marxists, etc. Publishes approximately five major articles per issue of significant importance in the field of interreligious dialogue. Uses book reviews, article abstracts, and news items of importance in ecumenical study field. Readers are scholars and clergy of mixed religious backgrounds—Catholics, Protestants, and non-Christians.

Articles should be limited to 20 to 30 pages of double-spaced, typewritten material. Query letters desirable. Guidelines available. No cash payment for material; authors receive one free copy of the journal and 40 tear sheets of their articles. Acknowledges articles immediately, but material is then sent to three associate editors knowledgeable about the topic; evaluations made in 2 or 3 months.

JOURNAL OF RELIGION AND AGING, The Medical Center, Department of Family Practice, 710 Center Street, Columbus, GA 31994-2299. Founded 1984. William M. Clements, Ph.D., Editor. A 100-page quarterly journal published by the Haworth Press, Inc., 28 East 22nd Street, New York, NY 10010, with a national circulation.

□The *Journal* prints academic and professional articles and has three main goals: to inform religious professionals (pastors, educators, chaplains, and counselors) about new developments in religious gerontology, to inform "secular" professionals (nurses, administrators, doctors, therapists) who work with elderly people and their families, and to focus the attention of the traditional academic disciplines within religion on human aging. Well-received articles: "Old Age in Ancient Near Eastern Literature," "The Therapeutic Use of Devotional Reading," "The Pastoral Care of Persons in Pain." Also publishes theology. Readers are adults, primarily clergy, with some scholars. Most are mainline Protestant, Roman Catholic, and Orthodox, in that order.

Articles should be 20 to 30 pages, double-spaced. Sample copies and guidelines available. Particularly interested in practical articles from chaplains, pastoral counselors, religious educators, and pastors. Query letters desirable; does not want reprints. Does not pay. Reports in 12 weeks.

KEY TO CHRISTIAN EDUCATION, 8121 Hamilton Avenue, Cincinnati, OH 45231. (513) 931–4050. Virginia Beddow, Editor. A 48-page quarterly magazine published by Standard Publishing.
☐*Key to Christian Education* is read by teachers, superintendents, ministers, directors of Christian education, youth ministers and leaders, Christian education professors, and editors. The popular phrase, "It's working!" describes in a nutshell the kind of material wanted. Articles should be filled with ideas that are working in the field of Christian education. Well-received articles: "Step by Step to Sunday School Success," "How to Keep a Church From Dying," "Applying Space-Age Management Techniques to Your Christian Education."
   Articles should be 700 to 2,000 words. Query letters not required. Sample copy and author's guidelines available. Pays on acceptance: $20 to $60 per article. Reports within 2 months.

LEAD, c/o The Wesley Press, Box 2000, Marion, IN 46952. (317) 674–3301. Founded 1915. Tom Armiger, Editor. A 4-page bimonthly newspaper sponsored by the Wesleyan Church, with a national distribution of 3,600.
☐*Lead* prints teacher-training and motivational articles, ideas for CYC clubs, and photos and illustrations. Camping articles have been well received. Readers are adult lay Wesleyans.
   Articles should be 500 words or more. Query letters are desirable; will consider reprints. No payment information or reporting time provided.

LEADERSHIP: A PRACTICAL JOURNAL FOR CHURCH LEADERS, 465 Gundersen Drive, Carol Stream, IL 60188. (312) 260–6200. Terry C. Muck, Editor. A 140-page quarterly journal with a national distribution of 85,000.
☐*Leadership* is "designed to speak to the everyday, practical needs of pastors, pastors' wives, church staff members, and lay decision-makers (elders, deacons, trustees, committee chairpersons). Material should be pertinent without being 'formula methodology.' " Material should use many examples and anecdotes, including personal ones. Readers are clergy and adult lay leaders, evangelicals, of mixed denominational backgrounds.
   Articles should be 3,000 to 5,000 words. Query letters desirable. Guidelines available. Puts a a high priority on quality of writing. Pays on publication: $200 to $350 per article, depending on length and substance. Reports in 4 to 6 weeks.

LIBERTY, 6840 Eastern Avenue N.W., Washington DC 20012. (202) 722–6691. Roland R. Hegstad, Editor. A 32-page bimonthly magazine published by the Religious Liberty Association of America and by the Seventh-Day Adventist Church, with a national distribution of 400,000.
☐*Liberty* is dedicated to the preservation of religious freedom. The Association advocates no political or economic theories. Subject areas include articles of current national and international import in the field of religious liberty. Most-wanted manuscripts deal with current issues or problems in the U.S., Canada, and around the world, wherever freedom of religion or conscience is being threatened. Manuscripts should answer—or ask—the question, "How is religious freedom being threatened, oppressed, protected, advanced, etc., in this event or issue?"
   Manuscripts should be no more than 2,500 words of high-quality writing, fully documented with footnotes and bibliography. Welcomes pictures when they relate to the article: photos usually purchased to accompany manuscripts, but on occasion, can also use photos on religious liberty themes: black-and-white glossies, 5″ by 7″ or larger or negatives. Sample copy available for $1.00 and author's guidelines available. Pays, on acceptance, an honorarium roughly approximating 6¢ per word for suitable articles. Pays $35 for good-quality, interesting, relevant photos; $100 and up for color negatives

suitable for inside or outside cover. Unless special arrangements are made prior to printing, no purchased photos will be returned. Reports in 3 weeks.

LIBRARIAN'S WORLD, P.O. Box 353, Glen Ellyn, IL 60138. (312) 668-0519. Founded 1970. Nancy Dick, Editor. A 36- to 40-page quarterly newspaper sponsored by the Evangelical Church Library Association, with a national distribution of 700.
□*Librarian's World* reviews books of all types and prints "articles that would be of interest to church librarians in regard to their work or in the fields of publishing and reading. However, we rarely publish articles because we cannot make payment for them and space is at a premium. Most articles have been reprints."
Sample copies available. Query letters desirable; will consider reprints. "As yet we have been unable to make payment for articles but hope this will be possible in the near future—probably around $25 per article."

LIGHT AND LIFE, 901 College Avenue, Winona Lake, IN 46590. (219) 267-7656. Lyn Cryderman, Managing Editor. A 36-page monthly magazine, the official publication of the Free Methodist Church of North America, with a national distribution of 50,000.
□*Light and Life* seeks "to proclaim the good news of Jesus Christ; to serve the needs of persons; to draw persons to Christ and the church; to stimulate Christian growth and responsible Christian living; and to present the message, ministries, and happenings of the Free Methodist Church." Prints first-person accounts of God's help in time of crisis, practical articles on Christian living, discipleship articles leading readers in Christian growth, humorous articles describing life in the church. Particularly needs solid doctrinal material with a Wesleyan-Arminian slant written on a lay level.
Articles should be 500 to 2,000 words. Query letters desirable. Author's guidelines available; sample copy $1.50. Pays, on publication, usually 4¢ per word. Reports in 4 to 6 weeks.

LIGHTED PATHWAY, 922 Montgomery Avenue, Cleveland, TN 37311. (615) 476-4512. Marcus V. Hand, Editor. A 28-page monthly magazine published by the Church of God Publishing House, with a national distribution.
□*Lighted Pathway* is for young people aged 13 to 25. Uses "positive, optimistic articles and stories showing youth involved in victorious Christian living. Any subject of concern to youth will be considered." Most subjects are relevant if properly handled; and today's youth are interested in more than clothes, fashion, careers, and dating. Well-received subjects include careers, travel, young celebrities in the field of music, sports, missions, and business.
Articles should be 800 to 1,600 words. Query letters helpful, but not required. Sample copies and author's guidelines available on request. Pays 2¢ to 4¢ per word, on acceptance. Reports within 30 days.

LIGUORIAN, One Liguori Drive, Liguori, MO 63057. (314) 464-2500. Rev. Norman J. Muckerman, C.SS.R., Editor; Francine M. O'Connor, Managing Editor. A 64-page monthly magazine of the Redemptorists, with a U.S. and Canadian circulation of 530,000.
□*Liguorian* is a pastoral Catholic magazine that seeks "to help readers live a fuller Christian life and to face their problems and difficulties from a Christian support background." Readers are mostly Catholic singles and families. Looking for articles that aid families, teens, children, and elderly readers to understand their Church and to recognize God's presence in their lives. Interested in activities of Catholics, outstanding parish activities, and ways to solve family problems from a Christian viewpoint. Prints fiction, nonfiction, stories of people, humor, articles that offer practical help for Christian living, and photos and illustrations with manuscripts. Uses very little poetry.
Articles should be 1,500 to 2,000 words. Prefers to read complete manuscripts unless article requires much research and legwork. Free sample copy and author's guidelines available. Pays 7¢ to 10¢ per word, on acceptance. Reports in 6 to 8 weeks.

LISTEN, 6401 The Paseo, Kansas City, MO 64131. (816) 333-7000, extension 244. Gail L. Ragle, Editor. A 4-page weekly children's paper of the Church of the Nazarene, with an international distribution of 70,000.

□*Listen* is the weekly Sunday story paper for preschool children of the Church of the Nazarene. Uses stories appealing to children aged 4 and 5. Subject areas include right living such as sharing, showing love, and taking turns; God's love and care; family relationships; respect for the Bible and the church.

Fiction should be 300 to 400 words. Free sample copy and author's guidelines available; send SASE with all requests. Pays on acceptance: 3½¢ per word, minimum payment $10. Also uses some poetry. Reports usually within 4 to 6 weeks.

LITURGY, 806 Rhode Island Avenue N.E., Washington, DC 20018. (202) 529-7400. Rachel Reeder, Editor. A quarterly journal published by the Liturgical Conference, with a national distribution of 4,500.

□*Liturgy* is published for the membership of the Liturgical Conference, a voluntary organization concerned with renewal of the life and worship of the Christian Church. Membership is ecumenical. Readers are scholars, clergy, and laity with particular interest in the renewal of worship forms and practices.

Short essays of 2,000 words or less preferred, but longer pieces will be considered. Writers should have pastoral experience and should study the magazine before submitting. Query letters helpful, guidelines available. A "modest stipend" is payable on publication. Acknowledges receipt immediately, but report on publication may take 2 months.

LIVE, 1445 Boonville Avenue, Springfield, MO 65802. (417) 862-2781. A weekly Sunday School paper for youth and adults, published quarterly by the Assemblies of God, with a national distribution of 208,000.

□*Live* seeks to show its readers how to put Christian principles into action in everyday living. Uses fiction that presents believable characters working out their problems according to Bible principles; articles with reader appeal, emphasizing some phase of Christian living, presented in a down-to-earth manner; biography or missionary material using fictional techniques; historic, scientific, or nature material with a spiritual lesson; fillers that are brief, purposeful, usually containing an anecdote and always with a strong evangelical emphasis. No Bible fiction accepted.

Fiction should be 1,200 to 1,800 words, nonfiction up to 1,000 words, fillers up to 500 words. Pays on acceptance, according to value of material and amount of editorial work necessary. Sample copy and "Suggestions for Writers" sheet available if request accompanied by a SASE.

THE LIVING CHURCH, 407 East Michigan Street, Milwaukee, WI 53202. (414) 276-5420. H. Boone Porter, Editor. A weekly magazine of 16 pages and up, published by The Living Church Foundation (Episcopal).

□*The Living Church* publishes "thoughtful and original articles on issues of current concern to Episcopalians at parish, diocesan, or national levels." Readers are both clergy and lay adults. Uses nonfiction with appropriate black-and-white photos and illustrations. Interested in interviews with persons doing effective ministries in parishes or communities.

Articles should be 2,000 to 3,000 words. Query letters helpful. Sample copy available. No payment for unsolicited material. Reports in 1 month.

THE LIVING LIGHT, 1312 Massachusetts Avenue N.W., Washington, DC 20005. Bernard L. Marthaler, Executive Editor; Mariella Frye, MHSH, Editor. A 98-page quarterly journal published by the U.S. Catholic Conference for 4,000 subscribers.

□*The Living Light* publishes "articles dealing with developments, trends, problems, and issues in the field of religious education and pastoral action." Readers are interested adults, Protestants and Orthodox, as well as Roman Catholics; scholars and clergy as well as laity. Articles are limited to nonfiction.

Articles should be approximately 2,500 words. Query letters encouraged. Sample copy available for $5.00. Pays $15 per published page, on publication. Reports in 2 to 3 weeks.

LIVING WITH CHILDREN, 127 Ninth Avenue, South, Nashville, TN 37234. Founded 1978. SuAnne Bottoms, Editor. A 52-page quarterly magazine sponsored by the Baptist Sunday School Board, with a national circulation of 48,000, distributed primarily through Southern Baptist Churches.
☐*Living With Children* prints articles and features containing practical information to aid parents in bringing up children ages 6 to 11, and which reflect a Christian approach to parenting. Readers are mostly parents. High-priority subjects include discipline, school, pets, spiritual concepts, parenting techniques, recreation and hobbies, teaching values to children, parent-child communication, self-esteem, motivation, death, teaching children responsibility, sibling rivalry, sex education, money management, education of children. Needs humorous articles dealing with living with children.

Articles should be either 850 words, 1,450 words, or 1,800 to 2,000 words. (Articles that do not meet these specifications are rejected.) Query letters desirable. Sample copies and guidelines available. Pays 4¢ per word for usable material on all-rights basis (first rights may be negotiated at a lower rate of pay). Reports in 10 weeks.

LIVING WITH HOPE, P.O. Box 428, Geneva, AL 36340. (205) 684–6159. Founded 1982. Lura Zerick, Editor. A 12-page quarterly newsletter with a national circulation of 1,000.
☐*Living With Hope* prints articles "that tell and show the victorious power of living a Christlike life; to encourage women to trust Him in all areas of their lives. He alone can help them rise above all that can bog down a life. All of us share what Jesus has done in our lives." Well-received articles: "Stretch Your Prayer Power," "From Pills to Power," "Please Forgive Yourself," "Who Do You Think You Are?," "Proverbs 31 Lady," "A Mother's Thanksgiving Prayer." Also prints fillers, poetry, devotions, and 2 book reviews and 1 puzzle per issue. Readers are largely women, of a number of evangelical denominations.

Articles should be 500 to 750 words; "will seldom use over 900 words." Reviews up to 300 words, meditations up to 200 words, fillers, 100 to 150 words. Sample copies and guidelines available. Particularly interested in book reviews, puzzles, and meditations. Query letters desirable but not essential; will consider reprints. Pays 3¢ per word for articles; 50¢ a line for poetry, $5 each for meditations and book reviews, $10 for puzzles. Reports in 4 weeks.

LIVING WITH PRESCHOOLERS, 127 Ninth Avenue, North, Nashville, TN 37234. (615) 251–2229. SuAnne Bottoms, Editor. A 52-page quarterly magazine published by the Baptist Sunday School Board of the Southern Baptist Convention, with a national circulation.
☐*Living With Preschoolers* uses articles and features that help parents enrich their understanding and guidance of preschoolers (infants through 5-year-olds). Appreciates articles that deal with a growth area of the child or personal growth of parents. Where possible, depending on subject matter, articles must have a clear Christian perspective and must be denominationally acceptable. Needs articles dealing with any subject of interest to parents of preschoolers. High-priority subjects include development of self-concepts, discipline, spiritual growth, parenting techniques, growth and development of preschoolers.

Articles should be typed, double-spaced, on a 55-character line. They are accepted only if they meet these specifications: 850 words for a 1-page article, 1,450 to 1,600 words for a 2-page article, 1,800 to 2,100 words for a 3-page article. Query letters desirable, but not required. Sample copy and author's guidelines available. Pays 4¢ per word, on acceptance.

LIVING WITH TEENAGERS, Baptist Sunday School Board, 127 Ninth Avenue, North, Nashville, TN 37234. (615) 251–2277. E. Lee Sizemore, Editor. A 50-page quarterly magazine published by the Southern Baptist Convention, with a national distribution.
□*Living With Teenagers* publishes articles for parents of teenagers. Articles must deal with an aspect of the parent-teen relationship and reflect a Christian perspective. Needs manuscripts that deal with the following parent-youth situations: communication, spiritual growth, leisure time/recreation, moral issues, loneliness, witnessing to youth, effects of both parents working, nutrition, fun times, teaching youth responsibility, preparing youth for marriage, sex education, aggressive youth, building self-concept in youth, overly submissive youth, handicapped youth, youth and their peers, teen pregnancy and unwed parents, drugs and alcoholism, youth and jobs, financial training, how to help youth relate to grandparents, brothers and sisters, moodiness and other characteristics of adolescence, school problems. Also prints poetry.

Articles should be 500, 1,000, 1,500, or 2,000 words. Free sample copy and author's guidelines available. Pays on acceptance: 4¢ per word, after editing. Reports in approximately 60 days.

THE LOOKOUT, 8121 Hamilton Avenue, Cincinnati, OH 45231. (513) 931–4050. Mark A. Taylor, Editor. A 16-page weekly magazine published by Standard Publishing, with a national distribution.
□*The Lookout* is a magazine about, by, and for members of adult Sunday School classes, as well as church attenders who aren't interested in Sunday School, but should be. Wants "first, stories about real people, individuals, or Sunday School classes; second, items that shed bibical light on matters of contemporary controversy; and third, items that ask, 'Why shouldn't I try this? Why couldn't our class accomplish that?' " Prints nonfiction, ideas that are working in the Sunday School and in the lives of its members, fiction that's as true to life as possible while remaining inspirational and helpful, inspirational and humorous shorts, photographs (black-and-white prints 4″ by 6″ or larger) and color slides or transparencies.

Articles and stories should be 750 to 1,800 words. Sample copy available for 50¢ postage. Pays 4¢ to 6¢ per word; for black-and-white prints, pays $5 to $25. If color slide is used on the cover, pays $50 to $135; for inside use, pays $10 to $100. Reports in 6 weeks. Uses second or reprint rights to articles previously published elsewhere.

LOVE LETTERS, P.O. Box 11510, Milwaukee, WI 53211. Founded 1982. Rita Bertolas, Publisher. A 16-to 20-page bimonthly magazine with a national distribution of 250.
□*Love Letters* is "an outlet for people to express how God's love has touched their lives." Uses mostly poetry, both free verse and rhymed; also prints short stories, inspirational thoughts, and prayers—all with the theme of expressing God's love in people's lives. Readers are adults and senior citizens of various evangelical, liberal, and mainline Protestant denominations.

Poems should be 30 lines, prose should be a maximum of 300 words. Author's guidelines available. No payment for material used, but author receives 2 free copies of issue in which contributions appear. Also interested in reprints.

THE LUTHERAN, 2900 Queen Lane, Philadelphia, PA 19129. (215) 438–6580. Edgar R. Trexler, Editor; Mark A. Staples, Features Editor. The 32-page bimonthly official magazine of the Lutheran Church in America, with a national distribution of 596,000.
□*The Lutheran* is published for a general lay readership, members of the Lutheran Church in America. News and features of the religious world, and especially of the congregations of the sponsoring church, make up most of the material in the magazine. Guidelines list four types of articles needed: 1) the church at work—stories describing the unique aspects of a specific church unit's program; 2) profiles—stories of individuals whose accomplishments reflect commitment to the Christian cause; 3) reflection—articles that explore the important issues related to Christian belief; 4) personal ex-

perience—stories that describe real-life encounters with adversity, family problems, frustrations, and opportunities of everyday living.

Articles should be 500 to 2,000 words, written for a wide general audience. They should be carefully researched, with liberal use of anecdotes. Query letters desirable. Sample copy and author's guidelines available. Pays $90 per printed page, on acceptance. Acknowledges receipt of manuscript; reports within 6 weeks.

LUTHERAN EDUCATION, 7400 Augusta, River Forest, IL 60305. (312) 771–8300, extension 380 or 381. Merle R. Radke, Editor. A 60-page journal, published 5 times a year and sponsored by Concordia College, with a national distribution of 3,800.
□*Lutheran Education* is published for teachers and administrators in Lutheran parochial schools, mostly those of the Lutheran Church—Missouri Synod. Interested in articles and news concerning educational methods, developments, curriculum, and administrative problems, especially in the parochial or Christian day school setting.

Articles should be 4 to 12 typewritten pages. Query letters desirable. No payment for material used. Reports in 4 weeks.

LUTHERAN FORUM, 308 West 46th Street, New York, NY 10036. (212) 757–1292. Glenn C. Stone, Editor. A 40-page quarterly magazine, published by the American Lutheran Publicity Bureau, with a national distribution of 5,000.
□*Lutheran Forum* seeks "articles on issues facing the church in its internal life and in its cultural/social context." Published for adults, mostly clergy and lay leaders of the several Lutheran synods and national church bodies. Prints only nonfiction material. Interested in news as well as feature material and uses photos frequently.

Articles should be 1,000 to 3,000 words. Query letters desirable. Sample copy may be purchased for $1.50. Pays on publication: $25 to $75 for articles, $12.50 to $15 for photos. Reports in 4 to 6 weeks.

THE LUTHERAN JOURNAL, 7317 Cahill Road, Edina, MN 55435. (612) 941–6830. Armin U. Deye, Editor. A 32-page quarterly magazine with a national distribution of 136,000.
□*The Lutheran Journal* seeks "wholesome and inspirational articles or stories, mainly for adults." This independent Lutheran magazine needs both fiction and nonfiction, some poetry, humor (if appropriate), and photos and illustrations. Prints a wide range of material of interest to members of the Lutheran church, mostly laity.

Articles should be 2,000 words or less. No query letters; complete manuscripts only. Sample copy available. Pays 1¢ to 2¢ per word, on acceptance. Reports within 4 to 6 weeks.

THE LUTHERAN LAYMAN, 2185 Hampton Avenue, St. Louis, MO 63139. (314) 647–4900. Walter E. Cranor, Editor. A 24-page newspaper published 8 times a year by the International Lutheran Laymen's League, with circulation in the U.S. and Canada of 118,000.
□*The Lutheran Layman* publishes news and features mainly about lay activity in Lutheran circles throughout the world. Especially interested in stories of people. Limited to nonfiction. Sponsor is Lutheran Church—Missouri Synod, but the newspaper reaches other Lutheran groups and beyond, to a general Protestant audience. Readers are primarily lay adults.

Articles should be 500 to 600 words. Query letters desirable. Pays, on publication, fees determined in advance with the authors. Also distributes calendars, tapes, *BCTN* Magazine, and a league leader's newsletter. Payment for above materials will be discussed at the time of assignment.

THE LUTHERAN STANDARD, 426 South Fifth Street, Box 1209, Minneapolis, MN 55440. (612) 330–3300. Lowell G. Almen, Editor. A magazine published 20 times a year by the American Lutheran Church, with a national distribution of 585,000.
□*The Lutheran Standard* "publishes material that communicates aspects of the faith to

its primary audience, the members and congregations of the American Lutheran Church. Also welcomes manuscripts that explore the connection between faith and personal concerns or social issues." Readers are adults, both clergy and laity of the church. Uses only nonfiction, and many photos and illustrations.

About one-third of the material used in the main feature section is produced by freelance writers. Articles should be 400 to 1,000 words. Query letters welcome. Sample copy and author's guidelines available. Pays about 10¢ a word, on acceptance. Reports in 3 weeks. *Ceased publication in 1987*

THE LUTHERAN WITNESS, 1333 South Kirkwood Road, St. Louis, MO 63122-7295. (314) 965-9000. Paul Devantier, Executive Director. A 32-page monthly, the official magazine of the Lutheran Church—Missouri Synod, with a national distribution of 440,000.

□*The Lutheran Witness* needs "parish stories that describe a particular unique ministry, thematic subjects dealing with moral and societal concerns, individual personalities that highlight the Christian life, parish and individual features usually related to the Lutheran Church—Missouri Synod." Readers are general laity, primarily adults; but also prints articles that appeal to youth and children. Also uses photos and illustrations.

Articles should be 450 to 600 words for a 1-page treatment, 1,200 to 1,500 for a 2- or 3-page treatment. No query letters. Copies of publication and sample articles available. Pays on publication: $30 per published page and $5 apiece for photos. Special consideration given for research or expense involved with preparation of some material. Reports within 1 week.

LUTHERAN WOMAN'S QUARTERLY, 4575 Canoe Drive, St. Louis, MO 63123. (314) 631-2400. Louise Mueller, Editor. A 48-page magazine published by the Lutheran Women's Missionary League (Lutheran Church—Missouri Synod), 3558 South Jefferson Avenue, St. Louis, MO 63118. National distribution of 300,000.

□*Lutheran Woman's Quarterly* is published primarily for the women of the Lutheran Church—Missouri Synod. "Features are usually personalized items of human interest with emphasis on a particular mission field or mission activity. Each issue has a basic theme centering on an issue, concern, or need of Lutheran women. News items, resource materials, and Bible studies are related to this theme."

General-feature articles should be 500 to 800 words. Most features are assigned or solicited by the editor. Query letters preferred. Sample copies available from the St. Louis address above. Does not pay for material used. Will pay for photos and artwork, which are usually commissioned. Reports as soon as possible.

LUTHERAN WOMEN, 2900 Queen Lane, Philadelphia, PA 19129. (215) 438-2200. Terry Schutz, Editor. A 32-page monthly magazine published by the Lutheran Church Women of the Lutheran Church in America, with a national distribution of 40,000.

□*Lutheran Women* prints both fiction and nonfiction, some poetry, concentrating on "articles and short stories addressing moral and social issues confronting Christian women today and showing women as strong, independent personalities." Examples of desired topics: parenting, women in the ministry, new life for the divorced woman, television and its values and dangers, world hunger. Especially interested in stories about minority women. Also uses photos.

Articles should be 700 to 3,000 words; average 1,500. No query letters. Sample copy and author's guidelines available. Pays $20 to $50 per article, on publication. Reports in 3 to 4 months.

MARIAN HELPERS BULLETIN, Association of Marian Helpers, Stockbridge, MA 01262. (413) 298-3691. Joseph J. Sielski, Editor. A 24-page magazine published quarterly by the Association of Marian Helpers, with an international distribution of 750,000.

□*Marian Helpers Bulletin* uses items of general interest to Roman Catholic clergy and general lay readers on religious matters, faith, lives of saints, accounts of some observances, jubilees, human-interest stories, devotion to the Lord, the Blessed Virgin Mary, and saints. Has many articles on hand, therefore not too interested in any new items.

Articles should be 500 to 1,000 words, maximum. Free sample copy available. Pays $25 to $50, on acceptance. Reports within a month or two.

MARRIAGE AND FAMILY LIVING, Abbey Press, St. Meinrad, IN 47577. (812) 357–8011. Kass Dotterweich, Editor. A monthly magazine published by the St. Meinrad Archabbey, with a national distribution of 40,000.

☐*Marriage and Family Living* uses material that promotes the growth and enrichment of Christian marriage and family living; mostly nonfiction, self-help material reassuring in nature. Needs in-depth material with religious overtones. Specifically, uses four different types of nonfiction articles: 1) informative and inspirational articles on all aspects of marriage and family life, especially relationship of husband and wife; 2) personal essays relating dramatic or amusing incidents that point up the human side of marriage and family life; 3) profiles of outstanding couples working in the family field, or successful programs in this field, and profiles of individuals who contribute to the betterment of marriage and family life; 4) interviews with authorities in the fields of marriage and family life (on current problems and new developments).

Articles average 1,500 to 2,000 words. Will accept 1,000 words, maximum is 2,500 words. Query letters desirable, but not required. Author's guidelines free on request. Buys first international serial rights, reprint rights, and book option; these rights can be assigned to the author by special agreement. Pays 7¢ per word, on acceptance. Black-and-white glossies and color transparencies purchased with or without manuscripts. Pays $15 for a magazine half-page, $30 for a full page. Requires model releases. Reports in 4 to 6 weeks.

MARYKNOLL MAGAZINE, Maryknoll, NY 10545. (914) 941–7590. Moises Sandoval, Editor. A monthly magazine of the Catholic Foreign Mission Society, with a national distribution of 1,200,000.

☐*Maryknoll Magazine* publishes articles on international issues and services, especially missionary activity, but also pieces on struggles against hunger, oppression, disease, and ignorance. Well-received subjects: disarmament, land use, and modern-day martyrs. Also uses stories of people and photos and illustrations.

Articles should be 1,000 to 1,250 words. Query letters required. Sample copy and author's guidelines available. Pays on acceptance: $75 and up for articles, $125 and up for black-and-white photo essays, $150 and up for color; $15 for stock black-and-white photos, $35 for color. Reports in 1 month.

MATURE LIVING, 127 Ninth Avenue, North, Nashville, TN 37234. (615) 251–2191. Jack Gulledge, Editor. A 50-page monthly magazine published by the Sunday School Board of the Southern Baptist Convention, with a national distribution of 190,000.

☐*Mature Living* publishes "stories and articles of human interest and warmth, consistent with Christian principles and aimed at the interests of a reading audience 60 years of age and older." Articles should be written in an informal style, give evidence of research, and should not talk down to readers. Nostalgia articles are good ("I remember when . . ."), as are 25-line profiles with action pictures that show notable achievements by the seniors described. Prints some fiction and cartoons, provided they laugh *with* and not *at* older people. Brief true accounts can go into the "Grandparents' Brag Board" column.

Articles should be 450 to 925 words, rarely more. Sample copy and author's guidelines available with SASE. Pays on acceptance: 4¢ per published word, $10 to $25 for black-and-white photos. Reports within 1 month.

MATURE YEARS, United Methodist Publishing House, 201 Eighth Avenue, South, Nashville, TN 37202. (615) 749–6438. Daisy D. Warren, Editor. A 64-page quarterly magazine published by the United Methodist Church for older readers, with a national distribution of 100,000.

☐*Mature Years* aims at a general reading public of senior citizens, mostly associated with the United Methodist Church. Prints a variety of materials—nonfiction articles dealing with all aspects of pre-retirement and retirement living. Also uses fillers (serious, humorous, inspirational), previously unpublished poems, fiction, photos, and cartoons. All material should relate to the readers' lives. Cannot use anything that pokes fun at older people or deals with depressing, unhealthy situations.

Articles and stories should be 1,200 to 1,800 words; fillers 500 to 800 words; poems under 16 lines. Photos should be black-and-white glossies. Query letters not necessary. Sample copy and author's guidelines available. Pays on acceptance: 4¢ per word for articles, stories, and fillers; 50¢ per line for poetry. Reports in 60 to 90 days.

The Mennonite, 600 Shaftesbury Boulevard, Winnipeg, Manitoba R3P OM4, Canada. Bernie Wiebe, Editor. A 24-page magazine published 24 times a year by the General Conference Mennonite Church, Box 347, Newton, KS 67114. (204) 888-6781.
☐*The Mennonite* looks for Anabaptist-Mennonite-oriented articles related to living in today's world. Articles expected to be overtly biblical for the general lay, adult, evangelical reader. Articles desired are stories of people, humor, features about current issues, meditations, poetry; also uses photos and illustrations. Writing style should be conversational, assuming an audience above average in intelligence, be picturesque and creative, showing theological literacy and familiarity with subject matter; sentences should be short. Particularly interested in articles on eschatology.

Articles should be 1,000 words; meditations 650 words or less; poetry "brief." Query letters desirable. Free sample copy and author's guidelines available. Pays on publication: 3¢ per word for feature and other articles, 35¢ per line for poetry, $15 to $20 for photos. Reports within 3 months.

Men's Ministries, Assemblies of God, Men's Ministries Department, 1445 Boonville Avenue, Springfield, MO 65802. (417) 862-2781, extension 1491. A 4-page bimonthly newspaper with a national distribution of 8,500.
☐*Men's Ministries* is for clergy and lay leaders of the Assemblies of God denomination. Uses nonfiction, stories of people, articles on men serving, how-to-do-it, and personal evangelism. Also uses photos and illustrations. Well-received articles: "Reaching Truckers for Christ," "Not Forgotten at Thanksgiving," "Senior Saints Want Activities," "Prison Ministry Profitable," "Blind Man Serves Too."

Articles should be 500 to 750 words. Query letters desirable. Sample copy on request. Reports immediately.

Message of the Open Bible, 2020 Bell Avenue, Des Moines, IA 50315. (515) 288-6761. Ray E. Smith, Editor. A 20-page monthly magazine of the Open Bible Standard Churches with a national distribution of 5,000.
☐*Message of the Open Bible* is an in-house denominational publication for evangelical adults. Articles speak to current issues or to the evangelical community in general.

Articles should be 800 to 1,600 words. Query letters desirable, but not required. Does not pay for material. Reports within 60 days.

Messenger of the Pentecostal Free Will Baptist Church, P.O. Box 1081, Dunn, NC 28334. (919) 892-4161. William L. Ellis, Editor. A 16-page monthly magazine with a national distribution of 5,000.
☐*Messenger* is the Advocate of Bible Holiness, official organ of the Pentecostal Free Will Baptist Church, Inc. Uses religious testimonial articles for its adult lay readers.

Article length is variable. Sample copy available.

Messenger of the Sacred Heart, 661 Greenwood Avenue, Toronto, Ontario M4J 4B3, Canada. (416) 466-1195. Rev. F. J. Power, S.J., Editor; M. Pujolas, Associate Editor. A 24-page magazine published 11 times a year by the Roman Catholic Apostleship of Prayer.

□*Messenger of the Sacred Heart* uses articles and short stories that reflect the lives and problems of their Roman Catholic readers.

Articles average 1,500 words in length. Free sample copy available on request. Pays 2¢ per word, on acceptance. Reports in 1 month. Also markets calendars and religious pictures; "we own them or pay suppliers when we buy them."

METAPSYCHOLOGY: THE JOURNAL OF DISCARNATE INTELLIGENCE, P.O. Box 30022, Philadelphia, PA 19103. Founded 1984. Mark Zweigler, Publisher; Tam Mossman, Editor. A 50-page quarterly journal with an international distribution.

□*Metapsychology* "assumes that revelation did not halt in New Testament times, but is still continuing. We are a forum and clearinghouse for answers and information—mainly of a metaphysical nature—obtained through automatic writing and trance mediumship." Issues are published in looseleaf format, so that subscribers may assemble their own ongoing series of "books." Goal is quality, not quantity: "Submissions must be up to the level of Jane Roberts's Seth material and of the ongoing Jacob sessions, which comprise part of each issue. Submissions that are dogmatic, judgmental, or claim to have the 'only' truth will not be considered." Subscribers only may submit questions to be answered by various discarnates in future issues.

Articles should be "primary material and first-person accounts, *not* commentary." Query letters required: enclose no more than 3 sample pages of material and SASE. All tapes and automatic writing must be transcribed and typewritten. Sample issue, which includes guidelines, is $5. Payment varies with length and quality, but always includes free year's subscription. Reports in 2 weeks.

METHODIST HISTORY, Box 488, Lake Junaluska, NC 28745. (704) 456–9432. Louise L. Queen, Editor. A 64-page quarterly magazine published by the Commission on Archives and History of the United Methodist Church.

□*Methodist History* publishes "articles on Methodist history that have not appeared in print before and deal with new sources of study. Priority is given to United Methodist history and secondly to other Methodist bodies." Deals with all phases of Methodist history—people, places, churches, organizations. Special priorities given to gathering history of ethnic groups within the Methodist Church and its tradition—blacks, Hispanics, Native Americans, Asian-Americans, etc.

Articles should be 5,000 to 7,500 words. Query letters requested. Sample copies available, within limits. No cash payment for material used, only extra copies of the issue in which the article appears. Reports as soon as possible after submission has been read by one or more experts.

MINISTRY: A MAGAZINE FOR CLERGY, 6840 Eastern Avenue, N.W., Washington, DC 20012. (202) 722–6000. Founded 1928. J. Robert Spangler, Editor. A 32-page monthly magazine sponsored by the Seventh-Day Adventist Ministerial association, with 17,000 subscribers and a maximum international distribution of 255,000.

□*Ministry* prints "practical, down-to-earth articles written to enhance the pastor's abilities in administration, counseling, preaching, Bible study, and other pastoral skills." Well-received articles: "Grief Recovery"; "Family Life Ministry That Works"; "Toward Better Preaching"; "From the Other Side of the Pulpit"; "Your Secretary, A Partner in Ministry"; "Dear Pastor, I Love You." Also prints devotions, Bible study, interviews, theology, and church growth materials. Readers are mainline and evangelical Protestant clergy.

Articles should be 6 to 9 pages, typed and double-spaced. Sample copies available. Particularly interested in articles directed to pastors' wives. Send complete manuscripts rather than query letters; no reprints. Pays on publication: approximately $25 per magazine page; most contributions earn $50 to $75. Reports in 6 weeks.

MISSIOLOGY, AN INTERNATIONAL REVIEW, Box 10,000, Denver, CO 80210. (303) 761–2482. Ralph R. Covell, Editor. A 128-page quarterly journal of the American Society of Missiology, with a national distribution of 3,000.

□*Missiology* is interested in articles dealing with the cross-cultural communication of the Christian faith as informed by the social sciences and related to the various traditions within the Christian movement—whether Orthodox, Catholic, Protestant, or Charismatic. Uses nonfiction and technical articles. Would like to see analysis of ecumenical/Orthodox/evangelical contemporary practices of missions. Well-received articles: "The Uniqueness and Universality of Jesus Christ," "American Catholic Missioners in China After World War II," "Music in the Early Evangelization of Mexico," "Missions and Cross-Cultural Conflict."

Articles should be 3,000 to 4,500 words. Query letters desirable. Free sample copy available. As a scholarly forum, *Missiology* is made up of contributed writings, most unsolicited; no remuneration, but 20 copies of article sent after publication.

MODERN LITURGY, 160 East Virginia Street, #290, San Jose, CA 95112. (408) 286–8505. Founded 1973. Ken Guentert, Editor. A 40-page magazine published 9 times a year (June through August and December-January issues are combined), with an international distribution of 16,000.

□*Modern Liturgy* prints articles on "Worship arts (visual arts, dance, drama, story, mime, etc.), liturgical theology, and prayer services for worship. Well-received articles: "Miracles of Jesus," "Peace and Worship," "Adult Initiation," "Imagination and Worship." Also prints fiction, poetry, profiles, and interviews. Readers are clergy and adult lay members of a number of denominations, chiefly mainline Protestant (Episcopal, Lutheran, Methodist) and some Roman Catholic; music directors and religious-education coordinators predominate.

Articles should be 1,300 to 1,500 words. Sample copies $3.00 and guidelines available. "If a theological article has been requested of you, use nontechnical terms and examples that untrained lay readers can understand." The editors avoid sexist language, but also "material which is self-conscious to the point of distraction." For particular areas of interest, write to Editor. Query letters preferred; no reprints. Pays 3¢ per word. Reports in 12 weeks.

MOODY MONTHLY, 2101 West Howard Street, Chicago, IL 60645. (312) 274–2535. Michael Umlandt, Managing Editor. A monthly magazine, averaging 132 pages, sponsored by the Moody Bible Institute, 820 North LaSalle Street, Chicago, IL 60610, with a national circulation of 225,000.

□*Moody Monthly* publishes a wide variety of material including fiction, nonfiction, stories of people, Bible doctrine, exposition. "It is impossible to write for us unless the writer has read us. Then he or she will know what we want."

Articles should be 1,000 to 2,500 words; 1,500 words is best. Reports within 10 days. Queries required; no unsolicited manuscripts accepted. Pays 5¢ to 10¢ per word, on acceptance. Free sample copy and author's guidelines available.

MOUNTAIN MOVERS, 1445 Boonville Avenue, Springfield, MO 65802. (417) 862–2781. Beverly Graham, Editor. A 16-page monthly magazine published by the General Council of the Assemblies of God, Division of Foreign Missions, with a national distribution of 150,000.

Does not accept freelance material. Only source of material is missionaries of the Assemblies of God.

THE MUSIC LEADER, 127 Ninth Avenue North, Nashville, TN 37234. (615) 251–2961. Derrell L. Billingsley, Design Editor. A 64-page quarterly magazine of The Sunday School Board of the Southern Baptist Convention, with a national distribution of 32,000.

□*The Music Leader* contains guidance materials, training aids, and enrichment for leaders of children and preschoolers. Relates directly to the quarterly magazines, *Music Makers* and *Young Musicians* for children and *Music Time,* the weekly leaflet for use in the home, with pre-schoolers. Readers are scholars, and clergy, and adult lay readers in Southern Baptist churches. Interested in articles for leaders on children and how they learn; methodology—singing, moving, instruments, creativity, vocal skills; "How We

Did It In Our Choir"; information about the Church music ministry and coming events; inspiration; choir organization; enlistment and training leaders; enlisting members; equipment, supplies and budget.

Articles should be 75 to 80 lines, or 150 to 170 lines typed, 40 characters per line; 250-line maximum. Sample copy and author's guidelines available. Pays 3½¢ per word, on acceptance. Reports in 2 weeks to 1 month.

MUSIC MAKERS, 127 Ninth Avenue, North, Nashville, TN 37234. Founded 1970. Jimmy R. Key, Editor. A 34-page quarterly magazine, sponsored by the Southern Baptist Convention, Baptist Sunday School Board, with an international distribution of 98,045.
□*Music Makers* prints music for children age 6 to 8: "songs of 1 page, 4 to 6 phrases long; range Middle C to fourth-line D; simple rhythm patterns, simple unison melodies, and simple accompaniments; tuneful, singable, and easy to learn." Readers are both children and lay adults, chiefly Southern Baptist.

Sample copies and guidelines available. Pays 4½¢ per word. Reports in 4 weeks.

MUSIC TIME, 127 Ninth Avenue, North, Nashville, TN 37234. (615) 251–2961. Derrell L. Billingsley, Editor. A 52-page quarterly magazine of The Sunday School Board of the Southern Baptist Convention, with a national distribution of 50,000.
□*Music Time* is for pre-schoolers, 4 and 5 years old. It uses extremely short, child-experience stories, poems, finger plays, music and art activities, and generally interesting articles and items for preschoolers and their parents.

Child-experience stories should be 15 to 30 typed lines, 48 characters per line. Poems average 8 to 12 lines. Free sample copy and author's guidelines available. Pays on acceptance: $9 to $12 per story, $5 to $9 per poem, $5 to $8 for music or art activities. Reports in 15 to 30 days.

MY DAILY VISITOR, 200 Noll Plaza, Huntington, IN 46750. (219) 356–8400. Patrick R. Moran, Editor. A 64-page pamphlet-sized bimonthly magazine published by Our Sunday Visitor, Inc., with a national distribution of 20,500.
□*My Daily Visitor* is a pocket-sized magazine containing spiritual reflections or meditations for each day of the month. The Mass scriptural readings and response head each page. Meditations are personal-interest and keyed to the liturgical and daily calendar and saints' days, patriotic holidays, etc. Readership is Roman Catholic youth, adults, and senior citizens.

Daily meditations should average 150 words; type meditation for one day per page. There are two guest editors per issue, who are assigned a year in advance. Query letters are required before these assignments are made; sample of contributor's writing is required. Sample copy available. Pays on publication: $100 for a series of monthly meditations. Reports in 2 weeks.

NETWORK, 806 Rhode Island Avenue, N.E., Washington, DC 20018. (202) 526–4070. A 24- to 34-page journal published 6 times a year with a national distribution of 8,000.
□*Network* is a Catholic social-justice lobby publication aimed at an audience of activist women and men concerned about the issues being lobbied for: nuclear disarmament, human rights abroad, national budget priorities, and the political process and the values that influence public policy.

Articles should be 2,500 to 5,000 words. Query letters desirable. Free sample copy and author's guidelines available. No payment for materials used. Reports within 2 weeks.

NEW OXFORD REVIEW, 1069 Kains Avenue, Berkeley, CA 94706. (415) 526–5374. Dale Vree, Editor. A 32-page monthly magazine published by New Oxford Review, Inc., with a national distribution of 7,753.
□*New Oxford Review* publishes articles on religious, cultural, and social justice issues, "with a special interest in fostering communication between orthodox Evangelicals and orthodox Catholics." It reaches an audience of adults—scholars, clergy, and laity—in a

wide variety of churches. Material is on subjects of scholarly interest, but written in a popular style. Nonfiction and short stories accepted.

Articles should be no more than 3,000 words. Query letters desirable. Sample copies available on request. No payment offered for material used. Reports within 2 months.

NEW WINE MAGAZINE, P.O. Box Z, Mobile, AL 36616. (205) 460–9010. Founded 1969. Dick Leggatt, Editor. A 36-page monthly magazine published by Integrity Communications, with an international distribution of 67,000.

□New Wine Magazine prints personal testimonies and teachings, profiles, interviews, and Bible study. Well-received articles have been on spiritual warfare and financial stewardship. Readers are lay adults of various Protestant denominations.

Articles should be 3 to 7 pages, typed, and double-spaced. Query letters desirable. Sample copy and author's guidelines available. Will consider reprints. Pays on publication: approximately $50 per published page, except for interviews or tape transcriptions. Reports in 10 to 15 weeks.

NEW WORLD OUTLOOK, 475 Riverside Drive, New York, NY 10115. (212) 870–3758. Arthur J. Moore, Editor. A 48-page magazine issued 11 times a year by the Education and Cultivation Division of the Board of Global Ministries of the United Methodist Church, with a national distribution of 40,000.

□New World Outlook is a missions magazine intended "to depict mission in the U.S.A. and around the world. A principal but not exclusive concern is to inform the church audiences about work and issues of the United Methodist Church. Articles deal with persons and projects and issues in society and the church, both overseas and in the United States. Also prints photos.

Articles should be 1,000 to 1,500 words. Query letters desirable. Free sample copy and author's guidelines available. Pays $50 to $150 per article, on publication; pays extra for photos. Reports on acceptance.

THE NORTHWESTERN LUTHERAN, 2929 North Mayfair Road, Milwaukee, WI 53222. (414) 771–9357. James P. Schaefer, Editor. A 16-page semimonthly magazine published by the Wisconsin Evangelical Lutheran Synod for a national distribution.

□The Northwestern Lutheran is published for adult lay readers, members of the Wisconsin Lutheran Synod Churches. All articles written by staff or by members of the churches of that communion. Material used must relate to the needs, interests, and theological point of view of that church.

Pays $25 per printed page.

OBLATES, 15 South 59th Street, Belleville, IL 62222. (618) 233–2238. Founded 1943. Fr. Don Ferguson, O.M.I., Editor. A 20-page bimonthly newsletter/magazine sponsored by Missionary Oblates of Mary Immaculate, with a national distribution of 450,000.

□Oblates prints "articles that inspire and motivate through expression of Gospel values in relation to everyday life." Well-received articles: "Prayer of Mid-Life," "A Little Mixed Up." Also prints fiction, and inspirational/religious poetry. "Readers are mostly middle-aged to older Americans looking for comfort, encouragement and, most of all, applicable Christian direction. All are Christian, most are Catholic . . . experienced, churchgoing folk who don't want to be preached at or scolded."

Articles should not exceed 600 words; best range is around 500. "Submissions should be tightly edited. Refrain from pompous or flowery prose." Sample copies and guidelines available. Query letters not needed; send original manuscripts (no reprints). Pays on acceptance: $60 for articles, $25 for poetry. Reports in 4 weeks.

THE OBLATE WORLD AND VOICE OF HOPE, P.O. Box 96, 907 Pasadena, San Antonio, TX 78291. (512) 736–1685. Rev. Emanuel Ballard, O.M.I., Editor. An 8-page bimonthly newspaper published by the Missionary Society of the Oblate Fathers of Texas with a national distribution of 140,000.

☐*The Oblate World and Voice of Hope,* a Roman Catholic newspaper, is read by clergy and lay adults.

Publishes mission stories of 1,000 to 1,600 words. Sample copies available. Pays 1¢ to 2¢ per word, on acceptance. Reports in 3 weeks.

ONE (formerly *Etcetera),* Nazarene Publishing House, 6401 The Paseo, Kansas City, MO 64131. (816) 333–7000, extension 277. A monthly tabloid-format magazine for 18- to 24-year-old singles, with a national distribution of 8,000.
☐*One* uses articles dealing with social issues, Bible study, personal spiritual development, and student interests geared toward the needs of college, university, and career singles.

Sample copy and author's guidelines available. Pays on acceptance. Reports in 10 to 12 weeks.

ON THE LINE, Mennonite Publishing House, 616 Walnut Avenue, Scottdale, PA 15683. (412) 887–8500. A weekly story paper for children aged 10 through 14, with a national distribution of 15,000.
☐*On the Line* seeks articles and stories that make the message of the Bible attractive, help children grow in an understanding of God, of themselves, and of other persons; help children feel they are worthy persons now, acceptable just as they are; help them grow toward a personal commitment to Christ; give help in handling problem areas of life; help children accept persons of other races and cultures as their equals; introduce them to the wonders of God's world in various forms—art, music, human relationships; help Mennonite children appreciate both their Christian heritage and Mennonite tradition and activities of the church program.

Articles and stories should be 750 to 1,000 words. Author's guidelines available. Buys puzzles and quizzes, appropriate verse from 8 to 24 lines, and professional-quality 8″ by 10″ photos. Pays about 3¢ per word.

THE OTHER SIDE, Box 3948, Fredericksburg, VA 22402. (703) 371–7416. Mark Olson, Editor. A 56-page monthly magazine with a national distribution of 16,000.
☐*The Other Side* publishes "articles on justice issues from a radical and Christian perspective; a few essays, but mostly personal-experience articles." Interested in material about personal experiences in working for justice as Christians. Reaches adult readers, both clergy and laity. Uses photos.

Articles should be 250 to 2,500 words. Query letters desirable. Sample copy available for $2.50; author's guidelines free. Pays on publication: $25 to $250 per article. Reports within 1 month.

OUR FAMILY, Box 249, Battleford, Saskatchewan SOM OEO, Canada. (306) 937–7344. Albert Lalonde, O.M.I., Editor. A 44-page magazine published monthly by the Oblate Fathers of St. Mary's Province, with a national distribution of 17,427.
☐*Our Family* is aimed at a Catholic family audience—average family men and women of both urban and rural backgrounds. A fair proportion of the readers have a professional background. Seeks vital, challenging, contemporary articles written in an unsophisticated, anecdotal style, about anything that concerns Christians as individuals or as families. Particularly needed: inspirational articles telling how people from all walks of life overcame obstacles, met sorrow, rose above failure, learned to conquer themselves and become more effective people through the living of Christian principles.

Articles should be 1,000 to 3,000 words; average length 2,000 words. Prefers to see finished manuscript. Author's guidelines free; send SASE with 42¢ postage; sample copy available for $1.50. Pays on acceptance: 7¢ to 10¢ per word for nonfiction; 7¢ to 10¢ per word for original short stories; 40¢ to 60¢ a line, depending on creativity, originality, and line length, for poetry that reveals people to themselves as humans and Christians (should be 4 to 30 lines). Also uses short anecdotes of 25 to 500 words. Prefers 8″ by 10″ black-and-white prints of good technical quality; pays $25 for inside use, $50 for cover use. Photographers who want more information should send for the free Photo Spec Sheet. Reports in 2 to 4 weeks.

OUR LITTLE FRIEND, Pacific Press Publishing Association, 1350 Villa Street, Mountain View, CA 94042. (415) 961–2323, extension 235. Louis Schutter, Editor. An 8-page weekly published for children ages 2 through 6 of the Seventh-Day Adventist Church with a national distribution of 66,000.
□*Our Little Friend* seeks "to aid in the character development of the child." Short, true-life stories are featured on heroism, adventure, nature, and purposeful everyday life. Stories should stress principles of right living such as health, temperance, honesty, truthfulness, courtesy, purity, respect, and love for parents and for God, and kindness to playmates and animals. Uses poetry, puzzles, short filler material, and special features. Small black-and-white photos submitted to illustrate a manuscript increase the chances of selling a story or poem. Do not send color pictures.
Stories should be 750 to 1,000 words. Free sample copy and author's guidelines available. Pays on acceptance: 1¢ per word for prose, 10¢ per line for poetry. Purchases small amount of freelance special feature art—must be of professional quality and preferably pen-line drawings. Music, crossword puzzles, maze and hidden-object puzzles must be camera-ready. Cannot accept pencil drawings. Artwork paid for on an individual merit basis. For front-page photo, pays $4 and up, 50¢ and up for one-time picture rental rights. Reports before the end of the month; does not read or buy manuscripts from June through August.

OUR SUNDAY VISITOR, 200 Noll Plaza, Huntington, IN 46750. (219) 356–8400. Founded 1912. Robert P. Lockwood, Editor. A 20-page newspaper published weekly. National circulation of 300,000.
□*Our Sunday Visitor* is a general-interest Roman Catholic news magazine dealing with the teachings of the church and how they apply to today's world. Prints interviews, profiles, nonfiction articles, devotions, and Bible study. Particularly needs intelligent, well-written articles on Catholic trends and society and family problem-solving. Well-received articles: "What to Do if Your Unmarried Daughter Becomes Pregnant," "When the Grandparents Come Home to Live," "TV Facts for Parents," "Euthanasia Today."
Articles should be 1,500 words. Writer's guidelines and sample copy available. Payment pre-arranged with author, on acceptance. Query letter desirable; reprints will be considered. Reports in 4 weeks.

PARISH FAMILY DIGEST, 200 Noll Plaza, Huntington, IN 46750. (219) 356–8400. Patrick R. Moran, Editor. A 48-page bimonthly magazine in 5" by 7½" digest format, published by Our Sunday Visitor, Inc., with a national distribution of 138,000.
□*Parish Family Digest* is family-oriented, uses interrelated items on schools, parish activities evolving around family, liturgical celebrations of family reception of sacraments, relations with senior citizens, services for the handicapped or undereducated. "Our Parish" feature calls for 250-word anecdotes relating to true experiences found in parishes—biographical or "unforgettable" character items, some historic (for example, the centennial of St. Patrick's Cathedral in New York or Minnesota's "Grasshopper Chapel"). Also prints satires of people, humor, education, travel (visits to shrines, etc.), and photos.
Fillers should be 100 to 250 words. Single-page features for "Our Parish" items should be 250 words. Query letter necessary only for liturgical or scriptural usage in manuscript. Free sample copy and author's guidelines available with SASE. Pays on acceptance: 5¢ per word, ranging from a total of $5 to $50 for maximum story length of 1,000 words. Reports in 2 weeks.

PARISH TEACHER, 426 South Fifth Street, Box 1209, Minneapolis, MN 55440. Published monthly (except July and August) by Augsburg Publishing House for church school teachers.

☐*Parish Teacher* seeks to provide its readers with ideas, articles related to teaching, devotional writings, review of new resources, and summaries of new education trends and methods for use in the classroom. Articles are needed in three general areas: teacher-helps that focus on the learner; teacher-helps that focus on methodology (including poetry, creative teaching styles, role-playing, photography, overhead projector, and planning sessions); and ideas useful in a class setting.

Feature articles should be approximately 700 to 750 words; ideas approximately 100 to 150 words. Author's guidelines available. Payment made for articles published.

PARTNERS, P.O. Box 15025, San Jose, CA 95115-0025. (408) 298-0965. Founded 1943. Lorry Lutz, Editor and Director of Communications. A 23-page quarterly magazine sponsored by the Christian Nationals Evangelism Commission, 1470 North Fourth Street, San Jose CA 95115. National distribution of 45,000.
☐*Partners* uses some assigned articles (though most are written in-house), profiles, interviews, missions, photos, and illustrations. No other information provided.

PARTNERSHIP, THE MAGAZINE FOR WIVES IN MINISTRY, 465 Gundersen Drive, Carol Stream, IL 60187. (312) 260-6200. Founded 1984. Ruth Senter, Editor. An 80-page semimonthly magazine sponsored by Christianity Today, Inc. Regional circulation of 35,000.
☐*Partnership* readers, "although a select group, represent a broad spectrum of education, background, experience, and expertise." Most are wives of local church pastors, elders, or lay leaders in a variety of denominations: evangelical, mainline and liberal Protestant, even Orthodox. Prints interviews, humor, fillers, photos and illustrations. "Interviews are well-received, but are done by house staff. Spiritual growth articles are well read."

All material "must be tightly focused to needs and interests of women who are wives of Christian ministers." Sample copy and *very* helpful guidelines available. Fillers should be 300 words, articles 1,200 to 2,000 words. Query letter desirable; will consider reprints. Pays $50 to $300, on acceptance. Reports in 4 weeks.

PASTORAL LIFE, Society of St. Paul, Canfield, OH 44406. (216) 533-5503. Rev. Ignatius W. Staniszewski, S.S.P., Editor. A 68-page monthly journal published by the Society of St. Paul, with a national distribution of 9,000.
☐*Pastoral Life* is published for Roman Catholic clergy and deals with the people and issues related to the clergy and their work in the church. "Designed to focus on the current problems, needs, issues, and all important activities related to all phases of pastoral work, ministries, and life." Avoids merely academic treatments on abstract and too-controversial subjects. Also features concise, pastoral homilies for Sundays and Holy Days.

Articles should be no longer than 3,500 words. Query letters appreciated. Sample copy and author's guidelines available. Pays 3¢ per word and up, on acceptance. Additional payments for reprints. Reports within 10 days.

PASTORAL RENEWAL, Box 8617, Ann Arbor, MI 48107. (313) 761-8505. Founded 1976. John Blattner, Editor. A 16-page monthly journal sponsored by the Center for Pastoral Renewal, with a national distribution of 14,000.
☐*Pastoral Renewal* prints analyses of, and advice regarding, pastoral care: analysis of contemporary Christian issues, practical and theoretical pastoral teachings, and teaching on basic Christian truths. Well-received articles: "Evangelizing Young People," "Islam's Threat to Christianity," "Growing in Manly Character," "Resolving Relationship Problems Among Leaders." Also prints interviews and theology. Readers are scholars, clergy, and general lay readers of all denominations.

Articles range between 800 and 3,000 words. Sample copies and guidelines available. Query letters desirable; will consider reprints. No payment. Reports in 2 weeks.

PENTECOSTAL EVANGEL, 1445 Boonville, Springfield, MO 65802. (417) 862–2781. Richard Champion, Editor; Harris L. Jansen, Managing Editor. A 32-page weekly magazine published by the Assemblies of God, with an international distribution of 300,000.

□*Pentecostal Evangel* is a denominational paper, the "voice" of the Assemblies of God. Choice of subjects should be made with this in mind. The *Evangel* goes into both Christian and non-Christian homes. Subjects should be significant and timely, and the material should be forceful and of definite spiritual value. Uses news and features of interest to Charismatic Christians: "devotional articles, true stories of soul winning, outstanding conversions, unusual answers to prayers, and physical healings, Bible studies, doctrinal articles, salvation messages, articles for the homemaker, moments of inspiration, seasonal articles, stories of people, poetry, and photos."

   Articles should be 500 to 2,000 words; poems up to 50 lines. Prefers to see entire manuscript. Sample copy and author's guidelines available. Pays on publication: 3¢ per word for first rights, 40¢ per line for poetry. Reports in approximately 3 months.

PERSPECTIVE, Box 788, Wheaton, IL 60187. (312) 293–1600. Lorraine Mulligan Davis, Editor. A 32-page quarterly magazine of Pioneer Clubs, with a national distribution of 20,000.

□*Perspective* is for the adult leaders of the Pioneer Clubs, conducted by lay men and women in local churches "to provide information that will aid the leader in personal growth, leadership skills, and understanding of children and youth." Material must deal specifically with adults leading children and youth in church/club settings. Many articles done on assignment; accepts only a few of the freelance manuscripts submitted. Also accepts how-to ideas, crafts, party, and service-project suggestions of 100 to 250 words. Writing must reflect understanding and knowledge of Pioneer Clubs. Well-received articles and topics: Experiences of a club leader working with first- and second-graders; "Growing New Guides," about training and recruiting club leaders; "Activities—More Than a Time-Filler."

   Articles should be 1,000 to 2,500 words, average 1,500. Query letters desirable. Sample copy and author's guidelines available for $1.50. Pays on acceptance: $7 to $10 for short filler projects/activities; $25 to $50 per article, depending on quality, length, and amount of editing required. Reports in 6 to 8 weeks.

PLUS: THE MAGAZINE OF POSITIVE THINKING, a 36-page monthly magazine published by the Foundation for Christian Living, P.O. Box FCL, Pawling, NY 12564; with a national distribution of 800,000. (914) 855–5000. Founded 1951. Donald T. Kaufman, Managing Editor.

□*Plus* is "dedicated to the advancement of Christianity as a practical way of life." Prints practical solutions to everyday problems and articles of faith and inspiration. Well-received articles: "Anger—Help or Hindrance?"; "Why Me?"; "Have a Terrific Time Living"; "How to Be at Peace With Yourself." Readers are general lay adults.

   Articles should be up to 3,000 words. Especially interested in short articles illuminating some specific aspect of positive living: "A warm, personal style keeps the reader interested and focused on how he can use this help in his own life. Anecdotes that are well-written, succinct, and visual work better than long-winded, preachy theories." Query letters desirable. Sample copies and explicit author's guidelines available. Will consider reprints. Pays up to $250, on publication. Reports in 6 weeks.

POCKETS, A DEVOTIONAL MAGAZINE FOR CHILDREN, 1908 Grand Avenue, P.O. Box 189, Nashville, TN 37202. Founded 1981. Judith E. Smith, Editor. A 32-page monthly (except January) magazine for children, with a national circulation of 80,000.

□*Pockets*'s purpose "is to open up the fullness of the Gospel of Jesus Christ to children 6 through 12, with a target reading age of 8 through 11." Prints fiction, nonfiction articles, poetry, devotions, and Bible Study. "Each issue is built around several themes with material that can be used by children in a variety of ways—Scripture stories, fiction, prayers, art, graphics, puzzles, and activities are included. Submissions do not need to be overtly religious."

Stories should be 1,000 to 1,800 words, poems 24 lines or less. Very precise, helpful guidelines and sample copy available. Particularly interested in "sensitive treatment of two difficult issues—nuclear threat and child abuse, either physical or emotional—in a fiction format. Story should help children name their fear, then deal with it. Seasonal material, both secular and liturgical, and material by children are also desired." Query letter not necessary; reprints will be considered. Pays on acceptance: 7¢ per word and up for stories and articles, $25 to $50 for poetry; $10 to $25 for activities. Reports in 2 weeks, "unless author is notified otherwise."

POWER FOR LIVING, Box 632, Glen Ellyn, IL 60138. (312) 668–6000. John Duckworth, Editor. An 8-page digest published quarterly in weekly sets by Scripture Press, with a national distribution of 400,000.

□*Power For Living* is the weekly adult paper in the Power/line quarterly take-home series, whose primary aim is "to make Christ relevant to adults in everyday life situations and to offer evidence that Christianity really works." Features unusual or colorful profile stories of Christians whose lives can be seen as an inspiration to others, subjects whose lives are packed with human interest. Anecdotes are a must. Wants strong, hard-hitting, true stories that show how God gives individual Christians power for living in situations as varied as the whole scope of human experience.

Articles should be 1,000 to 1,400 words. Query letters required. Free "Tips to Writers" available. Pays 5¢ to 10¢ per word on acceptance. Photos submitted should be 5" by 7" or larger; catch informal, unposed action; show people doing something pertinent to the story. Pays up to $25 for black-and-white photos, depending on quality. Reports in 4 to 6 weeks.

THE PRAYER LINE, P.O. Box 55146, Seattle, WA 98155. (206) 363–3586. Founded 1959. Rev. Jonathan E. Nisbet, Litt. D., Editor and President. A 4-page quarterly newsletter sponsored by the Prayer by Mail Society, Inc., with an international distribution of 5,000.

□*The Prayer Line* prints articles on prayer, devotions, theology, photos and illustrations. Readers are lay adult members of various denominations. Articles should be between 1,500 and 2,500 words. Sample copies available. Will consider reprints. Payment is per article, on publication, though many pieces are donated, as the Society is a nonprofit organization. Reports in 4 weeks.

THE PREACHER'S MAGAZINE, 6401 The Paseo, Kansas City, MO 64131. (816) 333–7000. Founded 1926. Wesley Tracy, Editor. A 64-page quarterly magazine sponsored by the Church of the Nazarene, Nazarene Publishing House, Box 357, Kansas City, MO 64141. Worldwide circulation of 17,000. (The *Magazine* is also distributed to pastors of other denominations who include their own insert.)

□*Preacher's Magazine* is Wesleyan-Arminian in theological persuasion and prints "how-to, instructional, motivational articles that will help the parish pastor do his job more effectively." Well-received articles: "Overcoming the Giant Despair," on dealing with the discouragements typical of pastoral work; "Celebration of the Discipline of Study"; "Pastoral Demands in Changing Times"; "Objectives for the Local Church"; "Holistic Missions"; "Leadership, Change, and the Gospel," an EPA winner. Also prints theology and Bible study. Readers are scholars and clergy of the Church of the Nazarene.

Articles should be between 1,500 and 2,500 words. Guidelines available. "Much of the magazine is on assignment. We get and purchase excellent, well-researched material on specific aspects of ministry and ministers." Query letters not necessary; "just let us see the material." No reprints. Pays on acceptance: 3¢ per word, except for Sermon Outlines (paid for individually, from $10 to $30). Reports in 9 weeks.

THE PRESBYTERIAN JOURNAL, P.O. Box 2330, Asheville, NC 28805. (704) 254–4015. William S. Barker, Editor. A 16- to 24-page weekly magazine with a national distribution of 20,000.

☐ *The Presbyterian Journal* prints news and articles pertaining to the people, churches, and issues of interest and concern to Presbyterian adults, both clergy and laity. Deals with both personal Christian experiences and theological issues, written from the evangelical perspective.

No longer wishes to receive freelance material, "as we are receiving more unsolicited manuscripts than are useful to us and convenient to process."

PRESBYTERIAN OUTLOOK, 512 East Main Street, Richmond, VA 23219. (804) 649–1371. George Laird Hunt, Editor. A 16-page weekly magazine published by Outlook Publishers, Inc., with a national distribution of 10,500.

☐ *Presbyterian Outlook* publishes news and articles of interest to the members of the Presbyterian Church (U.S.A.). Readers are both clergy and laity. Material is limited to nonfiction, reporting on "significant activities of the churches and issues that are or should be before the church."

Most writing done on assignment. Articles should be 1,000 to 2,000 words. Query letters desirable. Sample copies available. No payment for material used. Reports within 2 weeks.

PRESBYTERIAN SURVEY, 341 Ponce de Leon Avenue N.E., Atlanta, GA 30365. (404) 873–1549. Vic Jameson, Editor/Publisher. A magazine published monthly (except for combined issues in January-February and July-August) under the auspices of the Presbyterian Church (U.S.A.), with a national distribution of 178,000.

☐ *Presbyterian Survey* is intended primarily for families in congregations of the Presbyterian Church. The great majority of readers are laity with a wide range of ages, theological viewpoints, and involvement in the life of the church. Seeks to relate the Christian faith to the life of the people, to report on activities and decisions of the church that affect its congregations, and to enhance and support the church's undertakings. Most material is assigned, but does use freelance submissions, especially stories of individuals or groups who express their faith in significant ways. Uses photos, rarely uses poetry, and does not print fiction.

Articles should be 800 to 2,500 words; average is 1,500 to 2,000. Query letters desirable. Sample copy and author's guidelines available. Pays $50 to $200 per article, on acceptance. Reports in 60 days.

PRIMARY TREASURE, Pacific Press Publishing Association, 1350 Villa Street, Mountain View, CA 94042. (415) 961–2323 extension 235. Louis Schutter, Editor. An 8-page weekly published for children aged 7 to 9 by the Seventh-Day Adventist Church, with a national distribution of 66,000.

☐ *Primary Treasure* seeks to aid in children's character development. Desires short, true-to-life stories of heroism, adventure, nature, and purposeful everyday life. Should stress principles of right living such as health, temperance, honesty, truthfulness, courtesy, purity, respect, love for parents and for God, and kindness to playmates and animals. Also uses poetry, puzzles, short filler material, and special features. Small black-and-white photos submitted with a manuscript to illustrate a story or poem increase chances of sale. Do *not* send color pictures.

Manuscripts should be 600 or 1,200 words. Free sample copy and author's guidelines available. Pays on acceptance: 1¢ per word for prose, 10¢ per line for poetry. Reports on submissions before the end of the month, but does not read or buy any manuscripts during June, July, or August. Also purchases small amount of freelance special-feature art. Must be of professional quality, preferably pen-line drawings. Cannot accept pencil drawings. Music, crossword puzzles, maze, and hidden-object puzzles must be camera-ready. Artwork is paid for on individual merit basis. Front-page photos pay $5 and up; picture rental for one-time magazine rights only is 50¢.

PRO-CLAIMER, Box 1948, Rocky Mount, NC 27801. Founded 1972, under a different name. Linda Gillian, Associate Editor. A 4-page newspaper published 9 times a year, sponsored by Positive Action for Christ, with a national distribution of under 5,000.
□*Pro-Claimer* prints articles and stories with strong spiritual emphasis; material that presents biblical principles, written in a style understandable and attractive to today's teens. Well-received articles: on how to minister to old folks; on how to make and use spoon puppets; on relationships between teens and parents, other Christian teens, etc.—a series. Also publishes poetry, profiles, humor, interviews, and fillers. Readers are youth, Baptist and "nondenominational Bible-believers." (Various Protestant churches use Pro-Teen Bible Club material, also published by Positive Action.)

Articles should be 1,000 words for features and short stories, but shorter articles preferred. Sample copies and guidelines—undergoing changes to accommodate pending changes—available. "Pressing need: 1,000-word (preferably less) nonfiction pieces with substance, with biblical principles as the central theme, to fit columns. 'On Top' helps teens grow spiritually, 'On Guard' points out things they need to guard against, 'Square One' helps in their decision making." Query letters not necessary; will consider reprints. Pays $10 to $25 per article, usually on acceptance, sometimes on publication. Reports in 4 to 8 weeks.

PSYCHOLOGY FOR LIVING, Narramore Christian Foundation, Box 5000, Rosemead, CA 91105. (818) 288–7000. Founded 1955. Ruth E. Narramore, Editor. A 36-page monthly magazine with international distribution.
□*Psychology for Living* prints articles on "everyday personal and family problems." Well-received articles: "They Conquered Exhaustion: So Can You," "Helping the Homesick Camper," "Our Greatest National Asset." Readers are adults and senior citizens, clergy, and lay Protestants.

Articles should run 1 to 2 printed pages. Sample copies and guidelines available. Query letters not necessary; will consider reprints. No payment. Reports in 1 week.

PULPIT HELPS, 6815 Shallowford Road, Chattanooga, TN 37422. (615) 894–6060. Founded 1975. Joe B. Walker, Managing Editor. A 32-page monthly newspaper sponsored by AMG International, with a national circulation of 224,000.
□*Pulpit Helps* prints "material that is beneficial to ministers of evangelical churches." Prints humor, poetry, devotions, Bible study, theology, fillers, and photos and illustrations.

Query letters desirable; will consider reprints. No payment. Sample copy and guidelines available. Reports in 8 weeks.

PURPOSE, Mennonite Publishing House, 616 Walnut Avenue, Scottdale, PA 15683. (412) 887–8500. James E. Horsch, Editor. "A Christian weekly of general interest to young and old."
□*Purpose* seeks articles and short stories that are clearly written in terse, fast-moving style. These may deal with anything of concern and interest to Christians as disciples—helping them achieve the ideals of the Christian faith personally and in their relationships with others at home and at work, in the church, and in the community. Creative spiritual approaches to solution of social problems also welcome—focus on overpopulation, ecology, stewardship of resources, etc. Interested in articles and stories that show Christians putting their faith to work in day-to-day living, help readers with their beliefs and decision-making, show implications of following Christ in today's world, inspire interest in other peoples and cultures around the world, stress church loyalty and community responsibility, focus on hobbies, nature, travel, science, and seasonal topics from a Christian perspective.

Articles should be 350 to 1,200 words; short stories to 1,200 words. Sample copy and author's guidelines available. Buys appropriate verse, 4 to 12 lines long and 5″ by 7″ professional-quality photos. Pays up to 5¢ per word for unsolicited material; $4 to $12 for poetry; $7.50 to $25 for photos.

QUAKER LIFE, 101 Quaker Hill Drive, Richmond, IN 47374. (317) 962–7573. Jack Kirk, Editor. A 48-page magazine published monthly (except for combined issues in January-February and July-August) by Friends United Meeting, with an international distribution of 8,700.

□*Quaker Life* prints "articles clarifying the Quaker identity and furthering the Friends' message and mission in the world." Articles and materials related to tell the Quaker story. Designed for general lay reading audience of adults, largely members of the Society of Friends.

Most articles are solicited. No cash payment; author receives three complimentary copies of the magazine in which the article appears. Selected articles from the magazine are recorded on tape, in-house.

QUALITY PUBLICATIONS, Box 1060, Abilene, TX 79604. (915) 677–6262. Founded 1956. Bennie J. Whitehead, Owner; Johnny Ramsey, Editor. A 44-page monthly magazine sponsored by the Church of Christ, with a national distribution of 15,000.

□*Quality Publications* prints theology, devotions, Bible study, and religious materials for all ages. Readers include scholars, clergy, and general lay readers of various evangelical and mainline Protestant denominations.

Articles should be 4 to 5 pages, typewritten and double-spaced. Author's guidelines and sample copies available. Reports in 8 weeks.

QUIET REVOLUTION, 1655 St. Charles Street, Jackson, MS 39209. (601) 353–1635. Founded 1975. Chris Rice, Editor. A 12-page quarterly newspaper sponsored by the Voice of Calvary Ministries, with a national distribution of 13,500.

□*Quiet Revolution* prints "issues related to Christian community development, racial reconciliation, black leadership development, ministry among the poor, and biblical justice for the oppressed." Also prints profiles, interviews, Bible study, photos and illustrations. Readers are adults, mostly lay members of evangelical Protestant churches.

Articles should be 3 to 4 pages, typed and double-spaced. Sample copies and guidelines available. Query letters desirable; will consider reprints. Does not pay for articles. No decision time given.

R-A-D-A-R, Standard Publishing, 8121 Hamilton Avenue, Cincinnati, OH 45231. (513) 931–4050. Margaret Williams, Editor. A 12-page weekly Bible School paper for boys and girls.

□*R-A-D-A-R* seeks to reach children "with the truth of God's Word and to help them make it the guide of their lives." Prints fiction that reinforces Bible lessons presented in the Sunday School curriculum. In order to meet the particular needs, writers must request a theme list.

Stories should be 900 to 1,200 words; two-part stories a total of 2,000 words, with the hero of the story being an 11- or 12-year-old. Nature articles range from 500 to 800 words, as do articles on hobbies and handcrafts, animals, life in other lands, sports, science, seasonal subjects, etc. Articles should have a religious emphasis. Query letters unnecessary; prefers to receive entire manuscripts. Free sample copy and author's guidelines available. Pays 2¢ maximum per word, on acceptance. Additional payment made for photos. For verse and poetry (usually biblical, or about seasons or nature), pays 40¢ per line. For Bible puzzles and crosswords (mostly done on assignment) payment varies according to type of puzzle; for cartoons (of which approximately 10 to 12 are printed each year) pays $10 to $15. Reports in 4 to 6 weeks.

RAINBOWS, DREAMS AND BUTTERFLY WINGS, Shining Star Publications, Box 299, Carthage, IL 62321. (217) 357–3981. Founded 1982. Becky Daniel, Editor. A 32-page tabloid size newspaper, published 5 times yearly with a national distribution of 6,500.

□*Rainbows. . .* prints "unique ways of presenting the Bible to children, fun activities that will make students want to learn." Well-received articles have been on Bible heroes, developing positive self-concepts, Biblical bulletin boards, and seasonal ideas.

Also prints poetry, devotions, and Bible study. Readers are adults, lay members of evangelical and mainline Protestant denominations.

Articles should be "several activities that will fill an 11" by 17" page." Sample copies and guidelines available. "The King James version should be used unless you specify otherwise." Particularly interested in more preschool and primary-grade materials. No reprints. Pays "an average of $30 per page or an equivalent of Good Apple products. Rates can vary. Products are paid on acceptance, but if author chooses cash, payment will be on publication. Reports in 8 weeks.

THE REFORMED JOURNAL, 255 Jefferson Street S.E., Grand Rapids, MI 49507. (616) 459–4591. Jon Pott, Editor. A 32-page monthly magazine published by the William B. Eerdmans Publishing Co., with a national distribution of 3,000.
□*The Reformed Journal* prints "comment and opinion on the contemporary scene in the church, culture, and society from a Reformed perspective." Aimed at adults, primarily clergy and scholars, some laity—evangelicals of various Protestant denominations, mostly Reformed.

Articles should be from 8 to 11 typewritten, double-spaced pages. Query letters not required. Sample copy available. No payment for material used. Reports in 2 months.

RELIGIOUS BROADCASTING REPORT, P.O. Box 1129, Manassas, VA 22110. Founded 1983. Bruce H. Joffe, Editor and Publisher. A 4-page monthly newsletter with a national circulation of 2,000.
□*Religious Broadcasting Report* covers "the personalities and ministries affecting the church through religious broadcasting channels." Prints fillers and short, analytical insights into religious programming. Readers are adults, scholars, and clergy of mixed denominations.

Articles should be no more than 500 words. "Best news stories are brief—from 150 to 300 words." Query letters desirable; reprints not considered. For each short paragraph of news or insight, pays between $10 and $25, on publication. Reports in 4 weeks.

RELIGIOUS STUDIES REVIEW, Wilfred Laurier University, Waterloo, Ontario N2L 3C5, Canada. (519) 884–7300. An 80-page quarterly journal published by the Council on the Study of Religion.
□*Religious Studies Review* is devoted solely to the reviewing of books, mostly of a theological nature and of interest to the scholars and teachers of religion who are members of the theological and biblical societies in the Council.

The majority of the reviews are solicited. Query letters required. No payment for use of material.

RESOURCE (formerly *The Edge on Christian Education*), 6401 The Paseo, Kansas City, MO 64131. (616) 333–7000. Melton Wienecke, Editor. A quarterly magazine for church-school workers of the Church of The Nazarene.
□*Resource* uses motivational and informational articles of not more than 800 words on successful plans, programs, new ideas, and methods for better organization, outreach, evangelism, and improved teaching.

Author's guidelines available. Pays on acceptance. Reports in 10 to 12 weeks.

ST. JOSEPH MESSENGER AND ADVOCATE OF THE BLIND, 543 Pavonia Avenue, P.O. Box 288, Jersey City, NJ 07306. (201) 798–4141. Sister Ursula Maphet, CSJP, Editor. A 30-page quarterly magazine published by the Sisters of St. Joseph of Peace, with a national distribution of 50,000.
□*St. Joseph Messenger* deals with news about and things of interest to the supporters of the St. Joseph School for the Blind and the St. Joseph Nursing Home for the Blind. Freelance material, however, is mainly fiction and poetry. "Our greatest need is for good, contemporary, mainstream fiction that speaks to today and of today."

Feature articles should be 800 to 1,000 words; fiction can be somewhat longer. Sample copy and author's guidelines available. Pays on acceptance: a base rate of 1¢ per word or higher; pays $3 to $15 for poetry. Reports in 2 weeks. Also distributes calendars that are produced in-house.

ST. LUKE'S JOURNAL OF THEOLOGY, School of Theology, University of the South, Sewanee, TN 37375. (615) 598–5931. John M. Gessell, Editor. An 80-page quarterly journal with a national distribution of 2,500.
□*St. Luke's Journal* is "a journal of religious thought for clergy and laity who want to relate theological studies to contemporary issues. Provides a forum for discussion of the work of the ministry as this work is illumined by the work and experience of professionals and others in the field." Sponsorship is of Anglican/Episcopal background, but readers are from several denominations.

Articles should be less than 16 typewritten, double-spaced pages. Query letters desirable. Sample copy and author's guidelines available. No payment for material used. Reports in 2 months.

SCOPE, 426 South Fifth Street, Box 1209, Minneapolis, MN 55440. (612) 330–3413. Constance Lovaas, Editor. A 48-page monthly magazine published for American Lutheran Church Women, with a national distribution of 270,000.
□*Scope* is aimed primarily to be "an educational tool for women of the church. Prints Bible studies for use in women's groups, articles for inspiration and spiritual growth, information about the mission and concerns of the church, stories and articles geared to seasonal emphases." Uses nonfiction, very little poetry, and photos. Interested in any material that touches the lives of Christian women and their families. High premium on stories of people. Readers "have a wide range of lifestyles and a deep interest in all of life."

Brief articles of 800 to 1,000 words preferred. Free sample copy and author's guidelines available. Pays $40 to $75 per article, on acceptance. Reports in 1 month.

SEEK, 8121 Hamilton Avenue, Cincinnati, OH 45231. (513) 931–4050. Leah Ann Crussell, Editor. An 8-page weekly magazine, distributed quarterly by Standard Publishing Company, with a national distribution of 60,000.
□*Seek* is a colorfully illustrated take-home or pass-along weekly paper designed to appeal to older teens and modern adults. Articles printed show faith in action, victorious Christian living, first-person testimonies, answered prayer, historical figures with faith, and personality pieces. Articles must not be preachy or patronizing, must be wholesome, alive, vibrant, current, relevant, and have titles that demand that the articles be read. No poetry. Particularly needs personality pieces with photos to illustrate. Prefers 8″ by 10″ glossies with sharp black-and-white contrasts.

Articles should be 1,200 words; 1,500 words maximum. Query letters not necessary. Free sample copy and author's guidelines available. Pays 2½¢ per word, on acceptance. Pays up to $15 apiece for photos. Reports within 14 days.

SEVENTH ANGEL, Box 334, Pottstown, PA 19464. James A. Gittings, Editor. A 40- to 44-page monthly tabloid, a wholly-owned subsidary of J/S Arts and Features, Inc., with a national distribution of 4,000 paid and 15,000 unpaid copies.
□*Seventh Angel* prints "reportage on religion that is absolutely *free* of bias in favor of or against religion in any of its flavors. We want religion covered like City Hall." Prints religious news and personalities of all kinds, theology ("leading-edge stuff, no amateurs!"), poetry, and interviews. Well-received articles: "Law as a Structure For Freedom" by Roger Shinn, Bo Hodiak on EST, Jim Wright on schism in the Brazilian church, Dean Kelly on First Amendment problems. Readers are "center to left" scholars, clergy, and general lay readers of Roman Catholic and mixed Protestant denominations.

Articles should be 2,000 words tops, except for theology articles; average is about 800 words. Query letters desirable. Sample copies and author's guidelines available. Pay negotiable; top is $500, average is $150. Pays $85 for poetry, on publication. Reports in 3 weeks.

SHARING THE VICTORY, 8701 Leeds Road, Kansas City, MO 64129. (816) 921–0909. Skip Stogsdill, Editor. A 24-page bimonthly magazine published by the Fellowship of Christian Athletes, with a national distribution.

□*Sharing the Victory* is geared primarily for athletes and coaches, male and female, from the junior high to college level, with the aim of encouraging and enabling them to grow stronger in their faith. Uses both first- and third-person articles and profiles. Likes features on "name" athletes as well as third-stringers. Tries to feature a professional athlete, college athlete, high school athlete, and coach in each issue.

Articles should be 800 words. Publishes very little poetry. Sample copy and author's guidelines available for $1.00. Query letters are "extremely helpful, as all articles must fit our format and be seasonal." Uses a 2-page black-and-white centerspread sports photo each issue, plus a full-color slide and/or color print for front and back covers. Pays on publication: an average of $35 for articles and photos, more for exceptional pieces and full-page photos. Reports within 10 days at most on manuscripts and/or photos.

SHINING STAR BIBLE THINKER SHEETS, Shining Star Publications, Box 299, Carthage, IL 62321. (217) 357–3981. Founded 1984. Becky Daniel, Editor. A 48-page magazine published 5 times per year, with a national distribution of 5,600.

□*Shining Star* prints Bible work sheets that can be torn out and photocopied, and which present unique ways of introducing the Bible to children. Well-received sheets have been on Bible heroes, Christian values, seasonal ideas, Bible study, Bible puzzles, and creative writing. Also prints poetry, devotions, and educational materials. Readers are lay adults of various evangelical and mainline Protestant denominations.

Material should be sufficient to make up an 8½" by 11" worksheet. Sample copies and guidelines available. Particularly interested in seasonal ideas, Bible heroes, and positive self-concept. No reprints. Pay depends on content, but is approximately $10 per 8½" by 11" page, upon publication; or equivalent amount of products, on acceptance. Reports in 8 weeks.

SIGNS OF THE TIMES, P.O. Box 7000, Boise, ID 83707. (208) 467–7400. Founded 1874. Kenneth J. Holland, Editor. A 32-page monthly magazine, sponsored by the Seventh-Day Adventist General Conference, 6840 Eastern Avenue N.W., Washington DC 20012. Worldwide distribution of 400,000.

□*Signs of the Times* calls itself "a major evangelistic journal" and prints articles about "people who have overcome problems by putting the principles of the Bible into practice." Well-received articles have dealt with cancer, depression, child abuse, the threat of nuclear war, and divorce. Also prints poetry, profiles, interviews, devotions, fillers, Bible study, theology, photos and illustrations. Though most readers are lay adult Seventh-Day Adventists, *Signs of the Times* likes to "beam our articles at non-Christian young adults with little knowledge of the Bible."

Articles should be 1,700 to 2,000 words; shorter pieces should run from 700 to 1,000 words. Sample copies and extraordinarily helpful guidelines available. Query letters desirable; will consider reprints. Pays 10¢ per word, occasionally more, on acceptance. Reports in 2 weeks.

THE SINGING NEWS, P.O. Box 18010, Pensacola. FL 32505. (904) 434–2773. Janice D. Cain, Editor. A 40- to 44-page monthly tabloid newspaper with a national distribution.
□*The Singing News* is read by youth and adults of mixed Protestant denominations. Publishes feature and human-interest stories on gospel music personalities. Well-received articles have been "A Story From Galilee"; "The Reggie Vinson Story"; "Bob Ayala"; "George Beverly Shea, America's Beloved Gospel Singer"; "Gordon Jensen, Marching to the Beat of a Different Drummer."

Articles average 2,000 to 3,000 words. Query letters desirable. Free sample copy available. Pays 3¢ per word, on publication. Normally reports in 3 to 6 months.

THE SMALL GROUP LETTER, NavPress, P.O. Box 6000, Colorado Springs, CO 80934. Lani Carroll, Editor. A newsletter, published 10 times a year by the Navigators, 3820 North 30th Street, Colorado Springs, CO 80934.

□*The Small Group Letter* publishes nonfiction: Bible studies, devotional reading, curriculum, and "articles dealing specifically with small groups and small group leadership: practical, biblically-based articles to use as a resource for readers; application-oriented to help leaders of small Christian groups enhance the ministry of group Bible studies, etc." Readers are lay adults of various evangelical denominations.

Articles should be over 200 words and less than 1,000 words. Prefers to see entire manuscripts. Sample copies and author's guidelines available. Pays a flat fee for some articles; most are paid by the word. Reports in 4 weeks. Also interested in reprints.

SOJOURNERS MAGAZINE, P.O. Box 29272, Washington, DC 20017. (202) 636-3637. Jim Wallis, Editor. A 40-page monthly magazine of Sojourners Fellowship, with a national distribution of 53,000.

□*Sojourners Magazine* is interested in articles from a radical biblical perspective, from economics to politics to theology. Articles about Christian community, renewal of the church, and personal faith journeys sought; special emphasis on anti-nuclear and peacemaking issues. Also prints fiction, poetry, photos and illustrations, book and film reviews.

Articles should be 600 to 2,400 words; average is 1,200 to 1,800. Include a 2- or 3-sentence description of yourself with manuscript or cover letter, along with your address and a phone number. Sample copy and author's guidelines available on request. General policy is no payment. Usually reports within 6 weeks.

SOLO MAGAZINE, P.O. Box 1231, Sisters, OR 97759. Founded 1977. Jerry Jones, Editor. A 56-page quarterly magazine with a national distribution of 30,000.

□*Solo* prints "captivating, eye-catching, unusual approaches to old subjects . . . fascinating topics that might be especially interesting to Christian single adults, ages 25 through 45." Also prints profiles, interviews, humor, investigative journalism, photos and illustrations. "Average age of our readers is approximately 31; 40% are never-married, 40% divorced, 10% widowed, the remainder married. Sixty-five percent are women, nearly 70% have a college education."

Articles should be a maximum of 2,000 words; "shorter treatment is often required." Sample copy and guidelines available for $2.00 and large SASE. "We want to cover life-issues and felt needs of single adults aged 25 to 45. Topics do not have to be just for singles. Many life issues are relevant to all adults, regardless of marital status." Query letters a must; no unsolicited manuscripts accepted. "Seldom" considers reprints. Pays on publication: $10 to $50 for black-and-white photos; 5¢ per word for original material, 3¢ for reprints. Reports in 12 weeks.

SONLIGHT CHRISTIAN NEWSPAPERS, 4123 Narcissus Avenue, Lake Worth, FL 33461. Founded 1980. Dennis Lombard, Editor. *Sonlight* is a quarterly; *Neighbor News* a weekly. Ranging from 12 to more than 24 pages, they have a combined distribution of over 50,000 in southeastern Florida.

□*Sonlight* prints articles "calling churches to love, prayer, unity, revival, and harvest in end times; on body ministry, mission involvement, unique churches and ministries, opinion pieces on current moral issues, and restoration of New Testament Christianity." Temporarily suspended until mid-1985. Articles should be no more than 1,500 words; no fiction, poetry, or fillers.

□*Neighbor News* is a series of radically Christian community newspapers carrying hard local news, entertaining reader features, and "a wide variety of inspirational materials, features on moral issues, stories of faith and victory." Articles should be about 1,000 words. Also prints *many* fillers (clippings, jokes, wisdom, puzzles cartoons, reminiscences, history and Bible quizzes).

Readers of both publications are of all denominations. Guidelines available. Query letters required; considers only "major reprints, which we search for ourselves." Pays 2¢ to 10¢ per word, on publication. Reports in 1 to 2 weeks.

SOUNDINGS, AN INTERDISCIPLINARY JOURNAL, P.O Box 6309, Station B, Nashville, TN 37235. (615) 322–8171. Donald W. Sherburne, Editor. A 128-page quarterly journal published by Vanderbilt University and the Society for Values in Higher Education, with a national distribution of 1,750.
□*Soundings* publishes "scholarly articles that reflect both competence in a particular discipline and an interest in the values that dignify human life. Articles must be able to transcend the author's specialities in order to encourage dialogue among the various disciplines." Recent articles have dealt with medical ethics, human rights, literary criticism, and higher education.
Articles should be 10 to 25 typed pages, 30 pages maximum, and submitted in duplicate. Query letters not necessary. Sample copy and author's guidelines available. No payment for material used. Reports in 3 months.

SOURCE, c/o Church Ministries of the Pentecostal Assemblies of Canada. 10 Overlea Boulevard, Toronto, Ontario M4H 1A5, Canada. (416) 425–1010. Founded 1981. Rick Hiebert, Editor. A 28-page bimonthly magazine with a Canadian distribution of 3,000.
□*Source* is "designed for Christian education workers in the local church" and prints articles on issues in Christian education, testimonials on the importance of Sunday School, church, etc., and how-to ideas for Sunday School and evangelism. Well-received articles were on using high-tech equipment (computers, video) in Christian education, how to set up a resource center, and so forth. Also prints interviews and fillers. Readers are clergy and lay adult members of the Pentecostal Assemblies of Canada.
Feature articles should be from 700 to 1,100 words, fillers up to 700 words. Sample copies and guidelines available. "Since our primary market is the *Canadian* Christian educator, articles must not quote or rely extensively on American statistics or data." Query letters desirable; will consider reprints. Pays on publication: $10 for fillers, up to $25 for features. Reports in 6 weeks.

SOVEREIGN GOLD LITERARY MAGAZINE, P.O. Box 1631, Iowa City, IA 52244. Founded 1975. Gary J. King, Executive Editor and Publisher. A 100-page 5½" by 8½" quarterly newspaper (which may switch publication to every four months) with only 550 subscribers but approximately 5,000 to 10,000 readers worldwide.
□Prints articles and fiction with "high moral message, no offbeat, no abusive sex or sex *[sic]*. Prefers Christian-slanted stories, fiction or nonfiction." *Sovereign Gold's* poetry showcase booklet was "well received with many Christian poets and others therein. Several ministers participate and submit as well as others. Very unique but high moral quality publication." Readers include children, youth, adults and senior citizens, scholars, clergy, and lay readers of all denominations.
Fiction should be 500 to 1,500 words, "but will read all." Sample copies and guidelines available. Particularly interested in "some fiction with a Christian or good moral message, you know, one down-to-earth Christians can relate to. I hate hypocrisy or when someone cuts another faith down. Catholics and Protestants are humans! Bad language, swear words, and poor moral content will give your manuscript an unfavorable impression (with me)." Query letters preferred; will consider reprints only "if real good. It is a requirement that the words ORIGINAL, UNPUBLISHED be put on the sheet. This certifies to me that it has not been published or sent elsewhere." Payment "negotiable and if payment is made, by copy or copies, depending on the negotiations." Reports in 1 week.

SPIRITUALITY TODAY, Aquinas Institute, 3642 Lindell Boulevard, St. Louis, MO 63108. (314) 658–3882. Christopher Kiesling, O.P., Editor. A 96-page quarterly journal published by the Central Province of the Dominican Order, 1909 South Ashland Avenue, Chicago, IL, for a national distribution.

□*Spirituality Today* "aims at helping Christians respond to their call to full Christian life by providing them with greater understanding of their faith and its potentialities for abundant life in Christ by His Spirit." Readers are mainly Roman Catholics, most with some theological education, interested in a more thorough study of the Christian life than popular magazines provide. Articles may be theological, historical, biblical, biographical, analytical, inspirational—but must speak to the experiences of men and women today and be critical and probing. No poetry.

Articles should be 12 to 15 pages of typewritten, double-spaced material. Sample copy available for $1.00; author's guidelines free. Pays at least 1¢ per word, on publication. Reports in 2 or 3 months.

SPIRITUAL LIFE, 2131 Lincoln Road N.E., Washington, DC 20002. (202) 832-6622. Rev. Christopher Latimer, O.C.D., and Rev. Steven Payne, O.C.D., Co-Editors. A 64-page Catholic quarterly published by the Discalced Carmelite Fathers, with a national distribution of 17,000.

□*Spiritual Life* prints serious essays dealing with the manner in which men and women encounter God and live in His presence in the contemporary world. According to a survey, readers are interested in the following topics, in this order: 1) prayer in everyday life, 2) spiritual direction, 3) contemplative prayer, 4) Scripture, 5) faith experience, 6) liturgy, 7) community life, 8) forms of American spirituality, 9) religious life, 10) St. Teresa of Avila and St. John of the Cross.

Articles should be 3,000 to 5,000 words, occasionally longer or shorter. Query letters not necessary; prefers that text be sent in its entirety. Free sample copy and author's guidelines available. Pays $50 minimum on acceptance; generally about $10 per manuscript page. Reports within 2 weeks.

SPRINT [formerly *Looking Ahead*] c/o David C. Cook Publishing Company, 850 North Grove Avenue, Elgin, IL 60120. (312) 741-2400. Founded 1982. Kristine Miller Tomasik, Administrative Youth Editor. An 8-page quarterly magazine with a national distribution of 180,000.

□*Sprint* prints "very short, catchy articles reporting on teen involvement in church/community projects and interviews with outstanding teens or personalities of interest to teens; dealing with difficult situations and emotional needs of teens; etc. We are using the photo-feature format increasingly to treat these topics. All manuscripts should present a Christian approach to life." Readers are junior high school students of various denominations.

Fiction should be 1,000 to 2,000 words, articles 800 to 1,000 words. Sample copies and guidelines available. Query letters desirable; will consider reprints. Pays $65 to $75 for articles, $20 for glossy black-and-white photos, $50 for color transparencies. No reporting time given.

THE STANDARD, 2002 South Arlington Heights Road, Arlington Heights, IL 60005.(312) 228-0200. A 48- or 64-page magazine published 11 times a year by the Baptist General Conference, with a national distribution of 25,000.

□*The Standard* exists to promote and report the work of the boards of the Baptist General conference and its churches, and to encourage BGC members in their Christian living. Articles are almost exclusively by and about BGC members; accepts very few articles other than these.

Articles should be 1,000 to 2,000 words. Sample copy available. Pays 2¢ to 3¢ per word about the time of publication. Reports upon receipt.

STANDARD, 6401 The Paseo, Kansas City, MO 64131. (816) 333-7000, extension 363. Sheila Boggess, Editor. An 8-page weekly adult magazine of the Church of the Nazarene, with an international distribution of 185,000.

□*Standard* prints "quality leisure reading with a Christian emphasis" for all adult age groups. Articles and fiction should express values without being preachy. Prints fiction, first-person accounts sifted from personal crisis or everyday experience, vignettes, and poetry. Particularly needs material dealing with a variety of topics for all adult age groups, for single and married adults; topics particularly for men and for women. Poetry must have a Christian message either stated or strongly implied. Poetic style is left to the author's discretion (traditional forms, blank verse, free verse, Haiku, etc.).

Fiction should be 1,500 to 1,700 words, first-person articles 1,200 to 1,500 words; limit is 1,700 words. Free sample copy and author's guidelines available. Seasonal material should reach the office 10 months before circulation date of the periodical. If an article or story is better suited to another publication in the Nazarene offices, it will be referred. Pays on acceptance: 3½¢ per word for prose (from $30 to $50 total), 25¢ per line of poetry. Reports in 8 weeks.

STORIES, 14 Beacon Street, Boston MA 02108. Founded 1982. Amy R. Kaufman, Editor. A 64-page bimonthly magazine with a national distribution of 1,500.
□*Stories* prints short fiction exclusively and is "designed to encourage the writing of a particular kind of story described most accurately by the term 'affective fiction.' " Readers are lay adults.

Stories should range between 750 and 10,000 words. "Simplicity is achieved after a struggle, and universality is possible only to a degree, but we feel that these are the qualities most likely to evoke readers' sympathy and concern. Timelessness is another ideal we pursue by avoiding language and subjects that are fashionable. Translations and sharply perceptive humor interest us; romance, mystery, fantasy, science fiction, and political pieces generally do not." Sample copies and guidelines available only with SASE. Query letters will not be answered; no reprints. Pays an average of $150 per story. Reports in 10 weeks.

STORY FRIENDS, 616 Walnut Avenue, Scottdale, PA 15683. (412) 887–8500. Marjorie Waybill, Editor. A 4-page weekly take-home story paper for children aged 4 through 9, published monthly (4 issues at a time) by the Mennonite Publishing House, with a distribution in the U.S. and Canada of 14,000.
□*Story Friends* needs "stories that speak to the needs and interests of children of a variety of ethnic backgrounds. Stories of children relating to other children and adults with similar or dissimilar backgrounds, shut-ins, or handicapped people. Stories should provide patterns of forgiveness, respect, integrity, understanding, caring, and sharing, and increase the children's sense of self-worth through growing confidence in God's love for them as they are; help answer the children's questions about God, Jesus, the Bible, prayer, death, heaven; develop awe and reverence for God the Creator and for all His creation; avoid preachiness but have well-defined spiritual values as an integral part of each story; be plausible in plot; introduce children to followers of Jesus Christ; develop appreciation for the Mennonite heritage." Also uses some poetry.

Stories should be 365 to 700 words. Sample copy and author's guidelines available. Pays, on acceptance, 3¢ to 5¢ per word, or approximately $30 per 1,000 words. Reports within 2 weeks.

STRAIGHT, 8121 Hamilton Avenue, Cincinnati, OH 45231. (513) 931–4050. Dawn Brettschneider, Editor. A 12-page magazine for Christian teenagers published quarterly by Standard Publishing, and distributed weekly through churches.
□*Straight* fiction must be well-written and appeal to 13- through 19-year-olds. Main characters should be contemporary teens who cope with modern-day problems using Christian principles. Stories should be character-building, but not preachy. Conflicts must be solved realistically, with thought-provoking and honest endings. Nonfiction needs: devotional pieces, articles on current issues from a Christian point of view, and humor. Topics should be of interest to teens: school, family life, church, recreation, friends, part-time jobs, dating, and music. Artwork done on assignment. Photo needs: teen profiles, teen activities. Poetry accepted from teenage writers *only*.

Fiction should be 1,000 to 1,500 words; nonfiction 1,000 words. Free sample copy and author's guidelines available with SASE. Particular needs closely correlated with

Sunday School curriculum; submit seasonal material 12 months in advance. Pays on acceptance: 2¢ per word for first rights, 1¢ to 1½¢ per word for reprint rights. Reports in 4 to 6 weeks.

SUCCESS: CHRISTIAN EDUCATION TODAY, P.O. Box 15337, Denver, CO 80215. (303) 988–5300. Founded 1947. Edith Quinlan, Editor. A 32-page quarterly magazine published by Accent Publications, Inc.
□*Success: CET* seeks "to promote Christian education 'awareness' in local churches, colleges, and seminaries; and provide practical help to those active in the Christian education field." Considers articles on unique ministries, teaching activities, recreational activities, attendance-building programs, and success stories. Also solicits news on Christian education happenings throughout the nation as well as on mission fields; and inspirational, devotional stories.

Submissions should be 1,500 to 2,000 words; must be in keeping with traditional evangelical concept. Free sample copy and author's guidelines available upon request. Payment based on writing quality and value to total magazine.

SUNDAY DIGEST, David C. Cook Publishing Company, 850 North Grove Avenue, Elgin, IL 60120. (312) 741–2400. Judy Couchman, Editor. An 8-page weekly take-home paper for adults with a national distribution.
□*Sunday Digest* provides selected reading for Christian adults in evangelical churches. Articles are used that help readers better understand the Christian faith, inform them of issues affecting the Christian community, and challenge them to a deeper personal commitment to Christ. Interested in nonfiction, fiction, poetry, interviews, humor, short (too 500 words) inspirational pieces, and how-to articles. Avoids "preachy" fiction and "strained" humor.

Lead articles should be 1,200 to 1,500 words, features articles, 800 to 1,000 words. Query letters not required. Sample copy and author's guidelines available; send a SASE. Pays on acceptance: a minimum of 7¢ per word for articles, $15 minimum for poetry. Also interested in magazine reprints.

SUNDAY SCHOOL COUNSELOR, 1445 Boonville, Springfield, MO 65802. (417) 862–2781. Sylvia Lee, Editor. A 28-page monthly adult magazine, published by the Assemblies of God, with a national distribution of 38,000.
□*Sunday School Counselor* provides local Sunday School administrators and teachers with inspiration, information, and practical methods and program ideas. Prints nonfiction, stories of people, and photos and illustrations. Adults in Sunday School is a popular topic. Well-received articles: "Helping Children Cope With Death," "We Tore Up Our Quarterly," "Don't Feed Them Candy," "Home is Where the Hurt Is."

Articles should be 1,200 words; short fillers and ideas, 250 words tops. Prefers to see complete manuscript. Sample copy and author's guidelines available. Usually pays by the word, at 1½¢ to 3¢ per word on acceptance. Reports in 4 weeks.

TEAM, Box 7244, Grand Rapids, MI 49510. (616) 241–5616. Dale Dieleman, Editor. A 32-page quarterly published by the Young Calvinist Federation, with circulation in the United States and Canada of 2,000.
□*Team* is for volunteer leaders of church youth groups and promotes shared leadership, multicultural expression, and holistic ministry with youth. Shared ministry *with* youth emphasizes service. Publishes nonfiction: leadership skills, adolescent development, youth trends, rural and urban ministry issues and ideas, as well as various cultural (black, Hispanic, Asian, native American) perspectives on leadership and youth ministry. Prints photos and illustrations

Nonfiction articles should be 800 to 2,000 words. Free sample copy available; send 9" by 6" SASE. Pays $25 to $50, on acceptance. Reports in 4 weeks.

TEEN POWER, Box 632, Glen Ellyn, Il 60138. (312) 668–6000. Pam Campbell, Editor. An 8-page weekly take-home paper for teens aged 12 through 16, published quarterly

(4 issues at a time) by Scripture Press Publications, with an international distribution in the U.S., Canada, and Great Britain of 120,000.

□*Teen Power* is read primarily by junior high school students. Considers true stories that show how God is working in normal, everyday situations, as well as in the occasional crises in teens' lives. Particularly needs stories, quizzes, plays, allegories, poetry, and humorous material by teens. First-person as-told-to stories welcome. True stories need to include anecdotes, dialogue, and the teen's spiritual insights. Black-and-white photos should accompany manuscripts.

True stories and fiction should be 750 to 1,000 words. Plays, quizzes, and expository pieces should be 400 to 800 words. "Free Tips to Writers" packet available. Pays on acceptance: for all rights, 6¢ to 10¢ per word; for first rights, 4¢ to 7¢ per word, for second (reprint) rights, 3¢ to 5¢ per word.

TEENS TODAY, 6401 The Paseo, Kansas City, MO 64131. (816) 333–7000. Gary Sivewright, Editor. A weekly take-home paper published for Youth of the Church of the Nazarene, with an international distribution of 60,000.

□*Teens Today* publishes life-related Christian fiction directed to the junior and senior high-school-age audience of the Church of the Nazarene. Uses material on youth concerns: peers, parents, vocation, environmental and social issues, development of self, dating and sex.

Articles should be 1,200 to 1,500 words. No query letters. Free sample copy and author's guidelines available with SASE. Pays on acceptance: 3½¢ per word for first rights, 3¢ for reprint rights. Reports in 4 to 6 weeks.

TELLING THE TRUTH, Triple T. Christian Communication Center, 12814 U.S. 41 North, Evansville, IN 47711. (812) 867–2418. Donald R. Brown, Managing Editor. A 52-page magazine published quarterly by George Dooms Christian Communications.

□*Telling the Truth* is aimed at teenagers, with a combination of contemporary style and conservative biblical content. Message is of a Christian lifestyle for young people with a challenge to read and heed the Bible. "The purpose of this magazine is to creatively communicate Christianity to and through teenagers, endeavoring to introduce readers to Jesus Christ and to challenge Christian young people to become aggressively evangelistic, Bible-believing, and church-centered individuals." Each issue contains photography, artwork, and contributions written by teenagers.

Opportunities are open to teenagers to serve as campus correspondents for colleges and high schools anywhere in the world.

THEOLOGICAL STUDIES, Georgetown University, 37th and O Streets N.W., Washington, DC 20057. (202) 338–0754. Walter J. Burghardt, S.J., Editor. A 200-page quarterly magazine published by the Society of Jesus in the U.S., Jesuit Conference, 1717 Massachusetts Avenue N.W., Washington, DC 20036, for an international distribution of 7,100.

□*Theological Studies* is published for Roman Catholic clergy and scholars. Seeks "well-written, documented research in any of the theological disciplines, *i.e.,* biblical, historical, systematic, and pastoral theologies." Especially interested in "bulletins" and shorter pieces detailing recent developments in various theological areas.

Articles should average 11,000 words, bulletins up to 9,000 words, "notes" from 1,000 to 5,000 words. Query letters encouraged. Free copies are rare, but explicit 16-page instructions for contributors are available. No payment for materials used. Reports in 2 to 3 months.

THEOLOGY TODAY, P.O. Box 29, Princeton, NJ 08542. (609) 921–8300. Hugh T. Kerr, Editor. A 150-page quarterly theological journal with an international distribution of 10,000.

□*Theology Today* is published for an audience of scholars, clergy, and general lay readers of mixed backgrounds, mostly in liberal Protestant and Roman Catholic groups. Prints essays and articles on current issues related to theology and the Christian cause.

Has a theme for each issue. Well-received subjects: Church laity, the Bible and the church today, and recent Protestant and Catholic views on Scripture.

Most articles are assigned, but also considers freelance submissions. Length of articles varies according to subject and need. Query letters not required. Single sample copy available on request. Pays on publication, on a varied scale. Reports as soon as possible.

THOUGHT, A REVIEW OF CULTURE AND IDEA, Fordham University, Bronx, NY 10458. (212) 933–2233, extension 270. G. Richard Dimler, S.J., Editor. A 110-page quarterly journal with a national distribution of 1,300.

□*Thought* is "an eclectic Catholic journal of the humanities, covering the fields of literary criticism, current political affairs, and history. The material is scholarly, but strives to be eminently readable. Because of its many articles relating to such subjects as Catholic reform, religious and secular life, and ecumenism, *Thought* should prove of special interest to educated laymen of all faiths." Writers are expected to be authorities in the field of their writing, but must not write only to fellow professionals; material is addressed to nonprofessionals.

Articles should be limited to 20 double-spaced typewritten pages. Sample copy and author's guidelines available. No payment for material used. Reports in 4 to 6 months.

TIME OF SINGING, P.O. Box 211, Cambridge Springs, PA 16316. (814) 382–5911. Founded 1958, revived 1980. Charles A. Waugaman, Editor. A 32-page magazine published 3 times a year, sponsored by the High Street Community Church, P.O. Box 248, Conneaut Lake, PA 16316. National distribution of 250.

□*Time of Singing* "is designed to encourage the writing and sharing of original poetry which is Christian in the broadest possible interpretation of Jesus's statement, 'He that is not against us is with us.' We seek to provide satisfying reading experiences for those who enjoy inspirational poetry, resources for church bulletins and newsletters, and a platform from which Christian poets may share their writing." Poetry is biblical, seasonal, with a positive slant, and Christian in the widest sense. Issues frequently have a theme. Usually there is a Christmas issue, an Easter issue, and a summer issue, but not invariably so. Well-received was a choral reading based on 14 poems from previous issues in an Easter worship service. Readers are lay adults and clergy of different denominations.

Items mailed without return postage will not be returned. Guidelines free; back issue $1, current issue $3. Query letter not necessary, reprints may be considered. Pays one free copy. Reports in 4 to 6 weeks, but poems may be held for 1 year or more before publication.

TODAY'S CATHOLIC TEACHER, 2451 East River Road, Dayton, OH 45439. (513) 294–5785. Ruth A. Matheny, Editor-in-Chief. An 80- to 160-page magazine published 8 times a year for national distribution.

□*Today's Catholic Teacher* seeks out and publicizes the best in Catholic education in the country, and also offers how-to articles in general and religious education. Interested in nonfiction: stories of people and how-to articles. Well-received subjects include meditations for religious educators, in-service workshops, "13 Ways to Make Your Students Feel Loved," nurturing self-esteem, technology in Catholic schools.

Articles should be 1,200 to 1,800 words, with 1,200 words preferred. Query letters desirable, but not required. Sample copy available for $2.00; author's guidelines free with SASE. Pays $25 to $75 per article, on publication. Reports immediately on rejections; articles may be held several months for further consideration. Also markets filmstrips and tapes, for which payment varies considerably, depending on the material.

TODAY'S CHRISTIAN PARENT, 8121 Hamilton Avenue, Cincinnati, OH 45231. (513) 931–4050. Mildred Mast, Editor. A 32-page quarterly magazine published by Standard Publishing, with a national distribution of 30,000.

☐*Today's Christian Parent* prints devotional, inspirational, and informative articles for the family, on problems and pleasures of parenting and Christian child-rearing. Seeks refreshingly different articles on family situations, fresh new ideas or aspects of cogent problems. Needs articles for "Happenings at Our House." Well-received articles: "Family Bible Time," "No Christmas Feeling," "Successful Illness," "Have You Hugged Your Kid Today?" Uses very little poetry.

Articles should be 600 to 1,200 words. Also uses serious or humorous fillers and short pieces on family life. Free sample copy and author's guidelines available with 7″ by 10″ or larger SASE. Seasonal and special-day material should be received 9 months to 1 year in advance. Pays on acceptance, usually 2¢ per word. Reports in 6 weeks.

TODAY'S CHRISTIAN WOMAN, published by the Fleming H. Revell Company, 184 Central Avenue, Old Tappan, NJ 07675. (201) 768-8060. Dale Hanson Bourke, Editor. A bimonthly magazine of 100 pages or more, distributed through Christian bookstores and subscriptions, with a national circulation of 150,000.
☐*Today's Christian Woman* is read by "Christian women of all ages, married and single, homemakers and career women. Average reader is in her 30s or 40s, married, with one or more children, and lives in a suburban area. She considers herself an evangelical Christian." Prints personal-experience articles as well as discussion of relevant topics on women's roles and relationships. Fiction and poetry also included. Cooking, crafts, decorating, health, fashion, and beauty sections rely heavily on photos and illustrations.

Articles should be 1,700 to 2,000 words. Query letters required; unsolicited manuscripts returned unopened. Writers should include their qualifications for writing about the topic, or a brief sketch of their interests and writing experience. To receive sample copy of the magazine, send $3.50; author's guidelines also available. Pays approximately 10¢ per word, on acceptance. Reports in approximately 4 weeks.

TODAY'S PARISH, P.O. Box 180, Mystic, CT 06355. (203) 536-2611. Carol Clark, Editor. A 48-page magazine published 7 times a year by Twenty-Third Publications, with a national distribution of 20,000.
☐*Today's Parish* is directed to professional and volunteer leaders in Roman Catholic parishes as well as concerned parishioners. Prints articles on topics of specific interest to this readership: examples of real parish programs in areas of adult and childhood religious education, evangelization, social justice, liturgy, community-building, spirituality, etc. Also advice on management of money and personnel, planning techniques, needs assessment, evaluation, public relations, etc.

Articles should be 1,200 to 1,500 words. Query letters acceptable, but not required. Free sample copy and author's guidelines available. Pays on acceptance: $100 for full-length articles of good quality. Pays $25 for one-time use of black-and-white photos and $25 for four-color photos.

TODAY'S SINGLE, 915 West Wisconsin Avenue, #214, Milwaukee, WI 53233. (414) 271-6400. Founded 1980. Mrs. Rita Bertolas, Editor. An 8- or 12-page quarterly newspaper, sponsored by the ProBuColls Association, with a national distribution of 30,000.
☐*Today's Single* prints evangelical religious materials and items geared to single people, as well as devotions, Bible study, and photos and illustrations. Well-received articles included interviews with different individuals. Readers are evangelical singles.

Articles should be 400 to 500 words. Sample copies and guidelines available. Query letters desirable; will consider reprints. Pays 50¢ per column inch, on publication. Reports in 6 weeks.

TOGETHER TIME FOR TWOS AND THREES, 6401 The Paseo, Kansas City, MO 64131. Founded 1982. Janet E. Sawyer, Editor. A 4-page weekly take-home storypaper, sponsored by the Church of the Nazarene, with a national distribution of 23,000.
☐*Together Time* prints "stories which reinforce Sunday School concepts—action must be appropriate for 2- and 3-year-olds." Readers are children and their parents.

Stories should be 150 to 250 words, with a "short, catchy beginning, simple plot with a climax, and a satisfying conclusion. Setting, plot, and action should be realistic. Poetry should be 4 to 8 lines and not deal with symbolism. Cartoons should be directed to parents and involve children of several denominations: Nazarene, Wesleyan, Free Methodist, and Evangelical Friends. Crafts and activities should be simple and within the ability of the child if aided by the parent, or usable by the child if parent-made."

Sample copies and guidelines available. Query letters desirable. Pays $5 to $10 for stories, 25¢ per line (with a $2.50 minimum) for verse. Reports in 4 to 8 weeks.

TOUCH, Box 7244, Grand Rapids, MI 49510. (616) 241-5616. Joanne Ilbrink, Editor; Mary Jane Pories, Assistant Editor. A 24-page magazine for girls aged 9 through 14, published 10 months of the year by Calvinettes, an organization of over 600 girls' clubs throughout the United States and Canada; with an international distribution of 15,000.
□*Touch* looks for material that is fresh, that presents the Christian life realistically, and makes the readers see how Christian beliefs apply to their daily lives. Every piece should have a specific purpose or reason behind it; it should not merely entertain. Uses fiction, nonfiction, photos, games, puzzles, party ideas, short humorous pieces, and poetry. Themes are established and updated 6 months in advance; send for themes and deadlines sheet. Well-received articles: "A Season Without Love?" written for theme issue on feelings; "Joy is Where You Find It," written for theme issue on entertainment; "Lonely Are The Shy," written for theme issue on hangups.

Articles should be 900 to 1,200 words. Sample copy and author's guidelines available. Pays on acceptance: about 2¢ per word up to $35, depending on length, quality, and rights. For poetry, pays $5 to $25, depending on quality and use. For games and puzzles, pays $2.50 to $7.

TRIUMPH [formerly *Teen Action*] P.O. Box 17306, Nashville, TN 37217. (615) 361-1221. Mrs. Odell Walton, Editor; Larry D. Hampton, Editorial Manager. An evangelical youth magazine, published quarterly by the National Association of Free Will Baptists for national distribution.
□*Triumph* prints fiction and poetry. "Most articles teach a lesson without being preachy. Authors should couch a moral in a well-told story." Well-received articles: "The Fraternity Party," about college choice; "A Pig Named Ethel Mae," about responding to taunts; "I Can Always Be a Missionary," about understanding a missionary's task.

Articles should be 1,000 to 1,500 words. Query letters not necessary. Free sample copy and author's guidelines available. Pays $15 to $30 per article, on publication. Reports within 2 weeks.

TWIN CITIES CHRISTIAN NEWSPAPER, 1619 Portland Avenue South, Minneapolis, MN 55404. (612) 339-9579. Doug Trouten, Editor; Leonard and JoAnne Jankowski, Publishers. A 20-page biweekly tabloid newspaper serving the Christian community of Minneapolis and St. Paul, with 5,000 subscribers plus bookstore sales.
□*Twin Cities Christian Newspaper* is an independent, nondenominational evangelical newspaper, "designed for the born-again Christian in the Twin Cities area and suburbs. Prints consumer material to help the Christian in his individual and corporate spiritual life, and investigative articles on personalities, events, and legislation that have a particular significance to the evangelical." Also seeks interesting personality features on local people. The more current (news peg) the better. Also seeking articulate spokespersons for current issues (women in Army, abortion legislation, Christian day school movement, creationism, etc.).

Articles should be 750 to 1,000 words. Query letters required. No fiction, poetry, devotional material; not very interested in editorials or reviews. Sample copy available on request; include SASE. Pays on publication: 3½¢ per word; $5 each for black-and-white photos. Usually reports within 1 month.

THE UNITED CHURCH OBSERVER, 85 St. Clair Avenue, East, Toronto, Ontario M4T 1M8, Canada. Founded 1829. Hugh McCullum, Editor. A 56-page monthly magazine sponsored by the United Church of Canada, with 273,800 Canadian subscribers and approximately 575,000 readers.

□The *Observer* prints articles with "wide appeal: personal experience; Canadian- or global-oriented views of Christian issues, written in news-magazine style." Well-received articles have been on care for the dying, civil disobedience, the Medicare crisis, prayer, and workplace ethics. Readers are mainly adults, but include some children and youth, mostly lay members of mainline and liberal Protestant denominations.

Articles should be 1,000 to 1,500 words. Sample copies and guidelines (now being revised) available. Particularly interested in humor and personal stories. Query letters desirable; will consider reprints, if so indicated. Pay varies according to length, research, etc., but averages 10¢ to 20¢ a word. Reports in 6 weeks.

THE UNITED METHODIST REPORTER, P.O. Box 221076, Dallas, TX 75222. (214) 630–6495. Founded approximately 1840. The Rev. Spurgeon M. Dunnam III, Editor. A 4-page weekly newspaper sponsored by the United Methodist Church, with a national distribution of 500,000.

□*The United Methodist Reporter* prints 3 to 4 pages per issue of national church and religious news, feature, and opinion combined with local church pages. Feature articles "should be of interest to a broad-based, national, predominantly mainline Protestant readership." Readers are mainly adults and senior citizens.

Maximum-length articles of 1,000 words "acceptable only for religious news coverage, preferably cleared in advance, or *strong* religious news features." Sample copies and guidelines available. "A story about a distinctly Christian response to a human need is welcomed. We are particularly interested in how an individual's faith relates to what the person is doing and why he or she is doing it." Particularly interested in strong United Methodist and/or ecumenical features. Query letters desirable ("We do not guarantee use of, or payment for, any story unless arrangement is made ahead of time"). No reprints. Pays 4¢ per word, $10 minimum. Reports in 6 weeks.

UNITY MAGAZINE, Unity Village, MO 64065. (816) 524–3550. Pamela Yearsley, Editor. A 66-page monthly magazine published by the Unity School of Christianity, with an international distribution of 400,000.

□*Unity Magazine* publishes "spiritual and metaphysical poems and articles designed to inspire and inform. Devoted to the spreading of the truth of practical Christianity, the everyday use of the Christ principles. Material is designed to be constructive, friendly, unbiased as regards creed or sect, and positive and inspirational in tone. Uses articles on love, healing, health, understanding, and judgment—all metaphysically speaking." Also uses photos. Readers are adults.

Articles should be up to 2,500 words. No query letters. Because of the special approach, it is recommended that writers study the materials carefully before submitting. Free sample copy and author's guidelines available. Pays on acceptance: 2¢ to 5¢ per word for articles, $15 to $25 for black-and-white photos; $100 for color photos used on cover. Reports in 4 weeks.

THE UPPER ROOM, 1908 Grand Avenue, Nashville, TN 37202. (615) 327–2700. Mary Lou Redding, Managing Editor. An 80-page bimonthly booklet of daily readings, published in 43 languages and 61 separate editions, for a total international distribution of 3,000,000.

□*The Upper Room* seeks to provide daily readings for a wide audience of adults and youth, in several languages and editions. The readings are described as "personal sharing of experiences of God's love, power, and comfort; accounts of how God became real and how personal faith is relevant to daily work and relationships." Has an administrative affiliation with the Board of Discipleship of the United Methodist Church, but is "an international, interdenominational, and interracial publication." Meditations are provided for special days, but the pieces must stand apart from the holiday, since different countries celebrate different holidays in different fashions. Also publishes 2-page "Prayer Workshops" in each issue.

Meditations should be 250 words including text, title, reading, anecdote, prayer, author line, and intercession. No word games, acronyms, or poetry because of translation difficulties. Careful study of the writer's guidelines and sample copies recommended. Sample copy and author's guidelines available. No query letters except for "Prayer Workshop" pieces. Pays on publication: $10 per meditation, $50 and up for "Prayer Workshop" pieces.

VENTURE, Box 150, Wheaton, IL 60189. (312) 665–0630. David R. Leigh, Editor; Sharon Long, Associate Editor. A 32-page magazine published 8 times a year by the Christian Service Brigade.
□*Venture* readers (ages 12 through 18) are active in their Christian service Brigade Battalion groups run by their local churches. The magazine's goals are to speak to concerns of young men from a biblical perspective; to provide wholesome, entertaining reading; to promote the Battalion and respect for its leaders; and to present a positive image of Christian manhood. Uses true stories, fiction, puzzles, and quizzes.

Articles average 1,200 words. Query letters only. Sample copies available for $1.50 plus SASE. Pays 5¢ to 10¢ per word, on publication. Reports in 1 to 6 weeks.

VIRTUE, P.O. Box 850, Sisters, OR 97759. (503) 549–8261. William L. Carmichael, Publisher; Becky Durost, Managing Editor. An 80-page magazine published 8 times a year with a national distribution of 90,000.
□*Virtue* is aimed primarily at Christian homemakers. It seeks to inspire women in every aspect of their lives. Each issue offers articles on creative home management, self-improvement, spiritual enrichment, and family relationships. Articles should encourage the development of the whole woman, whether she is a homemaker full-time or is employed outside the home either full- or part-time. Inspirational rather than doctrinal in focus, articles should help women to be informed and to incorporate the truths of the Bible into every facet of life. Articles on all subjects should be presented in a practical, non-judgmental style, and articles on spiritual subjects should be applicable to everyday life.

Articles should run 1,000 to 1,500 words. Query letters required. Pays on publication: 5¢ to 8¢ per printed word for first rights.

VISIONS, 200 Noll Plaza, Huntington, IN 46750. (219) 356–1470. Marianna McLoughlin, Editor. An 8-page weekly magazine published during the school year by Our Sunday Visitor, Inc., with a national distribution of 40,000.
□*Visions* is geared toward Catholic youth in parochial school and CCD classes. Seeks articles that deal with faith interests of youth on the junior-high level, the meaning of faith in the life of young Christians today, and stories of people who witness to their faith. Uses fiction and nonfiction and general-interest features relating to the Catholic faith. Well-received articles: "Youth Clowns," about youth visiting nursing homes; "Courage to Conquer," about young people who overcome obstacles and handicaps; "Shoplifting"; "Pope John Paul II's Visit to U.S."; "Friendship Isn't a Game."

Articles average 250 to 700 words, short stories average 1,000 words. Sample copy and author's guidelines available. Buys all rights to manuscripts; however, rights can be reassigned upon request, and author can retain copyright. Pays $40 to $75 per article, on acceptance. Reports within 2 weeks.

VISTA, R.D. #4, West Middlesex, PA 16159. (412) 342–9857. Founded 1959. Patricia M. Leali, Editor. A 12- to 16-page bimonthly magazine sponsored by the Christian Church of North America, R.D. 2, Transfer, PA 16154, with 2,000 subscribers nationwide.
□*VISTA* prints articles "on the Christian as a consumer, an educator, a prayer warrior, a disciple, a parent, a government representative, an advocate for the poor and needy,

and mirror upon which the world can see Christ's image." Well-received articles: "Prayer"; "Christian Families"; "God is Able—To Heal, Deliver, and Aid." Also prints profiles, interviews, devotions, fillers, theology, photos and illustrations. Most readers are lay adult members of the CCNA, an evangelical Protestant denomination.

Articles should be 850 to 1,000 words. Sample copies and guidelines available. "We are always looking for devotional material or articles that address how the evangelical Christian can share Christ in everyday life—whether that be in the marketplace, at home, or in his church. We encourage support of your conclusions with Scripture." Query letters not required; will consider reprints. Always enclose SASE. No payment; no reporting time given.

VITAL CHRISTIANITY, Warner Press, Inc., P.O. Box 2499, 1200 East 5th Street, Anderson, IN 46018. (317) 644–7721. Arlo F. Newell, Editor-in-Chief; Richard Willowby, Managing Editor. A 32-page magazine for adults, published 20 times a year by the Church of God, with a national distribution of 35,000.

□ Vital Christianity is for adults "who want to learn more about the abundant life that is offered through Jesus Christ." Its three basic goals are "1) to evangelize the lost, 2) to inspire the believer, and 3) to inform all people of the work of the Church of God. Uses general religious material that is life-centered and scripturally sound. Provides doctrinal articles that explain the teachings of the Church in terms that lay people can easily understand. Highlights the personal experiences of people who have accepted Jesus Christ as their Lord and Savior and who have trusted Him to help them deal with real-life problems. Offers a variety of inspirational articles that give encouragement and practical guidance to Christian readers. Challenges the unsaved to accept Christ." No fiction used. Doctrinal articles should avoid being "polemic or preachy." Uses very little poetry, and what is used generally relates to one of the Christian holidays.

Articles should be 3 to 7 pages, typewritten, double-spaced. Query letters acceptable. Each issue follows a theme projected by the editorial division; listing of subjects provided on request. Sample copy and author's guidelines available for $1.00 postage. Pays on acceptance: approximately $20 for 2- to 3-page articles, approximately $50 for 4- to 7-page articles. Reports within 6 weeks. Also markets greeting cards, stationery, and calendars.

VOICE, P.O. Box 5050, 3150 Bear Street, Costa Mesa, CA 92626. (714) 754–1400. Nelson B. Melvin, Editor. A 40-page monthly magazine published by the Full Gospel Business Men's Fellowship, with an international distribution of 800,000.

□ Voice is evangelistic in nature, designed "as a witnessing tool to the non-Christian and a faithbuilder to the committed Christian." Three-quarters of its circulation is distributed in bundles sent to chapter meetings of the sponsoring group in 83 countries and distributed by them in their communities. Seeks manuscripts that are first-person testimonies to the power of God working in men's lives. Emphasis is on the baptism of the Holy Spirit. Readers are people of every denomination, the majority being Charismatics in the FGBMF.

Articles should be 2,000 words or less and center on personal testimonies. Free sample copy and author's guidelines available. 5¢ per word paid for material used.

THE WAR CRY, c/o National Publications, 799 Bloomfield Avenue, Verona, NJ 07044. (201) 239–0606. Lt. Colonel Henry Gariepy, Editor. The official organ of The Salvation Army, published weekly. Circulation 350,000 (Easter edition 1,800,000; Christmas edition 4,000,000).

□ The War Cry principally needs fiction with strong evangelical Christian emphasis (references to The Salvation Army not required, but any such references must be correct in every detail) and for Scripture-based inspirational and informational articles relating the Gospel to modern-day life. Also considers shorter fiction, meditations, personality sketches of Salvationists, short poems (particularly on Christmas and Easter themes), freelance photos, photo stories of Salvation Army activities and service.

Fiction should be 1,000 to 1,800 words; articles 800 to 1,500 words; meditations 800 to 1,500 words. Query letters advised. Sample copy and author's guidelines available. Pays approximately 4¢ per word, on acceptance. Higher rates paid for material selected for use in Christmas and Easter issues. Pays $10 to $35 for 8" by 10" photos.

WEE WISDOM, Unity Village, MO 64065. (816) 524-3550. Colleen Zuck, Editor. A monthly magazine for girls and boys published by Unity School of Christianity, with a national distribution of 100,000.

□*Wee Wisdom* is "a character-building magazine. Our goal is to help children develop their full potential. Short and lively stories, nature and science stories, puzzles, and projects are needed. Character-building ideals should be emphasized without preaching." Material should be readable by a third-grader. As with other Unity publications, it is recommended that prospective authors study the materials to learn the special approach of this group.

Articles should be 500 to 800 words. Sample copy and author's guidelines available. Pays 3¢ to 5¢ per word, on acceptance. Reports in 4 weeks.

WITH, Box 347, Newton, KS 67114. (316) 283-5100. Susan E. Janzen, Editor. A 32-page monthly magazine for Mennonite high school youth, with an international distribution of 7,000.

□*With* assists Mennonite youth to make a commitment to Jesus Christ and the Church amidst the complex and conflicting values they encounter in their world. Perspective is shaped by the Anabaptist/Mennonite tradition. Particularly interested in the problems 13- to 18-year-olds face, but rather than dealing with problems directly, likes to use nonmoralistic fiction or profiles of actual youth who can serve as models to their peers. Especially interested in articles about people, young and old, who are making a contribution to church and world or who are struggling with some of the issues of dating, being single, marriage, family relationships, school, care of body, meaning of discipleship, and commitment to church, peace, race relationships, lifestyle, college, vocation.

Nonfiction should be 1,200 to 1,500 words; fiction no more than 2,000 words. Prefers to see completed articles. Sample copy $1.25; author's guidelines free. Pays on acceptance: 4¢ per word average for prose; sliding scale for poetry. Reports in 1 to 2 months.

THE WITNESS, Box 359, Ambler, PA 19002. (215) 643-7067. Mary Lou Suhor, Editor. A 24-page monthly magazine published by the Episcopal Church Publishing Company, with a national distribution of 6,000.

□*The Witness* is published for an adult, mainline Protestant audience of liberal Christians, mostly Episcopalians, with a special interest in the social mission of the church. "Provides a forum for the reinterpretation of the radical biblical themes of judgment and grace in relationship to the social crises of our time—racism, sexism, classism, and imperialism." Recent topics included women's ordination, gay rights and the churches, liberation theology. Prints nonfiction, poetry, photos, graphics, and cartoons.

Articles should be 750 to 2,000 words. Query letters desirable. Free sample copy available. Pays $50 to $150 per article, on publication. Reports immediately.

THE WITTENBURG DOOR, 1224 Greenfield Drive, El Cajon, CA 92021. (619) 440-2333. Founded 1971. Mike Yaconelli, Editor. A 32-page bimonthly newspaper, sponsored by Youth Specialties, with a national distribution of 20,000.

□*The Wittenburg Door* prints short satirical pieces focusing on the church. Also prints poetry, nonfiction, and interviews. Readers are clergy and adult lay members of all denominations.

Articles should be 1,000 words maximum. Sample copies and guidelines available. Will consider reprints. Pays $35 to $50 per article, on publication. Reports in 12 weeks.

WOMAN'S TOUCH, 1445 Boonville Avenue, Springfield, MO 65802. (417) 862-2781. Elva J. Hoover, Editor. A bimonthly magazine published by the Department of Women's Ministries of the Assemblies of God, with a national distribution of 17,500.

☐*Woman's Touch* is especially interested in articles that show how women have been involved in Assemblies of God's Women's Ministries and, through this, have been helped or have been able to help someone in a special way. Also interested in articles that help women to solve practical home problems with the help of the Lord. Uses articles for and about the woman alone—widowed, never married, and divorced; articles dealing with family life; and devotional articles showing how God made a Scripture real to the author or the person written about. Also uses poems; stories of Assemblies of God missionaries; personal testimonies of God's healing power, grace in life, help in time of need; how-to articles and seasonal items.

Articles and stories should be 500 to 1,200 words. Query letters advised. Author's guidelines available. Some material assigned. Payment range varies.

WORKING FOR BOYS, Box A, Danvers, MA 01923. (617) 774-2664. Brother Alphonsus Dwyer, CFX, Editor. Submit articles to Brother Alois O'Toole, CFX, Associate Editor, 378 Main Street, Shrewsbury, MA 01545. A 28-page quarterly family and school magazine published by the Xaverian Brothers, with a national distribution of 16,000. ☐*Working For Boys* appeals mostly to Roman Catholic elementary-school children and their parents. Not a teenage magazine, though many teens read it. Prints articles of human interest, nature, biography, travel, religion, how-to, sports, etc. Fiction should be wholesome and conservative. Poems should not be more than 24 lines.

Articles should be no more than 1,200 words. Free sample copy and author's guidelines available. Pays on acceptance: 4¢ per word for articles and fiction, 40¢ per line for verse. Reports within 1 week.

WORLD CHRISTIAN, P.O. Box 40010, Pasadena, CA 91104. (818) 797-5320. Founded 1979. Gordon D. Aeschliman, Editor. A 48-page bimonthly magazine with a national distribution of 45,000. ☐*World Christian* prints "articles that articulate the lifestyle of people committed to radical discipleship on a global scale." Well-received articles: "World Christian Mandate," "Penetrating the Final Frontiers." Also publishes humor, interviews, photos and illustrations. Readers are youth, mainly evangelical Protestants.

Articles should be 1,500 to 2,500 words. Sample copies and guidelines available. Particularly interested in contributions from news editors. Query letters desirable; will consider reprints. No payment. Reports in 6 weeks.

WORLD CONCERN MAGAZINE, 19303 Freemont Avenue North, Seattle, WA 98133. (206) 546-7201. Mike McGregor, Editor. A 32-page bimonthly magazine with a national distribution of 90,000. ☐ *World Concern Magazine* prints articles related to global concerns, such as issues concerning world hunger and how supporters can fight hunger in their own neighborhood. Readers are adults of evangelical and other denominations.

Articles should be 800 to 1,000 words. Sample copies available. "It is very difficult to freelance for us, as most pieces are staff-written." Query letters desirable; will consider reprints. Pays $75 to $100, depending on length. Reports in 4 weeks.

WORLD ENCOUNTER, 2900 Queen Lane, Philadelphia, PA 19129. (215) 438-6360. James Solheim, Editor. A 36-page quarterly magazine published by the division for world mission and ecumenism of the Lutheran Church in America, with an international distribution of 8,000. ☐*World Encounter* is published for "adult and youth members of the Lutheran Church in America and the American Lutheran Church who have an interest in, and understanding of, the Lutheran Church's overseas mission and current social concerns in other parts of the world. Material must be theologically, sociologically, and anthropologically sound but written in a popular style. The focus is on what is happening in Lutheran groups." Prints nonfiction and photographs. Uses both human-interest features and provocative thought pieces. Especially interested in human development in the Third World and new forms of ministry in Africa, Asia, Latin America, and Europe.

Articles should be 750 to 1,800 words. Query letters necessary, since nearly all articles are assigned. Free sample copy and author's guidelines available. Pays on publication, with average of $200 for freelance features. Reports in 1 month.

WORLD VISION MAGAZINE, 919 West Huntington Drive, Monrovia, CA 91016. (213) 357-7979. David Olson, Editor. A 24-page bimonthly magazine with a national distribution of 1,000,000.

□ *World Vision Magazine* prints 1) human-interest stories of caring, active people (usually little-known Christians) and 2) opinion pieces. Uses humor related to cross-cultural ministry or lifestyle, with an evangelical humanitarian emphasis.

Need for freelance material is extremely limited. Articles should be 500 to 1,000 words. Query letters desirable. Free sample copy available. Pays 10¢ per published word, on acceptance. Reports in 2 months.

YAM, Box 7244, Grand Rapids, MI 49510. (616) 241-5616. Steven Geurink, Editor. A 16-page magazine published bimonthly by the Young Calvinist Federation, with a national distribution of 1,500.

□ *YAM* is designed for young adults aged 18 through 35. Material published must discuss young adults and their concerns (the single life, being married as a student, career choices, the Christian lifestyle) and ways to aid the group process. Particular needs include articles on the joys and struggles of living the young adult life; articles on Christian stewardship, discipleship, and world views.

Articles should be 750 words. Free sample copy available. Pays on acceptance: $25 to $50 for longer lead articles, $15 to $30 for area articles, $10 to $15 each for 4-part Bible studies, $15 to $25 for poetry, $10 to $15 for photos. Reports in 4 weeks.

YOUNG AMBASSADOR, Box 82808, Lincoln, NE 68501. (402) 474-4567. David Lambert, Managing Editor. A 64-page monthly published 11 times a year by the Back to the Bible Broadcast, with a national distribution of 80,000.

□ *Young Ambassador* is intended to aid the spiritual, emotional, and intellectual growth of 12- to 17-year-old Christian readers. All articles and fiction must be written in a style understandable and attractive to today's teens. "We rarely buy anything not written out of a thorough knowledge of contemporary youth culture—not that of 5 years ago. We are interested in *biblical* principles, not merely moral ones. Our greatest need is for high-quality, nonpreachy fiction, including some set in other times, other places, other worlds. Future themes include cars, cults, television, music, death, city life."

Articles should be 800 to 2,000 words; also interested in devotional articles of 300 to 800 words. Fiction should be 800 to 2,500 words, "but we buy few over 2,000 words." Theme sheets, writer's guidelines, and sample copy available on request; send 9" by 12" SASE. Pays on acceptance: 4¢ to 7¢ per word, depending on quality and difficulty; more for assigned pieces; $10 for poetry (from teens only); 3¢ per word for reprints. Pays up to $25 for black-and-white, up to $50 for color transparencies for inside editorial use, and $75 for color covers. Send SASE for photographer's guidelines. Reports in 6 to 8 weeks.

YOUNG MUSICIANS, 127 Ninth Avenue, North, Nashville, TN 37234. (615) 251-2944. Clinton E. Flowers, Editor. A 52-page quarterly magazine published by The Sunday School Board of the Southern Baptist Convention.

□ *Young Musicians* is for children ages 10 through 12 and publishes articles and stories about church music composers and hymn writers, also musical exercises, puzzles, and games. Theory pages (workbook type) accepted on a limited basis.

Article length desired: for 1-page story or article, 60 lines; for 2 pages, 120 lines; for 3 pages, 140 to 150 lines; all typed at 37 characters per line. Free sample copy and writer's guidelines available. Pays 4¢ per word, on acceptance. Reports usually within 1 week.

YOUNG SALVATIONIST, Salvation Army Publications, 799 Bloomfield Avenue, Verona, NJ 07044. (201) 239-0606. Captain Dorothy Hitzka, Youth Editor. A monthly magazine sponsored by the Salvation Army, with a national distribution of 46,000.

☐*Young Salvationist* is published for high-school students, with a pull-out section, "Young Soldier," for children. Lead articles carry Christian truths, but not in a preachy manner, and should deal with real-life issues facing teens today. "The lesson or point should be inherent in the article itself." Well-received articles were on cults, self-image, choosing friends, and "What is Real Love?" Also prints fiction, Bible study, fillers, and self-help articles.

Lead articles should be 800 to 1,200 words, fiction approximately 1,000 to 1,200 words. Sample copies and guidelines available. "Only material with a definite Christian message will be considered." Will consider reprints. SASE must accompany all submissions, or they will not be considered. "Please state whether your submission is for *Young Salvationist* or the 'Young Soldier' section." Pays 3¢ per word, on acceptance. Reports in 4 weeks.

YOUR CHURCH, 198 Allendale Road, King of Prussia, PA 19406. (215) 265–9400. Phyllis Mather Rice, Editor. A 48- to 64-page bimonthly magazine with national controlled circulation of 188,000.

☐*Your Church* is published for a widespread adult audience of clergy and lay readers of churches of all Protestant denominations—evangelical, liberal, and mainline. Limited to nonfiction and the general subject of the work of the Church. Uses practical articles on "church management, administration, the pastorate and its duties, special problems and needs, the pastor's spouse, personal devotions for pastors, money management, worship, liturgy, Christian education, counseling, and church architecture."

Articles should be 6 to 10 pages of typewritten material. Query letters desirable. Sample copy (enclose necessary postage) and author's guidelines available. Pays $6 per typewritten page, on publication. Reports in 3 months.

THE YOUTH LEADER, 1445 Boonville Avenue, Springfield, MO 65802. (417) 862–2781. Paul Tedesco, Editor. A 24-page, 8¼" by 11" periodical published 8 times a year by the Youth Department of the Assemblies of God, with a national distribution of 4,500.

☐*The Youth Leader* is aimed at adult leaders of teenagers to promote the role of creative leadership and provide programming materials. Uses skits, role plays, how-to-do-it, and why-do-we-do-it (rationale), Bible studies, discussion starters, fund-raising and party ideas, youth service activities and ideas. Uses some black-and-white photography. Particular subject needs: coping with the future, integrating vocation and faith, enhancing parent-teen relationships, raising social conscience as a Christian, material for youth services.

Articles should be 500 to 2000 words. Query letters desirable. Free sample copy and author's guidelines available. Pays on acceptance. The rate for manuscripts is determined by various factors: creativity, amount of editorial work required. Payment range per word: for creative writing such as a play, 3¾¢; for a skit, 3½¢; for research/analysis/ conclusions, 3¢ to 3¼¢; for service/activity idea, 2¾¢; for reportage accounts/narrative, 2½¢. Reports in 6 weeks.

YOUTH UPDATE, 1615 Republic Street, Cincinnati, OH 45210. (513) 241–5615. Founded 1982. Carol Ann Munchel, OSF, Editor. A 4-page monthly newsletter published by the St. Anthony Messenger Press, with a national distribution of 70,000.

☐*Youth Update* prints articles designed "to attract, instruct, guide, and challenge Catholics of high school age by applying the Gospel to modern problems and situations." Well-received articles: "Teen Alcoholism," "Anger," "Tension at Home." Also prints theology and photos. Readers are "students who vary in the scope of their religious education and in their reading ability. Aim to communicate with 15-year-olds with a C+ average. Avoid clichés and glib phrases, but aim more toward table talk than teacher talk."

Articles should be 2,500 words tops—roughly equivalent to 7 pages, double-spaced, of elite typeface. Sample copies and guidelines available. "We are open to a wide range of current and significant issues." Query letters desirable; will consider reprints. Pays 12¢ a word, or around $300 per article, "when requirements for publication are met." Reports in 4 to 6 weeks.

·THREE·
Writing Religious Books

This chapter lists publishers of religious books in the United States and Canada. Some of them are owned and operated by denominations or church groups and publish exclusively religious titles. Others are independent or family-owned publishers that do religious books. Some are general trade houses with religious departments that publish many religious books each year. Others are trade houses that only occasionally publish a religious title. However, all publishers listed below have indicated their interest in publishing *some* religious books. A few publishers listed in this chapter are interested in books of religious interest other than Christianity or Judaism.

Writing a book is a process quite different from writing a magazine article or a short piece for some other purpose. A book is a major venture, and the writer intending to tackle such a project will do well to consider carefully the information contained in each of the entries below. You will want to send for catalogs from the houses that seem likely to be interested in the kind of book you are writing. Many publishers also furnish author's guidelines.

Most publishers say that they prefer to begin with a query letter rather than a completed manuscript. This is standard procedure in book publishing, and the religious writer venturing into this field ought to follow it. Write a brief letter to the editor. Tell him or her your idea for a book. Give a brief, one-paragraph synopsis, and ask if he or she would be interested in seeing a portion or a whole manuscript (if you have already written it).

If the editor says yes to your query, probably the next step will be a formal proposal from you. This is an expanded query, in which you write more about your book, outline the contents, submit a sample chapter or two, discuss your idea of the market for the book, and give some indication of the time you will require to complete the task. You may want to indicate your anticipated needs for an advance or royalty.

If the publisher is still interested, the next step may be negotiations on a contract. The entries in this chapter give some clues as to the usual royalties and/or advances offered. In all cases, however, this matter is open to negotiation, as is much of the whole process of getting a book published. For this reason, many writers use agents to do their negotiating for them. Actually, it is not as complicated as it may sound, and if done with patience and cooperation, there is little to be feared. The publisher's objective is the same as the writer's—to publish the best book possible and to reach the greatest possible number of readers.

The business of publishing religious books has been expanding for several years. The increase in the number of religious bookstore outlets is due to the helpful counsel of such organizations as the Christian Booksellers Association and the Association of Evangelical Publishers. As you read the entries in this chapter, you will discover many different kinds of religious book publishers that have very different needs and objectives. Be sure that you try hard to match the subject and potential readership of your book with that of the publisher you choose.

Some of the publishers in this chapter publish books intended for a Jewish audience as well as Christian books, but most of the publishers of Judaica are entered under the listing in Chapter Four.

You will also find cross references within this chapter where a publisher is known by more than one name. For example, information on Scripture Press will be found under Victor Books, the name you find on the spine and title page of its publications. Spire Books will be found under Fleming H. Revell. On the other hand, Chariot Books will be found under David C. Cook. In all cases both names are entered in the alphabetical listing.

As with the chapter on periodical markets, we suggest you make good use of the indexes in the back of this book to help you find the publisher most likely to be interested in the kind of manuscript you intend to produce.

It hardly seems necessary, yet editors tell us that some words need to be said here, too, about being professional in the way that you submit manuscripts as well as the way that you write them for religious publishers. Reading some of the chapters in books suggested in Chapter Six, on resources for religious writers, will help you know how and what to do in submitting a book manuscript. We don't try to give complete guidance on that subject here, but the following list of the ten most common faults of book manuscripts will send up some warning flags. An editor compiled this list after some 20 years of reading book manuscripts. Take heed to these warnings about what *not* to do.

Ten Faults of Book Manuscripts

1. The manuscript is directed at no one. There is no focus, no special readership in mind.

2. The idea is out of date (or before its time).

3. There is no logical progression in the writing. Like Don Quixote, the manuscript goes in all directions at once.

4. The writing is sloppy. Unforgivable!

5. The author submits the manuscript to more than one publisher at a time without advising the publishers. Multiple submissions are sometimes permitted, but be sure the publishers know about them.

6. The manuscript is submitted to the wrong publisher. It would fit someone else's line but not ours. Query letters help avoid this.

7. Footnotes and other similar material are inaccurate or incomplete, which makes permissions and other necessary procedures difficult or impossible.

8. The author has a faulty or inadequate concept of the market at which the book is aimed.

9. An agent is used incorrectly. Agents can be helpful, but sometimes they get in the way if they are only duplicating the work of the author.

10. There is no table of contents.

A careful reading of these and other suggestions from book editors will go a long way toward helping you get your book published by one of the houses listed below.

◄PUBLISHERS►

ABBEY PRESS, St. Meinrad, IN 47577. (812) 357-8011. John T. Bettin, Editor. A Catholic book publishing house operated by St. Meinrad Archabbey; publishes 10 to 15 books a year, all of them paperbacks.

☐Abbey Press publishes mainly for an adult Roman Catholic audience, both clergy and laity, but reaches a general audience of Protestants as well. Limited to nonfiction, specializing in books of self-help and family enrichment from a Christian point of view. Successful titles: *When Your Child Needs a Hug* by Larry Losoncy, *When Opposites Attract* by John Drescher, *When God is at Home With Your Family* by David M. Thomas.

Most books are short, 96 printed pages and up. Query letters required before submitting manuscripts. Generally commissions books to meet needs; royalty rates and advances subject to negotiation. Reports in 3 weeks.

ABINGDON PRESS, 201 Eighth Avenue, South, Nashville, TN 37202. (615) 749-6301. Ronald P. Patterson, Vice-President. The official publishing house of the United Methodist Church. Publishes approximately 90 books a year, 85% paperbacks.

☐Publishes over a range of theological perspectives in five basic areas: reference books, lay books, family books, academic books, and professional books. Query letters preferred. Catalogs and guidelines available. Editors to contact: Reference, Carey J. Gifford; Lay, Mary Ruth Howes; Family, Ernestine Calhoun; Academic, Pierce S. Ellis: Professional, Don Hardy.

ACCENT BOOKS, P.O. Box 15337, Denver, CO 80215. (303) 988-5300. Robert R. Cook, Executive Editor. Publishes 16 to 24 paperback books a year.

☐Seeks to reach people for Christ and help them grow in their faith by showing biblical solutions to everyday human needs, problems, and desires. Approximately 85% of the books published are nonfiction for evangelical adults. Three elements must be evident in all manuscripts: pertinence/applicability to contemporary problems and needs; a solid, conservative, evangelical message; and editorial quality—manuscripts must be well-written, in a popular style that will hold the reader's attention. Do not submit sermons, manuscripts with a charismatic emphasis, dissertations, deeply technical Bible studies, devotionals, or subjects dealing with metaphysics, demonology, etc. Successful titles: *Up With America, Computer Bible Games, When Parents Cry, In the House of the Enemy.*

Prefers 30,000 to 60,000 word manuscripts, but they can go to 80,000 words if subject matter warrants. Query letters preferred, but sample chapters and outline may also be submitted. Catalogs and guidelines available for SASE. Reports in 6 to 8 weeks. Pays royalties, but not advances.

AGLOW PUBLICATIONS, P.O. Box I, Lynnwood, WA 98046-1557. (206) 775-7282. Gwen Weising, Editor. The publishing department of Women's Aglow Fellowship, International.

☐Has an audience of adult, charismatic Christian women, general lay readers. Seeks first-person women's testimonies, Bible studies, Bible-oriented manuscripts for books and booklets. Successful booklets: *Receive All God Has to Give, How to Walk in the Spirit, Setting the Captives Free;* Bible studies: *God's Daughter, God's Answer to Overeating, Spiritual Warfare.*

Booklets should be 5,000 or 10,000 words; books 25,000 to 50,000 words. Query letters desirable. Catalogs and guidelines available. Reports in 4 to 6 weeks. Purchases booklets outright; pays up to 7½% royalty on Bible studies.

ALBA HOUSE, 2187 Victory Boulevard, Staten Island, NY 10314. (212) 761-0047. Anthony L. Chenevey, Editor-in-Chief. Publishes 15 books a year, 90% of them paperbacks.

☐Alba House, sponsored by the Society of St. Paul, publishes for Roman Catholic adults—scholars, clergy, and general lay readers. Interested in books of Catholic theology, biblical topics, sociology, mental health, and family life; also interested in submissions of general nonfiction, devotional reading, biblical studies, curriculum, theological works, and some psychology. Also wants photos and illustrations. Successful titles: *Celibacy, Prayer & Friendship* by Kiesling; *Annulment: Do You Have a Case?* by Tierney; *Liturgy and Parish Life* by Krause.

Average length of manuscripts is 80,000 to 120,000 words. Send query letter first. Catalogs available. Pays 10% standard royalties; sometimes pays advances when requested. Manuscripts acknowledged on receipt; if interested, will reply and try to give an answer in 4 weeks.

THE ALBAN INSTITUTE, INC., Mount St. Alban, Washington, DC 20016. (202) 244-7320. Celia Allison Hahn, Editor. Publishes 8 paperbacks a year.
☐Seeks research on subjects like conflict management, clergy wives, female clergy, youth ministry, transitions (retirement, new pastorates), alcoholism, divorce among clergy, psychology, the process of replacing a minister. Successful titles: *Discover Your Conflict Management Style, The Pastor as Newcomer, New Beginnings: A Pastorate Start-Up Workbook.*

Manuscripts should be monographs of 40 to 60 pages, occasionally longer. Query letters and sample chapters preferred. Reports in 4 weeks. Pays flat fee or royalty of 5% to 10%. Interested in reprints.

ALLNUTT PUBLISHING, Box 879, Evergreen, CO 80439. (303) 670-3390. Frank Allnutt, Publisher. Publishes 3 books a year, mostly paperbacks.
☐Seeks fiction, biography and autobiography, and works about popular culture. Successful titles: *Salvation for a Doomed Zoomie, Unlocking the Mystery of the Force.* Readers are youth and lay adults of evangelical denominations.

Manuscripts should be 160 to 228 pages. Query letters preferred. Reports in 12 weeks. Pays either royalty or subsidy.

ALTERNATIVES, INC., 5263 Bouldercrest Road, Forest Park, GA 30051. (404) 961-0102. Harriette Grissom, Editor. Publishes 84 books a year, half of them paperbacks.
☐Seeks books on lifestyle; church, school, and family; social justice issues; and Christmas, Easter, and other holiday celebrations. Readers range from children to senior citizens of all denominations.

Query letters preferred. Reports in 6 weeks. Pays small flat fee. Interested in reprints.

ARBUTA HOUSE, Box 48, Abington, PA 19001. V. Kerry Inman, Editor. Publishes 7 paperbacks a year.
☐Seeks "fiction which is *very* subtly religious," Bible studies particularly, biography and autobiography, and curricula for adult study groups. "We are less than a year old." Audience is youth and adults, both clergy and lay members, chiefly Presbyterians.

Nonfiction manuscripts should be 200 typewritten pages; fiction can vary. Query letters preferred. Reports in 8 weeks. Payment varies. "We are interested in jointly financing books with writers in return for the writers having greater editorial control over the production of their books. We desire to have writers be an integral part of the company." Interested in reprints.

ARGUS COMMUNICATIONS, One DLM Park, P.O. Box 7000, Allen, TX 75002. Richard Duffield, Editorial Director; Rachel Meisel, Associate Editor. Publishes 6 to 8 religious books a year, all of them paperbacks.
☐Argus Communications publishes for an adult lay audience of all denominations. Interested in nonfiction, devotional reading, biblical studies, and other subjects that emphasize Christian living skills. Uses photos and illustrations. Wants "books by reputable authors that are directed to a general lay audience. Manuscripts should reflect an open-minded, upbeat attitude, with a strong emphasis on communicating

Christian values for the twentieth century." Successful titles: *Unconditional Love* by Jon Powell, *The Seventh Trumpet* by Mark Link.

Books vary in length; maximum is 75,000 words. Query letters required. Author's guidelines available. Pays royalties of 10% of net; advances negotiable. Reports in 1 month.

ASCENSION PRESS, 360 Church Street, Yalesville, CT 06492. (203) 269–9526. Rev. Alice B. Mann, Editor. Sponsored by the Order of the Ascension (Episcopal). Shipping manager at 3089 Emerald Street, Philadelphia, PA 19134. Publishes 3 books a year, all of them paperbacks.

☐Ascension Press seeks "books on parish development theory and method, specifically adapted to Anglican spirituality and the Episcopal Church." Successful titles: *Power From On High: A Model For Parish Life and Development* by Robert Gallagher, *Incorporation of New Members in the Episcopal Church: A Manual for Clergy and Lay Leaders* by Alice B. Mann. Readers are clergy and lay adults of various evangelical, liberal, and mainline Protestant denominations—especially Episcopalian.

Books should be 100 pages long. Outline/synopsis preferred. Pays flat fee, no advances. Also interested in reprints. Reports in 16 weeks.

AUGSBURG PUBLISHING HOUSE, 426 South Fifth Street, Box 1209, Minneapolis, MN 55440. (612) 330–3432. Roland Seboldt, Editor. The official publishing arm of the American Lutheran Church. Publishes 40 to 50 books a year for all age levels.

☐Numbers among its publications reference works, biblical studies, devotional readings, inspirational biographies—"any subject that applies Christian faith to life's problems." About three-fourths are books for general Christian readers: adult lay persons, youth, children of all denominations, leaning toward the evangelical or conservative approach. The other fourth of the books are for the professional (pastors) and academic market in seminaries and colleges. Nearly all are paperback originals.

For popular books aimed at the general reader, limit is 128 printed pages. For professional and academic books, no limit. Query letters preferred. Catalogs and guidelines available. Reports in 6 weeks. Pays on a 10% royalty base with escalated royalty negotiable. Pays advances.

BAKER BOOK HOUSE COMPANY, Box 6287, Grand Rapids, MI 49506. (616) 676–9185. Dan Van't Kerkhoff, Editor-in-Chief. Publishes 150 books a year, 60% of them paperbacks.

☐Seeks evangelical Christian literature ranging from academic to inspirational for a large audience of adults, youth, scholars, clergy, and general lay readers of evangelical, mainline Protestant, and mixed denominations. Subjects center on personal growth to biblical studies. Interested mostly in nonfiction—humor, devotional reading, reference works, biblical studies. Successful titles: *We Need Each Other* by Guy Greenfield, *Taming Tension* by Phillip Keller, *Happiness is a Choice* by Meier, *The King James Version Debate* by D.A. Carson, *Walking With the Giants* by Warren Wiersbe, *Uncle Ben's Quotebook.*

General trade books should be 96 to 200 printed pages; academic books, 160 to 320 pages. Catalogs and guidelines available. Reports in 3 to 4 weeks. Pays fees for booklets—$150 to $250; pays 7½% to 10% royalty for paperbacks, 10% to 12½% for hardcovers. Interested in inspirational, reference, and academic reprints.

BALLANTINE/EPIPHANY BOOKS, 201 East 50th Street, New York, NY 10022. Michelle Rapkin, Editor. Publishes 27 paperbacks a year.

☐Seeks "to provide a deeper understanding and new insight into ourselves and our spiritual lives; to enrich the Christian's life, bring the Gospel alive, and show how relevant God's word is in everyday life. We prefer nonfiction, but are more than willing to view proposals of fiction containing inspirational qualities." Successful titles: *The Joy of Living* by Willard Scott, *From Harper Valley to the Mountain Top* by Jeannie C. Riley, *Through the Night* by Eugenia Price. Target audience is adults and senior citizens, both clergy and lay members of all denominations. "We want books targeted not only to Christians, but to an audience at large with spiritual concerns."

Proposals with sample chapters preferred. Catalogs and guidelines available. "At this time, we are not interested in books for children or young adults, in fantasy, poetry, devotionals, or inspirational romance." Reports in 6 weeks. Pays royalties, usually of 6% to 100,000 copies and 8% thereafter, and advances. Interested in reprints.

A. S. BARNES, 9601 Aero Drive, San Diego, CA 92123. (619) 560–5163. Modeste Williams, Editorial Coordinator. Mainly a trade publisher. Publishes one or two religious titles a year.
☐Interested in religious books that appeal to general readers in the fields of history and biography. Readership is adult. Published: *Ten Women and God* by Lauderdale and Shelgren, *Truth Sets Free* by Kaylor, *Whence and Wherefore* by Zahavy. Howell-North Books, a branch of the company publishing Western Americana, does an occasional title of religious history.

Query letters not necessary. Catalogs available. Reports as soon as possible. Pays royalties and advances, negotiable.

BEACON PRESS, 25 Beacon Street, Boston, MA 02108. (617) 742–2110. Wendy J. Strothman, Director. A publishing operation of the Unitarian Universalist Association. Publishes 30 titles a year, half hardcover, half paperback.
☐"Committed to a bold program of scholarly and trade publishing aimed at responsible exploration of the human condition," Beacon Press seeks books with strong trade and academic market potential. Target audience is scholars, clergy, general laity, of a liberal theological stance. Interested in nonfiction, especially works that address important intellectual, social, and political issues. Successful titles: *Pure Lust: Elemental Feminist Philosophy, Sexism and God-Talk, Religion and America.*

Book manuscripts should be 200 to 400 pages. Query letters preferred. Catalogs available. Reports in 6 to 8 weeks. Pays standard royalties. Interested in paperback reprints, "particularly those that have course-adoption possibilities." Manuscripts may also be submitted to Marie Cantlon, Senior Editor.

BEACON HILL PRESS, P.O. Box 527, Kansas City, MO 64141. (816) 931–1900. Betty Fuhrman, Publishing/Editorial Coordinator; Evelyn Stenbock, Editorial Associate. Trade imprint of Nazarene Publishing House. Publishes 70 books a year, 80% of them paperbacks.
☐All theology and reference books written on assignment, as are Bible studies, curriculum, Christian education material, and missionary books. No mass market material, no autobiographies. Freelancers' best bets are Christian self-help or strong inspirational books. Rarely accepts fiction, poetry, children's books, or daily devotionals. "All books must appeal to our Wesleyan market." Successful titles: *Making the Bible Yours, The Faces of God, Making the Small Church Grow, More than I Do, Family Journey Into Joy.*

Paperback length should be 120 to 180 pages. Query letters "okay." Catalogs and guidelines available; SASE required. Reports immediately if not interested; 6 to 8 months required if book is to be considered. Royalty generally 10%. Advances only on assignment, on publication.

BETHANY HOUSE PUBLISHERS, 6820 Auto Club Road, Minneapolis, MN 55438. (612) 944–2121. Carol Johnson, Editor; Nathan Unseth, Assistant Editor. Publishes 40 to 50 books a year, the majority of them trade paperbacks.
☐This evangelical publisher seeks books in a broad range of categories; Bible reference work geared to families, Christian educators, and pastors *(Today's Handbook of Bible Times and Customs)*; personal growth/self-help such as *Telling Yourself the Truth* and *Free to Be Thin*; devotional books with unique, stimulating approaches geared to specific audiences *(Spiritually Single; Devotions for a New Mother)*; information and biblical answers

to contemporary issues such as cults, abortion, euthanasia, humanism, and divorce (*Hypnosis and the Christian; Who Broke the Baby?*); marriage and family books that nurture love and communication (*Helping Your Children Love Each Other; Please Tell Me How You Feel*); a young adult curriculum series called Building Books, with 34 lessons in a student workbook and accompanying teacher's guide; romantic/historical novels for adult women such as *The Wedding Dress* and *Love's Fragile Flame;* and Heartsong Books/Springflower Books, contemporary romances for teenage girls (specific guidelines available).

Catalog, general guidelines, and fiction guidelines available with SASE. Query letter with outline and 2 or 3 sample chapters. Royalty approximately 10%, 6% on mass market; advances negotiable.

BETHEL PUBLISHING, 1819 South Main, Elkhart, IN 46516. Pete Peterson, Senior Editor. Sponsored by the Missionary Church. Publishes 4 paperbacks a year.
☐Seeks fiction, devotional reading, and humor. Successful titles: *Spunky's Diary* by Janette Oke, *Cry for Peace* by Jean Springer.

Entire manuscripts of 40,000 words preferred. Catalogs and guidelines available. Reports in 8 weeks. Usually pays royalties, no advances.

BRANDEN PRESS, INC., 21 Station Street, Brookline, MA 02146. A general publisher.
☐Seeks books related to Eastern and African religions in conjunction with Christianity. Titles published include *The Hindu View of Christ, Modern Problems and Religion, God as Mother, Why I Became a Mormon, The Wisdom of Confucius, God in Africa.*

BRETHREN PRESS, 1451 Dundee Avenue, Elgin, IL 60120. (312) 742-5100. David Ellis, Book Editor. Sponsored by the Church of the Brethren. Publishes 10 books a year, 90% of them paperbacks. Toll-free: 1-800-323-8039.
☐Seeks two kinds of books: light, religion-oriented, but entertaining mass market paperbacks; and trade books on devotional, historical, biographical, or study themes. Interested in fiction, nonfiction, stories of people, humor, devotional reading, reference works, biblical studies, and curriculum. Target audience is general evangelical and mainline Protestants. Successful titles: *What About the Russians?* and *Computer Ethics.*

Manuscripts should be 100 to 225 typewritten pages. Catalogs and guidelines available. Reports in 6 weeks. Outright payments of $300 to $2,000.

BROADMAN PRESS, 127 Ninth Avenue, North, Nashville, TN 37234. (615) 251-2433. Thomas L. Clark, Editor-in-Chief. The publishing arm of the Southern Baptist Convention, under the supervision of the Sunday School Board. Publishes 100 titles a year, about half of them paperbacks.
☐Seeks books for a wide range of readers within and outside of the Southern Baptist Churches, appealing to evangelical and mainline Protestant groups of all ages, including scholars, clergy, and laity. List includes fiction, nonfiction, biographies, humor, devotional reading, reference works, biblical studies, and curriculum.

Book length varies from 96 to 200 pages, depending on the subject and market. Query letters preferred. Catalogs and guidelines available. Other editors to whom manuscripts may be sent: Juvenile and Youth, Grace Allred; Inspirational, Joseph Johnson; General Religious, Steve Bond, Forrest Jackson, Melody McCoy, or Harold Smith. Reports in 8 weeks. Pays 10% royalty, no advances. Interested in reprints, "if the title meets a need in our market."

WILLIAM C. BROWN COMPANY, PUBLISHERS, 2460 Kerper Boulevard, Dubuque, IA 52001. (319) 588-1451. Sandra J. Hirstein, Editor, Religious Education Division. This division of the Brown Company publishes primarily textbooks, 15 to 20 a year.
☐Seeks books primarily for use in Catholic schools. "Committed to the production of print resources that foster Christian learning and spiritual development, the division has grown in the last 14 years from an elementary-high school publisher to a full-service publisher of preschool through adult materials—mainly textbooks." Also in-

terested in books geared to the needs of catechists, religious educators, and directors of religious education programs.

Query letters preferred. Catalogs available, author's guidelines sent to contracted writers. Reports in 6 weeks. Pays both royalty and flat rates (on a work-for-hire basis); choice based on project size and author's ability to influence book sales. Also markets videocassettes and computer software, for which it pays royalties and flat fees.

BROWNLOW PUBLISHING COMPANY, INC., 6309 Airport Freeway, Fort Worth, TX 76117. Paul C. Brownlow, Vice President. Publishes 2 hardcovers a year.
□Seeks devotional reading and children's religious titles. Target audience is children and lay adults, mainly evangelical.

BUILDING BOOKS—*see* Bethany House Publishers.

CANEC PUBLISHING AND SUPPLY HOUSE, 85 St. Clair Avenue, East, Toronto, Ontario M4T 1M8, Canada. (416) 925–5931. R. L. Naylor, Head of House. The publishing operation of the United Church of Canada.
□Seeks manuscripts that appeal to an adult audience of clergy and general lay readers, mostly liberal or mainline Protestant. Interested in nonfiction, stories of people, devotional reading, reference works, worship resources, and biblical studies. Wants books with Canadian content, by Canadians, if possible.

Length of book varies with the need and subject. Query letters not necessary. Reports in 3 months. Either pays royalties or makes outright payments. Advances negotiable in special circumstances.

ARISTIDE D. CARATZAS, PUBLISHER, 481 Main Street, P.O. Box 210, New Rochelle, NY 10802. (914) 632–8487. Aristide Caratzas, Editor-in-Chief; Marybeth Sollins, Managing Editor. A general publisher that issues an average of 2 religious books a year.
□Seeks religious material appealing to a scholarly audience—works in history, biblical studies, theology, scholarly books, reference works, fiction that appeals to an adult audience of scholars and general readers.

Query letters requested. Catalogs available on request. Reports in 2 to 3 months.

CATHEDRAL PUBLISHERS, 324 East Fourth Street, Royal Oak, MI 48067. (313) 546–4510. A. Ingram, Editor. Publishes 1 or 2 paperbacks a year.
□Cathedral publishes primarily instructional books. Has a series on the denominations written by leaders of each group, a sermon series, prayer books, and a few other general titles. Readers are youth and adults of various denominations.

Books in the past have been commissioned, but is receptive to new ideas for future books. Query letters desirable. Catalog available. Pays on a royalty basis.

THE CATHOLIC UNIVERSITY OF AMERICA PRESS, 620 Michigan Avenue N.E., Washington, DC 20064. (202) 635–5052. Marian E. Goode, Manager. Publishes 5 hardcovers a year.
□Seeks scholarly works for the academic community in the fields of history, language and literature, philosophy and religion. Readers include adults, scholars, and librarians of the Roman Catholic Church. Successful titles: *Selected Plays of Lady Gregory; Metaphysical Themes in Thomas Aquinas; Origen: Spirit and Fire*, a translation.

Books average 250,000 to 300,000 words. Manuscripts not accepted without a query letter, two-page abstract of the manuscript, and curriculum vitae listing any previous publications. Catalogs available on request. Interested in reprints of scholarly works in Irish studies, philosophy, European history. Reports in 2 months after receipt of letter.

CBP PRESS, P.O. Box 179, St. Louis, MO 63166. (314) 371–6900. Herbert H. Lambert, Editor. Formerly Bethany Press. A division of the Christian Board of Publication, the publishing arm of the Christian Church (Disciples of Christ). Issues 10 to 15 books a year.

☐Seeks books for laity and clergy of the mainline Protestant denominations, and for some Roman Catholics. No fiction or poetry. Also publishes curriculum for several Protestant groups. Successful titles: *The New Testament Experience of Faith, Tools for Active Christians, Herbs and Spices of the Bible.*

Books are ordinarily 128 to 196 printed pages. Reports in 6 weeks. Pays royalties on net receipts, no advances.

CELEBRATION BOOKS—*see* The National Catholic Reporter Publishing Co.

CHARIOT BOOKS—*see* David C. Cook Publishing Co.

CHERISH ROMANCE BOOKS—*see* Thomas Nelson Publishers.

CHRISTIAN CLASSICS, INC., P.O. Box 30, Westminster, MD 21157. (301) 848-3065. John J. McHale, Editor. A Catholic publisher of 8 to 10 books a year.
☐Seeks well-written material on subjects of general interest in the field of religion. Interested primarily in devotional and biographical materials for a Catholic audience. Reprinted: *Lives of Saints,* and the *Summa Theologica of St. Thomas Aquinas.*

Books should be 120 to 250 pages. Query letters preferred. Catalogs available. Reports in 3 to 4 weeks. Pays royalties of 10% for hardcovers, 7% for paperbacks, some advances.

CHRISTIAN EDUCATIONAL PUBLISHERS, P.O. Box 2789, La Jolla, CA 92038. Arthur L. Miley, Editor. Publishes 35 paperbacks a year.
☐Seeks children and youth Sunday School curriculum and other works for children and youth—games, stories, craft ideas, etc. Target audience is children and youth of evangelical denominations.

"We do not accept unsolicited manuscripts. Write us a letter first, outlining the book." Reports in 6 weeks. Pays a flat fee, no advances.

CHRISTIAN SCHOOLS INTERNATIONAL, 3350 East Paris Avenue, S.E., Grand Rapids, MI 49508. (616) 957-1070. Sheri Haan, Director of Operations; Dr. Gordon Bordewyk, Editor. Publishes 40 textbooks a year for children and youth of an evangelical Calvinistic audience.
☐Seeks biblical studies and curriculum. Length of books varies. Catalogs and guidelines available. Reports on books commissioned in advance. Payment depends on the project. Advance paid on acceptance of proposal; balance paid upon submission of satisfactory manuscript; no royalties.

THE CHRISTOPHERS, 12 East 48th Street, New York, NY 10017. (212) 759-4050. Joseph R. Thomas, Editor. A Roman Catholic publisher of 2 paperbacks a year.
☐Target audience is adults of a variety of backgrounds. Also publishes calendars, appointment calendars, tapes, and pamphlets, but all materials are staff-written.

CISTERCIAN PUBLICATIONS, INC., WMU Station, Kalamazoo, MI 49008. (616) 383-4985. E. Rozanne Elder, Editorial Director. Sponsored by the Order of Cistercians of the Strict Observance, American region. Publishes 10 titles a year, 90% of them hardcovers. With reprints and split runs, however, paperbacks account for 40% of the total.
☐Seeks English translations of early and medieval Christian monastic texts and books studying or developing that tradition. " 'Monastic' means a way of life effectively separated from 'the world' and active ministry to the world, and centered in personal and liturgical prayer, asceticism, and manual labor." Interested only in manuscripts on monastic spirituality and history for adults, scholars, clergy, and general lay readers of Roman Catholic, Orthodox, and mixed denominations. Successful titles: *The Name of Jesus* by Irenee Hausherr, *St. Bernard of Clairvaux: Sermons on the Song of Songs, William of St. Thierry: The Mirror of Faith.*

Manuscripts should be 200 pages long. Catalogs and guidelines available. Reports in 1 month to a year, depending on readers and degree of specialization. Payment varies from no pay to royalty on sales; no advances.

CONCORDIA PUBLISHING HOUSE, 3558 South Jefferson Avenue, St. Louis, MO 63118. (314) 664–7000. Jaroslav J. Vajda, Adult Book Editor. The publishing arm of the Lutheran Church—Missouri Synod. Publishes 10 to 30 books a year.
☐Target audience is readers of a wide variety of ages and interests, scholars, clergy, and general laity. Seeks books described as "well-researched, authoritative, helpful works dealing with problems of coping, in keeping with the religious teaching of the Lutheran Church and based on sound moral values." Most are for evangelical or mainline Protestant church members. Emphasis is on books that are biblical or "helpful and practical." Successful titles: *The Power of Praise, Sarah, Daily Walk With God.*
   Books are usually 96 to 168 printed pages. Query letters encouraged. Catalogs and guidelines available. Manuscripts may also be addressed to Merv Marquandt, Family Book Editor, and Rodney Schrank, Music Editor. Reports in 6 to 8 weeks. Pays on royalty basis to single author of book, outright payment to multiple authors. Pays advance on acceptance of manuscript.

CONTEMPORARY DRAMA SERVICE, Box 7710, Colorado Springs, CO 80933. (303) 594–4422. Arthur Zapel, President. This division of Meriwether Publishing Ltd. publishes primarily religious drama, but also some religious books and secular materials for speech and drama activities.
☐Has published more than 300 religious plays, but is also interested in other participation resources for churches and schools, especially for religious holidays and for summertime retreats. Publishes for all age levels, both Protestant and Catholic audiences. Interested in church banners and other visual aids, group-participation games, and filmstrips, for which price is negotiable.
   Query letters suggested. Catalogs and guidelines available for $1 postage. Interested in reprints of nonfiction how-to books related to church activities and speech or drama. Reports in 4 weeks. Pays royalties of 10% or buys outright, depending on the work.

DAVID C. COOK PUBLISHING COMPANY, 850 North Grove Avenue, Elgin, IL 60120. (312) 741–2400. Cathy Davis, Managing Editor. Publishes 40 books a year, 80% of them paperbacks.
☐Target audience includes adults, children, youth, senior citizens, clergy, evangelical, and general readers. Seeks fiction, nonfiction, stories of people, humor, devotional reading, biblical studies, also photos and illustrations. "We are specializing and trying to reach new markets. We will also be experimenting with new fields." Chariot Books, their children's imprint, is looking particularly for Bible-based products that present scriptural truths in a unique and interesting manner. Markets three games based on *The Chronicles of Narnia.* Interested in books that are part of a series and junior novels for the 10- to 14-year-old. Successful adult titles: *Men in Mid-Life Crisis, Key to a Loving Heart.* For children: *The Picture Bible, More Stories From Grandma's Attic,* the "David and I Talk to God" series.
   Picture books should be 32 to 64 printed pages; books for the 8- to 10-year-old, under 20,000 words; adult books about 60,000 words. Query letters preferred for adult book manuscripts, plus first four chapters and a chapter-by-chapter synopsis. Catalogs available. Reports in about 4 months. Pays royalties of 7% to 12½%; pays half of advance when contract is signed, the other half when manuscript and its revisions are complete.

CORNELL UNIVERSITY PRESS, 124 Roberts Place, P.O. Box 250, Ithaca, NY 14850. (607) 257–7000. Walter H. Lippincott, Jr., Publisher; John G. Ackerman, Carol Betsch, Robb Reavill, Editors. Publishes 1 or 2 religious titles a year.
☐This scholarly publisher "wishes to produce sound serious works aimed not only at scholars but also at educated non-specialists." Interested in religion-oriented

manuscripts that appeal to a wide general audience in the areas of history, biography, theology, scholarly studies, philosophy of religion.

Catalogs and guidelines available. Query letters required. Submissions acknowledged in 2 weeks; definite decision takes 3 to 4 months. Pays on royalty basis, percentage depending "on economic considerations" and ranging from a waiver of royalties on first printing to 10% of list price for books of broad appeal.

CREATION HOUSE, 396 East St. Charles Road, Carol Stream, IL 60188. (312) 653-1472. Gordon Molsen, Publisher; Robert Walker, Janice Franzen, Editors. Publishes 3 or 4 religious paperbacks a year.
☐This nondenominational publisher seeks biography and autobiography, devotional reading, and general nonfiction. Successful titles: *Living With Jesus Today* by Juan Carlos Ortiz, *Leaning into the Wind* by Tozer. Target audience is lay adult members of mainline Protestant denominations.

Outline/synopsis or complete manuscripts of 175 to 200 pages preferred. Catalogs and guidelines available. Reports in 4 weeks. Pays royalty, but no advances.

CREDO HOUSE—*see* Regnery Gateway, Inc.

CROSSROAD PUBLISHING COMPANY, 370 Lexington Avenue, New York, NY 10017. Michael Leach, Executive Vice President; Frank Oveis, Managing Editor. Publishes 60 titles a year, 75% hardcover, 25% paperback.
☐Seeks nonfiction books on religion, spirituality, inspiration, theology, biography and autobiography, history, devotional reading, and reference works. Successful titles: *The Catholic Heritage* by Laurence Cunningham, *Troubador for the Lord* by Pam O'Neill, *In Memory of Her* by Elisabeth Schussler Fiorenza. Target audience includes scholars, clergy, and lay members of all Christian denominations.

Prefers to see outline/synopsis, sample chapters or complete manuscripts of 40,000 to 60,000 words. Reports in 6 weeks. Pays royalties on a sliding scale and advances.

CROSSWAY BOOKS, 9825 West Roosevelt Road, Westchester, IL 60153. (312) 345-7474. Jan Dennis, Editor; Ted Griffin, Senior Editor. All manuscripts should be sent to Shirley Kostka. Publishes some 20 books a year, 90% of them paperbacks.
☐Crossway Books seeks "Bible-oriented books relating biblical principles to contemporary issues and practical life." Interested in fiction, biography and autobiography, reference works, theological and devotional nonfiction, biblical studies, art and Christianity, current issues, family gift books, prayer, comfort, and Christian growth. Successful titles: *Bad News for Modern Man* and *The Great Evangelical Disaster* by Francis Schaeffer, *Dragon King Trilogy* and *Dream Thief* by Steven Lawhead. Readers include children, youth, adults and senior citizens; scholars, clergy, and general lay readers of evangelical, Roman Catholic, and mixed Protestant denominations.

Query letters preferred. Catalogs and writer's guidelines available. *Not* interested in poetry, books on prophecy, children's picture books, short stories, romantic fiction, essays, missionary biographies, commentaries, or exposés of well-known Christians. Pays royalties "as agreed in contract with author"; pays negotiable advances. Reports in 6 weeks.

C.S.S. PUBLISHING COMPANY, 628 South Main Street, Lima, OH 45804. (419) 227-1818. Wesley T. Runk, President; Rev. Michael Sherer, Editorial Director. Publishes 45 to 55 religious paperbacks a year.
☐Seeks "manuscripts that are contemporary, creative, and geared to the practical side of life for both clergy and laity." Deals primarily with subjects related to the life of the congregation, but also publishes books of help in daily living. Lists these areas of interest: preaching, youth programs, retreats, evangelism programs, counseling aids, worship, drama, stewardship, studies for Sunday Schools (youth and adult), devotional material for church seasons. Successful titles: *Lectionary Preaching Workbook, Susanna*

Wesley, Running Commentary. Target audience is clergy and lay readers of congregations of every denomination.

Ideal length of manuscript depends on subject: biblical and sermon types can be 200 to 300 pages; plays, worship and pastoral tools should be shorter—usually 20 to 40 pages. Query letters preferred. Catalogs and guidelines available. Reports in 6 to 8 months. Pays 6% to 8% royalties or buys outright for $25 to $300.

DISCIPLESHIP BOOKS—*see* Regnery Gateway, Inc.

DOUBLEDAY & COMPANY, INC., 245 Park Avenue, New York, NY 10167. (212) 953-4648. Robert T. Heller, Editorial Director of Religion Department. A general trade publisher that issues 50 to 60 religious titles a year, 60% of them hardcovers. Canadian address: 105 Bond Street, Toronto, Ontario M5B 1Y3.

□A very active religious book publishing department focuses on Catholic, evangelical, general Protestant, and Jewish interests. Books are aimed at adults—scholars, clergy, and laity. Interested in theology, spirituality, inspirational/devotional, reference, and Biblical studies. Successful titles: *Reaching Out; I've Got to Talk to Somebody, God;* the Anchor Bible series, and the Jerusalem Bible. Uses photos and illustrations where appropriate.

Length of manuscripts depends on subject; generally should be no less than 60,000 words. Query letters encouraged. Catalogs and guidelines available. Reports in 6 to 8 weeks. Pays royalties based on retail price and advances. Manuscripts can be addressed to the following editors: Evangelical (Galilee) and Catholic books, Robert T. Heller; Image Books, Patricia Kossmann; Judaica, Eve F. Roshevsky.

WILLIAM B. EERDMANS PUBLISHING COMPANY, 255 Jefferson Avenue, S.E., Grand Rapids, MI 49503. (616) 459-4591. Jon Pott, Editor-in-Chief; Charles VanHof, Managing Editor. Publishes 40 to 50 titles a year, 75% of them paperbacks.

□Books are mostly religious (Protestant) and are academic or theological, rather than devotional, inspirational, or celebrity-conversion. History and social studies titles are also academic, such as documentary histories of the states. Interested in nonfiction, reference works, biblical studies, works on theology, literature, the arts, and social sciences. Successful titles: *The Naked Public Square* by Rich John Neuhaus; *The Gospel of John* by F. F. Bruce; *Documentary History of America,* a 2-volume set by Edwin S. Gaustad. Target audience includes adults, scholars, clergy, evangelicals, and Protestants of mixed denominations.

Books should be 150 to 300 printed pages. Query letters preferred. Catalog available. Reports on queries in 3 weeks; on submissions in 4 months. Pays royalties of 7½% to 10%.

FARRAR, STRAUS AND GIROUX—*see* Chapter 4.

FORTRESS PRESS, 2900 Queen Lane, Philadelphia, PA 19129. (800) 523-3824. Harold W. Rast, Executive Editor; Norman A. Hjelm, Editor. The publishing arm of the Lutheran Church in America. Publishes about 80 books a year, many of them hardcovers.

□Has a broad publishing program appealing primarily to adults in mainline Protestant churches and Roman Catholics. Heavy emphasis on books for the academic market—colleges and seminaries as well as scholars and clergy. Subjects include all areas of interest: biblical studies, theology, church history, ethics, counseling and pastoral care, preaching, worship, devotional materials, and inspirational books for lay reading. Successful titles: *Introduction to the New Testament* by Helmut Koester, *The Rise of Christianity* by W. H. C. Frend, *Paul and His Letters* by Leander Keck.

Manuscripts can be of any length appropriate to the subject and market. Query letters encouraged. Catalogs available. Reports in 2 to 3 months. Pays standard royalties of 10% on hardcovers, 7½% on paperbacks; advances rare. Limited reprinting of classical theological works.

FRANCISCAN HERALD PRESS, 1434 West 51st Street, Chicago, IL 60609. (312) 254-4455. Rev. Mark Hegener, O.F.M., Managing Director. Sponsored by the Roman Catholic Order of Friars Minor (Franciscans); publishes 50 books a year, 80% of them hardcovers.

☐Franciscan Herald Press is interested in nonfiction, biblical studies, Franciscan topics, themes, history, and Roman Catholic disciplines of homiletics, theology, morals, Scripture, and history. Successful titles: *Human Existence: Medicine and Ethics* by William E. May, *Catechism of The Catholic Church: 2,000 Years of History* by Robert J. Fox, *Credo of Pope Paul VI: A Theological Commentary* by Candido Pozo, S.J.

Length desired is 20,000 to 50,000 words; hardcovers usually have a 5⅜" by 8" or a 6" by 9" trim size. Prefers "to select and commission manuscripts. Query letters are required." Has own style book. Royalties are 10% to 15% on scale of sales, on retail price of book, paid annually. Some advances are paid, depending on author and size of manuscript, from $200 to $500. Reports in 2 to 3 weeks.

FRIENDSHIP PRESS, 475 Riverside Drive, Room 772, New York, NY 10115. (212) 870-2585. Ward L. Kaiser, Senior Editor and Executive Director; Nadine Hundertmark, Editor. The trade publishing division of the National Council of Churches of Christ, as well as other participating church groups. Publishes 10 to 15 books a year.

☐Seeks to serve the program needs and mission opportunities of the member churches of the National Council. Each year's books follow the program's outlines and emphases as identified by these churches. Books appeal mostly to members of mainline Protestant churches and to some Roman Catholics—clergy and laity of all ages. Publishes some records, tapes, filmstrips, and other nonbook resources related to books and themes for each year. Successful titles: *Sojourn in Mosaic, Energy Ethics, Paradox and Promise in Human Rights.*

Most materials are written under assignment and few unsolicited manuscripts are considered. Query letters are invited to determine interest in specific topics or manuscripts. Catalogs and lists of projected study themes available.

FRIENDS UNITED PRESS, 101 Quaker Hill Drive, Richmond, IN 47374. (317) 962-7573. Earl J. Prignitz, Manager. Sponsored by the Friends United Meeting. Publishes 8 to 10 books a year, 95% of them paperbacks.

☐Publishes Quaker books primarily, but not exclusively. Audience mostly among the Friends—of all ages. Also has reprinted a number of worthy old books. Interested in nonfiction and devotional reading books. Successful titles: *Journal of George Fox*, edited by Rufus Jones; *Temptations of Jesus* by H. Thurman.

Manuscripts should be 100 to 150 pages. Query letters desirable. Catalog available. Reports on submissions in 2 to 3 months. Royalty payment varies from 5% to 12%.

GALILEE BOOKS—*see* Doubleday & Company, Inc.

THE K. S. GINIGER COMPANY, INC., 235 Park Avenue South, New York, NY 10003. Kenneth Seeman Giniger, President. Publishes 3 books a year, all of them hardcovers.

☐Publishes nonfiction: biography and autobiography, reference works, and devotional reading. "Most of our titles are conceived by us and commissioned to meet our requirements." Well-received titles: *A Treasury of Joy and Enthusiasm* by Norman Vincent Peale; *A Book of Condolences*, edited by Rachael Harding and Mary Dyson. Readers are general lay adults of Roman Catholic and various Protestant denominations.

Query letters with SASE preferred: "We are normally a closed market, but from time to time, our enthusiasm is sparked by a query." Pays royalties on a standard basis; pays advances on terms that vary. Reports in 4 weeks.

GOSPEL LIGHT PUBLICATIONS (REGAL BOOKS), Box 3875, Ventura, CA 93006. (805) 644-9721. Donald E. Pugh, Senior Editor; Carol Brown, Laurie Leslie, Associate Editors. Publishes 40 to 45 books a year, 95% of them paperbacks.

☐Regal Books are designed to help the reader understand the Bible and learn and grow in his or her faith. Publishes for evangelical laity—children, youth, and adults. Slant is conservative, built on belief in the Bible as the inspired word of God. Does *not* publish devotionals, short stories, booklets, pamphlets, tracts, or poetry. Successful titles: *Autobiography of God* by Lloyd J. Ogilivie; *A Distant Grief* by Kefa Sempangi; *Love, Acceptance, and Forgiveness* by Jerry Cook and Stan Baldwin.

Length desired is under 200 printed pages. Query letters required. Include a brief synopsis of your book, your reasons for writing the material, and why you believe it would be of interest or help to others. Also include a chapter-by-chapter outline of manuscript (brief paragraph of description and explanation under each chapter heading). If possible, also include two sample chapters, typed double-spaced. Catalogs and writer's guidelines available. Royalty or flat fee payment; advances paid very selectively—half on signing of contract, half on publication of book. Reports within 30 days.

GOSPEL PUBLISHING HOUSE, 1445 Boonville Avenue, Springfield, MO 65802. (417) 862-2781. Glen Ellard, Book Editor. Publishing arm of the Assemblies of God; issues 20 books a year, 90% of them paperbacks.

☐Gospel Publishing House issues titles for children, youth, adults, senior citizens, clergy, and general lay readers of the Assemblies of God Church. "Therefore, the doctrinal viewpoint of all books published is required to be compatible with our own." Generally publishes Bible study books and teacher helps for Christian believers. Would consider other types of books, including self-help, how-to, and biographical stories of people. "One of our big markets is the deaf and those who minister to the deaf." Particular need for books on biblical prophecy. Successful titles: *The Joy of Signing, Magnificent Strangers, The Christ-Centered Family, Practical Puppet Plays, The Sunday School Spirit, And He Gave Pastors.*

Radiant Life (a popular imprint of Gospel Publishing) books usually run 96 to 176 printed pages; more scholarly books up to 600 pages. Prefers, but does not require, query letters. Trade catalog and author's guidelines available. Usually royalty payment is 10% of retail price, lower for books sold at a quantity discount. Payments made in April and October. No advances. Reports in 3 to 4 months.

WARREN H. GREEN, INC., 8356 Olive Boulevard, St. Louis, MO 63132. (314) 991-1335. Warren H. Green, Editor-in-Chief. A general publisher that issues 1 or 2 religion-oriented titles a year.

☐Primarily a medical publisher and secondarily a publisher of scholarly works in philosophy. Interested in books on religious themes if they are combined with either subject.

Query letters required. Catalogs and guidelines available. Reports in 3 weeks. Pays royalties of 10% to 17%.

GREENWOOD PRESS, 51 Riverside Avenue, Westport, CT 06880. (203) 226-3571. James T. Sabin, Editor. A scholarly publisher that issues some religious titles.

☐Interested in religious books that appeal primarily to scholars. Looking for good reference works. Two recent series include "Contributions to the Study of Religion," an interdisciplinary and cross-cultural series designed to examine the world's religious groups and thoughts; and "Denominations in America," a series designed to provide single-volume references and research guides of major religious groups in the United States.

Query letters required; accepts no unsolicited manuscripts. Catalogs available. Author's guidelines for writers under contract. Reports in 3 months. Payment is by contractual agreement on a book-to-book basis.

HARPER AND ROW PUBLISHERS, INC., 1700 Montgomery Street, San Francisco, CA 94111. (415) 989-9000. Clayton E. Carlson, Publisher; John V. Loudon, Editorial Manager; John B. Shopp and Roy M. Carlisle, Editors. Publishes 65 to 70 religious books a year, 60% of them hardcovers.

☐Through its religious department, publishes "books that represent important religious groups, express well-articulated thoughts, combine intellectual competence and felicitious style, add to the wealth of religious literature irrespective of creedal origin, and aid the cause of religion without proselytizing for any particular sect." Seeks strong mainstream and evangelical academic books; mainstream books for the working minister; textbooks in religion and philosophy; serious theology and spirituality. Target audience is Jewish and Christian readers of all ages.

Query letters strongly encouraged. Catalogs available. Reports in 1 to 8 weeks. Royalty rates and advances are fully competitive with general trade and religious publishers. Occasionally reprints paperback editions of excellent books.

HARVEST HOUSE PUBLISHERS, INC., 1075 Arrowsmith, Eugene, OR 97402. (503) 343-0123. Eileen Mason, Managing Editor. Publishes 35 to 50 books a year, 90% of them paperbacks.
☐This evangelical publishing house is designed to publish books that "help the hurts of people"; thus the reason for its many how-to books. Also publishes study books, Bible-related and topical, that promote the cause of evangelical literature. Interested in non-fiction, stories of people, humor, devotional reading, biblical studies. "We do not consider ourselves to be a Fundamentalist house, but a strong evangelical publishing company, progressive and eager to proclaim the Gospel, even though sometimes only in small parts of a given book." Successful titles: *Layman's Bible Study Notebook; How to Study the Bible for Yourself; Spirit Controlled Woman; There's a New World Coming; Peace, Prosperity, and the Coming Holocaust; A Prophetical Walk Through the Holy Land.* Target audience is evangelical youth and adults.

Books should be 120 to 192 printed pages. Query letters required. Catalogs and guidelines available. Usually reports within 6 weeks. Annual royalty payments; percentage negotiable. Negotiable advances sometimes available.

HERALD PRESS, 616 Walnut Avenue, Scottdale, PA 15683. (412) 887-8500. Paul M. Schrock, General Book Editor. A division of the Mennonite Publishing House. Publishes 30 to 35 books a year, 80% of them paperbacks.
☐Seeks books for adults, youth, children, scholars, clergy, general laity. Emphasizes strong family life, Christian community, peace, a disciplined church, programs of evangelical and mission outreach concerned both with meeting spiritual needs and with alleviating poverty, injustice, and hunger. Particularly needs devotional/inspirational material with sparkle and wide appeal; and realistic adult fiction from a Christian perspective. Publishes fiction (especially for grades 4 through 9), stories of people, devotional reading, reference works, and biblical studies. Successful titles: *More-With-Less Cookbook* by Doris Janzen Longacre, *The Upside Down Kingdom* by Donald B. Kraybill.

Books vary widely in length, from 16-page pamphlets to 700 pages; most average 100 to 200 manuscript pages. Query letters required. Include one- or two-page typewritten summary of the nature of the book. Catalog available for 62¢ postage. Reports in 1 month. Pays 10% royalty of retail price up to 10,000 copies, escalates to 12% and 15%. No advances.

HORIZON HOUSE PUBLISHERS, Box 600, Beaverlodge, Alberta T0H 0C0, Canada. (403) 354-2818. K. Neill Foster and Eric Greenway, Editors. Sponsored by the nondenominational Evangelistic Enterprises; publishes 6 to 10 books a year, 80% of them paperbacks.
☐Horizon House publishes evangelistic books for general lay readers—fairly light reading that will appeal to the person on the street and books of issue/testimony/devotional orientation. Interested in branching out to more scholarly books and children's books. Publishes nonfiction, stories of people, humor, and devotional reading. Successful titles: *Dam Break in Georgia* by Foster and Mills, *How To Set Goals and Really Reach Them* by Lee.

Books average about 160 pages. Royalty payment rate depends on the manuscript. Acknowledges submissions immediately; reports within 1 month.

IDEALS PUBLISHING CORPORATION, 11315 Watertown Plank Road, Milwaukee, WI 53226. (414) 771-2700. James A. Kuse, Vice President.

☐Ideals Publishing is a secular house with a religious line. Looks for inspirational or middle-of-the-road religious books dealing with real-life problems, solutions, or answers. Publishes paperback books for adults, children, and senior citizens—all general lay readers. Interested in nonfiction, poetry, stories of people, devotional reading, and photos and illustrations. Successful titles: *Thank You, Lord, For My Home* by Gigi Graham Tchividjian, *A Time For Giving* by Jill Briscoe.

Length desired: for children's books, 10,000 words; adult books, 50,000 words; cookbooks, 250 recipes. Query letters required. Catalogs and writer's guidelines available. Rates of payment and advances vary. Reports in 6 to 8 weeks.

IMAGE BOOKS—see Doubleday & Company, Inc.

INTERVARSITY PRESS, Box 1400, Downers Grove, IL 60515. (312) 964-5700. James W. Sire, Editor-in-Chief; Andrew T. LePeau, Managing Editor. The publishing arm of Intervarsity Christian Fellowship, 233 Langdon, Madison, WI 53703. Publishes 45 books a year, 95% of them trade paperbacks.

☐Seeks books of interest to the academic community and to graduates; titles that integrate Christianity, life, and scholarly pursuits. Particularly need popular books by qualified professionals. Successful titles: *The Race* by John White, *Women at the Crossroads* by Kari Malcolm, *The Hard Sayings of Jesus* by F. F. Bruce, *Why Am I Afraid to Tell You I'm a Christian?* by Don Posterski. Target audience is adults and youth, scholars, clergy, and general laity of evangelical, mainline Protestant, and mixed denominations.

Manuscripts average 120 to 200 double-spaced pages; book limit is 90 to 400 double-spaced pages. Limit for booklet, 15 to 20 double-spaced pages; for pamphlet, 30 to 50 double-spaced pages. Query letters desirable. Catalogs and guidelines available. Reports within 3 months. Flat fee for booklets; 5% to 7½% royalty for pamphlets, 10% royalty for books. Also sells tapes, on which a 5% royalty is paid. Interested in reprints "occasionally."

JUDSON PRESS, Valley Forge, PA 19481. (215) 768-2116. Harold L. Twiss, Managing Editor. Publishes about 35 to 40 books a year, 90% of them paperbacks. The publishing operation of the American Baptist Churches in the United States.

☐Main interest is in books that serve as resources for church leaders, both laity and clergy—including professional guidebooks, lay manuals, inspirational books, and books for individual and group study. "We publish books with a religious theme for pre-school children, books of inspiration and devotion, books of Bible study, church manuals, and books about ethical and social issues from a Christian perspective." Successful titles: *Fingerplay Friends, Computers' New Opportunities for Personalized Ministry, Blue Collar Ministry.*

Average book length is 96 to 128 printed pages. Inspirational books tend to be shorter; children's books are usually 24 to 32 pages. Query letters, including outline or description of book, are desirable, but full manuscripts also reviewed. Author's guidelines available. Reports in 6 to 12 weeks. Pays on royalty basis, usually 10%. Pays advances on receipt of approved manuscript.

KEATS PUBLISHING, INC., 36 Grove Street, Box 876, New Canaan, CT 06840. (203) 966-8721. An Keats, Editor. A general trade publisher that releases about 20 religion-oriented titles per year.

☐Keats Publishing is interested in manuscripts qualifying as reference works with an evangelical point of view that appeal to the general reader, both youth and adults. Successful titles: *Daily Strengths for Daily Needs* by Mary W. Tileston, *In Tune With the Infinite* by Ralph Waldo Trine, *In His Steps* by Charles W. Sheldon.

Query letters required. Catalogs available on request. Pays royalties and advances. Reports as soon as possible. Also interested in reprints on nutrition, health, and inspiration.

JOHN KNOX PRESS, 341 Ponce de León Avenue N.E., Atlanta, GA 30365. (404) 873-1549. Walter C. Sutton, Editorial Director. A division of the Presbyterian Publishing House and one of two book publishing agencies operated by the Presbyterian Church (U.S.A.). Publishes 24 books a year, mostly paperbacks.
☐Seeks "books to inform, challenge, encourage, and strengthen Christian faith, in subject areas including biblical studies, ethics, theology, philosophy, psychology, counseling, and worship." Desires books of several kinds: textbooks and other instructional materials for seminaries, colleges, and churches; resources and tools for ministry; and books to help persons trying to live a Christian life.

Query first; send SASE for catalog and *Guidelines for a Book Proposal.* Address queries and proposals to Acquisitions Editor John G. Gibbs. Reports in 1 to 3 months.

KREGEL PUBLICATIONS, 733 Wealthy Street, S.E., P.O. Box 2607, Grand Rapids, MI 49501. (616) 451-4775. Robert L. Kregel, President; Paul W. Bennehoff, Editor. A nondenominational religious publisher that issues 20 titles a year.
☐Interested in evangelical books appealing to various audiences and age groups. Does not solicit new manuscripts: "We have a nine-page list of reprints of religious and philosophical books and sets that we are desirous of publishing as time and finances allow."

LAMB COMMUNICATIONS, 1616 South Fifth Street, Broken Arrow, OK 74012. Robert Lamb, Editor. Publishes 3 paperbacks a year.
☐Seeks devotional reading, biblical studies, poetry, and Bible-based teaching books. Successful titles: *The Lord's Supper—More Than a Ritual; Speaking Blood, Speaking Faith; The Blood of Jesus: A Foundation for Faith.* Target audience includes youth, adults, and senior citizens, both clergy and laity, of Roman Catholic and evangelical and mainline Protestant denominations.

Manuscripts should be a minimum of 24 pages; no maximum. Sample chapters preferred. Reports in 2 weeks. Payment negotiable; does not pay advances. Interested in reprints.

LIBRA PUBLISHERS, P.O. Box 165, 391 Willets Road, Roslyn Heights, NY 11577. (516) 484-4950. William Kroll, Editor. A general trade publisher with some religious titles.
☐Libra is primarily interested in books about the behavioral sciences. Publishes an occasional religious title related to these subjects.

Query letters encouraged. Pays 10% royalties; no advances. Reports in 3 weeks.

LIGHT AND LIFE PRESS, 999 College Avenue, Winona Lake, IN 46590. (219) 267-7161. Wilmer Bartel, Director. The publisher for the Free Methodist Church of North America.

LIGUORI PUBLICATIONS, BOOK AND PAMPHLET DEPARTMENT, One Liguori Drive, Liguori, MO 63057. (314) 464-2500. Christopher Farrell, C.SS.R., Editor-in-Chief; Roger Marchand, Managing Editor. Sponsored by the Congregation of the Most Holy Redeemer (Redemptorists), a Catholic order. Publishes an average of 45 titles a year: paperback originals and pamphlets.
☐Seeks spiritual, doctrinal, biblical, self-help, and educational materials. Looks for thought and language that speak to basic concerns of Catholic Christians. Successful titles: *Sharing the Faith With Your Child, Praying With Scripture, Experiencing God, Sin: A Christian View for Today.*

Send query letter or submit outline/synopsis and sample chapter. Photocopied submissions acceptable. Free book catalog for SASE. Reports in 3 to 5 weeks. Pays royalties on books; flat fees on pamphlets and teachers' guides.

LITTLE, BROWN AND COMPANY, INC.—*see* Chapter 4.

THE LITURGICAL PRESS, Collegeville, MN 56321. (612) 363–2213. Mark Twomey, Managing Editor. Sponsored by St. John's Abbey (a Benedictine group); publishes about 25 religious-oriented books a year, 90% of them paperback.
☐The Liturgical Press seeks biblical studies, devotional reading, and liturgy. "We generally are interested in manuscripts that are meaningful to the informed lay person with some interest in Scripture and liturgy." Successful titles: *Collegeville Bible Commentary (New Testament)*, *Preaching the Lectionary*, *The Ministry of Ushers*. Readers are scholars, clergy, and general adult lay readers of Roman Catholic and various mainline Protestant denominations.
Manuscripts of 200 pages or less are preferred. Dissertations, theses, and complicated scholarly manuscripts written for a limited audience are seldom published. Query letters preferred. Author's guidelines available. Usually pays royalty of up to 10%; sometimes a flat fee. Reports in 6 weeks.

LIVING FLAME PRESS, 123 Birch Hill Road, Locust Valley, NY 11560. (516) 676–4265. Katherine Quevedo, Editor; Jacqueline Seitz, Assistant Editor. Publishes 6 paperbacks a year.
☐Seeks devotional works. Successful titles: *The Born-Again Catholic* by Albert Boudreau, *Encountering the Lord in Daily Life* by Msgr. David Rosage. Target audience is lay Catholics.
Books should be 128 to 220 printed pages. Particularly interested in practical applications of faith to daily living. Send entire manuscripts. Catalogs and guidelines available. Reports in 8 weeks. Pays royalties, no advances.

LOIZEAUX BROTHERS, INC., 1238 Corlies Avenue, P.O. Box 277, Neptune, NJ 07753. (201) 774–8144. Marie D. Loizeaux, Editor. Publishes 5 to 10 books a year, 50% of them paperbacks.
☐Loizeaux Brothers is "a conservative, evangelical publisher, interested primarily in biblical commentaries." Does few titles per year, but "maintains a strong backlist of books of continuing value. Thus not actively seeking many submissions."
Catalogs available on request. Pays on a royalty basis; no advances. Reports in 5 months.

MASTER BOOK PUBLISHERS, P.O. Box 15908, San Diego, CA 92115. (619) 442–6671. Margie Brumbaugh, Editor; Dr. George Hillestad, Publisher.
☐Master Book Publishers seeks nonfiction biography and autobiography studies, reference works and scientific works detailing creation *vs.* evolution. Readers are children, youth, and adults, both scholars and general lay readers of evangelical Protestant denominations. Particularly interested in religious manuscripts for children and youth.
Manuscripts should be 152 to 300 pages. Sample chapters preferred. Catalogs and author's guidelines available. Pays royalties and occasional advances. Reports in 8 weeks. Also interested in reprints.

MERIWETHER PUBLISHING, LTD.—*see* Contemporary Drama Service.

MOODY PRESS, 2101 West Howard Street, Chicago, IL 60645. (312) 973–7800. Ella K. Lindvall, Managing Editor; Garry Knussman, Senior Editor, Academic Books; Jill Wilson, Adult Trade Editor. Publishing arm of Moody Bible Institute, 820 North LaSalle Street, Chicago, IL 60610. Publishes 75 to 100 books a year, 75% of them paperbacks.

□"Maintains leadership in evangelical Christian publishing by carefully, faithfully, and effectively promoting the education of believers, evangelization of unbelievers, and edification of the Church." Seeks books for evangelicals, written by evangelicals. Target audience includes children, youth, and adults. In addition to spiritual maturity and theological orthodoxy, the author's lifestyle must reflect the highest standard of biblical conduct. Mainly interested in the area of popular-level Christian fiction and nonfiction. Also publishes devotional reading, reference works, biblical studies, and curriculum.

Children's books should be 32 to 128 pages; popular, 128 to 250 pages; textbooks, 150 to 300 pages. Catalogs and guidelines available. Query letters preferred for academic books. Reports in 6 to 8 weeks. Royalty range depends upon author's experience and type of book. No advances. Also publishes maps of Bible lands.

MOREHOUSE-BARLOW COMPANY, INC., 78 Danbury Road, Wilton, CT 06897. (203) 762-0721. Stephen S. Wilburn, Editorial Director. A publisher of religious books and books oriented to the Episcopal Church. Publishes 20 to 25 books a year, most of them trade paperbacks.
□Seeks books and curriculum of interest to all ages and several denominations, although the foremost market is among the members and parishes of the Episcopal Church. Materials appeal to Roman Catholic market as well. Publishes books on theological topics, church history, spirituality, devotional reading, biblical studies, and curriculum. Uses photos and illustrations. Successful titles: *The Hospital Handbook, The Banner Book, What is Anglicanism?, A Priest's Handbook, Your Spiritual Growth Handbook.*

Books are usually at least 128 printed pages; how-to books and manuals may be 32 to 40 printed pages. Query letters are encouraged. Catalogs available. Reports as soon as possible. Pays 6% to 10% royalty. Also publishes calendars, appointment calendars, certificates, and church registers. Interested in reprints "in keeping with our editorial policies."

WILLIAM MORROW & COMPANY, INC., 105 Madison Avenue, New York, NY 10016. (212) 889-3050. A general publisher who issues approximately 3 religious titles a year.
□William Morrow is looking for religious books that appeal to a wide general audience on the topics of history, biography, scholarly studies, self-help, and other general topics.

Query letters required. Pays on a standard royalty basis. Reports in 6 to 8 weeks.

MORSE PRESS, P.O. Box 24947, Seattle, WA 98124. (206) 282-9988. Ronn Talbot Pelley, Editorial Director. Publishes 4 to 6 paperbacks a year.
□Seeks books for pastors and Sunday School classes; also publishes reference works, devotional reading, biblical studies, and curriculum on baptism, confirmation, and communion. Successful titles: *The Path of Life* by Luther G. Strasen, *Celebration!* by Richard Melheim. Target audience is children, youth, and adults, both clergy and laity, of the Lutheran Church.

Manuscripts should be 40,000 to 60,000 words. Query letters or sample chapters preferred. Catalogs available. Usually pays a flat fee, sometimes royalties, depending upon size and scope of project; pays advances. Reports in 12 weeks.

MOTT MEDIA, INC., PUBLISHERS, 1000 East Huron Street, Milford, MI 48042. (313) 685-8773. Leonard George Goss, Senior Editor. Publishes 15 to 20 books a year, both paperbacks and hardcovers.
□Seeks to produce and distribute "books that are prophetic for our times. Those books shall be orthodox in Christian doctrine, with sound exegesis and logical and practical application to all Christians." Needed are books on contemporary social issues, theology, doctrinal studies, lifestyle, family, devotional, Bible study, etc.

Query letter with outline and sample chapters desirable. Catalogs, guidelines, and information sheet available. Reports in 6 to 8 weeks. Advances negotiable.

MULTNOMAH PRESS, 10209 S.E. Division Street, Portland, OR 97266. (503) 257-0526. Rodney L. Morris, Editorial Manager. The publishing arm of the Multnomah School of the Bible. Publishes 20 to 30 books a year, 75% of them paperbacks.

☐Seeks innovative, challenging, encouraging books that minister by their biblical advice and contemporary insights. Interested in aids for studying the Bible; studies that grapple with issues confronting concerned Christians. Also interested in nonfiction, devotional reading, reference works, biblical studies, photos, and illustrations. Successful titles: *Growing Strong in the Seasons of Life* by Charles R. Swindoll, *Parables by the Sea* by Pamela Reeve. Target audience: adult laity and evangelicals of mixed denominations.

General books for lay persons should be 200 to 300 pages; devotional books, 100 pages. Payment by royalty. Also markets tapes, for which it pays royalty. Interested in reprints "similar in content to our new titles."

THE NATIONAL CATHOLIC REPORTER PUBLISHING COMPANY, P.O. Box 281, Kansas City, MO 64141. (816) 531-0538. William Freburger, Editor of Celebration Books imprint. Publishes 3 paperbacks a year.

☐The National Catholic Reporter Publishing Company is issuing, under the Celebration Books imprint, a line of pastoral resources for worship in the local church, for a primarily, but not exclusively, Roman Catholic audience.

No special policy on length of book. Query letters desirable. Pays on escalating royalty scale, beginning at 10% on the first 5,000 copies. No advances. Reports within 90 days.

NAZARENE PUBLISHING HOUSE—*see* Beacon Hill Press.

NEIBAUER PRESS, 20 Industrial Drive, Ivyland, PA 18974. (215) 322-6200. Nathan Neibauer, Editor. Has published 25 paperbacks for Protestant evangelical clergy.

☐A specialized publisher of books on self-help, stewardship, tithing, church enrollment and growth, fund-raising, communication literature for churches and related organizations, and reference works. Query letters required. Also distributes jewelry and tracts. Reports in 2 weeks.

NELSON-HALL PUBLISHERS, 111 North Canal Street, Chicago, IL 60606. (312) 930-9446. Peter Ferrara, Editor-in-Chief. A general publisher that issues approximately 5 religious books a year.

☐Seeks "serious nonfiction books of an educational nature, suitable for libraries and supplementary reading in higher education courses." Interested in books that appeal to all religious groups—Jewish, Catholic, Protestant, evangelicals. Looking for books in areas of history, biography, scholarly topics, self-help, reference works. Target audience is adults, primarily clergy and scholars.

Query letters required. Reports in 4 weeks. Pays on a standard royalty basis.

THOMAS NELSON PUBLISHERS, Nelson Place at Elm Hill Pike, Nashville, TN 37214. (615) 889-9000. Lawrence M. Stone, Editorial Vice President. Publishes 125 books a year, 65% of them paperbacks.

☐Seeks "books characterized by Orthodoxy (the message of God as revealed in Scripture and interpreted by the mainstream of historic Christian churches); validity (a specific and valid reason for existing); and quality." Wants books that realistically apply the Gospel to everyday life. Successful titles: *Tough Times Never Last But Tough People Do* by Robert H. Schuller; *Abortion and the Conscience of the Nation* by Ronald Reagan; *Three Steps Forward, Two Steps Back* by Charles Swindell. Interested in romantic fiction for Cherish Romance imprint; manuscripts should be submitted to Etta Wilson, Editor.

Length is determined by the book's goals. Query letters desirable; include in your outline a working title, a paragraph of what your book is about, and a chapter-by-chapter summary of its contents. Catalogs and guidelines available. Reports in 6 to 8 weeks. Usually pays royalties but sometimes (especially for gift books) makes outright payment. Advances available only to established authors. Also markets calendars and tapes.

NEW LEAF PRESS, P.O. Box 311, Green Forest, AR 72638. (501) 438–5288. Richard Nance, Editor. Publishes 8 to 10 books a year, 90% of them paperbacks.
□Desires books for evangelical adults, both clergy and laity, that minister wholeness to the Body of Christ. Interested in nonfiction, stories of people, and biblical studies. Successful titles: *I Gotta Be Me* by Tammy Bakker with Cliff Dudley, *Even Elvis* by Mary Ann Thornton, *The Todd Phenomenon* by Darryl E. Hicks and David A. Lewis.

Books should be 128 to 160 printed pages. Appreciates submissions of the complete manuscript. Catalogs available. Reports within 90 days. Payment of royalties is 10% on first 10,000 copies, 12½% on second 10,000 copies, and 15% thereafter. No advances.

OAK TREE PUBLICATIONS, INC., 9601 Aero Drive, San Diego, CA 92123. (619) 560–5163. Modeste Williams, Editorial Coordinator. An educational and general publisher that rarely publishes religious titles.
□Aims books at a wide, general audience of children, youth, and adults. Interested in fiction, nonfiction, stories of people, humor. Uses photos with some books. The publisher's philosophy is "to inform and entertain children, enlighten parents, and, in the process, contribute to their growth and understanding of the world around them."

Length of manuscripts varies: children's books are shorter. Query letters desirable. Catalogs available. Reports as soon as possible. Royalties are negotiable; pays advances.

OPEN DOOR MINISTRIES (formerly Open Door Press), 1044 Pershall Road, St. Louis, MO 63137. (314) 868–2203. A publisher of black Christian evangelical literature.
□Open Door Ministries is a house that for more than a decade has been distributing and publishing literature through a missionary organization. Publishes tracts and teaching aids; began a book-publishing line in 1979. Audience is general lay readers in the black community. Interested in devotional reading, biblical studies, curriculum, and other books related to Christian living in a black cultural context. Also interested in children's books.

Reports in 6 weeks. Also interested in reprints of any black-authored books that are out of print; for example, *Better Than I Was* by Frances Kelley, *I Want Somebody to Know My Name* by Cathy Meeks.

ORBIS BOOKS, Maryknoll, NY 10545. (914) 941–7590. Philip J. Scharper, Editor. Founded by the Maryknoll religious order, Orbis is sponsored by the Catholic Foreign Mission Society of America. Publishes 30 books a year, mostly paperbacks.
□Desires "to make Americans more aware of and responsive to the problems of the Third World: those emerging nations of Asia, Africa, and Latin America where two-thirds of the world's people live." Under its sponsorship, Orbis is most interested in the theology and religious development of these Third World countries. Although its books are published primarily for a Catholic readership, they appeal to scholars, clergy, and laity of all denominations interested in Third World developments. Successful titles: *Tribes of Yahweh; Puebla and Beyond; Black Theology, a Documentary History; Theology of Liberation.*

Manuscripts vary in length according to the needs of the subject being covered. Query letters preferred. Catalogs and material describing Orbis's purpose available on request. Reports in 6 weeks. Pays on a royalty basis of 7% to 10%. Pays some advances. Manuscripts may also be submitted to John Eagleson and Robert H. Quigley, Editors.

OXFORD UNIVERSITY PRESS, 200 Madison Avenue, New York, NY 10016. (212) 679–7300. Cynthia A. Read, Religious Books Editor. Canadian address: 70 Wynford Drive, Don Mills, Ontario M3C 1J9.
□Seeks general trade, scholarly, reference, college and seminary textbooks. Interested in works of original scholarship and books suitable for use as upper-level textbooks.

Subjects of particular interest: biblical studies, cultural history of religion, American religion. No fiction, poetry, or devotional/inspirational literature.

Query letters desirable. Send prospectus or table of contents and sample chapters with current resume.

PACIFIC PRESS PUBLISHING ASSOCIATION, P.O. Box 7000, Boise, ID 83707. Herbert E. Douglass, Ph.D., Editor. Sponsored by the General Council of Seventh-Day Adventists, 6840 Eastern Avenue N.W., Washington, DC 20012. Publishes 45 to 55 books a year, almost all of them paperbacks.

☐Seeks nonfiction: biography and autobiography, devotional reading, theology, curriculum, and "textbooks for within our own school system." Successful titles: *What Jesus Said About* by Morris Venden, *How to Survive the 80s* by Douglass and Walton, *The Cry of a Lonely Planet* by G. E. Vandeman. Target audience is children, youth, and adults, scholars, clergy and general laity, of both evangelical and mainline Protestant denominations, particularly the Seventh-Day Adventists.

Books range between 32 and 128 printed pages, with 96 being the average. Query letters, outlines, and sample chapters preferred. Catalogs and guidelines available. Reports in 12 weeks. Pays royalty of 7%, no advances.

PAULIST PRESS, 1865 Broadway, New York, NY 10023. (212) 265-4028. Kevin A. Lynch, C.S.P., Publisher; Donald Brophy, Managing Editor. A Catholic publisher that releases 110 to 115 books a year, 90% of them paperbacks.

☐Looking for "substantial works of theology and spirituality that are grounded in the Christian tradition and aimed at a broad ecumenical market." Also publishes some self-help books, prayer books, and books on art, film, and other cultural areas. Especially interested in popular theology and spirituality. Publishes some curriculum and books in religious educational field. Successful titles: *Afterlife* by Morton Kelsey, *The Community of the Beloved Disciple* by Raymond E. Brown, *Business Ethics* by Edward Stevens. Target audience is readers of all ages in Roman Catholic, liberal, and mainline Protestant churches.

Books are usually 100 to 300 pages. Query letters desirable. Reports in 4 weeks. Usually pays a 10% royalty on book-length manuscripts; sometimes pays $500 advance on publication. Also distributes calendars and audio and video tapes.

PELICAN PUBLISHING COMPANY, 1101 Monroe Street, Gretna, LA 70053. (504) 368-1175. James Calhoun, Executive Editor; Karen Trahan, Assistant Editor. A general trade publisher that issues some religious titles each year.

☐Is presently expanding its list of motivational self-help titles with a religious orientation and its list of Bible study books. Has an evangelical and Baptist orientation, but is seeking materials that appeal to a wide audience of children, youth, and adults; scholars, clergy, and lay readers. Looking for books in several subject areas: history, biography, biblical studies, reference works, devotional reading, and self-help.

Query letters preferred. Catalogs available. Reports take several months for unsolicited material. Usually pays 10% royalty, but authors with a track record in sales may receive a sliding-scale royalty. Also distributes greeting cards, for which 10% royalties are paid. Interested in reprints of an inspirational nature.

PENNSYLVANIA STATE UNIVERSITY PRESS, 215 Wagner Building, University Park, PA 16802. (814) 865-1327. John M. Pickering, Editorial Director. Publishes 2 religion-oriented titles a year.

☐A division of the University, the Press will consider scholarly nonfiction manuscripts on any subject, including religious studies in which Penn State offers courses. "The Press also has a continuing interest in history and sociology of religion, especially if it is comparative." Seeking scholarly books that appeal to a wide audience.

Query letters desired. Catalogs and guidelines available. Reports in 2 to 3 months. Pays on a royalty basis, usually 10% of net, sometimes with waiver of royalty on half of first printing. Interested in reprints "if scholarly and significant."

PICKWICK PUBLICATIONS, 4137 Timberlane Drive, Allison Park, PA 15101. (412) 487-2159. Dikran Y. Hadidian, Director/Editor. Publishes 6 or 7 religion-oriented titles each year.
☐Interested in religious books that appeal to a wide range of readers—Protestant, Catholic, evangelical—mostly scholars and seminarians, on topics of church history, biblical studies, theology, and other scholarly subjects.

Query letters required. Catalogs available. Reports in 2 months. Pays royalty of 8% to 10%.

PILGRIM PRESS, 132 West 31st Street, New York, NY 10001. (212) 239-8700. Marion M. Meyer, Senior Editor. The publishing arm of the United Church of Christ. Releases 15 to 20 religious titles a year, half of them paperbacks.
☐Publishes a wide variety of books for adult readers—scholars, clergy, laity; but mostly liberal or mainline Protestants. Has published books on church growth, Christian education, energy, politics, women's issues, gay rights, a handbook for church members, and collections of sermons. Successful titles: *Understanding Church Growth and Decline, Shopping Bag Ladies, Understanding Church Finances, The Sermon on the Mount.*

Manuscripts for general books should be 100 to 150 pages; scholarly books can run up to 300 pages. Query letters preferred. Catalogs and guidelines available. Reports in 1 to 6 months. Pays on royalty basis, 5% to 10%; advances negotiable. Interested in reprinting books "related to our indicated interests."

PINE MOUNTAIN PRESS, P.O. Box 19746, West Allis, WI 53219. A general publisher that occasionally issues a religious title.
☐Interested in religious books that appeal to a wide general audience on the subjects of history, biblical studies, and self-help. Religion is "a relatively new area, and thus we are open to suggestions within the parameters listed above." Target audience is youth and adults.

Query letters required. Reports in 6 weeks. Pays royalties of 10% of net cash received. Interested in reprints, which will be considered on an individual basis.

PLOUGH PUBLISHING HOUSE, Hutterian Society of Brothers, Rifton, NY 12471. (914) 658-3141. Johann Cristoph Arnold, Editor. Publisher of the Hutterian Society of Brothers. Publishes 3 or 4 books a year, half of them paperbacks.
☐"Offers books and pamphlets about the inner life, discipleship in community, marriage, education, Hutterian and Bruderhof history, songbooks, and records." Hutterians are a society of Anabaptist background and orientation. Plough books are aimed at adults and youth, clergy and laity. Books are limited to nonfiction; most are written by members of the Society; therefore, manuscripts are not being sought at present. Successful titles: *In the Image of God* by Heini Arnold, *Early Christians* by Eberhard Arnold, *God's Revolution* by Eberhard Arnold. Plough also publishes an occasional free magazine on Christian life and community news and views. Also distributes greeting cards, calendars, and records.

PRENTICE-HALL, INC., Englewood Cliffs, NJ 07632. (201) 592-2247 or 2248. Edward H. Stanford, Editorial Director; Mary E. Kennan, Editor for Steeple Books Division. A general publisher that issues many books on religious and metaphysical subjects.
☐This general commercial book publisher is interested in books that appeal to as diverse an audience as possible. Presently expanding acquisitions in the field of religion. Main interests are in biblical studies, then religious studies in specific areas such as psychology of religion. Seeks books in subject areas of history, the Bible, theology, and reference works. Most books should appeal to clergy and scholarly college audiences.

Appreciates any and all query letters. Catalogs and guidelines available. Readers' reports and editorial board consideration take 6 to 8 weeks. Pays 10% royalty on all copies sold; extra payment for photos.

PRINCETON UNIVERSITY PRESS, 41 William Street, Princeton, NJ 08540. (609) 452-4900. Interested in publishing 4 or 5 religion-oriented titles a year.
□Princeton University Press is a scholarly publishing house whose primary mission is to "disseminate works based on original research, mainly to an academic audience." Occasionally a book has general trade appeal, but all publications "must first and foremost stand as contributions to scholarship." Religious titles must also meet this test. Interested primarily in scholarly works in the areas of history, biography, and biblical studies. Has special interests in archeology, philosophy of religion, comparative religion, and Kierkegaard studies; appeal is mainly to scholarly readers.

Prefers query letters to precede submission of manuscripts. Catalogs and writer's guidelines available. Pays royalties ranging from none on first printing to a typical medium range of 5% to 15%, on a sliding scale. Reports on a preliminary editorial evaluation in 4 to 6 weeks, scholarly review in 3 to 4 months.

PROMETHEUS BOOKS, 700 East Amherst Street, Buffalo, NY 14215. Paul Kurtz, Editor. A general publisher that issues 1 or 2 religion-oriented books each year.
□Seeks religious materials that appeal to a wide audience, mostly oriented toward a liberal, humanistic point of view. Looking for books in history, biblical studies, scholarly subjects for an adult, scholarly audience.

Query letters are required. Reports in 6 weeks. Pays royalties.

RADIANT LIFE—*see* Gospel Light Publications.

RAINBOW BOOKS, P.O. Box 261129, San Diego, CA 92126. Arthur L. Miley, Publisher. Publishes 30 to 35 paperbacks a year.
□Seeks children and youth Bible studies, curriculum, and youth-interest material for evangelical churches.

Outline/synopsis preferred. Reports in 6 weeks. Pays flat fees.

RANDALL HOUSE PUBLICATIONS, 114 Bush Road, P.O. Box 17306, Nashville, TN 37217. (615) 361-1221. Harrold D. Harrison, Editor-in-Chief. Sponsored by the National Association of Free Will Baptists.
□Seeks biography and autobiography, reference works, biblical studies, devotional reading, theology. Also publishes a complete line of Sunday School and training curriculum (but written in-house). "Our market is primarily denominational. Our books have a strongly evangelical conservative tone." Successful titles: *I Looked For a Man . . . And Found One* by Lorene Miley, *More Chapel Messages* by Linton C. Johnson. Target audience includes children, youth, adults and senior citizens, scholars and clergy, of the Free Will Baptist denomination.

Query letters preferred. Reports in 6 weeks. Pays 10% royalty on assigned book manuscripts. Shorter assignments are negotiated for a flat fee. No advances.

REGAL BOOKS—*see* Gospel Light Publications.

REGNERY GATEWAY, INC., 940 North Shore Drive, Lake Bluff, IL 60044. (312) 295-8088. Douglas Hofmeister, Publisher. A general trade publisher with a major interest in Catholic-oriented scholarly publishing and general books for an evangelical Protestant market.
□Regnery Gateway publishes in the area of philosophy of religion and theology, oriented toward a Catholic adult audience—primarily clergy and scholars. Publishes both cloth and paperback books. Two new imprints being developed: Discipleship Books for the evangelical market and Credo House for books on religious issues of special interest to Catholics.

Query letters are absolutely necessary. "No phone calls, please, about manuscripts." Pays varying royalties depending on the author, subject, and market for each title.

RELIGIOUS EDUCATION PRESS, INC., 1531 Wellington Road, Birmingham, AL 35209. (205) 879-4040. Dr. James M. Lee, Editor; Mary Harrelson, Managing Director. A nondenominational publisher that issues 5 paperbacks a year.

☐Seeks serious, scholarly religious-education books. Successful titles: *Biblical Themes in Religious Education* by Joseph S. Marino, *The Religious Education of Older Adults* by Linda Jane Vogel. Target audience is scholars and clergy of all denominations.

Manuscripts should be 200 to 300 pages; entire manuscripts preferred. Reports in 6 weeks. Pays royalty of 7% to 10% of actual list price.

FLEMING H. REVELL COMPANY, 184 Central Avenue, Old Tappan, NJ 07675. (201) 768-8060. Gary Sledge, Editor-in-Chief; Norma F. Chimento, Managing Editor. Publishes 70 books a year, 55% of them hardcovers.

☐Seeks material attractive to adult evangelical Protestants and others of mixed denominational backgrounds; and occasionally, motivational material of general interest. Books should demonstrate a message of Christian salvation and biblical teaching. Interested in nonfiction. Publishes Spire Books, a paperback line. Successful titles: *Hide and Seek, Seeds of Greatness, Intended for Pleasure, Changepoints.*

Books should be 160 to 192 printed pages. Query letters desirable. Catalogs and guidelines available. Reports in 6 to 8 weeks. Royalty rates vary; some advances paid. Interested in reprints "that provide a depth of content matter reflecting original research not available today—on biblical themes or on issues of contemporary concern."

REVIEW AND HERALD PUBLISHING ASSOCIATION, 55 West Oak Ridge Drive, Hagerstown, MD 21740. (301) 791-7000. Richard W. Coffen, Book Editor. Publishes 20 to 30 books a year, 90% of them paperbacks.

☐Owned and operated by the Seventh-Day Adventist Church, seeks books for a wide audience of evangelical and mainline Protestants. Books must enhance Christian living within the Seventh-Day Adventist frame of reference. Interested in seeing "a Christian approach to mental health, good adult stories, nonfiction, stories of people, devotional reading, and biblical studies; books that advance the work of the church, including books with a fresh approach to doctrinal subjects, Bible history, and church history; books with an evangelical message; books that solve a problem; books dealing particularly with the needs and interests of youth; books promoting the various aspects of healthful living; stories of inspiration and adventure with a spiritual emphasis; character-building books for children; and books that present a Christian viewpoint of social and family problems." Successful titles: *Miss Doctor Lucy; On My Back, Looking Up; To Know God; Why Doesn't Anyone Care?*

Manuscripts should be 120 to 150 pages. Guidelines, "Ahem . . . As You Write Your Manuscript" free. Reports in 2 weeks to 2 months. Royalty of 7% to 10% paid annually. Token advance of $100 at signing of contract, upon acceptance. Also distributes Bible computer games; pays a royalty of 15%.

ROSS BOOKS, Box 4340, Berkeley, CA 94704. (415) 841-2474. A general publisher who occasionally issues a religious title.

☐Ross Books is interested in religion-oriented manuscripts that appeal to a wide general audience—books on history, self-help, scholarly subjects, and reference works for scholars and general readers.

Query letters required. Catalogs available. Pays advances and royalties of 8% to 10% of retail price. Reports in 3 months.

ROSS-ERIKSON, INC., 223 Via Sevilla, Santa Barbara, CA 93109. Shelly Lowenkopf, Editor; Buzz Erikson, Chief Executive Officer. Publishes 4 to 5 religious titles a year, 80% of them paperbacks.

☐Seeks "responsible and scholarly approaches to Eastern religions and cults." Successful titles: *An Open Path* by Jack Beeching, *Hindu Views and Ways* by A. Bharati, *Nepali Aama* by Brot Coburn. Target audience is scholars and adult laity of liberal and mixed denominations.

Manuscripts should be 250 to 350 typewritten pages. Query letters preferred.

Catalogs and guidelines available. "Note: we charge a $50 to $75 reading fee to cover cost of processing unsolicited manuscripts. Amount applied to payment if manuscript is published." Reports in 12 weeks. Pays 8% royalty or 20% of net trade income. Pays advances, on terms that depend on the manuscript. Interested in reprints.

WILLIAM H. SADLIER, INC., 11 Park Place, New York, NY 10007. (212) 227-2120. Elinor Ford, Publisher; William J. Reedy, Editor and Director, Adult Educational Division. Publishes 30 religious titles a year.
□"A leading publisher of Catholic catechetical materials for use in schools and parishes. The adult education division is especially interested in materials for adult religious education. Most materials are commissioned, but queries are welcome."
   Catalogs available. Reports in 6 weeks. Payment is negotiated. Also distributes training tapes for home and parish workshops; pays $300 flat fee for presenting a half-hour tape.

ST. ANTHONY MESSENGER PRESS, 1615 Republic Street, Cincinnati, OH 45210. (513) 241-5615. Rev. Norman Perry, O.F.M., Editor. Sponsored by the Franciscans of the Cincinnati Province. Publishes 6 to 10 paperback books a year.
□Seeks popular religious Roman Catholic education books of information, insight, inspiration, and practical spirituality. The books help adults understand their personal growth, faith, and current religious developments and movements. Publishes some books on saints and heroes, for children. Interested in nonfiction, books on religious and personal growth, continuing education material, and photos and illustrations. Successful titles: *The Good News About Sex, His Way, Living Room Retreat, Mirrors of God.*
   Ideal book length is 30,000 words, but publishes both longer and shorter works. Queries required. Reports in 4 to 6 weeks. Pays royalties of 6% to 8% and advances. Also distributes audio cassettes, paying a royalty of 10% on U.S. sales, 5% of Canadian sales. Interested in reprints "only if author is well-known, and there is a good reason—other than lack of interest—for the original publisher discontinuing publication."

SAINT MARY'S PRESS, Winona, MN 55987. (507) 452-9090. Stephan M. Nagel, Editorial Director. Sponsored by the Christian Brothers of Minnesota, 807 Summit, St. Paul, MN. Publishes 6 to 10 paperbacks a year.
□Primary editorial focus is on religious education materials for Roman Catholic high school students and their teachers. Terms and contracts are negotiated on an individual basis.

SCARECROW PRESS, INC., 52 Liberty Street, Metuchen, NJ 08840. (201) 548-8600. William R. Eshelman, President. A publisher primarily of reference books—indices, bibliographies, historical dictionaries, etc.—for libraries. Issues 4 or 5 religious titles a year.
□Interested in religion-oriented books of a scholarly nature, particularly those that might fit into one of three series: 1) American Theological Library Association Bibliography Series, 2) ATLA Monograph Series, or 3) Studies in Evangicalism. Lists of titles in these series are available.
   Query letters desired. Catalogs of backlist and of books in religion available. Reports in 2 weeks. Pays royalties of 10% of list price.

SCRIPTURE PRESS—*see* Victor Books.

SERENADE BOOKS—*see* Zondervan Publishing House.

SERVANT PUBLICATIONS, P.O. Box 8617, 840 Airport Boulevard, Ann Arbor, MI 48105. (313) 761-8505. Bert Ghezzi, Editor-in-Chief; Ann Spangler, Senior Editor. Publishes 25 books a year, almost all of them paperbacks.
□Seeks books of inspiration, Bible study, scripture meditation, prayer, the church in

the world today, and the charismatic renewal. Target audience consists of adults: clergy, laity, evangelicals, and Roman Catholics. Interested in nonfiction and biblical studies. Successful titles: *The Open Secret* by Hannah Whitall Smith, *On Fire With the Spirit* by John Bertolucci, *The Lord is My Shepherd* by David Rosage, *Love Has a Price Tag* by Elisabeth Elliot.

Query letters desirable. Catalog available. Reports in 30 to 60 days. Royalty varies. Interested in reprinting Christian classics, biography, and inspiration.

HAROLD SHAW PUBLISHERS, 388 Gundersen Drive, P.O. Box 567, Wheaton, IL 60189. (312) 665-6700. Luci Shaw, Editor-in-Chief. Address all manuscripts to Megs Singer, Managing Editor. Publishes 20 to 25 books a year, 85% of them paperbacks.
□Seeks Christian books with a message that needs to be expressed to the public. Books of high literary quality and an extra measure of creativity are desired, as well as manuscripts that deal with problems faced by Christians in today's society. Publishes nonfiction, devotional reading, reference works, biblical studies, and biographies for a target audience of orthodox Christian youth and adults and "thinking laypersons." Successful titles: *Walking on Water* by Madeleine L'Engle; *Finders Keepers* by Dee Brestin; *The Shaw Pocket Bible Handbook,* edited by Walter A. Elwell; *Where the Wind Begins* by Paula D'Arcy; *Flirting With the World* by John White; *Called and Committed* by David Watson; *The Achievement of C.S. Lewis* by Thomas Howard; *Creation in Christ* by George MacDonald, edited by Rolland Hein.

General titles should run approximately 150 to 200 pages. Query letters preferred. Catalogs available on request. Reports in 6 weeks. Usual royalty: 5% to 10% of actual retail price. With established authors or on commissioned books, advances—usually $300 to $500—may be offered. Interested in reprinting "books that are salable and fit into our guidelines."

SPIRE BOOKS—*see* Fleming H. Revell Co.

STANDARD PUBLISHING, 8121 Hamilton Avenue, Cincinnati, OH 45231. (513) 931-4050. Marjorie Miller, Director of New Products. Publishes 70 religion-oriented books a year, 75% of them paperbacks.
□Standard Publishing seeks religious-oriented children's stories and church curriculum; adult studies of Bible books and/or principles; how-to helps for Christian parents, teachers, and leaders; fiction, and devotional reading. Successful titles: *The Lord of Parables* by LeRoy Lawson, *Training For Service* by Orrin Root Anders; *Star of Bethlehem* by Anne Claire. Readers are children, youth, adults and senior citizens; scholars, clergy and general lay readers of evangelical Protestant denominations.

Query letters and outline/synopsis preferred. Length of manuscripts "varies." Catalogs and author's guidelines available. Royalty "depends on creativity involved—usually 5% to 10%. Flat fee is usually given for simple children's books; length and quality determines amount." Also pays advances. Reports in 12 weeks.

STEEPLE BOOKS—*see* Prentice-Hall, Inc.

STEIN AND DAY, Scarborough House, Briarcliff Manor, NY 10510. (914) 726-2151. Sol Stein, Editor-in-Chief; Benton Arnovitz, Executive Editor. A general publisher with an interest in publishing 2 or 3 religious titles a year.
□Seeks religious book manuscripts that appeal to a wide general audience. Has published in all religious areas, but has a slight emphasis on Judaica. Looking for books in history, biography, reference works. Successful titles: *Portrait of Jesus?: The Illustrated Story of the Shroud of Turin* by Frank G. Tribbe, *The Yiddish Song Book* by Jerry Silverman, *The Bar/Bat Mitzvah Planbook* by Lewit and Esptein. Books should appeal to both scholars and a general reading audience.

Query letters preferred. Reports in 2 to 4 weeks. Pays standard royalties and advances. Interested in reprinting books with continuing appeal suitable for mass market paperback and quality trade paperback format.

STEINER BOOKS, 72 Fifth Avenue, New York, NY 10011. (212) 924–6080. Bernard J. Garber, President; Andrew Flaxman, Editor. An affiliate of Multimedia Publishing Corporation. A general publisher with some interest in religious books.
□Steiner Books is interested in manuscripts that appeal to the general reader of religious materials in the subject areas of biography, self-help, fiction. Publishes 4 or 5 religious books a year; especially interested in those that deal with reincarnation and psychic phenomena.
Query letters preferred. Catalogs available. Usually pays royalties, but occasionally makes "outright purchase of an idea or synopsis for rewriting by the publisher." Reports in 1 month.

STRAWBERRY HILL PRESS, 2594 15th Avenue, San Francisco, CA 94127. (415) 228–6888. Jean-Louis Brindamour, Editor-in-Chief; Joseph Lubow, Editor. A general publisher that occasionally issues a religion-oriented book.
□Publishes for a general reading audience. Looks for material that appeals to religious groups in the subject areas of history, reference, devotionals, self-help, and scholarly studies.
Query letters required. Catalogs available with SASE. Reports in 2 months. Pays royalties of 10% of net; no advances. Also distributes greeting cards and hand-colored prints, which are bought for a flat fee. Interested in reprints "in the areas of self-help and inspiration, usually suited to a large audience."

CHARLES E. TUTTLE COMPANY, INC., 28 South Main Street, Rutland, VT 05701. (802) 773–8930. Florence Sakade, Editor-in-Chief. A general publisher with strong interest in religious books; publishes 2 or 3 a year.
□Charles E. Tuttle has a special interest in books that relate to religions in the Orient. "Always interested in well-researched original manuscripts of broad and/or scholarly appeal. Also interested in reprint possibilities of outstanding but long out-of-print books. Looking for books on Asia's culture, mores, and folkways, past, present, and future. Some Americana is included in our line, but rarely."
Query letters accompanied by outlines or sample chapters or complete manuscripts should be sent to the Tuttle address in Japan: Suido 1—Chome, 2-6, Bunkyo-Ku, Tokyo, Japan. Query letters preferred. Catalogs available from Rutland office for $1. Pays 10% royalties, and advances. Reports in 4 to 6 weeks.

TYNDALE HOUSE PUBLISHERS, 336 Gundersen Drive, Wheaton, IL 60187. (312) 668–8300. Dr. Wendell C. Hawley, Vice President and Editor-in-Chief. Publishes approximately 75 to 100 books a year.
□Works with materials that have a Christian emphasis. Interested in significant materials for the Christian public and relevant works for the non-Christian, wants inspirational material—first-person accounts, biblical novels, or self-help books. Interested in stories of people, devotional reading, reference works, biblical studies. Publishes only a few children's books. Generally does *not* publish Sunday School materials, sermon collections, books of poetry and music. Successful titles: *Norma, Hind's Feet in High Places, Effective Father, Strong-Willed Child.* Target audience is varied.
Catalogs and guidelines available. Reports in 6 to 8 weeks. "We can work with manuscripts on computer disk." Annual royalty payments, competitive with other publishers. Occasional advances, generally depending on whether a book is commissioned. Interested in reprinting "books that have had a good sale through a small or regional publisher; books whose content might appeal to the broader evangelical market."

VICTOR BOOKS, P.O. Box 1825, Wheaton, IL 60187. (312) 668–6000. James R. Adair, Executive Editor; Mark Sweeney, Director; Bee Shira, Associate Editor; Lloyd O. Cory, Reference Books; Carole Streeter, Acquisitions Editor. A division of Scripture Press Publications, Inc. Publishes 60 books a year.
□Seeks Bible-based books with a readable, contemporary message that lend

themselves to group study/discussion. Current need is for manuscripts that will help expand several successful series or can be used as reference materials. Must be biblically based, addressing problems that adults face; be enjoyable to read, containing contemporary anecdotes or similar material; written by someone who has credentials to write on the subject. Successful titles: *Healing for Damaged Emotions* by David Seamands, *Loving One Another* by Gene Getz. Target audience consists of children, youth, and adults, general lay readers in evangelical and mainline Protestant denominations.

Length of books varies, depending on format. Query letters desirable with a sample chapter or two and an outline. Author's guidelines available. Reports in 1 to 2 months. Royalty payments competitive.

WARNER PRESS, INC., 1200 East Fifth Street, Anderson, IN 46011. (317) 644-7721. Arlo E. Newell, Editor-in-Chief. Publishes 10 to 12 books a year, 80% of them paperbacks. □Warner Press, sponsored by the Publication Board of The Church of God, Anderson, Indiana, publishes books for youth, adults, and clergy of evangelical Protestant denominations—books on life experience, church, and religion, oriented to the Wesleyan-Armenian theological viewpoint. Theological books received only upon solicitation by the publishers. Scholarly works of a religious nature will be considered. Successful titles: *The First Century* by Barry Callen, *Receive The Holy Spirit* by Arlo F. Newell.

Books should be 86 to 120 manuscript pages. Query letters accepted. Guidelines available upon request. One-time purchase payment and/or royalty arrangement. Reports within 2 months.

G. R. WELCH COMPANY, LTD., 960 Gateway, Burlington, Ontario L7L 5K7, Canada. (416) 681-2760. Ian McPhee, Editor. A publisher and distributor of religious books. Publishes 20 to 30 titles a year, mostly paperbacks. □Company was founded in 1934 for distribution in Canada of foreign religious books. It currently represents 40 companies from the U.S. and Great Britain. Began publishing some of its own titles in 1977. Has two divisions, one for distribution of liberal and Roman Catholic books and one for evangelical books. Interested in nonfiction, biographies, devotional reading, reference works, and biblical studies. Successful titles: *People in Process* by Maxine Hancock; *The Corridors of Time* by Jane Scott; *God's Country* by Al Reimers; *Daily Study Bible*, 18 volumes. Target audience is adult readers of all denominations—scholars, clergy, and general lay readers.

Books should be 160 to 300 pages. Query letters encouraged. Catalogs and guidelines available. Reports in 1 month. Pays 10% royalty on hardcovers, 8% on paperbacks. Also distributes Beta and VHS videotapes, for which it pays a royalty.

THE WESTMINSTER PRESS, 925 Chestnut Street, Philadelphia, PA 19107. (215) 928-2700. Keith R. Crim, Editorial Director; Cynthia Thompson and James Heaney, Editors. The publishing arm of the Presbyterian Church (U.S.A.). Publishes 50 to 60 books a year, 90% of them paperbacks. □Seeks religious books and books on present-day social and ethical concerns for scholars, church professionals, church members, and general readers. "Books endeavor to stimulate the intellectual life of the churches and their educational institutions by representing the best thinking of the day on a broad range of religious, social, and cultural points of view. Authors are free to offer their own understandings of truth without being asked to subscribe to a particular creed or system of thought." Looking for material for academic use as well. Does not use fiction or poetry. Successful titles: *The Nature of Doctrine: Religion and Theology in a Postliberal Age* by George A. Lindbeck, *Unexpected News: Reading The Bible with Third World Eyes* by Robert McAfee Brown, *The Strength of the Weak: Toward a Christian Feminist Identity* by Dorothee Soelle, *Peace Thinking in a Warring World* by Edward LeRoy Long, Jr.

Books can be of any length appropriate to the subject. Query letters desirable. Catalogs and guidelines available. Reports in 90 days. Pays royalties on a negotiable scale; some advances. "We have done reprints of works by well-known authors (Eleanor Roosevelt, Charles Dickens, etc.). These are generally editorially generated."

WHITAKER HOUSE, Pittsburgh and Colfax Streets, Springdale, PA 15144. (412) 274-4440. Donna Arthur, Managing Editor. An independent Christian publisher. Publishes 40% contemporary originals and 60% classic reprints.
□Seeks both evangelical and pentecostal books for a general reading audience. Interested in teaching books using anecdotes and illustrations. Concentrates on authors with established ministries.

Manuscripts should be 300 pages, double-spaced. Query letters preferred; unsolicited manuscripts not accepted.

WINSTON/SEABURY PRESS, 430 Oak Grove, Minneapolis, MN 55403. (612) 871-7000. Wayne Paulson, Editorial Director; Miriam Frost, Managing Editor. A unit of CBS Publishing. Issues 50 to 60 general, religious, and academic books a year.
□Publishes religious titles in the scholarly, professional, and devotional fields and general books that help the reader improve the quality of his or her life. Books have sometimes been designed specifically for use in Roman Catholic, Episcopal, and Lutheran churches, but most materials are suitable for all denominations, meant for use at several age levels and for general lay reading. Some are curriculum or supplementary educational materials. Successful titles: *Catholicism, The Way of the Heart, Women's Reality, Self-Esteem: A Family Affair, Traits of a Healthy Family, Irish Blessing.*

Manuscripts vary in length, depending on intended use. Query letters desirable. Reports in 2 to 3 months. Manuscripts may also be submitted to Lisa Swanson, Editorial Assistant. Negotiates payment and advances on an individual basis.

WORD BOOKS, P.O. Box 1790, Waco, TX 76703. (817) 772-7650. Al Bryant, Managing Editor. A religious publisher. Issues 50 to 60 books a year, 90% of them paperbacks.
□Interested in "book manuscripts dealing with Christian growth, biblical studies for both laity and scholars, marriage and the family, Christian social concern from an evangelical and mainline denominational perspective, and the Christian lifestyle in a world of change and shortages." Successful titles: *Dropping Your Guard* by Charles R. Swindoll, *Approaching Hoofbeats* by Billy Graham, *Reagan Inside Out* by Bob Slosser, *Irregular People* by Joyce Landorf. Appeals to a wide range of readers of all ages (except children); scholars, clergy, and laity of all Christian backgrounds.

Average book for lay persons runs 160 pages or less. Biblical studies or reference works range up to 288 pages. Queries are suggested. Prefers completed to partial manuscripts. Catalogs and guidelines available. Manuscripts may also be submitted to Patricia Wienandt, Senior Editor. Reports in 2 months. Pays royalty of 10% to 15%. Advances as required, based on record of author and sales potential of proposed book. Also distributes greeting cards, calendars, records, and tapes, for which negotiable payment is made.

WORLD WIDE PUBLICATIONS, 1303 Hennepin Avenue, Minneapolis, MN 55403. (612) 338-0500. A publishing operation of the Billy Graham Evangelistic Association.
□Publishes paperback books designed for evangelical adults and youth: reference works, biographies, devotional reading, biblical studies. Does not accept freelance manuscripts.

YALE UNIVERSITY PRESS, 92A Yale Station, New Haven, CT 06520. (203) 436-7584. Edward Tripp, Editor-in-Chief; Charles Grench, Editor. Publishes 5 to 7 religious titles a year.
□All manuscripts submitted to this scholarly publishing operation "must be read by experts to determine the quality of the work and its contribution to scholarship." Interested in religious books in the subject areas of history, biblical studies, and other scholarly pursuits, and aimed at general readers of all denominations and faiths—both scholars and the general public. Especially interested in archaeology, biblical treatises, and religious history.

Queries, either by phone or letter, required. Catalogs and guidelines available. Reports in 2 weeks to 3 months. Pays on a royalty basis. Interested in reprinting "classic works for classroom use."

ZONDERVAN PUBLISHING HOUSE, 1415 Lake Drive S.E., Grand Rapids, MI 49506. (616) 698-6900. Cheryl Forbes, Executive Editor, General Books; Stanley Gundry, Executive Editor, Academic Books; Anne Severance, Editor, Inspirational Romance. Publishes 130 to 150 books per year, in both cloth and paperback.
□Zondervan publishes for a wide Christian audience, from textbooks to general trade books on almost every subject adaptable to biblical/Christian theology and practice. Nonfiction interests put emphasis on Christian discipline and commitment to biblical principles. Biblical content must be solid and subjected to thorough exegesis. Personal experience stories must be unusual and highly inspirational to a broad constituency. Fiction needs include mainstream fiction for adults, inspirational romance in both contemporary and historical areas, and limited young adult fiction. Imprints for romance lines are Serenade/Seranada and Serenade/Saga.

Nonfiction hardback books average 160 to 220 printed pages. Will print books as small as 96 pages—usually mass-market paperbacks or devotional items. Query letters required. Catalogs and author's guidelines available. Competitive royalty schedule averages 14% of net. Paperback royalties are negotiated. Advances are paid on a negotiated basis. Reports in 45 to 90 days.

·FOUR·

Writing for the Jewish Market

By Lionel Koppman
Director of Public Information for the Jewish Welfare Board (JWB)

In this chapter you will find a comprehensive annotated listing of Jewish periodicals and publishers of Judaica in the United States and Canada. As far as possible, we have described the kind of material each publishes and what each is seeking, especially from freelance writers.

For obvious reasons, the Christian market is much larger than the Jewish market, but the markets listed here are very diversified. They encompass not only the broad topic of religion, but also history, culture, the experiences of the Jewish people, and current happenings. The questionnaires and resulting entries reflect this wide diversification. As far as possible, we have also provided space for publisher and editors to describe the particular needs of their houses and periodicals.

Cautions and considerations in writing for a Jewish audience are generally the same as for all writing:

- Have a thorough knowledge of your audience.
- Know how much has already been written on the subject you are working on.
- Do you have a different angle?
- Is your material timely?
- Know the publisher to whom you are sending your manuscript. Take no chances! Query first, and send for sample copies of publications and author's guidelines, where available.
- Check your facts.
- Don't overwrite.
- Type your manuscripts, double-spaced, on one side of the sheet only.
- Always include a self-addressed, stamped envelope.

Would-be authors of Jewish-interest books are encouraged to read the excellent introduction to Chapter Three in this volume for procedures to follow in getting their books published. Read "10 Faults of Book Manuscripts"—and then read the list over again. Its points are deceptively simple; writers can save themselves much grief by following them.

In addition to writing for Jewish periodicals and authoring Jewish-interest books, writers may find that Jewish organizations can use their skills or they may discover outlets in radio or T.V. where there are a number of local and network programs devoted to issues of Jewish interest.

Writers should be aware that eight National Jewish Book Awards are conferred each year by the JWB Jewish Book Council. Information can be obtained from the council at 15 East 26th Street, New York, NY 10010. *Present Tense* magazine, also listed in this chapter, offers literary awards. Training for Jewish authors is available at writers' conferences conducted each year by the Jewish Students Press Network, 15 East 26th Street, New York, NY 10010 and through summer internships for young Jewish writers offered by the Jewish Telegraphic Agency, 165 West 46th Street, New York, NY 10036.

Queries and additional information on this chapter are welcomed. Additional information will be incorporated into future editions of this book.

◄PERIODICALS►

AGADA, 2020 Essex Street, Berkeley, CA 94703. (415) 848-0965. Reuven Goldfarb, Editor. A magazine published 3 times a year, with a national distribution of up to 600. □*AGADA* publishes stories, poetry, and translations of scriptural, Kabbalistic, rabbinic, or Hasidic writings and teachings (Divrei Torah), memoirs, essays, and illustrative graphic art. Also publishes photographs and works on Jewish mysticism. Readers are youth, adults, and senior citizens; scholars, rabbis, and general lay men and women of all branches of Judaism.

Average length of articles is about 1,800 words. Minimum is 500, maximum 6,000. Prefers to see complete manuscripts. Sample copy $5.75; writer's guidelines free. Authors are granted 2 free copies and a reduced rate on additional copies. Reports in 8 weeks.

ALGEMEINER JOURNAL, 404 Park Avenue South, New York, NY 10016. (212) 689-3390. Gershon Jacobson, Editor. A weekly Yiddish newspaper.
□*Algemeiner Journal* gives "concise, descriptive reports of contemporary Jewish life and events in the United States and throughout the world." Interested in Jewish issues and concerns, personalities, Jewish Americana, Israel, the Holocaust, Hasidism, Jewish folklore, book reviews, and photos.

Articles should be approximately 4 typewritten pages. Query letters required. Sample copies available. Pays $50 to $500 per article, on publication. Reports in 2 weeks.

AMERICAN JEWISH HISTORY, 2 Thornton Road, Waltham, MA 02154. (617) 891-8110. Marc L. Raphael, Editor. A quarterly magazine of historical research.
□*American Jewish History* publishes material based on original research that provides new insights into American Jewish life. Interested in Jewish Americana, the Holocaust, Sephardic Jewry, book reviews.

Average length of articles is 10,000 words. Query letters desirable. Sample copies available on request. No payment for materials used. Also distributes greeting cards; will consider reprints.

AMERICAN ZIONIST, 4 East 34th Street, New York, NY 10016. (212) 481-1500. Carol Binen, Managing Editor. A bimonthly magazine.
□*American Zionist* is interested in "current, intelligent discussions and factual presentations of situations in the Middle East, the relationship between Israel and America, and world Jewry." Also interested in articles on Jewish Americana and the Holocaust, book reviews, poetry, and photos.

Average length of articles is 1,000 to 2,500 words. Query letters not necessary. Sample copies available for $1. Pays 1 month after publication. Reports in 2 months.

AMIT WOMAN (formerly *The American Mizrachi Woman*), 817 Broadway, New York, NY 10003. (212) 477-4720. Micheline Ratzersdorfer, Editor; Ruth Raisner, Executive Editor. A magazine published by the major religious women's Zionist organization in the United States.
□*AMIT Woman* welcomes "articles on Jewish and Israeli themes: general-interest

pieces, historical material, interviews, nostalgia, Jewish photo features, articles on travel to Israel and Jewish communities throughout the world, personalities, the Holocaust, and Jewish humor." Departments using freelance material include Public Affairs and Book Reviews. Does special features on all Jewish holidays.

Length of features should be 1,000 to 2,000 words, book reviews 500 to 1,000 words. Detailed query letters required. Sample copies available. Submit seasonal material 6 months in advance. Pays $50 maximum per article, on publication. Reports in 2 months. Also distributes greeting cards, which are produced in-house.

BALTIMORE JEWISH TIMES, 2104 North Charles Street, Baltimore, MD 21218. (301) 752-3504. Gary Rosenblatt, Editor. A weekly magazine of regional interest.
□*Baltimore Jewish Times* is looking for high-quality material "of interest to a varied and intelligent readership, from humor to personality profiles to family issues." Interested in fiction with a Jewish theme, articles on Jewish issues and concerns, personalities, Jewish Americana, Israel, the Holocaust, converts to Judaism, Jewish humor, book reviews, photos, and art.

Articles average 750 words and up; features may run to 2,000 words. Query letters desired. Sample copies available for 60¢. Pays up to 5¢ per word, on publication. Reports in 2 to 3 weeks.

THE B'NAI B'RITH INTERNATIONAL JEWISH MONTHLY, 1640 Rhode Island Avenue N.W., Washington, DC 20036. (202) 857-6645. Marc Silver, Editor. A magazine with a circulation of 190,000.
□*The B'nai B'rith International Jewish Monthly* is interested in a wide variety of material, fiction with a Jewish theme, and articles of general Jewish interest, Jewish issues and concerns, Jewish Americana, Israel, the Holocaust, converts to Judaism, Chasidim, Jewish humor and folklore, Sephardic Jewry. Uses book reviews, poetry, and photos.

Articles range from 500 to 4,000 words. Sample copies available. Pays on publication. Reports in 6 weeks.

BROWARD JEWISH JOURNAL, P.O. Box 23909, Fort Lauderdale, FL 33307. (305) 563-3311. Dorothy Rubin, Publisher and Editor-in-Chief. A weekly newspaper.
□*Broward Jewish Journal* is interested in articles on Jewish issues and concerns, personalities, Jewish Americana, Israel, the Holocaust, Jewish humor, book reviews.

Articles should be 350 to 500 words. Query letters not required. Sample copies available. Payment for material open to discussion.

CALIFORNIA JEWISH PRESS, 6399 Wilshire Boulevard, Suite 511, Los Angeles, CA 90048. (213) 652-1300. Irving H. Shear, Editor-in-Chief. A semi-monthly tabloid newspaper.
□*California Jewish Press* is beamed toward business and professional leaders and is always interested in material about Jews with personal success stories and about happenings affecting Jewish communities around the world.

Articles should be 500 words. Writing must be tight. Query letters not necessary. Payment is in free copies and a byline.

CANADIAN ZIONIST, 1310 Greene Avenue, Montreal, Quebec H3Z 2B2, Canada. (514) 934-0804. Leon Kronitz, Editor. A magazine published bimonthly (except July and August) for 35,000 subscribers.
□*Canadian Zionist* is looking for "in-depth, serious articles or analyses on Israel, Zionism, the Middle East political situation, and general or Canadian Jewish issues and concerns." Also interested in articles on the Holocaust, book reviews, and material on intermarriage in Canada.

Articles should be 2,000 to 2,500 words. Query letters desired. Sample copies available. Pays approximately $100 per article, on publication. Reports in 3 weeks.

THE CLEVELAND JEWISH NEWS, 13910 Cedar Road, Cleveland, OH 44118. (216) 371-0800. Cynthia Dettelbach, Editor. A weekly newspaper.

□*The Cleveland Jewish News* is especially interested in "travel pieces and stories on unusual personalities." Concentration of news and articles on events and items of interest to the Cleveland area. Welcomes features on Jewish issues and concerns, Jewish Americana, Israel, the Holocaust, converts to Judaism, Hasidism, Jewish humor and folklore, and Sephardic Jewry. Also prints book reviews and photos.

Average length of articles is 2 to 3 pages of manuscript. Query letters desired. Sample copies available. Pays $20 to $25 per article, $10 for book reviews, on publication.

CHURCH AND SYNAGOGUE LIBRARIES, P.O. Box 1130, Bryn Mawr, PA 19010. (215) 853-2870. William H. Gentz, Editor; Bernard Deitrick, Book Review Editor. A 16-page bimonthly publication of the Church and Synagogue Library Association, with a national distribution of 2,600.

□*Church and Synagogue Libraries* is interested in feature articles, news, and fillers concerning the work of local libraries in churches and synagogues throughout the world. Also carries news of the sponsoring association as well as other library groups, particularly those associated with religious organizations. Especially interested in how-to articles and success stories of congregational libraries and librarians. Also uses photos and book reviews.

Articles should be 500 to 750 words. Fillers can be a paragraph or two; news items of varying lengths. Query letters welcome. Sample copies available. No cash payment for material used. Reports in 1 month.

COMMENTARY, 165 East 56th Street, New York, NY 10022. (212) 751-4000. Norman Podhoretz, Editor. An 80-page monthly magazine sponsored by the American Jewish Committee, with a national distribution of 45,000.

□*Commentary* is especially interested in "thoughtful essays on political, social, theological, and cultural themes." Seeks general articles and stories as well as material with Jewish content. Likes informational, historical, and thoughtful pieces. Also uses fiction and book reviews. Jewish-oriented material is about one-quarter of the magazine.

Articles should be 3,000 to 7,000 words; book reviews about 1,500 words; for fiction, length is flexible. Query letters desirable, but complete manuscripts can be submitted. Manuscripts may also be submitted to Brenda Brown, Non-Fiction Editor, or to Marion Magid, Fiction Editor. Pays approximately $500 to $1,000 for articles, $300 for book reviews, on publication. Reports in 4 weeks.

CONSERVATIVE JUDAISM, 3080 Broadway, New York, NY 10027. (212) 678-8060. David Wolf Silverman, Editor; Nina Cardin, Managing Editor. A quarterly magazine with a national distribution of 2,000.

□*Conservative Judaism* seeks "high-quality, original works that will stimulate rabbis both professionally and personally and be of interest to sophisticated lay people." Interested in Israel, Jewish issues and concerns, the Holocaust, converts to Judaism, Jewish Americana, book reviews, theology, ritual, prayer, feminism, and interreligious concerns. Readers are adults: scholars, rabbis, and general lay people, both men and women of Orthodox, Conservative, Reform, and Reconstructionist denominations.

Articles run from 500 to 5,000 words, 2,400 on the average. Prefers to see complete manuscripts. Sample copy $6.25; author's guidelines free. No payment for materials used. Reports in 3 weeks.

THE DETROIT JEWISH NEWS LTD. PARTNERSHIP, 17515 West 9 Mile Road, Suite 865, Southfield, MI 48075. (313) 424-8833. Gary Rosenblatt, Editor. A weekly newspaper with a local circulation of 16,750.

□*The Detroit Jewish News* wants articles of interest to the Metropolitan Detroit Jewish community—Jewish issues and concerns, personalities, Jewish Americana, Israel, the Holocaust, Hasidism, Jewish humor and folklore, Sephardic Jewry. Also uses book reviews and poetry.

Sample copies depend on availability. Pays by pre-arrangement.

FRIDAY of *The Jewish Exponent,* 226 South 11th Street, Philadelphia, PA 19102. (215) 893–5745. Jane Biberman, Editor. A monthly newspaper supplement with a national distribution of 70,000.

□*Friday* is interested in "short stories, interesting pieces on Jews in the arts: musicians, writers, composers, architects, personalities; historical pieces; poetry; and opinion pieces." Articles on Jewish issues and concerns especially welcome. Also interested in Jewish humor and folklore, and photos.

Articles should be 6 to 10 pages, but some may go to 20 pages. Query letters desirable. Sample copies available. Pays $50 to $200 on publication, depending on "importance and length." Reports within 3 weeks. Also see entry under *The Jewish Exponent.*

HADASSAH MAGAZINE, 50 West 58th Street, New York, NY 10019. (212) 355–7900. Alan M. Tigay, Editor. A magazine published 10 times a year for members of the Hadassah organization (subscriptions for nonmembers also available) with a national distribution of 345,000.

□*Hadassah Magazine* is interested in articles dealing with American and Israeli Jewish community and civic affairs. Uses short stories with strong plots and positive Jewish values and photos to illustrate articles and stories. No poetry.

Articles should be 1,500 to 3,000 words; fiction 3,000 words maximum. Prefers query letters. Pays 10¢ per word, on publication. Reports in 6 weeks. Also looking for reprints of interesting Judaica as well as Yiddish and Hebrew literature.

HERITAGE, FLORIDA JEWISH NEWS, P.O. Box 742, 207 O'Brien Road, Fern Park, FL 32730. (305) 834–8787 or 8277. Jeffrey Gaeser, Editor. A weekly newspaper with a local circulation of 6,000.

□*Heritage* is interested in a wide range of articles: Jewish issues and concerns, personalities, Jewish Americana, Israel, the Holocaust, converts to Judaism, Hasidism, Jewish humor and folklore, Sephardic Jewry, as well as book reviews, poetry, and photos. Looking for "unusual features about Jewish personalities or events written to give the reader a greater awareness of the strength of the Judaic heritage and tradition."

Articles should be 500 to 1,500 words. Query letters desirable, but not necessary. Sample copies available. Pays 50¢ to $1.50 per column inch, on publication.

JEWISH BOOK ANNUAL, 15 East 26th Street, New York, NY 10010. (212) 532–4949. Jacob Kabakoff, Editor. A yearbook published by JWB Jewish Book Council with a circulation of 1,200.

□*Jewish Book Annual* seeks "essays on subjects pertinent to Jewish culture and belles-lettres, bibliographies of books in English, Hebrew, and Yiddish; in America, Israel, and England." The annual is published for an adult audience of scholars, rabbis, and general readers of all Jewish groups and persuasions. Particularly interested in material on books, authors, and libraries.

Query letters desirable. Pays an honorarium of $100 per article, on publication.

THE JEWISH CHRONICLE (serving southern Westchester; formerly *The Yonkers Jewish Chronicle),* 122 South Broadway, Yonkers, NY 10701. (914) 423–5009 or 963–8457. Carolyn Weiner, Editor. A weekly newspaper.

□*The Jewish Chronicle* welcomes Jewish humor, cartoons, articles on personalities, Jewish Americana, and the Holocaust. Uses photos.

Articles should be less than 3 typewritten pages. Query letters not necessary. Sample copies available. No payment. Reports in less than a week.

JEWISH COMMUNITY BULLETIN, 6505 Wilshire Boulevard, Suite 505, Los Angeles, CA 90048. (213) 852–1234. Manuel Chait, Editor. A weekly newspaper sponsored by the Los Angeles Jewish Federation-Council with a regional circulation of 74,000.

□*Jewish Community Bulletin* is interested in Jewish issues and concerns, Jewish Americana, Israel, the Holocaust, converts to Judaism, Jewish humor and folklore, Sephardic Jewry, book reviews, and photos.

Average length of articles should be from 600 to 750 words. Sample copies available. Pays $25 per article, on publication. Reports as soon as possible.

JEWISH CURRENT EVENTS, 430 Keller Avenue, Elmont, NY 11003. Samuel Deutsch, Editor. A biweekly newspaper.

☐*Jewish Current Events* is interested in "items of Jewish content and/or concern; personalities; achievements, etc." Readers are children, adults, and rabbis. Welcomes material on Jewish Americana, the Holocaust, Israel, Hasidism, Sephardic Jewry, as well as book reviews and photos.

Looking for short pieces. Query letters not necessary. Pays varying rates, on acceptance. Reports in 2 weeks.

JEWISH CURRENTS, 22 East 17th Street, Suite 601, New York, NY 10003. (212) 924-5740. Morris U. Schappes, Editor. A monthly magazine.

☐*Jewish Currents* wants "material with a Jewish focus, expressive of a secular, progressive view of Jewish life and history." Interested in fiction with a Jewish theme and articles on Jewish issues and concerns, Jewish Americana, Israel, the Holocaust, Jewish humor and folklore, Sephardic Jewry, as well as book reviews and poetry.

Articles should be 2,000 to 3,000 words. Query letters desirable. Sample copies available. No payment for material used, but authors get 6 copies of issues in which their work is published and a one-year gift subscription. Reports in 6 weeks.

JEWISH DIGEST, 1363 Fairfield Avenue, Bridgeport, CT 06605. (203) 384-2284. Jonathan A. Levine, Editor. An independent monthly magazine.

☐*Jewish Digest* is devoted primarily to digests of articles from other magazines. Interested in Jewish issues and concerns, Jewish Americana, Israel, Jewish humor, and other subjects.

Copies available on request. Pays for original articles.

JEWISH EXPONENT, 226 South 16th Street, Philadelphia, PA 19102. (215) 893-5700. Al Erlick, Managing Editor. A weekly newspaper published by the Federation of Jewish Agencies of Greater Philadelphia, with a national distribution of 70,000.

☐*Jewish Exponent* is interested in Jewish issues and concerns, personalities, Jewish Americana, Israel, the Holocaust, converts to Judaism, Hasidism, Jewish humor and folklore, Sephardic Jewry. Also prints book reviews and photos.

Average length of articles 500 to 1,000 words. Query letters desirable. Sample copies available. Pays on publication: $35 to $100 per article, depending on length and subject matter. Also see entry for *Friday* of the *Jewish Exponent*.

JEWISH FRONTIER, 15 East 26th Street, New York, NY 10010. (212) 683-3530. Mitchell Cohen, Editor. A monthly magazine published by the American Labor Zionist Movement.

☐*Jewish Frontier* is interested in all aspects of American and world Jewish political and cultural life, with a special emphasis on Israel. Welcomes fiction with a Jewish theme, articles on Jewish issues and concerns, Jewish Americana, Israel, the Holocaust, Jewish humor and folklore, and Sephardic Jewry. Also uses photos and book reviews.

Articles should be 1,500 to 2,000 words, book reviews 800 words. Query letters useful. Sample copies available. "Carefully examines all submissions, whether solicited or not." Pays on publication: $15 for poems, $25 for book reviews, $35 for fiction, $100 for articles. Reports "quickly."

THE JEWISH GUARDIAN, G.P.O. Box 2143, Brooklyn, NY 11202. (212) 384-4661. Pinchus David, Editor. Circulation 10,000.

☐*The Jewish Guardian* is interested in "A) any devout piece with substance, B) anti-Zionist articles with an Orthodox Jewish point of view, C) pieces that are critical of wayward movements in Judaism."

No limit on article length. Query letters desirable. Sample copies available. Pays on acceptance. Reports within 1 week.

THE JEWISH NEWS, 60 Glenwood Avenue, East Orange, NJ 07017. (201) 678-3900. Charles Baumohl, Editor. A weekly newspaper with a national distribution of 28,000. □*The Jewish News* seeks "human-interest features and in-depth articles on subjects of Jewish concern," including Israel, Jewish humor and folklore, the Holocaust, Jewish Americana, and Jewish photographs and artwork. Readers are children, youth, adults and senior citizens, scholars, rabbis, and lay people of all Jewish denominations.

Articles should be 1,200 words on the average; limits are roughly 600 and 2,500 words. Prefers to see complete manuscripts. Sample copies available. Pays $25 to $150 per article, on publication. Reports in 4 weeks.

JEWISH PRESS FEATURES, Jewish Student Press Service, 15 East 26th Street, Suite 1350, New York, NY 10010. (212) 679-1411. Joyce Fine, Editor. □*Jewish Press Features* is a monthly press service that carries "feature articles and investigative pieces on any issue of concern to the Jewish community, for distribution to subscribing Jewish university student and community publications." Interested in articles on personalities, Jewish Americana, Israel, the Holocaust, converts to Judaism, and Sephardic Jewry. Also prints book reviews and photos.

Articles range from 350 to 2,000 words; average 1,000. Query letters desirable. Sample articles available. Pays $15 per book review, $30 per article, on publication.

THE JEWISH QUARTERLY REVIEW, Dropsie College, 250 North Highland Avenue, Merion, PA 19066. A scholarly journal edited by the Faculty of Dropsie College and issued 4 times a year. □*The Jewish Quarterly Review* prints articles and book reviews within the fields of Hebraica and Semitica of purely academic concerns. Interested in the origins of Hasidism and Sephardic Jewry, research related to medieval Jewish history, and poetry. Welcomes articles by scholars wishing to become known.

Average length of articles is 15 pages. Sample copy and author's guidelines available. Query letters desirable. No payment for material used. Reports "anywhere from one day to 3 years." Also accepts advertising. Contact W. R. Johnson, Advertising Manager.

THE JEWISH REPORTER, incorporating *The Stamford Jewish Voice*, Box 3038, 1035 Newfield Avenue, Stamford, CT 06905. (203) 322-6935. Arlene Kay, Contributing Editor. A regional newspaper with a circulation of 4,000. □*The Jewish Reporter* publishes local Jewish Federation and organization news, features about world Jewish communities and personalities, material on Jewish issues and concerns, Israel, arts and crafts.

Articles should be 500 to 750 words. Query letters desirable. Sample copies available. No payment for material used. Reports in 6 weeks.

THE JEWISH STAR, P.O. Box 9112, Birmingham, AL 35213. (205) 956-3929. Margie Rudolph, Editor-Publisher. A monthly newspaper. □*The Jewish Star* is interested in regional and national items relating to Jewish issues and concerns, personalities, Jewish Americana, Israel, the Holocaust, Jewish humor and folklore. Also prints book reviews and photos.

Articles should be no more than 3 manuscript pages. Sample copies available. No payment for material used. Reports "when space is available."

JOURNAL OF PSYCHOLOGY AND JUDAISM, 1747 Featherston Drive, Ottawa, Ontario K1H 6P4, Canada. (613) 731-9119. Dr. Reuven P. Bulka, Editor. A journal published twice yearly with a distribution of about 1,000. □*Journal of Psychology and Judaism* publishes "research findings and theoretical studies on the dialogue and interface of Judaism and psychology." Particularly interested in the Holocaust and in "contributions toward developing a clinical approach consistent with Jewish values." Readers are scholars, rabbis, and general lay readers of all branches of Judaism.

Prefers to see complete manuscripts. Articles should be 12 to 15 pages (5,000 to 7,000 words). Free sample copies are "handled by Human Sciences Press, and are up to their discretion"; author's guidelines are on the inside flap of the journal. No payment for materials used. Reports in 10 weeks.

THE JOURNAL OF THE NORTH SHORE JEWISH COMMUNITY, 140 Washington Street, Salem, MA 01970. (617) 744–5672. Barbara Wolf, Editor. A fortnightly newspaper with a local circulation of 8,000.
□*The Journal of the North Shore Jewish Community* uses local news and features of trends, outstanding pilot programs, political analysis, cartoons, and humor. Interested in fiction with a Jewish theme, articles on Jewish issues and concerns, Jewish Americana, Israel, converts to Judaism, Hasidism, Jewish humor, and Sephardic Jewry. Uses photos.
   Articles range from 500 to 3,000 words; average 2,000. Query letters desirable. Pays on publication: $15 to $60 per article, $5 to $15 per photo. Reports in 4 weeks.

JUDAISM, 15 East 84th Street, New York, NY 10028. Robert Gordis, Editor. A quarterly magazine published by the American Jewish Congress with a national distribution of 4,500.
□*Judaism* carries "discussions relevant to the religious, moral, and philosophical concepts of Judaism and their relevance to the problems of modern society." Interested in fiction with a Jewish theme and articles on Jewish issues and concerns, Israel, the Holocaust, converts to Judaism, Hasidism, Jewish folklore, and Sephardic Jewry. Also prints book reviews and poetry.
   Articles should be not more than 7,000 to 8,000 words. Query letters desirable. Sample copies available. No payment for material used. Reports in 2 weeks.

JWB CIRCLE, 15 East 26th Street, New York, NY 10010. (212) 532–4949. Lionel Koppman, Executive Editor. The magazine of JWB, the Association of Jewish Community Centers, YMHAs and YWHAs and camps in the United States and Canada.
□*JWB Circle* carries feature articles on community projects and programs that involve Jewish community centers, Jewish federations and other agencies; experiences of Jews in the United States; Jewish culture, with emphasis on the performing arts, books, music, films, etc.; the community center movement in Israel, Europe, and South America. Welcomes authoritative articles on trends and their impact on communal agencies such as the Jewish community centers, fiscal management of nonprofit organizations, leadership development, etc. Good photos a must.
   Articles should be 750 to 1,000 words. Query letters desirable. Sample copies available. Payment is the prestige of a byline, plus free copies. Reports in 3 weeks.

KEEPING POSTED, 838 Fifth Avenue, New York, NY 10021. (212) 249–0100. Aron Hirt-Manheimer, Editor. A magazine published 6 times a year by the Union of American Hebrew Congregations.
□*Keeping Posted* is published for youth and adults and written in a popular style. Each issue focuses on a different theme.
   Average article is 2,000 words. Query letters essential; authors should get a list of themes for the year and directions from the Editor. Sample copies available. Pays $100 per article, on publication. Reports within 1 week.

KENTUCKY JEWISH POST AND OPINION, 1551 Bardstown Road, Louisville, KY 40205. (502) 459–1914. Jeff Lebensbaum, Editor. A weekly newspaper.
□*Kentucky Jewish Post and Opinion* is looking for "articles about Jewish people who live in Kentucky, come to Kentucky for some reason and are of interest to Jews locally." National and international news is used, but written elsewhere. The Kentucky edition carries 6 pages of Kentucky news in a 20-page paper. Particular need for sports news.
   Articles should be 500 to 1,000 words. Query letters desired. Sample copies available. Pays guest writers. Reports in 2 weeks.

LILITH, 250 West 57th Street, New York, NY 10019. A magazine for women.
☐*Lilith* is interested in "high-quality, lively writing: fiction, poetry, drama and nonfiction of people, issues, and developments of interest and concern to Jewish women."

Feature articles should be 1,000 to 3,000 words; 1,500 to 2,000 words preferred. Author's guidelines available. Pays $25 to $50 honorarium. Reports "as soon as decision is reached on manuscript."

MENORAH: SPARKS OF JEWISH RENEWAL, 7041 McCallum Street, Philadelphia, PA 19119. Arthur I. Waskow, Editor. A monthly magazine.
☐*Menorah* is looking for "descriptions of creative, innovative Jewish life practices—political, religious, cultural; e.g., a solar 'Eternal Light,' an 'Interfaith Center for Reversing the Arms Race,' tzedakah collectives, new approaches to Pesach, emergence of Jewish dance and body movements." Interested in articles on Jewish issues and concerns, poetry, and illustrations—particularly line drawings for holidays, etc.

Articles average 500 to 1,500 words. Since the paper is typically 8 pages, brevity and vividness are important. Query letters desirable. Sample copies available. No payment for material used. Reports in 2 weeks.

M'GODOLIM, 2921 East Madison Street, #7RWM85, Seattle, WA 98112–4237. Keith S. Gormezano, Editor. A quarterly magazine with a variable distribution of 180 to 200.
☐*M'godolim* prints fiction with a Jewish theme; articles about Israel, Jewish issues and concerns, Jewish Americana, converts to Judaism, and Sephardic Jewry; poetry and Jewish humor. Also prints black-and-white drawings. Readers are scholars, rabbis, and general lay adult men and women of all persuasions—Orthodox, Conservative, and Reform.

Articles should be 400 to 1,000 words. Prefers to see complete manuscripts. Sample copy $2.00. No payment for materials published. Reports in 8 weeks.

MIDSTREAM, 515 Park Avenue, New York, NY 10022. (212) 752–0600. Joel Carmichael, Editor. A monthly Jewish review magazine with a national distribution of 10,000.
☐*Midstream* is interested in articles analyzing political and cultural concerns (past, present, and future) facing Israel and Jews throughout the world, fiction with Jewish themes, Jewish issues and concerns, personalities, Jewish Americana, the Holocaust, converts to Judaism, Hasidism, Jewish humor and folklore, and Sephardic Jewry. Also uses book reviews and poetry.

Average length of manuscripts is 3,000 to 4,000 words. Prefers completed manuscripts. Submissions should be accompanied by a short biographical sketch of the author. Sample copies available. Pays 5¢ per word, on publication. Reports within 2 month.

MOMENT, 462 Boylston Street, Boston, MA 02116. (617) 536–6252. Leonard J. Fein, Editor. Circulation 25,000.
☐*Moment* describes itself as "a magazine of Jewish affairs" and welcomes any submissions of high quality that have Judaic content. Interested in fiction with a Jewish theme, articles on Jewish issues and concerns, personalities, Jewish Americana, Israel, converts to Judaism, Jewish humor and folklore, world Jewry, and poetry.

Articles should be 2,000 to 3,000 words, but length is flexible. Query letters desirable. Sample copies available. Pays $150 to $300 per article, on publication. Reports in 4 to 6 weeks.

NOAH'S ARK, A MAGAZINE FOR JEWISH CHILDREN, c/o 6330 Gulfton, #460, Houston, TX 77081. (713) 771–7143. Debbie Dubin and Linda Block, Editors. A monthly newsmagazine.
☐*Noah's Ark* is used as a supplement to English-language Jewish newspapers and is also mailed directly to individual subscribers and in group orders to religious schools and synagogues. Uses puzzles, games, stories, current events, and other feature

material that appeals to Jewish children and their teachers and parents. "Items should convey information in a fun, easy-to-digest way. No didactic teaching." Looking for short holiday stories. Also, if written for elementary-school-age children, fiction with a Jewish theme, articles on Jewish issues and concerns, personalities, Jewish Americana, Israel, the Holocaust, Jewish humor and folklore, worldwide Jewry, and book reviews.

Prefers articles to be 400 to 600 words. Query letters not required. Pays 5¢ per word. Reports within 1 month.

OMAHA JEWISH PRESS, 333 South 132nd Street, Omaha, NE 68154. (402) 334-8200. Morris Maline, Editor-in-Chief. A weekly newspaper.
□*Omaha Jewish Press* is interested in material of local and regional interest on Jewish issues and concerns, personalities, Jewish Americana, Israel, the Holocaust, converts to Judaism, Hasidism, Jewish humor and folklore, Sephardic Jewry, as well as book reviews, photos and cartoons.

Articles should be 2 to 5 typewritten pages. Query letters desirable. Sample copies available. Pays on acceptance. Reports in 1 month.

OTTAWA JEWISH BULLETIN AND REVIEW, 151 Chapel Street, Ottawa, Ontario, Canada. (613) 232-7306. Cynthia Engel, Editor. A biweekly newspaper.
□*Ottawa Jewish Bulletin and Review* is interested in news feature material of interest to Canadians, dealing with Israel and the Diaspora. Also "occasionally accepts opinion pieces and creative writing." Uses book reviews, poetry, photos, as well as articles on Jewish issues and concerns.

Articles should be 200 to 400 words. Query letters desirable. Sample copies available. Rarely pays for contributions. Reports as soon as possible.

PIONEER WOMAN, 200 Madison Avenue, New York, NY 10016. (212) 725-8010. Judith A. Sokoloff, Editor. The magazine of Pioneer Women/Na'amat, of the Women's Labor Zionist Organization of America.
□*Pioneer Woman* publishes information about the sponsoring organization's work in Israel (day care, vocational training for women, women's rights, community centers, etc.), Israel in general, Jewish issues, worldwide women's issues, occasional fiction with a Jewish theme, articles reflecting the seasons and holidays, and book reviews. Also welcomes articles on women's issues and social issues in the United States, personalities, Jewish Americana, the Holocaust, Jewish humor and folklore. Prints photos.

Average length of articles is 1,500 to 2,500 words. Query letters and manuscripts desired. Sample copies available. Pays 8¢ per word, on publication.

PRESENT TENSE, 165 East 56th Street, New York, NY 10022. (212) 751-4000. Murray Polner, Editor. A 64-page quarterly magazine of world Jewish affairs, sponsored by the American Jewish Committee, with a national distribution of 45,000.
□*Present Tense* deals with Jewish life and features reportage and personal journalism. The primary interest of the magazine is nonfiction articles on Jewish issues and concerns, personalities, Jewish Americana, Jewish humor, and Sephardic Jewry. Well-received articles: "Women Rabbis—How Are They Doing?," "Irving Howe—A Profile," "The World of the Half-Jew." Also prints photos.

Articles should be 1,500 to 3,000 words. Query letters necessary. Sample copies $3.00. Pays $100 to $250 per article, on acceptance. Reports in 4 to 6 weeks. Also interested in reprints.

REFORM JUDAISM, 838 Fifth Avenue, New York, NY 10021. (212) 249-0100. Aron Hirt-Manheimer, Editor. A magazine published by the Union of American Hebrew Congregations with a national distribution of 275,000.
□*Reform Judaism* is interested in articles about Reform Judaism or topics that would be of interest to the movement or its members. Wants articles on Jewish issues and concerns, Jewish Americana, Israel, the Holocaust, converts to Judaism, and Jewish humor.

Articles should be 750 to 1,500 words. Query letters desirable. Sample copies available. No payment for material used. Reports within 1 week.

RESPONSE, 15 East 26th Street, Suite 1350, New York, NY 10010. (212) 679-1411. A quarterly magazine.

☐*Response* publishes "essays that challenge conventional assumptions about American Jewish communal and religious life. Attuned to the arts, havurot, new lifestyles, and emerging Jewish institutions." Interested in articles on Jewish issues and concerns, Jewish Americana, and Israel. Uses book reviews and poetry.

Articles should be 1,500 to 7,500 words. Query letters desirable. Sample copies available. Send SASE with articles. No payment for material used.

RHODE ISLAND JEWISH HISTORICAL NOTES, 130 Sessions Street, Providence, RI 02906. George Kellner, Ph.D., Editor. A yearbook of the Rhode Island Jewish Historical Association.

☐*Rhode Island Jewish Historical Notes* prints articles, most of which are written by persons familiar with Jewish life in Rhode Island. Interested in vignettes of individuals, institutions, living history through tapings, etc., material centered on Jewish life in Rhode Island, Jewish issues and concerns, Jewish Americana, and photos.

No payment for material used.

SHOFAR, 43 Northcote Drive, Melville, NY 11747. Send all manuscripts and correspondence to Alan A. Kay, Ed.D., Editor, 777 Oak Lane, East Meadow, NY 11554. A magazine published 8 times a year for Jewish children aged 8 through 13, with an estimated distribution of 10,000.

☐*Shofar* "is a magazine for children that will heighten Jewish identity and pride, increase the joy of being Jewish, and capture the attention of 8- through 13-year-olds. The subtitle of the magazine—'For Jewish Kids on the Move'—suggests its contemporary format in stories and pictures." Seeks fiction with a Jewish theme, articles about Jewish issues and concerns, poetry, Jewish folklore, personalities, Jewish Americana, short plays on Jewish themes, and puzzles. Readers are of all persuasions.

Articles should be 500 to 750 words. Query letters and complete manuscripts welcome. Free sample copy and author's guidelines available. Pays 10¢ per word (maximum of $150) plus 5 free copies. Reports in 6 to 8 weeks.

THE SOUTHERN JEWISH WEEKLY, P.O. Box 3297, Jacksonville, FL 32206. (904) 355-3459. Isadore Moscovitz, Editor and Publisher. A weekly newspaper with a regional distribution of 28,500.

☐*The Southern Jewish Weekly* prints "news of interest to *Southern* Jewish readers"—lay people of Orthodox, Conservative, and Reform congregations. Interested in fiction with a Jewish theme, Israel, Jewish humor, photos, personalities, and Jewish Americana.

Articles should be 500 words. Prefers to see complete manuscripts. Sample copy available for SASE. Pays $10 to $50 or lifetime subscription, on acceptance. Reports in 1 week.

STUDIES IN BIBLIOGRAPHY AND BOOKLORE, Hebrew Union College, 3101 Clifton Avenue, Cincinnati, OH 45220. (513) 221-1875. Herbert C. Zafren, Editor. An annual magazine.

☐*Studies in Bibliography and Booklore* uses scholarly bibliographical studies and bibliographies for scholars and rabbis. No payment for articles.

THE UFORATZTO JOURNAL, 770 Eastern Parkway, Brooklyn, NY 11213. (212) 778-4270. Rabbi Mayer S. Rivkin, Editor. A magazine issued two or three times a year.

☐*The Uforatzto Journal* welcomes articles on Jewish issues and concerns, Israel, Hasidism, and other Jewish themes.

Articles should be 5,000 words or less. Pays on publication.

VIEWPOINTS, c/o Canadian Jewish Congress, 1590 Avenue Docteur Penfield, Montreal, Quebec H3G 1C5, Canada. (514) 931-7531. Morton Weinfeld, Chairman; William Abrams, Editor. A quarterly magazine, the joint project of *The Canadian Jewish News* and the Canadian Jewish Congress.

□*Viewpoints* "aims to provide a national vehicle for the independent expression of opinion on matters of interest to the Canadian Jewish community. We are open to all viewpoints in Canadian Jewish life. We welcome articles, fiction, and poetry of quality."

Articles range from 2,500 to 4,000 words. Query letters desirable. Sample copies available. Unsolicited manuscripts must be accompanied by SASE. Reports within 2 to 4 weeks.

WESTERN STATES JEWISH HISTORY, 2429 23rd Street, Santa Monica, CA 90405. (213) 450-2946. Norton B. Stern, Editor.

□*Western States Jewish History* is interested in articles on Jews, Judaism, and Jewish communities west of the Mississippi, including Western Canada, Alaska, Hawaii, the Pacific, Mexico and Central America.

Length of articles ranges from 3 to 50 pages. Query letters desirable. Sample copies $5.00. No payment for material used. Reports in 2 weeks.

WISCONSIN JEWISH CHRONICLE, 1360 North Prospect Avenue, Milwaukee, WI 53202. Andy Muchin, News Editor. A weekly regional newspaper.

□*Wisconsin Jewish Chronicle* is interested in material of local and regional interest on personalities, Israel, and Jewish religious and social issues.

Articles should be 750 to 1,000 words. Query letters desirable. Sample copies available. Pays $25 per article, on publication.

YIVO ANNUAL OF JEWISH SOCIAL SCIENCE, 1048 Fifth Avenue, New York, NY 10028. (212) 535-6700. David G. Roskies, Editor. A biennial publication.

□*Yivo Annual of Jewish Social Science* publishes "scholarly studies on Ashkenazic Jewry, the mass immigration from Eastern Europe, the Holocaust." Also interested in scholarly contributions to Jewish issues and concerns.

Articles should be essay-length—15 to 50 typewritten pages. Query letters desirable. No cash payments, but provides 25 free offprints. Reports in 2 months.

YOUNG ISRAEL VIEWPOINT, 3 West 16th Street, New York, NY 10011. (212) 929-1525. Yaakov Kornreich, Editor. A newspaper with a circulation of 35,000.

□*Young Israel Viewpoint* is interested in "pieces on a wide range of Jewish topics to interest a sophisticated audience, securely educated, with an Orthodox lifestyle and outlook." Interested in fiction with a Jewish theme, articles on Jewish issues and concerns, personalities, Jewish Americana, Israel, the Holocaust, converts to Judaism, Hasidism, Jewish folklore, and Sephardic Jewry. Uses book reviews, photos, and poetry.

Articles should be 200 to 400 words, features and fiction, 1,000 words. Query letters desirable. Sample copies available. No payment for material used. Reports in 1 month.

YOUNG JUDAEAN, 50 West 58th Street, New York, NY 10019. (212) 355-7900. Mordecai Newman, Editor. A magazine published 8 times a year with a circulation of 4,000.

□*Young Judaean* welcomes "almost any material of Jewish and/or Zionist interest written on a level understandable and enjoyable for 10- to 12-year-olds." Interested in fiction with a Jewish theme, Jewish issues and concerns, Jewish personalities, Jewish Americana, Israel, the Holocaust, Hasidism, Jewish humor and folklore, Sephardic Jewry, book reviews, photos, and poetry.

Nonfiction articles should be 500 to 1,500 words, 500 to 1,000 words for fiction. Sample copies available for 75¢. Pays $20 to $40 per article, on publication. Reports in 2 weeks. Also interested in reprinting "Jewish material for youngsters, especially that which is related to Israel."

◄PUBLISHERS OF JUDAICA◄

ADAMA BOOKS, 306 West 38th Street, New York, NY 10018. (212) 594–5770. Founded 1983. Esther Cohen, Publisher; Pamela Nelson, Managing Editor. Publishes 6 to 8 books of Jewish interest a year, 60% of them paperbacks.

☐Adama Books seeks to publish "quality books, alternative books that deal with a freedom of thought. We deal with a broadly-based definition of Judaism." Topics of interest include modern Bible studies; Israel; Jewish history, thought, humor, liturgy and prayer; Jewish Americana; the Holocaust; women's rites and rituals; and books of photographs. Audience includes children, youth, adults and senior citizens, scholars, rabbis, and lay readers of all branches of Judaism. Successful titles: *The Shalom Seders,* three alternative Haggadahs in one volume; *Teenagers Themselves; Samed: Journal of a West Bank Palestinian.*

Length of books varies. Prefers to see query letters, outline/synopsis, sample chapters, or complete manuscript, depending on the project. Catalogs available. Query for future needs and interests. Pays standard author's royalty and sometimes advances, on signing. Reports in 4 to 6 weeks.

ALTERNATIVES IN RELIGIOUS EDUCATION, INC., 3945 South Oneida Street, Denver, CO 80237. (303) 758–0954. Audrey Friedman Marcus and Rabbi Raymond A. Zwerin, Editors. Publishes educational materials and 4 to 12 books a year.

☐Alternatives in Religious Education publishes for adults, youth, and children of all Jewish denominations. Seeks "unusual and innovative materials for Jewish educational settings—mini-courses, games, books, ditto paks, teacher materials." Plans to branch out into trade books. Interested in subjects pertaining to the Bible, Hasidism, the Holocaust, Israel, Jewish history, liturgy, and prayer, as well as biographies of Jewish personalities. Successful titles: *The Jewish Family: Past, Present, and Future* by Paulette Benson and Joanne Altschuler (a mini-course); *The Jewish Teacher's Handbook* by Audrey Friedman Marcus; *The Jewish Life Cycle Game* by Nachama Skolnik; *Bible People,* Books One, Two, and Three (workbooks) by Joel Lurie Grisharer.

Length of books varies according to the type of material. Query letters desirable. Prefers finished manuscripts for mini-courses. Wants educationally sound materials that require little editing. Catalogs available. Pays 10% royalty. Reports in 3 months. Also markets tapes and songbooks on holidays, symbols, and Bible heroes and heroines, for which it pays a flat fee or royalty. Also interested in reprinting Jewish children's books.

BANTAM BOOKS, INC., 666 Fifth Avenue, New York, NY 10019. (212) 765–6500. Nessa Rapoport, Editor for Jewish Bookshelf; Grace Bechtold and Brad Miner, Editors for Religion and Inspiration. Publisher of hardcovers and paperbacks; issues several books of Jewish interest and numerous Christian titles each year.

☐Bantam Books' Jewish Bookshelf features books on Judaism, general fiction, and nonfiction. Christian books are nonsectarian and deal with family life and contemporary issues.

Query letters desired, along with sample chapters and outline. Payment rates vary. Reports as soon as possible.

BEHRMAN HOUSE, INC., 1261 Broadway, New York, NY 10001. (212) 689–2020. Neal Kozodo, Editor, The Library of Jewish Studies. Publishes about 22 books a year, 90% of them paperbacks.

☐Behrman House's Library of Jewish Studies is interested in "textbooks for use with students of religious schools or day schools between grades 1 and 12, college texts and collections of primary sources, books intended for use as instructional tools in adult education in synagogues and Jewish community centers, reference books on Jews and Judaism." Subjects of special interest are the Bible; the Holocaust; Israel; Jewish Americana; Jewish history, thought, liturgy, and prayer. Successful titles: *Hebrew and Heritage* by David Bridger; *My People: Abba Eban's History of the Jews,* adapted for religious schools by David Bamberger; *Exploring Our Living Past,* edited by Jules Harlow.

Length of books ranges from 124 to 400 pages. Query letters desirable. Catalogs available. Payment varies; advances negotiable. Reports in 2 to 4 weeks.

BIBLIO PRESS, P.O. Box 22, Fresh Meadows, NY 11365. Publishes adult Jewish women's studies, guides, and books—all nonfiction or monographs.
☐Biblio Press seeks academics and women who know the religious field for assigned research projects on topics where gaps in Jewish women's materials exist. No general religion publications sought—all must be Judaic-centered even when designed for a general market. No poetry or novels. Also sells relevant books of other publishers.

Query first for publication list of 7 books published since 1979. Small press royalty arrangement and/or lump sum on acceptance of manuscript. Also distributes 18" by 24" posters of Jewish women in history, which "we buy from the very few producers of same." Also interested in reprinting biographies or histories of Jewish women.

BLOCH PUBLISHING COMPANY, 19 West 21st Street, New York, NY 10010. (212) 989-9104. Publishes about 15 books a year, half of them paperbacks.
☐Bloch Publishing Company is interested in "all topics for all ages relating to Judaism, with the exception of poetry." Publishes for a wide range of audiences—adults, youth, and children; scholars, rabbis, general lay readers, in all branches of Judaism. Interested in books on the Bible; biographies of Jewish personalities; Hasidism; the Holocaust; Israel; Jewish Americana, history, humor, thought, liturgy, and prayer.

Query letters required. Catalogs available. Pays royalties of 5% to 10%. Reports within 1 to 3 months. Also interested in reprinting books on Judaica.

MARTIN BUBER PRESS—*see* Revisionist Publishers.

CAMBRIDGE UNIVERSITY PRESS, 32 East 57th Street, New York, NY 10022. (212) 688-8885. David Emblidge, Editor. A general trade publisher.
☐Cambridge University Press publishes books about Judeo-Christian religious practice and about other religious traditions. Especially interested in books on the Bible.

Books are usually 200 to 300 pages in length. Pays royalty of 10% of list price.

CARROLL & GRAF PUBLISHERS, INC., 260 Fifth Avenue, New York, NY 10001. (212) 889-8772. Founded 1983. Kent Carroll, Publisher. Publishes 10 Jewish-oriented books a year, 20% of them hardcovers, 80% paperbacks.
☐Carroll & Graf Publishers seeks "quality fiction and history." Successful titles: *Jews Without Money* by Michael Gold, *Justice at Nuremberg* by Robert Conot, *Three Cities* by Sholem Asch. Target audience is adult scholars and general lay readers of mixed Jewish denominations.

Prefers to see outlines or synopses. Catalogs available. No limits to the length of manuscripts. Pays royalty of 6% to 10% and advances on signing. Reports in 4 weeks. Also interested in reprints.

CCAR PRESS, 21 East 40th Street, New York NY 10016. (212) 684-4990. Founded 1889. Rabbi Elliot L. Stevens, Director of Publications. The publishing arm of the Central Conference of American Rabbis, the Press issues 3 to 6 titles a year of Jewish interest, 65% of them hardcovers.
☐The CCAR Press is "the largest publisher of Jewish liturgy in the world. Besides prayerbooks for many occasions, the Press publishes guides to Jewish practice and professional volumes for rabbinical interest and use." Mainly interested in Jewish thought, liturgy, prayer, and guides to practice. Successful titles: *A Passover Haggadah,* illustrated by Leonard Baskin; *Gates of Prayer,* a clothbound prayerbook; *The Five Scrolls,* illustrated by Leonard Baskin. Readers are mainly Reform rabbis.

Prefers query letters or outline/synopses. Sample chapters are "okay, but *no* entire manuscripts." Catalogs available. "We do *not* publish any works in the field of education." Usually pays a flat fee, but royalties are subject to negotiation; also pays advances. Reports in "a few weeks."

CORNELL UNIVERSITY PRESS, 124 Roberts Place, P.O. Box 250, Ithaca NY 14851. (607) 257-7000. Walter H. Lippincott, Jr., Director; Bernhard Kendler, Editor. Publishes some Judaica.

☐Cornell University Press seeks "to publish works of scholarship. We are self-supporting and must publish some books that are income-producers—the more the better. Our favorite kind of book is a sound, responsible scholarly work that appeals to nonscholars as well." Audience includes scholars and general adult readers. Interested in books on Hasidism, the Holocaust, Israel, the philosophy of religion, Jewish history and thought. Successful title: *Judaism and The American Idea* by Milton Konvitz.

Length of books is very flexible, depending on the nature of the subject—usually 70,000 to 100,000 words. Query letters required. Pays on a royalty basis; percentage depends on economic considerations. Range from a waiver of royalties on part or all of first printing to 10% of list price on books of broad appeal. Pays advances if anticipated sales justify them. Initial consideration takes 2 weeks; final report in 3 to 4 months. "In principle, we're interested in reprinting books (in cloth or paperback) in the areas in which we concentrate, when we believe there exists a substantial market for them."

CROWN PUBLISHERS, INC., One Park Avenue, New York, NY 10016. (212) 532-9200. Carole Baron, Editor of Judaica. A general publisher who releases 1 or 2 books on Jewish topics each year, all of them hardcovers.

☐Crown Publishers is interested in Judaica that appeals to a wide variety of adult readers. Subjects of interest include Hasidism; and Jewish Americana, fiction, humor, and thought.

Query letters required. Pays royalties and advances. Reports in 4 to 6 weeks.

JONATHAN DAVID PUBLISHERS, 68-22 Eliot Avenue, Middle Village, NY 11379. (212) 456-8611. Rabbi Alfred J. Kolatch, Editor.

☐Jonathan David publishes books on the Bible, Israel, Jewish Americana, and Jewish humor for an audience of youth, adults, and scholars.

Reports within 4 weeks. Also interested in reprinting "any book suitable for the Jewish market."

DECALOGUE BOOKS, 7 North MacQuesten Parkway, P.O. Box 2212, Mount Vernon, NY 10550. (914) 664-7944. William Brandon, Publisher. A publisher of Judaica.

☐Decalogue Books is interested in history, biography, biblical studies, scholarly works, theology, and reference works. Uses some photos.

Query letters desirable. "All authors are on a royalty schedule." Reports in 8 weeks. Also interested in "books of lasting value that deserve to be reprinted."

DOUBLEDAY & COMPANY, INC., 245 Park Avenue, New York, NY 10167. (212) 953-4648. Robert T. Heller, Executive Editor, Religion Department; Eve Roshevsky, Editor, Jewish and General Religion. A general publisher that issues 8 to 10 books a year on Judaica, most of them hardcovers.

☐Doubleday publishes for a wide audience of children, youth, and adults—scholars, rabbis, and general lay readers. Interested in Bible studies; family celebrations; religious traditions and observances; celebrity biographies and autobiographies; the Holocaust; and Jewish Americana, humor, and fiction. Especially interested in unusual nonfiction material on the Holocaust. Successful titles: *How to be a Jewish Grandmother, Over and Above* by Laura Hobson, *1,000 Questions and Answers about Judaism.*

Length desired: 300-page minimum for fiction, 400 pages and up for nonfiction. Gift or poetry books may be shorter. Catalogs and author guidelines available. Pays advances and royalties. Reports in 3 to 6 weeks.

FAIRLEIGH DICKINSON UNIVERSITY PRESS, 285 Madison Avenue, Madison, NJ 07940. (201) 377-4050. Founded 1967. Harry Keyishian, Editor. A scholarly publisher.

☐Fairleigh Dickinson University Press publishes books in the Littman Library of Jewish Civilization Series. Successful titles: *Survey of Jewish Affairs, 1982; Life and Work of Susan Isaacs; Jews in Black Perspective* by J. R. Washington, *The Exalted Faith* by Abraham IBN David.

Books should be 200 to 500 pages. Query letters or entire manuscripts welcome. Catalogs and author's guidelines available. Pays royalties, no advances. Especially interested in women's studies. Will consider reprints. Reports in 12 to 15 weeks.

FARRAR, STRAUS AND GIROUX, 19 Union Square West, New York, NY 10003. (212) 741-6900. A general publisher.
☐Farrar, Straus and Giroux publishes mostly nonreligious books, but has in the past published books of general interest written from the perspective of a variety of religious faiths.

Query letters not necessary. Catalogs available. Pays on a royalty basis. Reports as quickly as possible.

FLEET PRESS CORPORATION, 160 Fifth Avenue, New York, NY 10010. (212) 243-6100. Susan Nueckel and P. Scott, Editors. A general publisher that publishes an occasional book on Judaica.
☐Seeks materials that appeal to a wide public readership of adults—primarily reference works and history.

Query letters required. Payment varies. Reports in 2 months.

FORTRESS PRESS, 2900 Queen Lane, Philadelphia, PA 19129. (215) 848-6800. Founded 1856. Norman Hjelm, Editor; Jane Stone, Sales Administrator; Hal Rast, John Hollar, and Davis Perkins, Editors. Publishes 10 Jewish-interest books a year, 75% of them hardcovers.
☐Fortress Press publishes biblically-based Hebrew scriptures of the Old Testament for text and studies, as well as Jewish thought and history. Successful titles: *Prophecy and Society in Ancient Israel* by Robert R. Wilson; *History of Israel in Old Testament Times* by S. Herrmann; the Foundations of Judaism Series—*Messiah in Context, Midrash in Context, Torah.* Readers are scholars and rabbis of various branches of Judaism. Specific interests include biblical studies in the Old and New Testaments, early Christianity, Reformation studies, ethics, theology, and critical studies in religion.

Hardcovers should be 300 to 350 pages, paperbacks, 100 to 250 pages. Query letters and outline/synopses preferred. Catalogs available. Also interested in reprints. Reports in 4 weeks.

SAMUEL FRENCH, INC., 45 West 25th Street, New York, NY 10010. (212) 206-8990.
☐Samuel French is a drama publisher interested in both short and long plays, very few religious, none on biblical subjects.

Pays on a royalty basis for both book sales and productions.

HARPER AND ROW, PUBLISHERS, INC., 1700 Montgomery Street, San Francisco, CA 94111. (415) 989-9000. John Loudon, Editorial Manager. A general publisher of religious books, some Judaica.
☐Harper and Row is interested in "mainstream books on Jewish life and tradition, and Bible and Jewish thought that appeal to a broad market." Successful titles: *The Jewish Way in Love and Marriage* by Maurice Lamm, *The Book of Letters* by Lawrence Kushner, *Profiles in American Judaism* by Marc Lee Raphael.

Query letters desirable. Pays advances and royalties. Reports in 1 to 8 weeks. Also interested in reprinting (in trade paperback) strong books with excellent backlist potential.

HARVARD UNIVERSITY PRESS, 79 Garden Street, Cambridge, MA 02138. (617) 495-2600. Maud Wilcox, Editor. Publishes some Judaica.
☐Harvard University Press is "primarily interested in scholarly books for the academic

and serious nonfiction markets." In Judaica, interested in biographies of Jewish personalities, Israel, Jewish history and thought. Successful titles: *Gershom Scholem* by David Biale and *Less Than Slaves* by Benjamin Ferencz, both winners of the National Jewish Book Awards; *Bernard Berenson: The Making of a Connoisseur* by Ernest Samuels; *Einstein: A Centenary Volume,* edited by A. P. Fench.

Query letters encouraged. Catalogs available. Pays on an annual royalty basis.

HEBREW UNION COLLEGE PRESS, Hebrew Union College, Cincinnati, OH 45220. (513) 221-1875. Michael A. Meyer, Editor.

☐Hebrew Union College Press publishes studies in its Monograph Series and works on contemporary Jewish relevance in its Jewish Perspective Series. Target audience includes primarily rabbis and scholars. Interested in books on the Bible; Jewish history, thought, liturgy, and prayer; and "first-rate works of Jewish scholarship." Well-received titles: *From Reform Judaism to Ethical Culture: The Religious Evolution of Felix Adler* by Benny Kraut, *The World of a Renaissance Jew: The Life and Thought of Abraham ben Mordecai Farissol* by David B. Ruderman, winner of the National Jewish Book Award for Jewish History.

Books should be 200 to 500 pages in length. Query letters required. Catalogs available. No payment for material used; author receives free copies of the book. Reports in 6 months.

HOLIDAY HOUSE, INC., 18 East 53rd Street, New York, NY 10022. (212) 688-0085. Margery Cuyler, Editor.

☐Holiday House is interested in children's books.

Query letters desirable. No original art, please. Pays on a royalty basis. Reports in 2 months.

INDIANA UNIVERSITY PRESS, Tenth & Morton Streets, Bloomington, IN 47405. (812) 335-4203. John Gallman, Director; Robert Mandel, Assistant Director.

☐Indiana University Press has embarked on an ambitious program of publishing books of Jewish interest. In the last 2 years, it has published 8 titles, on subjects ranging from the predicament of Jews in wartime Warsaw to the image of Jews in Hollywood films. Several series of Jewish books are planned—on Jewish literature and culture, the modern Jewish experience, and Jewish political and social studies.

Query letters required. Catalogs available. Reports in 3 to 8 weeks.

JETSAND PUBLISHERS, LTD., P.O. Box 17052, West Hartford, CT 06117. (203) 658-1423. Founded 1979. A publisher of Kosher cookbooks, all of them paperbacks.

☐Jetsand Publishers, Ltd.'s successful titles include *Not Chopped Liver! The Kosher Way to Cook Gourmet* and *It's All Fish!*

Audience includes adults and senior citizens of the Orthodox, Conservative, and Reform branches of Judaism.

KAR-BEN COPIES, INC., 11216 Empire Lane, Rockville, MD 20852. (301) 984-8733.

☐Kar-Ben Copies is "looking to expand" its library of modern, creative books for Jewish children and their families on Jewish themes—fiction and nonfiction. Successful titles: *Come, Let us Welcome Shabbat; My Very Own Jewish Home; My Very Own Haggadah.*

Average length of books is from 32 to 48 pages. Query letters desirable. Catalogs available on request. Pays royalties of 5% to 10%. Reports in 30 days. Also distributes calendars, ditto paks, and worksheets, for which a flat fee is paid.

KTAV PUBLISHING HOUSE, 900 Jefferson Street, Box 6249, Hoboken, NJ 07030-7205. (201) 963-9524. Bernard Scharfstein, Secretary-Treasurer. Publishes 30 to 35 Jewish books a year, 80% of them hardcovers.

☐KTAV Publishing House is interested in "the entire gamut of Judaica, from the juvenile to the esoteric," for all ages and all branches of Judaism.

Query letters required. Catalogs available. Rates of payment vary depending on the subject and the manuscript. Reports within 4 weeks. Also distributes stationery, records, and tapes and is interested in reprints.

LITTLE, BROWN AND COMPANY, INC., 34 Beacon Street, Boston, MA 02106. (617) 227-0730. A general publisher.
□Little, Brown is looking for "high-quality books on a wide range of subjects," for audiences of all ages and all types. Submissions only from previously published authors.
  Length of books depends on subject. Novels or major works of nonfiction should be 50,000 words or more; juvenile books shorter. Query letters required; does not consider complete manuscripts. Author's guidelines available. Pays on negotiated royalty basis; advances also negotiable. Reports in 3 to 4 months.

MACMILLAN PUBLISHING COMPANY, 866 Third Avenue, New York, NY 10022. (212) 702-2000. George Walsh, Editor.
□"We are publishers of general trade books, fiction and nonfiction, with both an adult and a children's division." Successful titles: *Jewish History Atlas* by Gilbert, *The Macmillan Bible Atlas* by Aharoni and Avi-Yonah, *The Macmillan Atlas of the Holocaust* by Gilbert.
  Does not accept unsolicited manuscripts.

MICAH PUBLICATIONS, 255 Humphrey Street, Marblehead, MA 01945. (617) 631-7601. Founded 1975. Dr. Roberta Kalechofsky, General and Literary Editor. Publishes 2 Jewish books a year, all of them paperbacks.
□Micah Publications is interested in "the values of scholarship and learning, the rediscovery of language as drama, the creation of usable metaphors for our contemporary world. We regard publishing as a partnership: the writer writes, we publish." Topics include Jewish thought and history. "We are interested in superbly written fiction and scholarly work. We will publish anything that meets these standards, regardless of genre or whether it is religious or not." Well-received titles: *Encounters with Israeli Authors, The Book of Tziril: A Family Chronicle, The Jewish Cat Book—A Different Breed* (though "not our usual kind of publication"). Audience includes scholars, rabbis, and general lay adults of all branches of Judaism.
  Doesn't like "to judge a book by its length, though the economics of publishing make us partial to books around 300 pages." Prefers to see sample chapters. Catalogs available. "Essentially, we break even on our costs, so royalties are simply not within our economic arrangement. Neither do we ever accept subsidies from writers. After expenses are paid off, if there is money made—which is rare—we share it equally." Reports in 3 months.

NIGHTINGALE RESOURCES, Box 322, Cold Spring, NY 10516. Founded 1981. Send submissions to Lila T. Gold. Publishes "no set number" of trade books.
□NightinGale Resources publishes "at this point, facsimiles of documents of history in English with new material written currently establishing the original work in time and place." Successful title: *The Jewish Manual*, a facsimile of the first Jewish cookbook in English, first published in 1846. Readers are "anyone interested in Jewish history."
  Specifically interested in "any topic not hackneyed or worked to dreariness." Query letters desirable. Reports as quickly as possible. Also interested in reprints.

OXFORD UNIVERSITY PRESS, 200 Madison Avenue, New York, NY 10016. (212) 679-7300. Cynthia A. Read, Religious Book Editor. Publishes general trade, scholarly, reference, college and seminary textbooks, and some Judaica.
  Query letters desirable. Send prospectus or table of contents and sample chapters with current résumé.

PAULIST PRESS, 545 Island Road, Ramsey, NJ 07446. (201) 825-7300. Founded 1890. Rev. Kevin Lynch, C.S.P., Editor and President; Donald Brophy, Managing Editor.

Publishes 4 Jewish-interest books a year, 25% of them hardcovers, the rest paperback.
☐Paulist Press publishes books for Jewish and Christian readers interested in knowing and understanding each other's faiths. Subjects of interest include Bible studies, Jewish thought, and Jewish/Christian dialogue books. Successful titles: *Soloveitchik on Repentance*, Pinchas Peli, Editor; *Dictionary of Jewish-Christian Dialogue*, Leon Klenicki, Editor; *Judaism* by Stuart Rosenberg.

Query letters and outline/synopses preferred. Also interested in reprints. Pays royalties, and advances on signing. Reports in 4 weeks.

PHILOSOPHICAL LIBRARY, INC., 200 West 57th Street, New York, NY 10019. (212) 265-6050. Founded 1941. Joseph Sullivan, Editor; Mrs. Rose Morse, Director. Publishes 5 to 10 Jewish books a year, most of them hardcovers.
☐Philosophical Library publishes "mostly philosophy and religious books. No special criteria, all aspects, all religions, all philosophies." Interested in books on Bible studies; Israel; Jewish thought, history, and fiction; the Holocaust; Jewish Americana; and biographies of Jewish personalities. Well-received titles: *Anti-Semitism: Causes and Effects* by Grosser and Halperin, *The Real Jewish World: A Rabbi's Second Thoughts* by Rosenberg, *Special Counsel* by Charney. Audience is scholars and general lay adults of all branches of Judaism.

Finished books should be 128 pages and up. Prefers to see complete manuscripts. Catalogs and author's guidelines available. Payment varies. Reports in 3 weeks.

PROMETHEUS BOOKS, 700 East Amherst, Buffalo, NY 14215. (716) 837-2475. Founded 1969. Paul Kurtz, Editor; Doris Doyle, Trade Editor; Stephen Mitchell, College Editor. Publishes 2 to 3 Jewish books a year, 50% of them hardcovers.
☐Prometheus Books publishes books on philosophy, ethics, humanism, education, and the social sciences. Interested in books on Bible studies, Jewish thought and fiction, the Holocaust, and biographies of Jewish personalities. Well-received titles: *Israel's Defense Line* by I. J. Kennan, *Raoul Wallenberg* by Harvey Rosenfeld, *Humanistic Judaism* by Rabbi Sherwin Wine.

Books should be 200 to 300 pages. Query letters desirable. Catalogs available. Pays royalties of 10% and advances. Also interested in reprints. Reports in 8 weeks.

REVISIONIST PRESS PUBLISHERS (also includes Martin Buber Press), G.P.O. Box 2009, Brooklyn Heights, NY 11202. Bezalel Chaim, Editor. Publishes 14 books a year.
☐Revisionist Press is interested in "Jewish history, especially the Holocaust; Medieval Jewish history; history of the Jewish Khazars; Jewish ethnography and ethnology, cinema, anarchism and individualism; Jewish libertarian socialism; history of the Jews of New York; biography; Jewish history of the modern period; the Jewish existential movement; Jewish pacifism." Successful titles: *The Eclectic Anarchism of Erich Muhsam* by Lawrence Baron, *Revisionist Historians and German War Guilt* by Warren Morris. "We are now beginning an ambitious translation program involving the translation of hundreds of works from Yiddish into English. This is a unique program, and we welcome manuscripts in this area. We also need translations on Jewish subjects from Hebrew, German, French, and Spanish."

Length of manuscripts varies from 60 to 800 pages. Query letters desirable, but not necessary. List of publications available. Pays royalty of 10% of net selling price. Reports in 2 to 3 weeks.

ROSSEL BOOKS, 44 Dunbow Drive, Chappaqua, NY 10514. (914) 238-8954. Founded 1979. Seymour Rossel, President. Publishes 6 to 8 Jewish books a year, 75% of them hardcovers.
☐Rossel Books is "dedicated to servicing the modern Jewish American reading public with trade and textbooks to suit the needs of the community at large." Interested in books on Bible studies; Israel; Jewish thought, fiction, and humor; Jewish Americana; biographies of Jewish personalities; Hasidism; the Holocaust; Jewish history, liturgy and prayer; Hebrew texts for American students; and photos and illustrations. Well-

received titles: *Genocide: Critical Issues of the Holocaust, Torah From Our Sages: Pirke Avot, Promise of a New Spring: the Holocaust and Renewal.* Audience is scholars, rabbis, and general lay readers of all ages, mostly of the Conservative and Reform branches of Judaism.

Children's books should be 48 to 64 pages, adult trade books from 208 to 356 pages. Query letters desirable. Catalogs available. Pays royalties on trade books, flat fees for texts. Also interested in reprints. Reports in 4 to 6 weeks.

SCHOCKEN BOOKS, INC., 200 Madison Avenue, New York, NY 10016. (212) 685-6500. Emile Capouya, Chief Editor; Bonny V. Fetterman, Judaica Editor. Publishes 15 books a year on Judaica.
□Schocken Books publishes books for people interested in Jewish issues and topics, scholars as well as general readers; also course-adoption books. Specific subjects of interest include biblical studies; Jewish history; philosophy and rabbinical thought; biography; Israel and Zionism; the Holocaust and anti-Semitism; Hasidism and mysticism; Jewish life, literature, and culture. Successful titles: *On Being a Jewish Feminist*, edited by Susannah Heschel, and *The Zionist Dream Revisited* by Amnon Rubenstein.

Query letters desired. Pays standard industry scale. Reports within 8 weeks.

SEPHER-HERMON PRESS, INC., 53 Park Place, New York, NY 10007. (212) 349-1860. Samuel Gross, President and Chief Editor.
□Sepher-Hermon Press is interested in "nonfiction works of substance written with a view compatible with traditional Judaism, yet of interest to the intelligent reader of Judaica, regardless of affiliation." Subjects of primary interest are the Bible, biographies of Jewish personalities, Hasidism, the Holocaust, and Jewish history. Audience includes scholars, rabbis, and general adult readers of all persuasions. Looking especially for competent translations of classic rabbinic works from Hebrew. Successful titles: *The Minhagim* by Abraham Chill, *The Jews of Rhodes* by Mark D. Angel, *Gates of Mercy* by Louis E. Kaplan.

Minimum length of books is 150 pages. Query letters required. Catalogs available. Pays on a 10% to 20% royalty basis. Reports in 2 months.

SHULSINGER SALES, INC., 50 Washington Street, Brooklyn, NY 11201. (212) 852-0042. Leah Weinman, Editor. Publishes 4 or 5 books a year, all of them paperbacks.
□Shulsinger Sales is interested in books for youth and children of all branches of Judaism. Especially wants children's books about Jewish holidays. Well-received titles: *Twins Visit Israel, Holiday Fun Book, Holiday Coloring Book.*

Books should be 16 to 48 pages. Catalogs available. Pays on royalty basis. Reports in 1 month.

STATE UNIVERSITY OF NEW YORK PRESS, State University Plaza, Albany, NY 12246. (518) 473-7602. Founded 1965. William Eastman, Editor; Michele Martin, Editor, Jewish Literature Series. Publishes 7 or 8 Jewish books a year in dual editions—both paperback and hardcover.
□SUNY Press publishes scholarly monographs evaluated by an editorial board of scholars. Specific topics of interest include Jewish thought, Hasidism, Jewish history, hermeneutics, mysticism, religion, and literary criticism. Successful titles: *The Slayers of Moses* by Susan Handelman, *At The Crossroads: Essays on Ahad Ha'am* by Jacques Kornberg, *The Jews of Vienna* by Marsha Rosenblit.

Query letters or outline/synopses preferred. Catalogs available. Pays on a royalty basis, no advances. Reports in 12 weeks.

STEIN AND DAY PUBLISHERS, Scarborough House, Briarcliff Manor, NY 10510. (914) 762-2151. Sol Stein, President and Editor-in-Chief; Benton M. Arnovitz, Executive Editor. A general publisher who issues some Judaica and occasionally works with a Christian focus.

☐Stein and Day is interested in a wide range of Jewish subjects, including biographies of Jewish personalities, the Holocaust, Israel, Jewish Americana, fiction, history, humor, and thought. Audience is general adult readers. Successful titles: *The Jewish Mystique, Just Because They're Jewish, The Book of Jewish Lists, Jewish Responses to Nazi Persecution, The Warsaw Diary of Adam Czerniakow, Theomatics, Portrait of Jesus?: The Illustrated Story of the Shroud of Turin.*

Average length of manuscripts is 60,000 to 150,000 words. Query letters required. Pays standard royalties and advances. Reports in 2 to 6 weeks. Also interested in reprinting works "for which we can anticipate a sizable and long-lasting commercial market in trade paperback and mass-market paperback formats."

TEMPLE UNIVERSITY PRESS, Philadelphia, PA 19122. (215) 787–8787. Michael Ames, Editor-in-Chief and Assistant Director. Publishes 2 books a year of Jewish interest, all of them in hardcover, half with simultaneous paperback editions.
☐Temple University Press publishes "scholarly books on social issues, American history, comparative policy, women's studies, ethnic studies, also regional books and photographic books. Topics of Jewish interest include Israel, Jewish Americana, Hasidism, photos and illustrations." Readers are scholars and general lay readers of all branches of Judaism.

Query letters with outline/synopsis and sample chapters preferred. Catalogs available. Pays royalties and occasionally advances. Reports in 6 weeks.

TRANSACTION BOOKS, Rutgers University, New Brunswick, NJ 08903. (201) 932–2280. Irving Louis Horowitz, President. Publishes 12 to 14 books of Jewish interest a year.
☐Transaction Books publishes "primarily on subjects in social science, political science, international relations, anthropology and culture, economics and technology." In Judaica, interested in books on the Holocaust, Israel, Jewish history and thought. Well-received titles: *Taking Lives: Genocide and State Power* by Irving Louis Horowitz; *In God We Trust,* edited by Thomas Robbins; *Studies of Israeli Society,* edited by Ernest Krausz; *Global Economics and Religion* by James Finn; *Mainstream and Margins* by Peter I. Rose; *The Letters and Papers of Chaim Weizmann,* Series B, by Barnet Litvinoff; *Jews in Soviet Culture* by Jack Miller; *Anti-Semitism in America* by Harold E. Quinley and Charles Y. Glock; *Political Theory as Public Confession* by Peter Dennis Bathory.

Books should be from 200 to 400 pages in length. Query letters encouraged. Catalogs available. Payment negotiable. Reports in 2 months. Also interested in reprinting scholarly books on the social sciences and on the sociology and politics of religion.

UNION OF AMERICAN HEBREW CONGREGATIONS, 838 Fifth Avenue, New York, NY 10021. (212) 249–0100. Founded 1883. Aron Hirt-Manheimer, Editor; Steven Schnur, Managing Editor. Publishes 15 books of Jewish interest a year, of which 20% are hardcovers, 80% paperbacks.
☐Union of American Hebrew Congregations publishes books on Bible studies, Israel, and Jewish thought and history. "All materials conform to our religious school and adult series curriculum." Successful titles: *The Torah: A Modern Commentary, Inside the Synagogue, The Jewish Home Detectives.* Readers are children, youth, and adults; both rabbis and general lay readers, of the Conservative and Reform branches of Judaism.

Query letters, outline/synopsis, and sample chapters preferred. Catalogs and author's guidelines available. Specifically needs books for intermediate and high school curriculum. Pays royalties and advances. Also interested in reprints. Reports in 3 weeks.

UNITED SYNAGOGUE BOOK SERVICE, 155 Fifth Avenue, New York, NY 10010. (212) 533–7800. Founded 1913. Dr. Morton K. Siegel, Editor; Joseph B. Sandler, Director. Publishes 5 books of Jewish interest a year, half of them paperbacks.
☐United Synagogue Book Service publishes "volumes which have educational value and reflect the Conservative approach to Judaism." Topics of interest include Bible studies, Israel; Jewish thought, liturgy, and prayer; the Holocaust; Jewish history; and religious school texts in all categories. Readers are children, youth, and adults, both rabbis and general lay readers of the Conservative branch of Judaism.

Length of manuscripts vary depending on the particular topic or objective of the book. Prefers to see outline/synopsis and sample chapters. Pays royalties of 10% or a flat fee, negotiated in each instance.

THE UNIVERSITY OF ALABAMA PRESS, P.O. Box 2877, Tuscaloosa, AL 35486. (205) 348-5180. Malcom M. MacDonald, Director. Publishes the Judaic Studies Series, which focuses on theology and history.
☐The University of Alabama Press is interested in historical, theological, and sociological works of scholarly merit in the areas of American religion and Judaic studies.

Query letters desirable. Catalogs and explicit author guideline available. Pays on a royalty basis. Reports in 6 to 8 weeks. In general, does not seek reprints, "but we would entertain the notion of reprinting a truly fine work in the area of American religious history of Judaic studies."

UNIVERSITY OF CALIFORNIA PRESS, 2120 Berkeley Way, Berkeley, CA 94720. (415) 642-4247. Founded 1893. James H. Clark, Director; Dan Dixon, General Editor. Publishes 6 books of Jewish interest a year, all of them hardcovers.
☐University of California Press publishes "predominantly scholarly books that are subject to preliminary outside review by noted scholars and are then presented for final acceptance to a faculty editorial board of 17 members representing the nine campuses of the University." Topics of interest include Israel, and Jewish thought and history. Successful titles: *Theories of Modern Art* by Herschel Chipp, *Ishi in Two Worlds* by Theodora Kroeber, *The Teachings of Don Juan* by Carlos Castaneda.

Ideal length for manuscripts is 400 double-spaced pages, but acceptable submissions may run from 175 pages to over 1,000, "since our chief criterion is quality." Query letters with outline/synopsis, and sample chapters preferred. Author's guidelines available. Royalty ranges from no royalty on the first printing to 10% on the first 5,000 copies, 12½% on the next 5,000, and 15% thereafter; very seldom pays advances. Also considers reprints. Reports in 12 to 24 weeks.

UNIVERSITY PRESS OF AMERICA, 4720 Boston Way, Lanham, MD 20706. (301) 459-3366. Founded 1974. James E. Lyons, Managing Editor; Elizabeth Carnes, Marketing Manager. Publishes 12 to 18 Jewish-interest books a year, in simultaneous hardcover and paperback editions.
☐University Press of America publishes scholarly books exclusively. Manuscripts are written by recognized authorities, almost entirely academics. Topics include Jewish thought and history. Readers are adult scholars of all branches of Judaism. Successful titles: *Notes on Moral Theology* by Richard McCormick; *Justice and War in the Nuclear Age,* edited by Phil Lawler; *Reformed Faith and Politics,* edited by Ron Stone.

No set figure for length of manuscripts. Query letters preferred. Author's guidelines and catalog available on request. Pays 5% to 15% royalty, depending on quantity of books sold; pays no advances. Also interested in reprints. Reports in 12 weeks.

VANGUARD PRESS, INC., 424 Madison Avenue, New York, NY 10017. (212) 753-3906. Bernice S. Woll, Chief Editor.
☐Vanguard Press is interested in high-quality nondenominational fiction and nonfiction. Successful titles: *The History of Anti-Semitism* by Leon Poliakov, *Yoshe Kalb* by I. J. Singer, *Love and Knishes* by Sara Kasdan. Primary audience is scholars and general adult readers.

Books should be 250 to 350 pages. Query letters required. Pays advances and royalties. Reports in 10 to 12 weeks.

YALE UNIVERSITY PRESS, 92A Yale Station, New Haven CT 06520. (203) 432-4969. Founded 1908. Edward Tripp, Editor-in-Chief; Charles Grench, Editor. Publishes 5 Jewish-interest books a year.
☐Yale University Press publishes "scholarly books for a broad readership." Especially

seeks "strong-selling books." Successful titles: *Chronicle of the Lodz Ghetto* by Lucjan Dobroczyki, *Introduction to the Code of Maimonides* by Isadore Twershy, *Jewish Expression* by Judah Goldin.

Manuscripts should be no longer than 400 double-spaced typed pages, including notes and frontmatter. Query letters preferred. Samples of catalog and guidelines for manuscript preparation available. Pays a royalty of nothing to 15%, usually 5% to 10% of list. Usually pays advances, part on signing, part on acceptance of manuscript. Also interested in reprints. Reports in 4 to 6 weeks.

·FIVE·

Branching Out: Other Opportunities in Religious Publishing

The market for religious writing is rapidly expanding—the opportunities around us are multiplying every day. Three earlier chapters in this book have examined the largest and most obvious fields in some detail. In this chapter, we look at some lesser known (or at least less tried) opportunities. Some are right at your doorstep, in your own community, or in your region of the country; others are in your own denomination or faith group. This chapter is filled with names and addresses of places that need religious writers. Some are bound to fill your needs—or more accurately, perhaps you can fill theirs.

More than that—as you read this chapter, many other places will come to mind as you begin to plan for further expansion of your writing. The field is limited only by your time and energy. We urge you to make the most of your opportunities as a religious writer.

Since the publication of the first edition of *Religious Writer's Marketplace,* several people have written to suggest unusual opportunities for religious publication. Read on!

·WRITING FOR THE LOCAL CONGREGATION·

One obvious, yet often overlooked, writing opportunity available to almost everyone is in the local church or synagogue.

Writing for your local church will give you valuable experience and a chance to make a special gift of your writing talent. Once you start looking, you'll find a wide range of writing opportunities. Your pastor will almost certainly appreciate some help. And you'll gain by building a file of published samples of your work plus some good ideas you can try out in larger (and better paying) markets. The following suggestions from *The Christian Writer's Newsletter,* quoted here, are used by permission of the publisher. The article entitled, "Ten Ways to Write for Your Home Church" is by Barbara Uittenbogaard of Cherry Hill, New Jersey. Consider the following possibilities:

1. Learn speedy, accurate note taking by serving as secretary of your church group. Volunteer to write announcements of the group's activities for the church bulletin.

2. The next time it's your turn to lead the worship service for your circle or Bible study group, use your poems and meditations.

3. Volunteer to substitute occasionally in the church school. Use the opportunity to try out your children's stories or songs and to experiment with craft ideas you can later develop into articles.

4. Direct and produce your own play with a cast recruited from the junior or senior high youth group or a vacation Bible school class.

5. Ask your pastor if you could write prayers for church services. Experiment with prayers of confession and praise and with litanies for special Sundays, such as Mother's Day, or special concerns, such as world hunger.

6. Create a slide show highlighting the history of your church or explaining the religious symbols in the sanctuary.

7. Try writing news articles, feature stories, or book reviews for your church newsletter. If no newsletter exists, volunteer to be the first editor.

8. Study local newspapers to determine the kinds of church events considered newsworthy. Submit press releases and articles accompanied by crisp black-and-white photographs.

9. Write and design a brochure publicizing your church's youth programs or mission work.

10. Learn business and technical writing by helping church-related agencies write proposals and reports.

◄WRITING FOR REGIONAL PUBLICATIONS◄

Another large market that the serious religious writer should investigate are the many regional publications, especially among the major denominations. Usually rather substantial publications, they appear frequently—some are weeklies. All are looking for news and features, and they represent a vast opportunity for the religious writer—right at your doorstep.

Most regional publications do not pay for material used, but some do, and once you become known as a writer in your area, other opportunities will present themselves. Investigate first the papers of your own denomination, as each paper prefers to use people who understand their church and its special needs. These publications are set up to serve a certain area and are interested almost exclusively in stories about people and events in that area; you will want to consider this important fact in writing for them.

The following pages list the area or regional papers of four national church bodies: Roman Catholic, Episcopal, Southern Baptist, and Methodist, which have the largest number of regional publications. Other churches also have regional papers, or regional supplements to their national papers. Send for sample copies and get to work!

◄ROMAN CATHOLIC DIOCESAN PAPERS◄
(listed alphabetically by state and city)

Alabama

ONE VOICE, P.O. Box 10822, Birmingham, AL 35202.
THE CATHOLIC WEEK, P.O. Box 349, Mobile AL 36601.

Alaska

INSIDE PASSAGE, 419 Sixth Street, Juneau, AK 99801.

Arizona

DIOCESE OF PHOENIX NEWSPAPER, 400 East Monroe, Phoenix, AZ 85004.

California

THE TIDINGS, 1530 West Ninth Street, Los Angeles, CA 90015.

THE OBSERVER, P.O. Box 2079, Monterey, CA 93940.
THE CATHOLIC VOICE, 2918 Lakeshore Avenue, Oakland, CA 94610.
DIOCESE OF ORANGE BULLETIN, 2811 East Villa Real Drive, Orange, CA 92667.
CATHOLIC HERALD, 5890 Newsman Court, Sacramento, CA 95819.
SOUTHERN CROSS, P.O. Box 81869, San Diego, CA 92138.
THE MONITOR, 441 Church Street, San Francisco, CA 94114.

Colorado

DENVER CATHOLIC REGISTER, P.O. Box 1620, Denver, CO 80201.
CATHOLIC CROSSWINDS, 1001 North Grand Avenue, Pueblo, CO 81003.

Connecticut

CATHOLIC TRANSCRIPT, 785 Asylum Avenue, Hartford, CT 06105.

Delaware

THE DIALOG, Box 2208, Wilmington, DE 19899.

District of Columbia

CATHOLIC STANDARD, P.O. Box 4464, Washington, DC 20017.

Florida

THE VOICE, 9401 Biscayne Boulevard, Miami, FL 33238.
THE FLORIDA CATHOLIC, Box 3551, Orlando, FL 32802.
SOUTHERN CATHOLIC, 855 West Carolina Street, Tallahassee, FL 32301.

Georgia

THE GEORGIA BULLETIN, 680 West Peachtree Street N.W., Atlanta, GA 30308.
THE SOUTHERN CROSS, 601 East Sixth Street, Waynesboro, GA 30830.

Hawaii

HAWAII CATHOLIC HERALD, 1184 Bishop Street, Honolulu, HI 96813.

Idaho

IDAHO REGISTER, P.O. Box 2835, Boise, ID 83701.

Illinois

THE MESSENGER, P.O. Box 327, Belleville, IL 62222.
THE CHICAGO CATHOLIC, 155 East Superior Street, Chicago, IL 60611.
THE CATHOLIC POST, P.O. Box 1722, Peoria, IL 61656.
THE OBSERVER, 921 West State Street, Rockford, IL 61102.
JOLIET CATHOLIC EXPLORER, Route 53 & Airport Road, Romeville, IL 60441.
TIME AND ETERNITY, 514 East Lawrence Street, Springfield, IL 62703.

Indiana

THE MESSAGE, P.O. Box 4169, Evansville, IN 47711.
THE HARMONIZER, P.O. Box 11169, Fort Wayne, IN 46856.
GARY SUNDAY VISITOR, P.O. Box M–356, Gary, IN 46401.
THE CRITERION, P.O. Box 1410, Indianapolis, IN 46206.
LAFAYETTE SUNDAY VISITOR, P.O. Box 1603, Lafayette, IN 47902.

Iowa

THE CATHOLIC MESSENGER, 201 West Second Street, Davenport, IA 52801.
THE CATHOLIC MIRROR, Box 10372, Des Moines, IA 50306.

THE WITNESS, 1229 Mount Loretta, Dubuque, IA 52004.
THE GLOBE, 1825 Jackson Street, Sioux City, IA 51105.

Kansas

THE SOUTHWEST KANSAS REGISTER, Box 1317, Dodge City, KS 67801.
EASTERN KANSAS REGISTER, 2220 Central, Kansas City, KS 66110.
NORTHWESTERN KANSAS REGISTER, P.O. Box 958, Salina, KS 67401.
THE CATHOLIC ADVANCE, 424 North Broadway, Wichita, KS 67202.

Kentucky

THE MESSENGER, P.O. Box 268, Covington, KY 41012.
THE RECORD, 701 West Jefferson Street, Louisville, KY 40202.

Louisiana

THE CHURCH TODAY, P.O. Box 7417, Alexandria, LA 71306.
CATHOLIC COMMUNICATOR, P.O. Box 14746, Baton Rouge, LA 70808.
THE MORNING STAR, P.O. Box 3223, Lafayette, LA 70502.
CLARION HERALD, P.O. Box 53247, New Orleans, LA 70153.

Maine

THE CHURCH WORLD, P.O. Box 698, Brunswick, ME 04011.

Maryland

THE CATHOLIC REVIEW, 320 Cathedral Street, Baltimore, MD 21203.

Massachusetts

THE PILOT, 49 Franklin Street, Boston, MA 02110.
THE ANCHOR, 410 Highland Avenue, Fall River, MA 02722.
THE CATHOLIC OBSERVER, P.O. Box 1570, Springfield, MA 01101.
THE CATHOLIC FREE PRESS, 47 Elm Street, Worcester, MA 01609.

Michigan

THE MICHIGAN CATHOLIC, 2701 Chicago Boulevard, Detroit, MI 48206.
THE CHALLENGE, P.O. Box 14082, Jefferson Station, Detroit, MI 48214.
THE CATHOLIC WEEKLY, 1628 Lambden Road, Flint, MI 48501.
WESTERN MICHIGAN CATHOLIC, 650 Burton Southeast, Grand Rapids, MI 49507.
UPPER PENINSULA CATHOLIC, P.O. Box 548, Marquette, MI 49855.
THE CATHOLIC WEEKLY, P.O. Box 1405, Saginaw, MI 48605.

Minnesota

OUR NORTHLAND DIOCESE, P.O. Box 610, Crookston, MN 56716.
THE CATHOLIC OUTLOOK, 215 West Fourth Street, Duluth, MN 55806.
ST. CLOUD VISITOR, P.O. Box 1068, St. Cloud, MN 56302.
THE CATHOLIC BULLETIN, 244 Dayton Avenue, St. Paul, MN 55102.
THE COURIER, P.O. Box 949, Winona, MN 55987.

Mississippi

MISSISSIPPI TODAY, P.O. Box 2130, Jackson, MS 39205.

Missouri

THE CATHOLIC MISSOURIAN, P.O. Box 1107, Jefferson City, MO 65102.
THE CATHOLIC KEY TO THE NEWS, P.O. Box 1037, Kansas City, MO 64141.
ST. LOUIS REVIEW, 462 North Taylor Street, St. Louis, MO 63108.
THE MIRROR, M.P.O. Box 847, Springfield, MO 65801.

Montana

EASTERN MONTANA CATHOLIC REGISTER, P.O. Box 2107, Great Falls, MT 59403.
WESTMONT WORD, P.O. Box 1729, Helena, MT 59624.

Nebraska

WEST NEBRASKA REGISTER, P.O. Box 608, Grand Island, NE 68802.
SOUTHERN NEBRASKA REGISTER, P.O. Box 80329, Lincoln, NE 68501.
THE CATHOLIC VOICE, 6060 Northwest Radial, Omaha, NE 68104.

New Hampshire

CONCERN, 153 Ash Street, Manchester, NH 03105.

New Jersey

CATHOLIC STAR HERALD, 1845 Haddon Avenue, Camden, NJ 08101.
THE BEACON, P.O. Box 1887, Clifton, NJ 07013.
THE ADVOCATE, 37 Evergreen Place, East Orange, NJ 07018.
EASTERN CATHOLIC LIFE, 101 Market Street, Passaic, NJ 07055.
THE MONITOR, P.O. Box 3095, Trenton, NJ 08619.

New Mexico

PEOPLE OF GOD, 7208 Arvada Northeast, Albuquerque, NM 87110.
THE VOICE OF THE SOUTHWEST, P.O. Box 7, San Fidel, NM 87049.

New York

THE EVANGELIST, 39 Philip Street, Albany, NY 12207.
THE TABLET, 1 Hanson Place, Brooklyn, NY 11243.
WESTERN NEW YORK CATHOLIC VISITOR, 100 South Elmwood Avenue, Buffalo, NY 14202.
LONG ISLAND CATHOLIC, 115 Greenwich Street, P.O. Box 700, Hempstead, NY 11551.
NORTH COUNTRY CATHOLIC, Box 326, Ogdensburg, NY 13669.
COURIER-JOURNAL, 114 South Union Street, Rochester, NY 14607.
THE CATHOLIC SUN, 257 Onondaga Street, Syracuse, NY 13202.

North Carolina

NORTH CAROLINA CATHOLIC, 300 Cardinal Gibbons Drive, Raleigh, NC 27606.

North Dakota

DAKOTA CATHOLIC ACTION, P.O. Box 128, Williston, ND 58579.

Ohio

CATHOLIC TELEGRAPH, 100 East 8th Street, Cincinnati, OH 45202.
CATHOLIC UNIVERSE BULLETIN, 1027 Superior Avenue Northeast, Cleveland, OH 44114.
THE CATHOLIC TIMES, P.O. Box 636, Columbus, OH 43216.
HORIZONS, 1900 Carlton Road, Parma, OH 44134.
STEUBENVILLE REGISTER, P.O. Box 160, Steubenville, OH 43952.
CATHOLIC CHRONICLE, P.O. Box 1866, Toledo, OH 43603.
CATHOLIC EXPONENT, 315 Ohio One Building, Youngstown, OH 44503.

Oklahoma

THE SOONER CATHOLIC, P.O. Box 32180, Oklahoma City, OK 73123.
EASTERN OKLAHOMA CATHOLIC, Box 520, Tulsa, OK 74101.

Oregon

CATHOLIC SENTINEL, 2816 East Burnside Street, Portland, OR 97214.

Pennsylvania

LAKE SHORE VISITOR, P.O. Box 4047, Erie, PA 16512.
THE CATHOLIC ACCENT, P.O. Box 850, Greensburg, PA 15601.
THE CATHOLIC WITNESS, P.O. Box 2555, Harrisburg, PA 17105.
THE CATHOLIC REGISTER, Box 126C, Logan Boulevard, Hollidaysburg, PA 16648.
THE CATHOLIC STANDARD AND TIMES, 222 North 17th Street, Philadelphia, PA 19103.
PITTSBURGH CATHOLIC, 110 Third Avenue, Pittsburgh, PA 15222.
CATHOLIC LIGHT, 300 Wyoming Avenue, Scranton, PA 18501.

Rhode Island

THE VISITOR, 184 Broad Street, Providence, RI 02903.

South Carolina

THE CATHOLIC BANNER, P.O. Box 5287, Columbia, SC 29250.

South Dakota

WEST RIVER CATHOLIC, Box 678, Rapid City, SD 57709.
THE BISHOP'S BULLETIN, P.O. Box 665, Yankton, SD 57078.

Tennessee

COMMON SENSE, 1325 Jefferson Avenue, Memphis, TN 38104.
TENNESSEE REGISTER, 2400 21st Avenue, South, Nashville, TN 37212.

Texas

WEST TEXAS CATHOLIC, 1800 North Spring, Amarillo, TX 79107.
SOUTH TEXAS CATHOLIC, 1200 Lantana, Corpus Christi, TX 78407.
THE TEXAS CATHOLIC, 3915 Lemmon Avenue, Dallas, TX 75219.
TEXAS CATHOLIC HERALD, 1700 San Jacinto, Houston, TX 77002.
WEST TEXAS ANGELUS, 116 South Oakes, San Angelo, TX 76902.

Utah

INTERMOUNTAIN CATHOLIC REGISTER, P.O. Box 2489, Salt Lake City, UT 84110.

Vermont

VERMONT CATHOLIC TRIBUNE, 351 North Avenue, Burlington, VT 05401.

Virginia

ARLINGTON CATHOLIC HERALD, 200 North Glebe Road, Arlington, VA 22203.
CATHOLIC VIRGINIAN, 14 North Laurel Street, Richmond, VA 23261.

Washington

THE PROGRESS, 910 Marion Street, Seattle, WA 98104.
INLAND REGISTER, P.O. Box 48, Spokane, WA 99210.
CENTRAL WASHINGTON CATHOLIC, P.O. Box 505, Yakima, WA 98907.

West Virginia

THE CATHOLIC SPIRIT, P.O. Box 951, Wheeling, WV 26003.

Wisconsin

THE COMPASS, Box 1825, Green Bay, WI 54305.

TIMES-REVIEW, P.O. Box 937, La Crosse, WI 54601.

CATHOLIC HERALD, P.O. Box 1176, Madison, WI 53701; and P.O. Box 1572, Milwaukee, WI 53201; and 1512 North 12th Street, Superior, WI 54880.

Wyoming

WYOMING CATHOLIC REGISTER, P.O. Box 4279, Casper, WY 82604.

Canada

WESTERN CATHOLIC REPORTER, 10562 109 Street, Edmonton, Alberta T5H 3B2.

BRITISH COLUMBIA CATHOLIC, 150 Robson Street, Vancouver, British Columbia V6B 2A7.

THE NEW FREEMAN, P.O. Box 6609, Street A., St. John, New Brunswick E2L 4S1.

THE MONITOR, P.O. Box 986, St. John's, Newfoundland A1C 5M3.

DIOCESAN NEWS, P.O. Box 1689, Charlottetown, Prince Edward Island C1A 7N4.

THE CATHOLIC TIMES, 2005 St. Marc Street, Montreal, Quebec H3H 2G8.

PRAIRIE MESSENGER, Box 190, Muenster, Saskatchewan S0K 2Y0.

◄EPISCOPAL DIOCESAN PAPERS◄
(listed alphabetically by state and city)

Alabama

CENTRAL GULF COASTLINE, 950 Government Street, Mobile, AL 36604.

THE ALABAMA CHURCHMAN, 27 Four Winds, Northport, AL 35476.

Alaska

THE ALASKA EPIPHANY, 1205 Denali Way, Fairbanks, AK 99701.

Arizona

ARIZONA NEWS, P.O. Box 13647, Phoenix, AZ 85002.

Arkansas

THE ARKANSAS CHURCHMAN, 3609 Meadow Drive, Pine Bluff, AR 71603.

California

SAN JOAQUIN STAR, 4159 East Dakota, Fresno, CA 93726.

THE EPISCOPAL NEWS, P.O. Box 2164, Los Angeles, CA 90051.

PACIFIC CHURCHMAN, 1804 Clemens Road, Oakland, CA 94602.

THE MISSIONARY, 1916 Woodstock Way, Sacramento, CA 95825.

CHURCH TIMES, 2728 Sixth Avenue, San Diego, CA 92103.

THE MISSION BELL, 532 Center Street, Santa Cruz, CA 95060.

Colorado

THE COLORADO EPISCOPALIAN, P.O. Box 18–M, Capitol Hill Station, Denver, CO 80218.

Connecticut

GOOD NEWS, 1335 Asylum Avenue, Hartford, CT 06105.

Delaware

COMMUNION, 2020 Tatnall Street, Wilmington, DE 19802.

District of Columbia

WASHINGTON DIOCESE, Mount St. Alban, Washington, DC 20016.

Florida

FLORIDA EPISCOPALIAN, 12581 Mandarin Road, Jacksonville, FL 32223.
SOUTHERN CROSS, 8550 126th Avenue North, Largo, FL 33543.
THE NET, 525 Northeast 15th Street, Miami, FL 33132.
DIOCESE, P.O. Box 790, Winter Park, FL 37290.

Georgia

DIOCESE, 2744 Peachtree Road Northeast, Atlanta, GA 30305.
EPISCOPAL CHURCH IN GEORGIA, P.O. Box 2205, Savannah, GA 31402.

Hawaii

HAWAIIAN CHURCH CHRONICLE, Queen Emma Square, Honolulu, HI 96813.

Idaho

THE IDAHO MESSENGER, 923 H Street, Rupert, ID 83350.

Illinois

ADVANCE, 65 East Huron Street, Chicago, IL 60611.
ILLINOIS CHURCHMAN, 411 Washington Street, Pekin, IL 61554.
LIGHT, 348½ South 24th Street, Quincy, IL 62301.

Indiana

THE CHURCH MILITANT, 1100 West 42nd Street, Indianapolis, IN 46208.
THE BEACON, 117 North LaFayette Boulevard, South Bend, IN 46601.

Iowa

THE IOWA EPISCOPALIAN, Rural Route, Bondurant, IA 50035.

Kansas

THE PRAIRIE SPIRIT, P.O. Box 1383, Salina, KS 67401.
KANSAS CHURCHMAN, 835 Southwest Polk Street, Topeka, KS 66612.

Kentucky

THE CHURCH ADVOCATE, 530 Sayre Avenue, Lexington, KY 40508.
THE BISHOP'S LETTER, 421 South Second Street, Louisville, KY 40202.

Louisiana

ALIVE!, P.O. Box 4046, Alexandria, LA 71301.
CHURCH WORK, P.O. Box 15719, New Orleans, LA 70175.

Maine

THE NORTHEAST, 143 State Street, Portland, ME 04101.

Maryland

MARYLAND CHURCH NEWS, 105 West Monument Street, Baltimore, MD 21201.
EASTERN SHORE CHURCHMAN, Box 11, Church Hill, MD 21623.

Massachusetts

EPISCOPAL TIMES, 1 Joy Street, Boston, MA 02108.
THE PASTORAL STAFF, 37 Chestnut Street, Springfield, MA 01103.

Michigan

WESTERN MICHIGAN CHURCHMAN, 2600 Vincent Avenue, Kalamazoo, MI 49008.
THE RECORD, 4800 Woodward Avenue, Detroit, MI 48201.
THE CHURCH IN HIAWATHALAND, 322 South 5th Street, Escanaba, MI 49829.

Minnesota

SOUNDINGS, 309 Clifton Avenue South, Minneapolis, MN 55403.

Mississippi

THE CHURCH NEWS, P.O. Box 1636, Jackson, MS 39205.

Missouri

THE DIOCESAN BULLETIN, Box 23216, Kansas City, MO 64141.
INTERIM, 1210 Locust Street, St. Louis, MO 63103.

Montana

THE EPISCOPAL EVANGEL, 515 North Park Avenue, Helena, MT 59601.

Nebraska

THE NEBRASKA CHURCHMAN, 924 Elm, Gordon, NE 69343.

Nevada

THE DESERT CHURCHMAN, P.O. Box 1807, Elko, NV 89801.

New Hampshire

NEW HAMPSHIRE CHURCHMAN, P.O. Box 108, Milford, NH 03055.

New Jersey

THE VOICE, 24 Rector Street, Newark, NJ 07102.
THE CHURCH NEWS, 808 West State Street, Trenton, NJ 08618.

New Mexico

THE RIO GRANDE EPISCOPALIAN, P.O. Box 6068, Santa Fe, NM 87502.

New York

THE ALBANY CHURCHMAN, 19 Stonybrook Road, Rexford, NY 12148.
EPISCOPAL CHURCHFACTS, 1114 Delaware Avenue, Buffalo, NY 14209.
TIDINGS, 36 Cathedral Avenue, Garden City, NY 11530.
THE EPISCOPAL NEW YORKER, 1047 Amsterdam Avenue, New York, NY 10025.
DIOCESE, 935 East Avenue, Rochester, NY 14607.
THE MESSENGER, 310 Montgomery Street, Syracuse, NY 13202.

North Carolina

THE HIGHLAND CHURCHMAN, Box 5074, Asheville, NC 28803.
THE COMMUNICANT, P.O. Box 17025, Raleigh, NC 27619.
CROSS CURRENT, RD 2, Box 27, Williamston, NC 27892.

North Dakota

THE SHEAF, 2315 North University Drive, Fargo, ND 58102.

Ohio

INTERCHANGE, 412 Sycamore Street, Cincinnati, OH 45202.
CHURCH LIFE, 2230 Euclid Avenue, Cleveland, OH 44115.

Oklahoma

OKLAHOMA'S MISSION, P.O. Box 1098, Oklahoma City, OK 73101.

Oregon

OREGON EPISCOPAL CHURCHMAN, P.O. Box 467, Lake Oswego, OR 97034.
OREGON TRAIL CHURCHMAN, Box 1648, Nyssa, OR 97913.

Pennsylvania

NEWSBEAT, 826 Delaware Avenue, Bethlehem, PA 18015.
FORWARD, 145 West 6th Street, Erie, PA 16501.
THE CHURCHMAN, 221 North Front Street, Harrisburg, PA 17108.
DIOCESAN NEWS, 1930 Chestnut Street, Philadelphia, PA 19103.
NEWSLETTER, 325 Oliver Avenue, Pittsburgh, PA 15222.

Rhode Island

THE RHODE ISLAND CHURCHMAN, 275 North Main Street, Providence, RI 02903.

South Carolina

PIEDMONT CHURCHMAN, P.O. Box 1789, Columbia, SC 29202.
JUBILATO DEO, 3212 Seabrook Island Road, St. John's Island, SC 29455.

South Dakota

SOUTH DAKOTA EPISCOPAL CHURCH NEWS, Box 367, McLaughlin, SD 57642.

Tennessee

TENNESSEE CHURCHMAN, P.O. Box 3553, Knoxville, TN 37917.

Texas

EPISCOPAL CHURCHMAN, 1630 North Garrett Avenue, Dallas, TX 75206.
THE TEXAS CHURCHMAN, P.O. Box 44, Friendswood, TX 77546.
THE ADVENTURE, P.O. Box 1067, Lubbock, TX 79408.
THE CHURCH NEWS, Box 6885, San Antonio, TX 78209.

Utah

DIOCESAN DIALOGUE, 1710 Foothill Drive, Salt Lake City, UT 84108.

Vermont

THE MOUNTAIN ECHO, P.O. Box 3, Greensboro, VT 05841.

Virginia

JAMESTOWN CHURCHMAN, 600 Talbot Hall Road, Norfolk, VA 23505.
THE VIRGINIA CHURCHMAN, 110 West Franklin Street, Richmond, VA 23220.
THE SOUTHWESTERN EPISCOPALIAN, P.O. Box 2279, Roanoke, VA 24009.

Washington

OLYMPIA CHURCHMAN, P.O. Box 12126, Seattle, WA 98102.
COLUMBIA CHURCHMAN, North 4734 Driscoll Boulevard, Spokane, WA 99208.

West Virginia

MOUNTAIN DAYSPRING, 206 East Second Street, Weston, WV 26452.

Wisconsin

FOND DU LAC CLARION, P.O. Box 149, Fond du Lac, WI 54935.
THE MILWAUKEE CHURCHMAN, W207–56910 High Bluff Drive, Muskego, WI 53150.
THE HERALD, Box 477, Rice Lake, WI 54868.

Wyoming

THE WYOMING CHURCHMAN, P.O. Box 874, Newcastle, WY 82701.

SOUTHERN BAPTIST
◄STATE AND REGIONAL PAPERS◄
(listed alphabetically by state)

Alabama

ALABAMA BAPTIST, 3310 Independence Drive, Birmingham, AL 35209.

Alaska

ALASKA BAPTIST MESSENGER, Star Route "A," Box 1791, Anchorage, AK 99507.

Arizona

BAPTIST BEACON, 400 West Camelback Road, Phoenix, AZ 85013.

Arkansas

ARKANSAS BAPTIST NEWSMAGAZINE, Box 525, Little Rock, AR 72203.

California

CALIFORNIA SOUTHERN BAPTIST, P.O. Box 5168, Fresno, CA 93755.

Colorado

ROCKY MOUNTAIN BAPTIST, 7393 South Alton Way, Englewood, CO 80112.

District of Columbia

CAPITOL BAPTIST, 1628 16th Street N.W., Washington, DC 20009.

Florida

FLORIDA BAPTIST WITNESS, 1230 Hendricks Avenue, Jacksonville, FL 32207.

Georgia

CHRISTIAN INDEX, 2930 Flowers Road, South Atlanta, GA 30341.

Hawaii

HAWAII BAPTIST, 2042 Vancouver Drive, Honolulu, HI 96822.

Illinois

ILLINOIS BAPTIST, P.O. Box 3486, Springfield, IL 62708.

Indiana

INDIANA BAPTIST, P.O. Box 24038, Indianapolis, IN 46224.

Iowa

IOWA SOUTHERN BAPTIST NEWS, 2400 86th Street, Des Moines, IA 50322.

Kansas
BAPTIST DIGEST, 5410 West 7th, Topeka, KS 66606.

Kentucky
WESTERN RECORDER, Box 43401, Middletown, KY 40243.

Louisiana
BAPTIST MESSAGE, Box 311, Alexandria, LA 71301.

Maryland
MARYLAND BAPTIST, 1313 York Road, Lutherville, MD 21093.

Massachusetts
NEW ENGLAND BAPTIST, P.O. Box 688, 5 Oak Avenue, Northboro, MA 01532.

Michigan
MICHIGAN BAPTIST ADVOCATE, 15635 West Twelve Mile Road, Southfield, MI 48076.

Minnesota
MINNESOTA-WISCONSIN SOUTHERN BAPTIST, 519 16th Street S.E., Rochester, MN 55901.

Mississippi
BAPTIST RECORD, P.O. Box 530, Jackson, MS 39205.

Missouri
WORD AND WAY, 400 East High, Jefferson City, MO 65101.

Nevada
NEVADA BAPTIST, 895 North Center Street, Reno, NV 89501.

New Mexico
BAPTIST NEW MEXICAN, Box 485, Albuquerque, NM 87103.

New York
NEW YORK BAPTIST, 500 South Salina Street, Syracuse, NY 13202.

North Carolina
BIBLICAL RECORDER, P.O. Box 26568, Raleigh, NC 27611.

Ohio
OHIO BAPTIST MESSENGER, 1680 EAST BROAD, COLUMBUS, OH 43203.

Oklahoma
BAPTIST MESSENGER, 1141 North Robinson, Oklahoma City, OK 73103.

Oregon
NORTHWEST BAPTIST WITNESS, 1033 North 6th Avenue, Portland, OR 97232.

Pennsylvania
PENN-JERSEY BAPTIST, 4620 Fritchey Street, Harrisburg, PA 17109.

South Carolina

BAPTIST COURIER, P.O. Box 2168, Greenville, SC 29602.

South Dakota

NORTHERN PLAINS NEWS, P.O. Box 1278, Rapid City, SD 57709.

Tennessee

BAPTIST AND REFLECTOR, P.O. Box 347, Brentwood, TN 37027.

Texas

BAPTIST STANDARD, P.O. Box 226330, Dallas, TX 75222.

Utah

UTAH-IDAHO SOUTHERN BAPTIST WITNESS, 8649 South 1300 East, Sandy, UT 84092.

Virginia

RELIGIOUS HERALD, P.O. Box 8377, Westhampton Station, Richmond, VA 23226.

West Virginia

SOUTHERN BAPTIST IN WEST VIRGINIA, 801 Sixth Avenue, St. Albans, WV 25177.

◄UNITED METHODIST REGIONAL PAPERS◄
(listed by geographical jurisdictions)

North Central Jurisdiction

CENTRAL ILLINOIS UNITED METHODIST, P.O. Box 2050, Bloomington, IL 61701.
DIMENSIONS, 518 Lewis Street, Burlington, WI 53105.
EAST OHIO TODAY, 29 East Main Street, Dalton, OH 44618.
HAWKEYE UNITED METHODIST, 1019 Chestnut Street, Des Moines, IA 50309.
HOOSIER UNITED METHODIST, 1100 West 42nd Street, Indianapolis, IN 46208.
MICHIGAN CHRISTIAN ADVOCATE, 316 Springbrook Avenue, Adrian, MI 49221.
MINNESOTA UNITED METHODIST, 122 West Franklin Avenue, Room 400,
     Minneapolis, MN 55404.
NORTHERN ILLINOIS UNITED METHODIST, 77 West Washington Street, Room 1806,
     Chicago, IL 60602.
THE PRAIRIE FLAME, 1721 South University, Fargo, ND 58103.
WEST OHIO NEWS, 471 East Broad Street, Suite 1106, Columbus, OH 43215.

Northeastern Jurisdiction

CENTRAL NEW YORK UNITED METHODIST, 210 Hill Street, Chittenango, NY 13037.
CIRCUIT RIDER, 5124 Greenwich Avenue, Baltimore, MD 21229.
EASTERN PENNSYLVANIA UNITED METHODIST, P.O. Box 820, Valley Forge, PA 19482.
THE LINK, 900 South Arlington Avenue, Room 112, Harrisburg, PA 17109.
MAINE UNITED METHODIST, P.O. Box 277, Winthrop, ME 04364.
NEW YORK NEWS, 30 Reid Avenue, Port Washington, NY 11050.
NORTHERN NEW YORK UNITED METHODIST, 129 Madison Avenue, Watertown,
     NY 13601.
PENINSULA UNITED METHODIST COMMUNICATOR, 139 North State Street, Dover,
     DE 19901.
SOUTHERN NEW ENGLAND REPORTER, 566 Commonwealth Avenue, Boston,
     MA 02215.
UNITED METHODIST RELAY, 21 North Main Street, Cranbury, NJ 08512.
THE VOICE, 3 Orchard Road, Binghamton, NY 13905.

WEST VIRGINIA UNITED METHODIST, P.O. Box 2313, Charleston, WV 25328.
WESTERN NEW YORK CONFERENCE COMMUNICATOR, 8499 Main Street, Buffalo, NY 14221.
WESTERN PENNSYLVANIA UNITED METHODIST, 223 Fourth Avenue, 2nd Floor, Pittsburgh, PA 15222.
ZION'S HERALD, United Methodist Center, 566 Commonwealth Avenue, Boston, MA 02215.

South Central Jurisdiction

ARKANSAS UNITED METHODIST, P.O. Box 3547, Little Rock, AR 72203.
CENTRAL TEXAS METHODIST, 1600 Thomas Place, Fort Worth, TX 76107.
CONTACT, 2420 North Blackwelder, Oklahoma City, OK 73106.
CROSSFIRE, 151 North Volutsia, Wichita, KS 67214.
INTERCHANGE, P.O. Box 4187, Topeka, KS 66604.
LOUISIANA UNITED METHODIST, P.O. Box 3057, Baton Rouge, LA 70821.
MISSOURI EAST UNITED METHODIST, 4625 Lindell Boulevard, Suite 424, St, Louis, MO 63108.
MISSOURI WEST METHODIST, 1512 Van Brunt Boulevard, Kansas City, MO 64127.
NEBRASKA MESSENGER, P.O. Box 4553, Lincoln, NE 68504.
NEW MEXICO UNITED METHODIST, 209 San Pedro, NE, Albuquerque, NM 87108.
NORTH TEXAS METHODIST, 1928 Ross Avenue, Dallas, TX 75201.
NORTHWEST TEXAS METHODIST, 1415 Avenue M, Lubbock, TX 79401.
OKLAHOMA INDIAN MISSIONARY ADVOCATE, P.O. Box 60428, Oklahoma City, OK 73146.
REPORTERO [Spanish language], P.O. Box 28098, San Antonio, TX 78284.
SOUTHWEST TEXAS METHODIST, P.O. Box 28090, San Antonio, TX 78284.
TEXAS METHODIST, 5215 South Main Street, Houston, TX 77002.

Southeastern Jurisdiction

FLORIDA UNITED METHODIST, P.O. Box 3767, Lakeland, FL 33802.
HOLSTON UNITED METHODIST, P.O. Box 1178, Johnson City, TN 37601.
KENTUCKY UNITED METHODIST, P.O. Box 5107, Lexington, KY 40555.
LOUISVILLE UNITED METHODIST, 1115 South Fourth Street, Louisville, KY 40203.
MEMPHIS UNITED METHODIST, 575 Lambuth Boulevard, Jackson, TN 38301.
MISSISSIPPI UNITED METHODIST ADVOCATE, P.O. Box 1093, Jackson, MS 39205.
NORTH CAROLINA CHRISTIAN ADVOCATE, P.O. Box 508, Greensboro, NC 27402.
SOUTH CAROLINA UNITED METHODIST ADVOCATE, 4908 Colonial Drive, Room 207, Columbia, SC 29203.
TENNESSEE UNITED METHODIST, P.O. Box 120607, Nashville, TN 37212.
UNITED METHODIST CHRISTIAN ADVOCATE, 909 Ninth Avenue West, Birmingham, AL 35204.
VIRGINIA ADVOCATE, P.O. Box 11367, Richmond, VA 23230.
WESLEYAN CHRISTIAN ADVOCATE, P.O. Box 54455, Atlanta, GA 30308.

Western Jurisdiction

CALIFORNIA-NEVADA UNITED METHODIST, 231 West Myrtle Street, Hanford, CA 93230.
CIRCUIT WEST, 2076 230th Street, Torrance, CA 90501.
GREAT LAND NEWSCACHE UNITED METHODIST, 3421 Perenosa Bay Drive, Anchorage, AK 99502.
NORTHWEST UNITED METHODIST, 2729 72nd Southeast, Mercer Island, WA 98040.
ROCKY MOUNTAIN UNITED METHODIST, 2200 South University Boulevard, Denver, CO 80210.
THE UNITED METHODIST, 1505 Southwest 18th Avenue, Portland, OR 97201.
YELLOWSTONE UNITED METHODIST, 1307 Cherry Drive, Bozeman, MT 59715.

◄WRITING FOR NONPROFIT ORGANIZATIONS◄

Many nonprofit, charitable organizations in every community have a religious sponsor or orientation. Most need help preparing materials for their members, writing promotional material, and getting the word out to the media about their organizations. Nonprofit organizations represent another opportunity to do religious writing.

The author of this book has written for several such organizations and is currently involved with at least three of them. Here is one suggestion of what can be done. Recently, a friend recommended me to the John Milton Society for the Blind to help put together a pamphlet on the Bible and blindness. After I had done this one task for them, they also asked me to prepare a brochure on Helen Keller's religious faith, in anticipation of the celebration of the 100th anniversary of her birth. (She was one of the founders of the Society and was its president for 30 years—two facts the Society wanted to emphasize during the anniversary celebration.)

In the process, the Society also came up with the idea of writing a story for magazines on Miss Keller's Christian faith. They sent this story to several publications; many used it in part or whole. Many of the publications that used the story do not pay for submissions and were happy to get this article from the John Milton Society.

After I finished the story, the Society asked me to search their files and old minutes for vignettes on Miss Keller and her faith that would be suitable as filler in other publications. These reached an even wider audience. In addition, my association with the Society has stimulated my interest in religious work with the blind, and I have written two other stories on blindness that have been accepted by magazines.

Why not scour your town for such groups and offer them your services as a writer? They may not pay you at first, or they may pay very little, but such groups are used to paying for professional services and are very much in need of writers. Whether you get paid or not, the rewards that come from doing something for a worthwhile cause are great—and you do get your name in print. Try it!

◄MARKETING RELIGIOUS POETRY◄

Because marketing religious poetry is different in many respects from marketing other kinds of writing, it seems appropriate to have a separate section in this chapter to deal with this subject.

In poetry writing, financial rewards are small and recognition is hard to come by. Therefore, it is essential that you not waste your time, effort, and money on futile submissions.

As you study the entries in Chapters Two, Three, and Four you will note dozens of publishers that consider poetry for publication. You will, likewise, find some entries that say that no poetry is accepted. Follow these instructions carefully.

If you are serious about getting your poetry published, you will want to do more than simply study these entries and then submit your work. You will want to get some of the literature that gives instruction on poetry marketing and lists the places where it may be submitted. One recent book you will want to consider purchasing is *The Poet's Marketplace* by Joseph J. Kelly, published by Running Press, 125 South 22nd Street, Philadelphia, PA 19103 ($9.95). This book lists more than 400 little magazines, chapbook publishers, literary reviews, university presses, and major book publishers that accept poetry. Entries tell you exactly what each publisher is looking for. In addition, a chapter lists contests for poets, societies where poets may receive marketing help, and grants available to poets.

Two other books are highly recommended: *The Poet's Handbook* by Judson Jerome, Writer's Digest Books, Cincinnati, OH 45242 ($10.95) for its practical help in all aspects of poetry writing and marketing; and *Pathways for the Poet* by Viola Jacobsen Berg, published by Mott Media, Milford, MI 48042 ($9.95) for its specific help for religious poets.

You will want to investigate poetry associations such as the American Poetry Association, Dept. RW–85, Box 2279, Santa Cruz, CA 95063. They sponsor an annual poetry contest and also periodically publish a volume of religious poetry, *Words of Praise,* on an invitational basis. A great many of the poets they publish in other anthologies are also concerned with religious themes.

You will want to watch for announcements of poetry contests in various newsletters and magazines for writers such as *The Writer* and *Writer's Digest,* as well as in other religious sources.

Christian poets will want to join the Society of Christian Poets, Box 214, Van Buren, AR 72956. This association has a monthly newsletter, runs regular contests for poets, and publishes an annual report that lists dozens of marketing sources for poetry that you will find nowhere else. In addition, membership in the society gives you regular contact with Christian poets in all parts of the country.

In order to give religious poets additional information and inspiration for marketing their work, we asked Patti Garr, the founder of the Society of Christian Poets, to give us some information on the marketing of religious poetry. Her words follow here:

"The demand for religious poetry is on the increase. A search for serenity by many people is the thrust and motivation behind its growing popularity. The door was opened hundreds of years ago by a psalmist named David and carried on through the intervening years by a long succession of poets moved by God to write. Learning how to take advantage of the new interest in poetry is necessary in order to reach the market that is all around us.

"Getting published in local newsletters, bulletins, and newspapers should be your first step; therefore, your immediate area is the place to start. Begin in your own back yard.

"Newspapers are usually the best stepping stone for beginning poets, since their guidelines and needs are not as limited as those of other publications. Literary publications should also be considered. These often use much poetry. They usually pay only in free copies, but it is a start.

"Large commercial magazines use some poetry as well, but usually vague or faddish verse. However, you might want to try to get your foot in the editorial door with some seasonal submissions here. Short fillers written in poetic fashion are also a possibility.

"Religious magazines are probably your best bet. Search the entries in this volume, and consult the indexes to find those that will accept poetry. Be sure to consider their desires concerning the type of poetry published. One of the best poetry columns currently being published in religious magazines is called 'Quiet Heart' and appears regularly in *Decision Magazine.*

"Religious poets will not want to limit their submissions to religious magazines. Writing fine adaptable-line poetry geared to all types of readers through secular publications is an important ministry.

"Poets should continue to develop their own inner resources. Encouragement from organizations that motivate is important as well. Join a critique group of religious writers and continue your education in writing good poetry. Stress the positive things in your career and capitalize on past victories by adapting these methods to win at future efforts."

◄CREATING CARTOONS AND CARTOON ARTICLES◄

by Larry Neagle, *cartoonist and author, Fort Worth, Texas*

Cartoons! What do you think of when you see that word?

Most of us think of our favorite newspaper comic strip, or of the comic books our kids leave in the worst places, or of those one-shot boosts of mirth found in many magazines, or of Walt Disney-type animation on the screen.

All of these can be good fun; but the Christian writer with cartooning ability ought to see something else—a chance to retread research material through cartoons and cartoon articles.

I chanced upon the benefits of cartoons almost 10 years ago. Toward the middle of the year, I received the acceptance letter for my ninth published article. Somewhat over 40 hours of work on a 1,200 word piece had just netted me the sum of "free gratis." Somehow the per-hour return there left something to be desired. There had to be a way to turn all that work into income!

I thought I knew what it was. Earlier that year, I'd seen a two-page article in a Sunday School magazine. It consisted of six cartoons, each with a small amount of text, built around the idea of "How to Goof at Giving a Lecture." It had looked like something to consider, so I'd saved it. Maybe I could do something like that with my as-yet-unrewarded labor—a how-to on time management for minsters.

I pulled the article from my files and studied it. Here's the form that emerged: six points, minimally worded, stated backwards (with "pay attention to audience reaction" becoming "ignoring audience reaction"), each illustrated with a simple but funny cartoon.

I'm not a great artist. And to do a successful cartoon or cartoon article, you needn't be either. The two keys are an idea and humor. The idea I had for my first try is stated above. The humor was somewhat harder. What's funny to one person is not always funny to another. During the years I have learned to rely on eight devices for humor: satire, fantasy, exaggeration, reverse ideas, unusual use of an object, understatement, balloon-busting, and sarcasm. There are many examples of each of these ideas in my cartoons.

The form for submission I worked out on my own. I decided to use a separate page for each step, with a cartoon rough idea and a text on each page. I used a cover page for the necessities of name, address, title, and rights being sold.

Finding markets was not hard. I went through my market guides (such as the one you hold in your hands) looking for magazines that would be interested in *both* my subject *and* in cartoons. From there I went to sample copies to get a feel of the magazines' personalities. Then I wrote query letters.

After a few hours of work, my time management research became "How to Waste Time in the Ministry." The first place that I sent it, *Church Management: The Clergy Journal,* bought it. Since then, my work has been a regular feature of their magazine. In addition, I have sold more than 130 other cartoon articles to such periodicals as *The Alliance Teacher, Church Training, The Deacon, Freeway, Hicall, Lighted Pathway, Looking Ahead, Pentecostal Conquerors, Triumph,* and *Young Salvationist.* Some were slanted to ministers, others to Sunday School workers, still others to youth.

What about pay? I've received as little as $15, and as much as $250 for one submission. The average is around $75—not bad dividends for retreaded research material!

◄WRITING GREETING CARDS►

Many religious writers have found greeting cards a good market for their talents. Cards are a means of expressing not only the sender's love, but also God's love to the recipient. Several companies specialize in religious cards, and many general publishers use religious messages and verse for special occasions.

Stores indicate that customers are looking for cards that communicate concern for others, that contain a meaningful message and have a freshness of appearance. Religious and inspirational cards are definitely a part of this market.

If you plan to write for the greeting card market, study publishers' needs carefully and request their instructions about how to submit your material. These differ greatly. The National Association of Greeting Card Publishers, however, gives the following general guidelines: Verses and messages should be typed, double-spaced, each one on a 3" by 5" or 4" by 6" card. Use only one side of the card, and be sure to put your name and address in the upper left-hand corner. Keep a copy of any verse or idea you send. (It's also advisable to keep a record of what you've submitted to each publisher.)

Always enclose a SASE, and do not send out more than ten verses or ideas in a group to any one publisher.

The National Association of Greeting Card Publishers issues a booklet for freelancers, *Artists and Writers Market List,* with the names, addresses, and editorial guidelines of greeting card companies. Sending a self-addressed stamped envelope to the Association at 600 Pennsylvania Avenue S.E., #300, Washington, DC 20003.

You may also want to study this market further by getting one of the following books that have been prepared for greeting card writers: *A Guide to Greeting Card Writing* edited by Larry Sandman, published by Writer's Digest Books (Cincinnati); or *Writing and Selling Greeting Cards* by Carl Goeller, published by The Writer, Inc. (Boston). Both sell for $10.95.

Christmas is, of course, the biggest season for sending cards, but don't forget the many other occasions throughout the year—Easter, Mother's and Father's Days, birthdays, graduation, weddings, anniversaries, and such religious observances as Confirmation and First Communion. Sympathy cards are also sought. Note in the list below that some companies specialize in Jewish holiday messages.

Establishing yourself in this market requires talent, determination, and lots of work—because the competition is keen. Professional writers are also on the staffs of many companies, but freelance material is definitely sought. Query publishers to find out themes that are open at each of them. Send for the "tip sheets" or "market letters" that some of them issue.

The following publishers do some religious material—some of them a great deal, others only for Christmas or other special holidays. Special emphases are indicated in the parentheses.

ABBEY PRESS, Box 128, St. Meinrad, IN 47577 *(Catholic).*
AMERICAN GREETINGS CORPORATION, 10500 American Road, Cleveland, OH 44144.
ARGUS COMMUNICATIONS, One DLM Park, Box 7000, Allen, TX 75002.
ARTFORMS CARD CORPORATION, 725 County Line Road, Deerfield, IL 60015 *(Jewish).*
BLUE MOUNTAIN ARTS, INC., P.O. Box 4549, Boulder, CO 80306 *(Inspirational but not religious).*
BROWNLOW PUBLISHING CO., INC., P.O. Box 3141, Fort Worth, TX 76105.
CREATIVE GRAPHICS COMPANY, P.O. Box 123, La Mirada, CA 90638.
DAYSPRING, OUTREACH PUBLICATIONS, Box 1010, Siloam Springs, AR 72761.
THE EVERGREEN PRESS, Box 4971, Walnut Creek, CA 94596 *(Christmas).*
D. FORER AND COMPANY, INC., 105 East 73rd Street, New York, NY 10021 *(Christmas).*
GIBSON/BUZZA, GIBSON GREETING CARDS, 2100 Section Road, Cincinnati, OH 45237.
HALLMARK CARDS, Kansas City, MO 64141.
IDEALS PUBLISHING CORPORATION, 11315 Waterton Plank Road, Milwaukee, WI 53201.
LEANIN' TREE PUBLISHING COMPANY, Box 9500, Boulder, CO *(Christian verse).*
MISTER B GREETING CARD COMPANY, 3305 Northwest 37th Street, Miami, FL 33142 *(Christmas, Jewish).*
MORNING STAR CARDS, 810 First Street South, Hopkins, MN 55343.
NORCROSS/RUSTCRAFT GREETING CARD COMPANY, 950 Airport Road, West Chester, PA 19380.
OATMEAL STUDIOS, Box 138, Rochester, VT 05767 *(Christmas).*
RED FARM STUDIOS, P.O. Box 347, Pleasant Street, Pawtucket, RI 02862 *(Christmas).*
VAGABOND CREATIONS, 2560 Lance Drive, Dayton, OH 45409 *(Christmas).*
WARNER PRESS, P.O. Box 2499, Anderson, IN 46011 *(Christian).*

◄WRITING FOR NEWSPAPERS AND SYNDICATES►

by K. Maynard Head, *author and columnist, Cumberland Gap, Tennessee*

Writing for newspapers, for the most part, has been left to the secular writer. This does not imply that there is no need for commentators on the daily news that affects each of us; there is definitely a fertile field in the nation's newspapers for the Christian writer.

In this country, newspapers are classified as either daily or weekly—the latter group including those that may be published more often than once a week, but not every day. The daily papers have access to wire services and can afford to hire staff writers, so the opportunity to write for this market is not as great as in the weekly field.

Most smaller newspapers are eager to find and develop the writing skills of freelancers. Opportunities for writing feature articles and columns are available in most towns, since staff writers are often overworked and the need for material is constant.

The weekly column is an excellent way to become a writer for a newspaper in your area. The column with a moral twist has been used effectively by a number of Christian writers and has often been the springboard for magazine articles and books.

The first step in writing for newspapers is to approach the editor of the local paper with your idea. He may prefer to see a single article in order to determine your writing style and interest. Let him or her know your background and/or interest and suggest a possible story.

You may get an immediate assignment, but more likely, you will be asked to submit a piece on speculation. If you display your best efforts at this time, you may be given additional assignments.

If your interest is in writing a column, be prepared to show the editor samples of your writing—and some completed columns. Since a column occupies a definite place in the paper each week, the editor will depend on you to supply copy for that space on a regular basis. The column will appear under the same heading each time it is published, and the length of each submission should be approximately the same. The 500-word column has been very successful in many instances.

Once your column has appeared for several months in your local newspaper, it may be time to branch out to others. Follow the same procedure in approaching other editors as you did with the first, but this time take or send clips of your column as it appears in print. If you offer the column to distant cities, your best approach may be to mail a package containing a cover letter explaining the column, samples of the materials, a rate card or sheet and, of course, an SASE for return of your material.

Or you may want to work through a syndicating agency, some of which are suggested below. My own weekly column, "Mountain Moments," has been syndicated since 1975 and now appears in 275 newspapers in 17 states. There is opportunity out there to be pursued!

There are also a number of publications to assist the aspiring columnist in locating markets. Some of them are:

WRITER'S & PHOTOGRAPHER'S GUIDE TO NEWSPAPER MARKETS by Joan and Ronald Long, Helm Publishing, Box 10512, Costa Mesa, CA 92627. This book contains a guide list of Canadian and U.S. dailies, weeklies, and monthlies as well as religious, collegiate, and other specialty papers.

SYNDICATED COLUMNISTS by Richard Weiner, published by the author at 888 Seventh Avenue, New York, NY 10019. The book lists columnists and syndicates.

HOW TO SYNDICATE YOUR OWN NEWSPAPER COLUMN by W. P. Williams and Joseph H. Van Zendt, Contemporary Books, Inc., 180 North Michigan Avenue, Chicago, IL 60601.

EDITOR AND PUBLISHERS YEARBOOK: A complete listing, this annual publication is the Bible of the newspaper business and can be ordered from *Editor and Publisher* at 575 Lexington Avenue, New York, NY 10022.

Once your column and features have appeared in local newspapers, it may be time to seek out a syndicate for help in marketing. The following is a partial list:

CONTEMPORARY FEATURES SYNDICATE, P.O. Box 1258, Jackson, TN 38301. Seeking material on self-help, a natural for religious writers.

RELIGIOUS NEWS SERVICE, 43 West 57th Street, New York, NY 10019. Supplies material to both religious and secular publications. Interested in both Jewish and Christian news and features.

NATIONAL CATHOLIC NEWS SERVICE, 1312 Massachusetts Avenue N.W., Washington, DC 20005. Interested in news, features, photos—any material suitable for their major customers, Catholic weekly newspapers.

DICKSON FEATURE SERVICE, 17700 Western (#69), Gardena, CA 90248. Write for guidelines on religious material.

The following syndicates specialize in news and features of Jewish life:

JEWISH CHRONICLE NEWS SERVICE, 235 West 102nd Street, New York, NY 10025.

JEWISH STUDENT PRESS SERVICE, 15 East 26th Street, Suite 1350, New York, NY 10010.

JEWISH TELEGRAPHIC AGENCY, and SEVEN ARTS FEATURE SYNDICATE, 165 West 46th Street, New York, NY 10036.

◄WRITING CURRICULUM►

The curriculum and new products divisions of denominational and some nondenominational publishing houses produce a wide assortment of religious teaching materials, new products, and variety items. The possibilities are as limitless as your ideas: Sunday school curricula, vacation Bible school courses, church-time materials, teacher training aids, coloring books, "dot-to-dot" activities, puzzles, quiz books, games, crafts, puppets, and bulletin board ideas.

First, visit your local religious bookstore or supply house to see what is on the market. You may find a publisher whose established line of products fits your proposal. Then, query the New Products Editor or the Curriculum Editor of any of the following houses. Find out their policy on freelance submissions, because many of these houses use staff writers. Below is a list of producers of Christian curriculum materials.

ABINGDON PRESS, 201 8th Avenue South, Nashville, TN 37202. *(United Methodist)*

AMERICAN BAPTIST BOARD OF EDUCATION MINISTRIES, Valley Forge, PA 19481.

AUGSBURG PUBLISHING HOUSE, 426 South Fifth Street, Minneapolis, MN 55415. *(American Lutheran Church)*

THE BRETHREN PRESS, 1451 Dundee Avenue, Elgin, IL 60120.

BROADMAN PRESS, 127 Ninth Avenue North, Nashville, TN 37243. *(Southern Baptist Sunday School Board)*

CONCORDIA PUBLISHING HOUSE, 3558 South Jefferson, St. Louis, MO 63116. *(Lutheran Church—Missouri Synod)*

DAVID C. COOK PUBLISHING COMPANY, 850 North Grove Avenue, Elgin, IL 60120.

FORTRESS PRESS, 2900 Queen Lane, Philadelphia, PA 19129. *(Lutheran Church in America)*

FREEWILL BAPTISTS, P.O. Box 1088, Nashville, TN 37202.

GOSPEL PUBLISHING HOUSE, 1445 Booneville, Springfield, MO 65802. *(Assemblies of God)*

GOSPEL LIGHT PUBLICATIONS, Box 3875, Ventura, CA 93006.

GRADED PRESS, 201 Eighth Avenue, South, Nashville, TN 37202. *(United Methodist)*

HERALD PRESS, 616 Walnut Avenue, Scottdale, PA 15638. *(Mennonite)*

JUDSON PRESS, Valley Forge, PA 19481. *(American Baptist)*

JOHN KNOX PRESS, 341 Ponce de Leon Avenue Northeast, Atlanta, GA 30308. *(Presbyterian)*

LIGHT AND LIFE PRESS, 999 College Avenue, Winona Lake, IN 46590. *(Free Methodist)*

MESSENGER PUBLISHING HOUSE, P.O. Box 850, Joplin, MO 64801. *(Pentecostal Church of God)*

NAZARENE PUBLISHING HOUSE, 6401 The Paseo, Kansas City, MO 64131.

OUR SUNDAY VISITOR, INC., Noll Plaza, Huntington, IN 46750.

PACIFIC PRESS, 1350 Villa Street, Mountain View, CA 94040. *(Seventh-Day Adventist)*

PAULIST PRESS, 1865 Broadway, New York, NY 10023. *(Catholic)*

THE SALVATION ARMY, 120 West 14th Street, New York, NY 10011.

SCRIPTURE PRESS, 1825 College, Wheaton, IL 60187.

STANDARD PUBLISHING COMPANY, 8121 Hamilton Avenue, Cincinnati, OH 45231.

SUCCESS WITH YOUTH PUBLICATIONS, P.O. Box 27028, Tempe, AZ 85252.

UNION GOSPEL PRESS, P.O. Box 6059, Cleveland, OH 44101.

UNITED BRETHREN PUBLISHING, 302 Lake Street, P.O. Box 650, Huntington, IN 46750.

WARNER PRESS, 1200 East Fifth Street, P.O. Box 2499, Anderson, IN 46011. *(Church of God)*

WESLEY PRESS, Box 2000, Marion, IN 46952.

WESTMINSTER PRESS, 925 Chestnut Street, Philadelphia, PA 19107. *(Presbyterian)*

WINSTON/SEABURY PRESS, 430 Oak Grove, Minneapolis, MN 55403.

Writers of Jewish religious education materials will find several possible publishers listed in Chapter Four.

Religious writers will also want to know about the several denominations that produce curriculum materials cooperatively. One of the largest such programs has been in progress for several years under the supervision of the Joint Education Development (JED) Program of these churches: Presbyterian Church U.S.A., Christian Church (Disciples), Cumberland Presbyterian Church, Reformed Church in America, Evangelical Covenant Church, Church of the Brethren, Episcopal Church, Moravian Church, Presbyterian Church of Canada, United Church of Canada, and the United Church of Christ. Anyone interested in writing curriculum for these courses—JED materials are written on assignment—should contact one of the denominations listed or Dr. Robert Koenig, JED Editor-in-Chief, 132 West 31st Street, New York, NY 10001.

There are also many curriculum writing possibilities with publishers who produce materials for Christian day schools sponsored by churches. Write to one of these organizations for a list of potential publishers:

ASSOCIATION OF CHRISTIAN SCHOOLS INTERNATIONAL, P.O. Box 4097, Whittier, CA 90607.

CHRISTIAN SCHOOLS INTERNATIONAL, 865 28th Street, Grand Rapids, MI 49508.

EVANGELICAL TEACHER TRAINING ASSOCIATION, Box 327, Wheaton, IL 60187.

◄WRITING FOR MUSIC PUBLISHERS►

There is a continuing need for religious music for choirs, musical groups, and educational purposes. Some of this is in a traditional form. In addition, contemporary Christian music (Gospel music) is popular in many quarters. There is also a need for new liturgical worship music. There is also a very wide range of audiences who like music—from children to teens, to young marrieds to mature audiences.

Religious music publishers say they are looking for "viable, committed artists who can verbally get the message across" in their chosen medium. Before sending off any material, it is best to query publishing houses for their interests and submission requirements. Generally, music publishers also appreciate both a demo record or tape of a new song and a complete four-part harmony manuscript with both words and music.

Several denominational publishing houses issue music and should be queried as well. If you are interested in writing hymns or converting your poetry to hymn forms, you would do well to join the Hymn Society of America and receive their quarterly publication, *The Hymn.* Dues are $18 per year. You will receive information about workshops, contests, and other material relevant to Christian hymnody. Write: Hymn Society of America, Wittenberg University, Springfield, OH 45501. Writers of all types of music will want to investigate a helpful book, *The Songwriter's Guide to Writing and Selling Hit Songs,* published by Prentice-Hall at $6.95.

If you are interested in writing Gospel music, you will want to contact some of the following publishers:

ALEXANDRIA HOUSE, Box 300, Alexandria, IN 46001.

THE BENSON PUBLISHING HOUSE, 365 Great Circle Road, Nashville, TN 37228.

Hope Publishing Company, 380 South Main Place, Carol Stream, IL 60187.
Lexicon Music, Inc., P.O. Box 1790, Waco, TX 76703.
Lillenas Publishing Company, 2923 Troost Avenue, Kansas City, MO 64141.
Lorenz Publishing Company, 501 East Third Street, Dayton, OH 45401.
Manna Music, Inc., 2111 Kenmere Avenue, Burbank, CA 91504.
Maranatha Music, P.O. Box 1396, Costa Mesa, CA 92626.
Masterpiece Music, P.O. Box 5322, Garden Grove, CA 92645.
The Sacred Music Press, 501 East Third Street, Dayton, OH 45401.
Singspiration Music, 1415 Lake Drive S.E., Grand Rapids, MI 49506.
Sparrow Records, Inc., 8025 Deering, Canoga Park, CA 91304.
Tempo Records, Inc., 1900 West 47th Place, Mission, KS 66205.
Truine Music/Trigon Music, P.O. Box 23088, Nashville, TN 37202.
Word Records/Music, 4800 West Waco Drive, Waco, TX 76796.

◄WRITING FOR DRAMA PUBLISHERS►

Religious drama offers specialized and somewhat limited, yet exciting, possibilities for the religious writer. Drama is flourishing in churches across the nation. Drama on Jewish themes is also growing. Colleges and universities with a religious background are becoming aware of the educational, spiritual, and outreach possibilities of drama. Further indication of the opportunities available to religious playwrights are: the development of full-time Christian performing groups, the recent appearance of more playwriting contests, the growing interest in Jewish theme drama, and the emergence of clearing houses that serve as a link between the amateur, educational, and professional components of the movement.

Religious drama writers should watch the prize offer announcements in writers' publications. Also, dramatic associations of interest to playwrights include the Dramatists Guild, 234 West 44th Street, New York, NY 10036 and the Theatre Communications Group, 355 Lexington Avenue, New York, NY 10017. The latter publishes the annual *Dramatist's Sourcebook*.

The following is a list of publishers of drama that the playwright can query for their needs and submission requirements:

Of Jewish Interest

American Jewish Theatre, c/o 92nd Street TM-YWHA, 1395 Lexington Avenue, New York, NY 10028.
Jewish Repertory Theatre, 344 East 14th Street, New York, NY 10003.

Of Christian and General Interest

Abingdon Press, 201 8th Avenue, South, Nashville, TN 37202.
Agape Drama Press, Ltd., P.O. Box 1313, Englewood, CO 80110.
Augsburg Publishing House, 426 South Fifth Street, Minneapolis, MN 55415.
Baker's Plays, 100 Chauncy Street, Boston, MA 02111. John Welch, Editor.
Broadman Press, 127 Ninth Avenue, North, Nashville, TN 37234.
Contemporary Drama Service, Arthur Meriwether Inc., Box 7710, Colorado Springs, CO 80933.
C.S.S. Publishing Company, 628 South Main Street, Lima, OH 45804.
Fortress Press, 2900 Queen Lane, Philadelphia, PA 19129.
Higley Publishing Corporation, P.O. Box 2470, Jacksonville, FL 32203.
Judson Press, Valley Forge, PA 19481.
Lamb's Players Theatre, 500 Plaza Boulevard, P.O. Box 26, National City, CA 92050.
Lillenas Publishing Company, Box 527, Kansas City, MO 64141.
Meyer and Brother Publishers, 1414 South Wabash Avenue, Chicago, IL 60605.
Paulist Press, 545 Island Avenue, Ramsey, NJ 07446.

RON REED, 25718 North Hogan Drive, #C6, Valencia, CA 91355.
SCRIPTURE PRESS PUBLICATIONS, INC., 1825 College Avenue, Wheaton, IL 60187.
STANDARD PUBLISHING, 8121 Hamilton Avenue, Cincinnati, OH 45231.
WALTERICK PUBLISHERS, 3207 State Avenue, Kansas City, KS 66102.
WORD, INCORPORATED, 4800 West Waco Drive, Waco, TX 76710.

◄WRITING FOR RADIO AND TELEVISION►

There are also growing numbers of opportunities for writers in religious radio and television. New religious stations continue to be organized. In addition, public-service stations and public-service programs on commercial stations often deal with religious topics or are sponsored by community religious organizations. All of these programs need writers.

Because opportunities in this field are usually local, we will not attempt to list any stations or programs here. The best source of such information for the writer is the *Directory of Religious Broadcasting,* an annual publication that lists information about programs and stations in all localities. This directory can be ordered for $29 from the National Religious Broadcasters, Box 2544, Morristown, NJ 07960. Phone: (201) 428–5400.

Two other sources of information about religious radio and TV are the following:

THE DIRECTOR OF AUDIO-VISUAL COMMUNICATION NATIONAL COUNCIL OF
    CHURCHES, 475 Riverside Drive, New York, NY 10115.
PROTESTANT RADIO AND TV CENTER, INC., 1727 Clinton Road N.E., Atlanta, GA
    30329.

◄WRITING FOR FILM PRODUCERS►

The religious film market continues to present several opportunities to the talented, determined writer. New ideas and materials are needed constantly. Although breaking into this area of the business is not easy, it is possible. Before submitting any material, prepare a complete résumé, listing your credentials, experience, availability, fields of interest, background, and credits. Sample scripts you've written should accompany the query, and possibly a one-page story-synopsis of the material you propose. Most companies listed below produce 16–mm films and sound filmstrips for the interdenominational church market for audiences of all ages. Be sure to query them first for particular needs and submission guidelines.

The serious writer in this field will also want to study books and other guides to the preparation of material for film use, such as *Writing for Film and Television* by Steward Bronfeld, published by Prentice-Hall at $4.95. *Christian Film and Video* is a newsletter that reviews the latest in Christian productions as well as the classics in the field. For a sample copy, write editor Mark Fackler at 501 East Seminary, Wheaton, IL 60187.

The following companies indicate they are interested in seeing material for Christian films and filmstrips:

KEN ANDERSON FILMS, Box 618, Winona Lake, IN 46590. (219) 267–5774. Ken
    Anderson, President. Religious material with evangelical bias.
CATHEDRAL FILMS, INC., P.O. Box 4029, Westlake Village, CA 91359.
CONCORDIA PUBLISHING HOUSE, Product Development Division, 3558 South
    Jefferson Avenue, St. Louis, MO 63118. (314) 664–7000.
CONTEMPORARY DRAMA SERVICE, Arthur Meriwether, Inc., Box 7710, Colorado
    Springs, CO 80933.
DAVID C. COOK PUBLISHING COMPANY, 850 North Grove Avenue, Elgin, IL 60120.
CORNERSTONE PICTURES, 2800 Washington Street, Avondale Estates, GA 30002.
FAMILY FILMS, 14622 Lanark Street, Panorama City, CA 91402. Paul R. Kidd, director
    of product development.

GOSPEL FILMS, INC., Muskegon, MI 49443. (616) 773–3361.

MARK IV PICTURES, INC., OF IOWA, 5907 Meredith Drive, Des Moines, IA 50322. (515) 278–4737.

OUR SUNDAY VISITOR, INC., Audiovisual Department, 200 Noll Plaza, Huntington, IN 46750. Richard D. Hawthorne, audiovisual manager.

WORLD WIDE PICTURES, 1201 Hennepin Avenue, Minneapolis, MN 55403.

Canada

FAITH FILMS, LTD., 224 Cayer Street, Box 1096, Coquitlam, British Columbia V3J 6Z4.

◄CONSIDER SELF-PUBLISHING►

by E. Jane Mall, *author, newsletter editor, and publisher, Corpus Christi, Texas*

Self-publishing was once regarded as something people with no talent resorted to. Little old ladies with family diaries self-published; serious writers did not. This is no longer true. Self-publishing has become highly respectable and should be considered as an option by any writer. Usually this entails a manuscript of book length, but you may want to consider smaller items. I've done a bit of it myself with my newsletter, *Church Secretary Swap Shop* and my Church Mouse Press.

Don't, however, approach self-publishing as a last-ditch effort, or as a way to get even with all those short-sighted publishers, or as a way to make a lot of money. Think of it as a way to let others know that you are a serious writer and that people will pay to read what you write.

With this in mind, there are a few important points to consider before you make a decision to self-publish. First, it would be wise to do some practical reading on self-publishing. There are some good books on the subject (all self-published, too!):

The Publish-It-Yourself Handbook by Bill Henderson, Pushcart Press, P.O. Box 845, Yonkers, NY 10701 ($12.50).

The Self-Publishing Manual by Dan Poynter, Para Publishing, P.O. Box 4232, Santa Barbara, CA 93103 ($14.95).

Publish It Yourself by Charles Chickadel, Trinity Press, Box 1320, San Francisco, CA 94101 ($5.95).

How To Publish Your Own Book by L. W. Mueller, Harlo Press, 50 Victor, Detroit, MI 48203 ($7.95).

You may not want to invest in all of these books, so look them up in your library or borrow them from a writer friend before you buy a copy.

You can also receive excellent information on self-publishing from the National Writers' Press, 1450 South Havana, Suite 620, Aurora, CO 80012. Also *Inkling,* the newsletter for writers (P.O. Box 128, Alexandria, MN 56308) has an annual November issue on self-publishing that you may want to investigate.

Next, consider the value of the book or other material you have written. You must believe in its worth and be convinced there is a market of buyers interested in the subject of your book. One way to confirm this belief is to submit your manuscript to at least three publishers and hope they will tell you their reasons for rejection. Study these reasons carefully and determine whether or not you can (or should) make revisions—and submit the manuscript again.

What makes you think your book will sell as a self-published book when no publisher will take a chance on it? There can be a valid answer. If you can convince yourself that your book will have a market and that you will be proud to have your name on the cover, you might well consider self-publishing.

However, there are other factors to consider. As a self-publisher, you will be in charge of *all* of the aspects of the editing, publishing, and marketing of your book. If you have had some experience in advertising, marketing, and public relations, it will be a big plus. If these areas don't interest you at all, perhaps you would be wise to forget self-publishing.

You must also consider the investment of time and money that will be involved in the whole project. If you cannot carry out or get help in the distribution of your book, you may end up with a garage or basement full of copies.

The various steps necessary in the process such as obtaining copyright, an ISBN number, and giving your publishing venture a name, are all outlined in the books on self-publishing above. All of these must be considered as you venture into self-publishing.

Is it a good idea to self-publish? Perhaps. Mark Twain, Walt Whitman, and Edgar Allan Poe, among others, all published themselves at one time. If you are able to successfully publish and market your book, it will be a major accomplishment. You probably won't be famous or wealthy, but you will have made an important statement. You will have told a lot of people that you are a serious writer, that you believe in what you are doing, and that an audience for your work does exist. It's a beginning.

Dan Poynter, author of one of the books on self-publishing mentioned above, lists 10 reasons why you "must" self-publish your book. They are well summarized in this quotation: "A self-published book has a better chance of success because it is under the control of someone who cares—the author."

SIX

Getting Help: Additional Resources for the Religious Writer

Why should a fledgling writer invest time and money in a writer's conference, seminar, workshop, or correspondence course to talk about writing? Why buy and read books about writing? Why not spend the time practicing instead?

It is true that no amount of listening or reading will put your words on paper or provide the trial and error necessary to make you a published author. It's a little like a carpenter sitting in a lecture hall, listening to a woodworker discuss the craft while the carpenter's own tools lie idle at home. But anyone who has attended a conference, bought books on writing, taken a correspondence course, or enrolled for training at a local school knows that time spent on learning the basics puts the beginning writer far ahead. There are at least 10 advantages to the writer who seeks help from such sources:

1. *The writer gets a good introduction to the business end of publishing.* Unless you understand the pressures of the editorial process, you are unable to appreciate fully why material is needed on time, why royalties are established at the present scale, and why editors ask for clean, neat manuscripts with proper spacing.

2. *The writer learns how to slant the material for different audiences.* A writer researching a project can use the same research for a variety of markets and audiences. This makes investment of time and money for research pay multiplied dividends.

3. *The writer learns to master the techniques.* Public school and college courses in English composition usually do not offer the kind of concentrated study of writing techniques that a producing, selling author should learn to handle with ease. Such techniques include the use of metaphor, simile, onomatopoeia, alliteration, flashback, and many more.

4. *The writer shares the experiences of veteran writers.* Writing is hard work. The commiseration of fellow craftsmen is of inestimable value to the suffering wordsmith. It might seem a small matter, but just knowing that someone else has had similar experiences can encourage a writer who might think he or she is the only one enduring the agony.

5. *The writer learns to spot trends.* A writer's success often depends on market trends. A good book or article ahead of its time is rejected just as easily as one written behind the times, after the market has been glutted by literature on a given subject.

6. *The writer gets help in keeping records.* Everything from cost-cutting techniques to tips on tax deductions can be learned from writing teachers.

7. *The writer can get to know other writers* in the same locality and take advantage of opportunities for fellowship through writers' clubs.

8. *The writer's awareness of market potentials can be greatly increased* as he or she learns of new book or magazine publishing houses.

9. *A writer can learn which reference books, magazines, and pamphlets are important.*

10. *Finally, the writer's natural talent can be sharpened through the discipline of study.*

Working through a well-organized program can be a shortcut to success. "Iron sharpeneth iron; so a man sharpeneth the countenance of his friend." (Proverbs 27:17). As a student, the writer has the counsel of a trusted mentor to offer sympathy when rejections prevail, and to help celebrate when victory is won.

Get help! Light is the task when many share the toil. This chapter can show you how.

—Norman B. Rohrer, Director
Christian Writers' Guild

◄AREA CHRISTIAN WRITERS' CLUBS, FELLOWSHIP◄ GROUPS, AND CRITIQUE GROUPS

Writers' groups are a valuable part of a writer's experience. Purposes and goals common to most groups include: 1) To join in fellowship and share inspiration with other Christian writers; 2) to share news of markets, sources, and resources; 3) to share ideas, enthusiasm, motivation, and experience; 4) to share critiquing, receive help, and perfect writing; 5) to encourage beginning writers to complete stories, articles, and books and to submit their work to publishers, 6) to write, produce, and be published as writers sharing their lives, experiences, and faith with others.

Although secular groups have been established for years in many parts of the country, the increase in clubs for religious writers is a recent trend. There are exactly six times as many groups listed here as there were in the first edition of *Religious Writer's Marketplace!*

This list was prepared by Sally Stuart, based on a questionnaire sent to all groups of which we were aware. Groups listed with no information besides their leaders did not return their questionnaires. In many of these cases, we also did not have the group's official name and therefore just list them under the generic title of "Christian Writing Group."

Alabama

THE WRITING ACADEMY, INC. Leader: Olga Williams, 913 Terrace Acres, Auburn, AL 36830. (205) 821–7647. Purpose: To provide motivation, instruction, and peer support for writers as they share their Christian perspective, particularly serving those who undertake individual and cooperative ventures of producing materials for the church (interdenominational). Three classes of memberships: charter, regular, associate. Conducts an annual seminar in August for members at Yahara Center, Madison, Wisconsin.

Alaska

EAGLE RIVER CHRISTIAN WRITERS' CRITIQUE GROUP. Leader: Marilyn Morgan, 2830 Teklanika Drive, Eagle River, AK 99577. (907) 694–2053. Meets one Thursday a month, 9:30 A.M., at the Chugiak United Methodist Church, Mile 18½ Old Glenn Highway. About 3 to 6 members. Membership open. Purpose: To critique each other's writing and improve marketing possibilities.

Arizona

ARIZONA CHRISTIAN WRITERS' CLUB. Leader: Donna Goodrich, 648 South Pima Street, Mesa, AZ 85202. (602) 962-6694. Meets first Saturday of each month (except holiday weekends, then second Saturday), 10 A.M. to noon, at Phoenix Christian High School, Room 9, 1751 West Indian School, Phoenix, AZ. Approximately 20 participants. Membership open. $1 per month dues includes newsletter. Purpose: To share writing, set monthly goals, critique manuscripts, and suggest markets.

CHRISTIAN WRITERS' CLUB. Leader: Rev. Paul Miller, 39 West Palmdale, Tucson, AZ 85714.

MESA CHRISTIAN WRITERS' CLUB. Leader: Donna Goodrich, 648 South Pima Street, Mesa, AZ 85202. (602) 962-6694. Meets second Thursday of each month, 1 P.M. to 3 P.M., at Mesa Public Library Auditorium, 64 East 1st Street, Mesa, AZ 85201. About 10 to 15 participants (more in the winter). Membership open. Members pay $1 monthly dues, which includes their newsletter. Purpose: To share writing, set monthly goals, critique manuscripts, and suggest markets.

PHOENIX CHRISTIAN WRITERS' CLUB. Leaders: Mary Lou Klingler and Jan Potter, 1056 East Pueblo Road, Phoenix, AZ 85020. (602) 944-9479 or (602) 246-2810. Meets second Thursday of month (except August), 7:15 P.M., at Bethany Bible Church, Room 108, 6060 North 7th Avenue, Phoenix, AZ 85013. Approximately 25 members. Membership open. Purpose: "To encourage, inspire, and learn to write our best for the glory of God."

PRESCOTT CHRISTIAN WRITERS' FELLOWSHIP: Leader: Pauline Dunn, 1840 Iron Springs Road, No. A2F, Prescott, AZ 86301. (602) 778-7342. Meets last Saturday of the month, 9 A.M. to 11 A.M., usually at Dorothy Galde's home, 140 South Bradshaw, Apt. 1, Prescott. About 10 to 15 participants. Membership open. Purpose: "To encourage each other to persist and improve our writing for Christian publishers and publications. To learn through seminars, guest speakers, and study of a text."

Arkansas

CHRISTIAN WRITERS' CLUB. Leader: C. B. Jensen, Route 7, Box 390, Beautiful View Acres, Mountain Home, AR 72653. (501) 425-7151.

CHRISTIAN WRITERS' CLUB. Leader: Thelma McMillon, 1301 North Scenic Acres Drive, Horseshoe Bend, AR 72512.

SOCIETY OF CHRISTIAN POETS. Founder: Patti Garr, Box 214, Van Buren, AR 72956. (501) 474-8913. Meets the third Thursday of each month, 7 P.M., in Van Buren Municipal Complex. Over 100 members. Membership open; nondenominational. Purpose: To encourage inspirational poets. Sponsors poetry contests and sends a newsletter about every four months.

California

CHRISTIAN WRITERS' GROUP. Leader: Judy Bacchetti, 3665 Dolbeer, Eureka, CA 95501.

CHRISTIAN WRITERS' GROUP. Leader: Patricia A. Chapman, c/o Simpson College, 801 Silver Avenue, San Francisco, CA 94134.

CHRISTIAN WRITERS' GROUP. Leader: Kenneth L. Dodge, 2956 Rollingwood Drive, San Pablo, CA 94806.

CHRISTIAN WRITERS' GROUP. Leader: Sharon Johnson, 143 Clinton Street, 9, Garden Grove, CA 92640. (714) 554-4749.

CHRISTIAN WRITERS' GROUP. Leader: Catherine Lawton, 116 Sussex Drive, Santa Rosa, CA 95401.

CHRISTIAN WRITERS' GROUP. Leader: Rev. LeRoy Reedy, 1598 Caramay Way, Sacramento, CA 95818.

CHRISTIAN WRITERS' GROUP. Leaders: Dr. & Mrs. Nelson Sheets, 6612 Gulf Crest Drive, San Diego, Ca 92119.

DIABLO VALLEY CHRISTIAN WRITERS' GROUP. Leader: Peggy Parker, 2275 Trotter Way, Walnut Creek, CA 94596. (415) 934-3221. Meets second and fourth Mondays of each month, 7:30 to 9:30 P.M., at Community Presbyterian Church, Danville. Membership open. Purpose: To encourage and critique one another's writing efforts and to share information on markets and workshops.

GREATER SACRAMENTO CHRISTIAN WRITER'S WORKSHOP. Leader: Carla Atkinson, 730 Santa Rita Way, Sacramento, Ca 95825. (916) 485-9813. Meets monthly on the second Wednesday, 1:15 to 3:15 P.M. at Sylvan Oaks Library, 6700 Auburn Boulevard, Citrus Heights. About 30 participants. Membership open. Purpose: To provide fellowship with other writers, marketing information and guidance in writing, emphasizing Christian publications, and speakers who inspire and offer technical information. Sponsors a writers' workshop in August.

LITERATURE MINISTRY PRAYER FELLOWSHIP. Leader: Ethel Herr, 731 Lakefair Drive, Sunnyvale, Ca 94086. (408) 734-4707. Membership in this nationwide group is restricted to Christians who will sign a prayer covenant. Sends quarterly prayer bulletin and needs sheet to all members. Purpose: To provide prayer support for writers and editors in the Christian writing industry.

LODI WRITERS' ASSOCIATION. Leader: Dee Porter, 606 Daisy, Lodi, Ca 95240. (209) 334-0603. Meets fourth Monday of each month, 7:30 to 9:30 P.M., at Carnegie Library, Pine Street (next to City Hall), Lodi. About 25 participants (75 on mailing list). Membership open. Purpose: To inspire and educate all writers of all categories of publication.

SAN DIEGO COUNTY CHRISTIAN WRITERS' GUILD. Convenor: Sherwood E. Wirt, Box 1171, El Cajon, CA 92022. Nine critique groups meet monthly throughout the greater Los Angeles/San Diego area. About 250 participants in all. Membership open. Purpose: Mutual encouragement and exchange of information. Sponsors spring and fall banquets, a summer picnic and a fall workshop. Sends a monthly newsletter to members.

SANTA BARBARA CHRISTIAN WRITERS' GUILD. Leader: Kay Strom, 1025 Camino del Retiro, Santa Barbara, CA 93102. (805) 964-1458. Meets last Thursday of the month, 7:30 P.M. Meeting location rotates to members' homes. About 25 participants. Membership open. Purpose: Some instruction, special speakers. Mostly critique of members' work and mutual encouragement.

SANTA CLARA VALLEY CHRISTIAN WRITERS. Leader: Ethel Herr, 731 Lakefair Drive, Sunnyvale, CA 94086. (408) 734-4707. Contact Ms. Herr for information on area critique groups. Membership open. Purpose: To provide instruction, inspiration, encouragement, and prayer support for Christian writers. Sponsors an annual seminar in Christian writing the third Saturday of October.

SUTTER-BUTTES CHRISTIAN WRITERS' FELLOWSHIP. Advisor: Bonnie Wheeler. Leader: Lou Ella Vaughn, 2032 Blevin Road, Yuba City, Ca 95991. (916) 674-5436. Meets second Saturday of each month, 9 A.M. to noon, at Calvary Temple Church, Highway 20, Yuba City. About 20 participants. Membership open. Purpose: To edify beginners, critique manuscripts, in love and honesty, and spread the Good News through writing.

Colorado

CHRISTIAN WRITERS' GROUP. Leader: Gail Emmans, 1080 Lilac Street, Broomfield, CO 80020.

CHRISTIAN WRITERS' GROUP. Leader: Dr. Norman R. Oke, 205 North Murray Boulevard, No. 44, Colorado Springs, CO 80916.

Connecticut

CHRISTIAN WRITER'S FELLOWSHIP—NEW LONDON AREA. Leaders: Vi Merritt, 20 Rock Ridge Road, Waterford, CT 06385, and Sharon Roberts, 12 Johnston Court, Waterford, CT 06385. (203) 442-7472 or (203) 447-1540. Meets one Tuesday per month, 7 P.M. to 9 P.M. at Vi Merritt's home. Approximately 12 participants. Membership open. Purpose: To share inspirational writing advice (from books, magazines, or conferences). Members are encouraged to bring something they've written that month to share with the group.

Florida

CENTRAL FLORIDA CHRISTIAN SCRIBES. Leader: Elisabeth S. McFadden, 64-A South Lake Drive, Leesburg, FL 32788. (904) 589-4763. Meets second Thursday of each month, September through May. Meets 3 P.M. to 5 P.M. in September, November, January, and March, and 7 P.M. to 9 P.M. in October, February, April, and May. Forest Lake Seventh-day Adventist Church, Route 436 (Semoran Boulevard), Forest City. Occasionally meets elsewhere; phone to verify location. About 12 to 15 members. Membership open. Purpose: To help prepare manuscripts for publication, critique material, encourage use of talent, and spread the Good News of salvation.

FORT MYERS FLORIDA WRITERS' GROUP. Leader: S. Kimbrough, P.O. Box 456, Alva, FL 33920. (813) 728-2557. Meets first Tuesday of each month, at First Christian Church, Fort Myers.

GOOD NEWS NETWORK. Leader: Tina Thaggard, 1826 Linhart Avenue, Fort Myers, FL 33901. (813) 334-3412. Meets first Tuesday of each month, 6:30 P.M. to 9 P.M. at First Christian Church, 2016 McGregor Avenue, Fort Myers. Approximately 10 to 13 participants. Membership open. Purpose: To encourage and inspire Christians to write, share markets, critique works, and offer market suggestions.

Georgia

CHRISTIAN WRITERS' GROUP. Leader: Rev. Robert E. Maner, 1619 North Lee Street, Valdosta, GA 31601.

Idaho

CHRISTIAN WRITERS' GROUP. Leader: Margaret Bull, 802 3rd Street, Lewiston, ID 83501.

CHRISTIAN WRITERS' GROUP. Leader: Thelma Gray, Route 2, Box 269, Moscow, ID 83403.

CHRISTIAN WRITERS' GROUP. Leader: Laura Ruby, 1925 Center Street, Maries, ID 83861.

TREASURE VALLEY FELLOWSHIP OF CHRISTIAN WRITERS. Leader: Barbara J. Webb, 1711 Vista Avenue, Route 2-Box 2430, Fruitland, ID 83619. (209) 452-3886. Usually meets second Tuesday of each month at the above address. Group of 6 to 8. Membership open. Purpose: "To gain new insights into writing, submitting, and publishing our work; sharing lives, experiences, and Jesus Christ with others."

Illinois

CHRISTIAN WRITERS' GROUP. Leader: Bob Johnson, 208 East Winter, Danville, IL 61832.

CHRISTIAN WRITERS' GROUP. Leader: Chaplain Faith Jones, 1322 East Jackson, Springfield, IL 62703.

CHRISTIAN WRITERS' GROUP. Leader: Diane Skinner, Route 3, Shelbyville, IL 62565.

CHRISTIAN WRITERS' GROUP. Leader: Glenn J. Sneed, Royalton, IL 62983.

Indiana

BROWN CO. CHRISTIAN WRITERS CLUB. Leader: Evelyn Gladding, SW 3-17, Box WS 427, Nineveh, Indiana 46164. (317) 878-5434. Meets third Monday of each month, except December, 7:30 P.M., at Community Room of Coop. Building, Old Schoolhouse Way, Nashville. About 20 participants. Membership open. Purpose: To offer fellowship, encouragement, and suggestions to Christian writers.

CHRISTIAN WRITERS' CLUB OF MICHIANA. Leader: Susan Smeltzer, 134 North Tuxedo Drive, South Bend, IN 46617. Meets fourth Tuesday of each month, 7 P.M., at Bowen Library, Bethel College, 1001 West McKinley Avenue, Mishawaka, IN 46545. Approximately 20 to 25 members. Membership open to Christian writers. Purpose: To enjoy fellowship with Christian writers, share markets and resources. Encourage writers to complete manuscripts and submit them to publishers. Pursue professional skills, techniques, and ethics of writing. Programs include critique groups, speakers, workshops, and participation in local college workshops and seminars.

CHRISTIAN WRITERS' GROUP. Leader: David Duff, Logos Creations, First Church of the Nazarene, 601 North Shortridge Road, Indianapolis, IN 46219.

CHRISTIAN WRITERS' GROUP. Leader: Aileen Karg, 1004 Cottage Avenue, Crawfordsville, IN 47973.

CHRISTIAN WRITERS' GROUP. Leader: Mrs. Royce Stewart, Route 2, Box 29, Seymour, IN 47247.

FIVE SENSES CHRISTIAN WRITERS' CLUB. President: Mary Emmans, 16226 Darden Road, Granger, IN 46530. (219) 272-3421. Meets first Monday of each month, 7 P.M. Sends newsletter to all members. Nondenominational. Purpose: To enjoy fellowship, inspire Christian writers, share market news, sources and resources, ideas and enthusiasm, and motivation and experience.

FORT WAYNE CHRISTIAN WRITERS' CLUB. Leader: Linda R. Wade, 739 West Fourth Street, Fort Wayne, IN 46808. (219) 422-2772. Meets second Tuesday of each month, 7 P.M., Fairfield Nazarene Church, 2502 Fairfield Avenue, Fort Wayne. July and August meetings usually breakfast at a local restaurant; Christmas meeting is a dinner/social in a home. About 20 members. Membership open. Purpose: To learn, evaluate, critique, and market manuscripts. Members are encouraged to submit manuscripts to publishers and must bring something to read at each meeting.

WRITING FOR KIDS CLUB. President: Rose Goble, P.O. Box 298, Star City, IN 46985. (219) 595-7531. Membership open.

Iowa

CHRISTIAN WRITERS' GROUP. Leader: Mrs. Ramon Vanderpool, 1230 North 24th Street, Fort Dodge, IA 50501. (515) 576-5025.

INTERSTATE RELIGIOUS WRITERS' ASSOCIATION. Leader: Rev. Marvin E. Ceynar, Box 308, Dumont, IA 50625. (515) 857-3752. This organization, formerly the Iowa Religious Writers' Association, now includes members from bordering states as well. Does not meet regularly, but sponsors two Christian writers' workshops each year and an annual dinner in Des Moines.

OMAHA COUNCIL BLUFFS WRITERS' CRITIQUE GROUP. Leader: Dee Barrett, 16 Susan Lane, Council Bluffs, IA 51501. (712) 322-7692. Meets second Friday of the month at noon (bring a sack lunch) at South Omaha Library, 23rd and M Streets, Omaha. About 6 to 10 participants. Membership open to writers, even to non-Christians. A second group in this area meets on the third Monday of the month, 7 P.M. to 9 P.M., at First Nazarene Church, 2601 Avenue A, Council Bluffs.

QUAD-CITIES CHRISTIAN WRITERS. Leader: Clare Johnson, 412 Lamphere Drive, Blue Grass, IA 52726. (319) 381-4419. Meets first Monday of the month, 7:30 P.M., at the home of Norman Ross, 918 East 13th Street, Davenport, IA 52803. About 10 participants. Membership open. Purpose: To encourage better writing in the inspirational/religious markets.

Kansas

CHRISTIAN WRITING GROUP. Leader: Shirley Burr, 506 Hampton Road, Wichita, KS 67206.

MID-AMERICA FELLOWSHIP OF CHRISTIAN WRITERS. Leader: Aggie Villanueva, 15503 Midland Drive, Shawnee, KS 66217. (913) 268-4480. Meets third Tuesday of each month, 6:30 P.M. to 9:30 P.M., at the above address. The group is small, but membership is open. Purpose: To critique, study, and encourage. This group also sponsors a biennial writers' conference.

Kentucky

CHRISTIAN WRITING GROUP. Leader: James F. Sorrel, 1146 Putnam Street, Newport, KY 41071.

JACKSON CHRISTIAN WRITERS' CLUB. Leader: Rev. Louis A. Bouck, Vancleve, KY 41385. (606) 666-5006. Meets Fridays, 7 P.M., at Breathitt County Public Library, 1024 College Avenue, Jackson, KY 41339. 16 members. Membership open. Purpose: To improve personal writing abilities and produce quality materials for publication, and to enjoy Christian fellowship.

OHIO VALLEY FELLOWSHIP OF CHRISTIAN WRITERS. Leader: Irmgard L. Williams, Route 6-Box 108, Adams Lane, Henderson, KY 42420. (502) 826-8203 or 826-4144. Meets third Monday of each month, 7 P.M., in the lounge of Kiddie Kastle, 434 9th Street, Henderson, KY. About 10 participants. Membership open to people from Kentucky and Indiana. Purpose: To inspire writers to develop their writing skills for the glory of God by support and instruction.

Maine

CHRISTIAN WRITING GROUP. Leader: Anita Fordyce, R.D. 1, Box 178, Monmouth, ME 04259.

Maryland

ANNAPOLIS FELLOWSHIP OF CHRISTIAN WRITERS. Leader: Jeri Sweany, P.O. Box 411, Annapolis, MD 21404. (301) 267-0924. Meets fourth Monday of the month, 7:30 P.M. at Evangelical Presbyterian Church of Annapolis, Ridgely Avenue and Wilson Road, Annapolis. Meetings average 15 participants. Membership open. Purpose: To provide a Christ-centered fellowship to inspire writers to develop their writing skills and to encourage them to use these skills for the glory of God.

Massachusetts

THE BERKSHIRE AREA CHRISTIAN WRITERS FELLOWSHIP. Director: Susan Downs, 961 Wilbraham Road, Springfield, MA 01109. (413) 783-8243. Meets first Monday of every month at 6 P.M. $2 per month membership fee. Nondenominational. About 25 members. Membership open. Purpose: To help members improve their writing skills through lessons or films dealing with writing technique; sharing market information; critiquing; and providing books on writing, publishers' guidelines, and sample copies.

CHRISTIAN WRITERS' GROUP. Leader: J. Grant Swank, Jr., 28 Main Street, Walpole, MA 02081.

Michigan

CHRISTIAN WRITERS' GROUP. Leader: Shirley J. Ruder, 5721 Gun Lake Road, Hastings, MI 49058.

CHRISTIAN WRITING GROUP. Leader: John A. Wright, 3173 School, Weidman, MI 48893.

Minnesota

MINNESOTA CHRISTIAN WRITERS GUILD. President: Joyce K. Ellis, 8441 Hiawatha Avenue, Eden Prairie, MN 55344. (612) 934-7042. Meets third Monday of each month, September through May (second Monday in December), 7:15 P.M., at Grace Church of Richfield, 7101 Nicollet Avenue, Richfield. Approximately 85 members. Membership open. Purpose: To create an atmosphere of fellowship, to inspire writers to "do all to the glory of God" (I Corinthians 10:13), and to instruct them in fulfilling their highest potential. Meetings include speaker or panel, usually editors or experienced writers, who cover writing topics.

Missouri

CARTHAGE WRITERS' GUILD. President: Margaret Pyle, P.O. Box 824, Carthage, MO 64836. Meets second Wednesday of each month, 1:30 P.M., at First Methodist Church, Carthage. About 15 participants. Membership open. Purpose: Education and fellowship. Co-sponsors an all-day writing workshop with The Missouri Arts Council each fall. The workshop offers 4 to 6 classes on writing in a scenic setting.

CHRISTIAN WRITING GROUP. Leader: Reba Fitz, 202 Ballman, Ferguson, MO 63135.

CHRISTIAN WRITING GROUP. Leader: Carol Patterson, Route 1, Box 347, Harrison-ville, MO 64701.

CHRISTIAN WRITING GROUP. Leader: Margaret Owen, 207 North 67th Street, Gladstone, MO 64118.

CHRISTIAN WRITING GROUP. Leader: Celeste Rhea, 7527 Flora Avenue, Maplewood, MO 63143.

CHRISTIAN WRITING GROUP. Leader: William L. Poteet, 411 McArthur Avenue, Union, MO 63084.

CHRISTIAN WRITING GROUP. Leader: Dr. Carl Selfridge, 601 Mill, Lamar, MO 64759. (417) 682-3462.

CHRISTIAN WRITING GROUP. Leader: Earl A. Vansickle, 628 Maryvue Drive, Maryville, MO 64468.

CHRISTIAN WRITING GROUP. Leader: Dr. Earl C. Wolf, 10832 Fuller, Kansas City, MO 64134.

ST. CHARLES CHRISTIAN WRITERS' CLUB AND WORKSHOP. Leader: Vesta Ward, 629 Maran Drive, St. Charles, MO 63301. (314) 946-5391. Meets fourth Thursday of each month, 10 A.M. to 2 P.M., at above address. About 6 to 10 participants. Membership open. Purpose: To encourage, critique, teach, share markets, and support members. "We are a share-and-care group."

Montana

MONTANA CHRISTIAN WRITERS. Leader: Margaret Ferguson, 1030 Hauser Boulevard, Helena, MT 59601. (406) 442-9939. Meets first Monday of the month, 7 P.M., and third Saturday of the month, 10 A.M. About 15 participants. Membership open. Purpose: To encourage and educate members and edit their manuscripts.

Nebraska

CHRISTIAN WRITERS' GROUP. Leader: Mary Anne Miller, 803 Academy Avenue, York, NE 68467.

REWRITERS. Convenor: Wayne C. Lee, Lamar, NE 69035. (308) 882–2291. Meets fourth Monday of each month, 7 P.M., in members' homes. About 12 members. Membership open. Purpose: To improve writing and marketing.

THESAUREAN'S WRITERS CLUB. Leader: Sylvia Chalupsky, Box 172, Burwell, NE 68823. (308) 346–4771. Meets fourth Wednesday of the month, 1:30 P.M., in members' homes. 7 members. Membership open. Purpose: To encourage, share, and support one another in achieving writing goals. "Our motto is: 'Writing is the expression of the soul.'"

Nevada

CHRISTIAN WRITING GROUP. Leader: Cheryl Ochman Williams, 3505 Tabor, North Vegas, NV 89030.

RENO AREA CHRISTIAN WRITERS. Leader: Leita Twyeffort, 3251 Rockwood Drive, Sparks, NV 89431. (702) 331–2744. Meets second Tuesday of every month, 7 P.M., at Sparks First Church of the Nazarene, 2200 El Rancho Drive, Sparks. About 12 to 15 members. Membership open. Purpose: Critiquing, sharing information and encouragement.

New Hampshire

THE LAKE REGION WRITER'S CLUB. Leader: Pat Assimakopoulos, P.O. Box 1618, Wolfeboro, NH 03894. Membership open. Purpose: Critiques, fellowship and, encouragement.

THE WORDSMITHS: A CHRISTIAN WRITERS' FELLOWSHIP. Leader: Cynthia S. Vlatas, 5 Jeremy Lane, Hudson, NH 03051. (603) 882–2851. Meets second and fourth Tuesdays of each month, 7 P.M., at Chandler Branch Library, 257 Main Street, Nashua. Ten members. Membership open; newly formed at the end of 1984. Purpose: To provide a place for Christian writers of all levels to be encouraged and improve writing skills. Activities include manuscript critiquing, writing assignments, special speakers. Nondenominational. Annual dues $10. A lending library is available to members.

New Jersey

SOUTH JERSEY CHRISTIAN WRITER'S FELLOWSHIP. Leader: Sandi Cleary, 308 Clark Place, Northfield, NJ 08225. (609) 646–5694. Critique group meets second Thursday of the month, 7 P.M., at the above address; market research group meets fourth Saturday of the month, 1 P.M. Call phone number above for location. Membership restricted to Christian writers who are actively writing and publishing, and to serious beginners. Purpose: To provide encouragement, motivation, and practical assistance through critique sessions and market research meetings.

New Mexico

CHRISTIAN WRITERS' GROUP. Leader: Hazel Cage, Box 285, Mesilla Park, NM 88047.

SOUTHWEST CHRISTIAN WRITERS' ASSOCIATION. Leader: Patricia A. Burke, 3204 Coronado Avenue, Farmington, NM 87401. (505) 327–1962. Meets third Saturday of the month, 2 P.M. to 4 P.M., at the above address. Has more than 20 members. Membership open. Purpose: To teach skills required to write for the Christian market, provide materials, and critique members' work.

New York

BROOKLYN WRITERS' CLUB. Leader: Ann Dellarocco, Box 184, Brooklyn, NY 11214. (718) 837–3484. Meets Mondays, 6:30 P.M. to 8 P.M., at New Utrecht Brooklyn

Public Library, 86th Street, and 18th Avenue, Brooklyn. About 125 members. 20 to 25 at weekly meetings. Membership open. Purpose: Sharing, workshop, fellowship, critique of manuscripts, marketing information.

CHRISTIAN WRITERS' CLUB. Leader: Marjorie L. Comfort, 645 East State Street, Olean, NY 14760.

CHRISTIAN WRITERS' CLUB. Leader: Rev. Carlton D. Hansen, 855 Long Pond Road, Rochester, NY 14612.

NEW YORK CHRISTIAN WRITERS' GROUP. Coordinator: Gwen Lam, 165 West 66th Street, New York, NY 10023. (212) 787-4845. Meets first Friday of each month, 7 P.M. to 9 P.M., in members' homes. About 16 members. Membership open to those interested in pursuing religious writing. Purpose: 1) To read and offer constructive criticism of one another's manuscripts to develop professionalism and refine writing skills; 2) to share market news and help with marketing; and 3) to provide prayer support, fellowship, and encouragement.

North Carolina

CHRISTIAN WRITERS' CLUB. Leader: David F. Browning, P.O. Box 4311, 749 Cedarbrook Drive, Rocky Mount, NC 17801. (919) 442-7119.

Ohio

CHRISTIAN WRITERS' GROUP. Leader: Jayne Schooler, 505 Southline Drive, Lebanon, OH 45036.

DAYTON AREA CHRISTIAN SCRIBES. President: Beth Anne Davis; Secretary: Lois Pecce, P.O. Box 613, Dayton, OH 45459. (513) 433-6470 or (513) 435-0220. Meets second Thursday of the month, 7 P.M., at Kettering College of Medical Arts, 3737 Southern Boulevard, Kettering. Approximately 45 members. Membership open. Purpose: To provide a conducive and congenial atmosphere in which writers may develop their skills, grow in confidence through Christ, and enhance and strengthen their ministry by mutual sharing. Nondenominational.

OHIO FELLOWSHIP OF CHRISTIAN WRITERS. Chairman: Frances Simpson, 233 West Church Street, Marion, OH 43302. (419) 389-2561. All denominations welcome. Meets September through May, excluding December. Usually meets third Saturday of each month, 9:30 A.M. to 11:30 A.M. (quarterly newsletter gives exact dates). Membership open. Purpose: Fellowship, sharing ideas, and critiquing manuscripts.

STATELINE CHRISTIAN WRITERS' CLUB. Leader: Esther M. Jetter, 3191 State Route 49, Fort Recovery, OH 45846. (419) 375-4238. Meets third Saturday of every month, 10 A.M., in office of Fort Recovery Industries, Star Route 49, Fort Recovery. About 8 to 10 participants. Membership open. Purpose: To encourage new or published writers, study writing skills, share market information and materials (books, magazines, tapes).

Oklahoma

CHRISTIAN WRITERS' GROUP. Leader: Shirlene Braswell, 4501 College, Bethany, OK 73008.

CHRISTIAN WRITING GROUP. Leader: Rev. Ricky Short, 418 East "B" Street, Waurika, OK 73573.

TULSA CHRISTIAN WRITERS' CLUB. President: Norma Jean Lutz, Box 213, Inola, OK 74036. (918) 543-2641. Meets second Thursday of each month at Martin East Regional Library, 2610 South Garnett, Tulsa. Membership open; dues are $5 per year. Interdenominational. Purpose: To inspire writers to sharpen their skills and to be encouraged in their Godly calling.

Oregon

CHRISTIAN WRITING GROUP. Leader: Rev. Fletcher Galloway, 5923 North Minnesota Avenue, Portland, OR 97217.

COASTAL FELLOWSHIP OF CHRISTIAN WRITERS. Leader: Beth Dickinson, Route 1, Box 325, OR 97391. (503) 336-3410. Meets first Tuesday of each month, 7:30 P.M., at Toledo Public Library. Eight members. Membership open. Purpose: "Fellowship, share, encourage, learn, write, produce, submit, and be published as we share our lives, our experiences, and Jesus Christ with others."

NEW HOPE WRITERS' GUILD. Leader: Geneva Ijima, 20349 South LeLand Road, Oregon City, OR 97045. (503) 656-3632. Meets first Wednesday of each month at New Hope Community Church. Approximately 15 members. Membership open. Purpose: Growth and training for newer writers. Share short devotional time, marketing news, and writing tips. Divide into groups for critiquing.

OREGON ASSOCIATION OF CHRISTIAN WRITERS. Consulting Director: Sally E. Stuart, 3280 Southwest 170th Avenue, No. 1613, Beaverton, OR 97006. (503) 658-4104. Meets three times annually: January in Salem, May in Eugene, and October in Portland, on a Saturday, 8:30 A.M. to 4 P.M. Membership open, nonmembers welcome. Annual dues, plus registration fees for meetings. About 250 members, 100 additional participants. Purpose: To encourage new writers, to offer speakers in various fields of writing, to promote writing through workshops, and to encourage participants to go home and write.

PROFESSIONAL WRITERS' CRITIQUE GROUP. Leader: Salley E. Stuart, 3280 Southwest 170th Avenue, No. 1613, Beaverton, OR 97006. (503) 658-4104. Meets first Monday of the month, 7 P.M., in members' homes. About 10 members. Membership by invitation only. Purpose: To provide encouragement, prayer support, market aid, and professional manuscript critiquing.

SPEAKERS & WRITERS, INK. Director: Anne Hesse, P.O. Box 1925, Lake Oswego, OR 97034. (503) 635-2662. Corporate Board: Ruby MacDonald, Pat Rushford, Lauraine Snelling, Sally E. Stuart. Open to all writers and speakers; paid membership required. Purpose: Professional training organization. Provides a speakers' bureau. Helps members learn their craft and set up local writers' groups. Holds an annual conference in the Portland area (write for details).

TWENTIETH CENTURY SCRIBES. Hostess: Ruth Griffin, 17551 Southeast River Road, Milwaukee, OR 97222. (503) 654-3772. Meets second Monday of the month, 7:30 P.M., at the above address. About 7 members. Membership open. Purpose: To encourage and critique constructively.

Pennsylvania

CHRISTIAN WRITERS' GROUP OF LEHIGH VALLEY. President: Patricia Wood, 349 East Main Street, Bath, PA 18014. (215) 837-9758. Meets monthly in members' homes. Small group. Nondenominational. Membership open. Purpose: To encourage, train, and support writers in this ministry.

CHRISTIAN WRITERS' GROUP. Leader: Linda Brickajlik, 819-A Forest Road, Perkasie, PA 18944.

CHRISTIAN WRITERS' GROUP. Leader: Rev. Bud Reedy, 923 Cocoa Avenue, Hershey, PA 17033. (717) 533-6805.

CHRISTIAN WRITING GROUP. Leader: Mary P. Hunsberger, P.O. Box 3206, Bethelehem, PA 18017.

CHRISTIAN WRITERS' GROUP. Leader: Shirley Stevens, 347 Bank Street, Sewickley, PA 15143. (412) 741-6253.

GREATER PHILADELPHIA CHRISTIAN WRITERS' FELLOWSHIP. Leader: Marlene

Bagnull, 316 Blanchard Road, Drexel Hill, PA 19026. (215) 626–6833. Usually meets fourth Thursday of the month, 9:30 A.M. to noon (September through May), at Rose Tree Park Church of the Nazarene, 1810 North Providence Road, Media, PA. About 8 to 15 participants. Membership open. Purpose: "To encourage one another and to develop the gift God has given us. This is accomplished through a sharing/teaching format." Nondenominational.

WRITERS IN THE SPIRIT. Chairman: June Caldwell, R.D. 2, Box 179B, Oil City, PA 16301. (814) 676–6885. Meets first Tuesday of the month, excluding holidays.

YORK CHRISTIAN WRITERS. Coordinator: Rita Holler, 100 Greenwood Road, York, PA 17404. (717) 792–0228. Meets second Monday of each month, 7 P.M., at 159 East Market Street. Interdenominational. Annual dues $12. Membership open. Purpose: To encourage and enlighten Christian writers through organized critiquing.

Tennessee

CHRISTIAN WRITERS' GROUP. Leader: Jack Conn, 4020 Guinn Road, Knoxville, TN 37921. (615) 483–8377.

CHRISTIAN WRITERS' GROUP. Leader: Virginia Jensen, 60 Lester Avenue, No. 307, Nashville, TN 37210.

Texas

CHRISTIAN WRITERS' GROUP. Leader: Gale M. Brazier, 2729 South Broadway, Apartment 288, Tyler, TX 75701.

CHRISTIAN WRITERS' GROUP. Leader: Deborah Lawrence, 2425 Navajo, Pampa, TX 79065.

CHRISTIAN WRITERS' LEAGUE OF AMERICA. National Coordinator: Marilyn Olivarez, Route 2, Box 266A, Harlingen, TX 78550. (512) 425–2011. Chairman of Board of Directors: Noel W. Dudley, 1604 East Taylor, Harlingen, TX 78550. (512) 428–2823. Harlingen chapter meets first Sunday of the month (except during summer months), 2 P.M., at Harlingen public library. Members and chapters across the country, with about 250 members nationwide. Local chapter is about 30 members. Membership open. Organized about 10 years ago to encourage Christian writers throughout the United States. They publish a quarterly newsletter, Currents, and a magazine, *Channels*. They also sponsor biennial writers' conferences.

CHRISTIAN WRITERS' LEAGUE OF EAST TEXAS. Founder: Lee Longenecker, Longview, TX. Affiliate of the Christian Writers' League of America.

TRINITY VALLEY CHRISTIAN WRITERS. President: Marie Clingerman, 2813 Mimosa Drive, Richland Hills, TX 76118. (817) 284–0411. Meets third Saturday of each month, 1 P.M. to 3 P.M., at James Robison Headquarters, 1801 West Euless Boulevard, Euless, TX. About 50 participants. Membership open. Purpose: To instruct, encourage, and bring together area writers, perpetuating God-given talent.

Utah

UTAH CHRISTIAN WRITERS' FELLOWSHIP. Leader: Jill L. Potter, 1646 East Trevino Road, Sandy, UT 84092. (801) 571–5657. Meets third Thursday of each month, 7:30 P.M., in members' homes. About 14 members. Membership is restricted to Christian writers who profess a personal relationship with Christ, and believe the Bible to be the one and only inspired word of God. Purpose: "To give encouragement to Christian writers and to help enable them to reach their full potential as they write in the name of Christ to spread the hope of our Lord throughout the world."

Virginia

CHRISTIAN WRITING GROUP. Leader: Reeford Chaney, 3910 Monza Drive, Richmond, VA 23234.

Washington

CHRISTIAN WRITERS. Leader: Shirley Waite, 1004 Pleasant, Walla Walla, WA 99362. (509) 525–5592. Meets first Monday of each month, 1:30 P.M., in members' homes. About 15 members. Membership open. Purpose: To encourage and critique one another.

CHRISTIAN WRITERS' GROUP. Leader: G. Franklin Allee, 221 Crestwood Drive, Richmond, WA 99352.

CHRISTIAN WRITERS' GROUP. Leader: Golda V. Leighty, Aladdin Route, Box 56B, Colville, WA 99104.

SEATTLE CHRISTIAN WRITERS' FELLOWSHIP. Leader: Dr. Mary Hammack, 12521 Eleventh Avenue, Northwest, Seattle, WA 98177. (203) 362–5956. Meets second Saturday of each month, 10 A.M. to noon, at North Seattle Alliance Church, 2150 North 122nd, Seattle. Fifteen or 16 participants. Membership open. Purpose: To critique members' writing.

WASHINGTON CHRISTIAN WRITERS' FELLOWSHIP. Founder: Elaine Wright Colvin, P.O. Box 11337, Bainbridge Island, WA 98110. (206) 842–9103. Meets monthly on Saturdays. Membership open.

WENATCHEE CHRISTIAN WRITERS' FELLOWSHIP. Leader: Millie Hynes, 211 Ridgemont Drive, East Wenatchee, WA 98801. (509) 884–3279. Meets fourth Thursday of each month, 7:30 P.M. (call above phone number for location). About 30 participants. Membership open. Purpose: To enjoy fellowship, encourage, inspire, share market information, critique, and offer workshops and speakers.

WHATCOM CHRISTIAN WRITERS' CLUB. Contact: Judy Clotemaker, 840 East Pole Road, Lynden, WA 98264. (206) 354–2636. Meet at Dutch Mothers Restaurant (in Upper Room), 12:00 to 2:00 P.M. second Thursday of each month, September to May.

Wisconsin

WISCONSIN FELLOWSHIP OF CHRISTIAN WRITERS. Leader: Janice Hamilton, 1921 Greenwich Lane, Janesville, WI 53545. (608) 756–9685. Meets fourth Tuesday of the month (except December), 7:30 P.M., at Randolph Street Church of the Nazarene, 1710 Randolph Road, Janesville. About 15 members. Membership open to Christians, high school age or older. Purpose: "To encourage Christian writers; to see more of our members published; and to discover the ministry of writing."

Australia

INABURRA CHRISTIAN WRITERS' FELLOWSHIP. Inaburra Complex, Bodella Crescent, Menai, N.S.W. 2234, Australia. Meets bimonthly from February on the second Sunday of the month, 2 to 4 P.M. Contact and secretary is Miss Merle Cox, P.O. Box 38, Sutherland, N.S.W. 2232.

Canada

CHRISTIAN WRITERS' CLUB. Leader: Roy Austin, 1411 Loch Lomond Road, St. John, New Brunswick, E2J 1Z8.

FRASER VALLEY CHRISTIAN WRITER'S GROUP. Meets monthly at 2082 Geneva Court, Abbottsford, BC V2T 3Z2. Chairman: Helen Lescheid. Phone: (604) 852–3148 or (604) 859–7530.

New Zealand

CHRISTIAN WRITERS' GUILD. Leader: William Hathornthwaite, Box 2928, Second Floor, Grand Building, 9-11 Princess Street, Auckland 1, New Zealand. Purpose: To encourage Christian writers, uncover markets, suggest resources and training possibilities. Publishes a newsletter and sponsors an annual one-day writers' seminar.

West Indies

CARIBBEAN CHRISTIAN WRITER'S GUILD. Leader: William M. Almack, Box 239, Bridgetown, Barbados, West Indies. (809) 426–6795. Organized October 1984; first workshop sponsored in 1984. Purpose: To train new writers, encourage developing writers and represent them to publishers.

CHRISTIAN WRITERS' GROUP. Leader: Peter Lee Sam, c/o Olive Lee Sam, 6 Weekes Trace, Mission Road, San Juan, Trinidad, West Indies.

◄CHRISTIAN WRITERS' CONFERENCES◄ AND WORKSHOPS

At conferences, successful freelance writers and well-known religious editors and publishers help perfect God-given abilities, develop new talents, and cultivate writing interests. Held annually or biennially across the nation, these conferences and workshops have become the lifeline of the working and selling writer. Approximately 6,000 men and women attend the more than four dozen Christian writers' conferences and workshops throughout the United States, Canada, and other countries. You'll want to explore the possibilities of these conferences by sending for their free brochures. In the following entries, if a month is given, it is the usual time of year the conference is held.

In addition to the conferences and workshops listed below, two series of such training sessions are held by Norman Rohrer, director of the Christian Writer's Guild, and Thomas Noton, editor and publisher of *The Christian Writer.* Write for information on these one-day seminars: Norman Rohrer, Write-to-be-Read Workshops, 260 Fern Lane, Hume, CA 93628; or Thomas Noton, *The Christian Writer,* P.O. Box 5650, Lakeland, FL 33807.

Alaska

SCHOOL OF CHRISTIAN WRITING. Anchorage, June. Biennial. Write: Doug Walker, Alaska Bible College, Box 289, Glenallen, AK 99588.

Arizona

STATEWIDE CHRISTIAN WRITERS' WORKSHOP. Phoenix, first week in November. Write: Donna Goodrich, 648 South Pima Street, Mesa, AZ 85202.

California

BIOLA UNIVERSITY WRITERS' CONFERENCE. LaMirada, June. Write: Dr. Lowell Saunders, Biola University, 13800 Biola Avenue, LaMirada, CA 90639.

CENTRAL CALIFORNIA CHRISTIAN WRITERS' GUILD. October. Write the Guild at P.O. Box 1677, Clovis, CA 93613.

FOREST HOME SCHOOL OF CHRISTIAN WRITING. Forest Falls. Beginners, June; others, October. Write: West Harty, Forest Home Christian Conference Center, Forest Falls, CA 92339.

FULL GOSPEL, NOR-CAL WORKSHOP. Yuba City, November. Write: Mrs. Lou Vaughn, 2032 Blevin Road, Yuba City, CA 95991.

MOUNT HERMON CHRISTIAN WRITERS' CONFERENCE. Mount Hermon, Easter week. Write: David R. Talbott, Box 413, Mount Hermon, CA 95041.

NOR-CAL CHRISTIAN WRITERS' WORKSHOP. Sacramento, August. Write: Darlene Bogle, 24361 Soto Road, Hayward, CA 94544.

ORANGE COUNTY CHRISTIAN WRITERS. October. Write: Maureen Taylor, 5321 West Keelson Avenue, Santa Ana, CA 92704.

SAN DIEGO CHRISTIAN WRITERS' GUILD WORKSHOP. October. Write the Guild at Box 1171, El Cajon, CA 92022.

SANTA CLARA VALLEY SEMINAR IN CHRISTIAN WRITING. San Jose area, October. Write: Ethel Herr, 731 Lakefair Drive, Sunnyvale, CA 94086.

Illinois

CHRISTIAN WRITERS' INSTITUTE CONFERENCE AND WORKSHOP. Wheaton, June. Write: Becca Anderson, 396 St. Charles Road, Wheaton, IL 60188.

MISSISSIPPI VALLEY WRITERS' CONFERENCE. Rock Island, June. Write: David Collins, 3403 45th Street, Moline, IL 61265.

WRITE TO PUBLISH WORKSHOPS. Chicago, June. Two workshops: one for unpublished authors, one for published. Write: Carolyn Klingbell, Moody Bible Institute, 820 North LaSalle Street, Chicago, IL 60610.

Indiana

CHRISTIAN WRITERS CONFERENCE OF NEW HARMONY. New Harmony, biennial January. Write: Keryx Ministries, c/o Walter Wangerin or Mark Kroeger, P.O. Box 3238, Evansville, IN 47731.

MARION COLLEGE CHRISTIAN WRITERS' CONFERENCE. Marion, May/June. Write: Marion College, Marion, IN 46953; or Linda Wade, 739 West Fourth Street, Fort Wayne, IN 46808.

Iowa

INTERSTATE RELIGIOUS WRITERS' ASSOCIATION. Clear Lake, April and October. Write: Rev. Marvin Ceynar, Box 308, Dumont, IA 50626.

Kansas/Missouri

NAZARENE WRITERS' CONFERENCE. Biennial, August. Write: Dr. J. Fred Parker, Nazarene Publishing House, Box 527, Kansas City, MO 64141.

Massachusetts

GORDON COLLEGE CHRISTIAN WRITERS' CONFERENCE. Wenham, June. Write: Bob Dagley, Gordon College, Wenham, MA 01984.

Michigan

ANDREWS UNIVERSITY CHRISTIAN WRITERS' CONFERENCE. Berrien Springs, July. Write: Dr. Kermit Netteberg, Andrews University, Berrien Springs, MI 49104.

MARANATHA CHRISTIAN WRITERS' SEMINAR. Muskegon, June. Write: Sandra Aldrich, Maranatha Biel and Missionary Conference, Muskegon, MI 49441.

Minnesota

DECISION SCHOOL OF CHRISTIAN WRITING. Minneapolis, August. Write: Lori J.P. Sorensen, *Decision* Magazine, P.O. Box 779, Minneapolis, MN 55440.

Missouri/Kansas

MID-AMERICA FELLOWSHIP OF CHRISTIAN WRITERS. Kansas City, biennial, May. Write: Sally Stone, 201 S.E. 88th, Kansas City, MO 64155.

New Jersey

COMMUNICATION THROUGH THE WRITTEN WORD. Princeton, April. Write: Dr. Jack Cooper, Princeton Theological Seminary, Princeton, NJ 08540.

New Mexico

SOUTHWEST CHRISTIAN WRITERS' SEMINAR. Farmington, September. Write: Patricia Burke, 3204 Coronado Avenue, Farmington, NM 87401.

North Carolina

BLUE RIDGE CHRISTIAN WRITERS' CONFERENCE. Black Mountain, July/August. Also began inspirational romance writers' conference in 1984. Write: Yvonne Lehman, P.O. Box 188, Black Mountain, NC 28711.

Ohio

AKRON MANUSCRIPT CLUB WRITERS' CONFERENCE. Akron, May. Write: Vivian M. Preston, 248 4th Street N.W., Barberton, OH 44203.

CHRISTIAN WRITERS' CLINIC. Cincinnati, biennial, October. Write: Marjorie Miller, Standard Publishing Company, 8121 Hamilton Avenue, Cincinnati, OH 45231.

Oregon

WARNER PACIFIC COLLEGE CHRISTIAN WRITERS' CONFERENCE. Portland, March. Write: Dr. Dale W. Mark, Warner Pacific College, 2219 Southeast 86th, Portland, OR 97215.

Pennsylvania

WRITING FOR PUBLICATION WORKSHOP. Pittsburgh, April/May. Write: Continuing Education Office, Pittsburgh Theological Seminary, Pittsburgh, PA 15206.

ST. DAVID'S CHRISTIAN WRITERS' CONFERENCE. St. David's, June. Write: Gayle G. Roper, R.D. #6 Box 112, Coatesville, PA 19320.

South Carolina

ANDERSON COLLEGE WRITER'S CONFERENCE. Anderson, July. Write: Robert L. Richardson, Anderson College, 316 Boulevard, Anderson, SC 29621.

Tennessee

CHRISTIAN WRITERS' GRAND OLE WORKSHOP. Nashville, July. Write: Dr. John Warren Steen, 6511 Currywood Drive, Nashville, TN 37205.

FREE WILL BAPTIST WRITERS' CONFERENCE. Nashville, May. Write: H.D. Harrison, Free Will Baptist College, Box 17306, Nashville, TN 37217.

SOUTHERN BAPTIST WRITERS' WORKSHOP. Nashville, July. Write: Bob Dean, P.O. Box 24001, Nashville, TN 37203.

Texas

BRITE SCHOOL OF CHRISTIAN WRITING. Dallas/Ft. Worth, May. Write: Verna Berry, 7517 Terry Court, Fort Worth, TX 76118.

CHRISTIAN WRITERS' LEAGUE OF AMERICA. Harlingen. Biennial conference sponsored by local chapter. Write: Marilyn Olvarez, Route 2, Box 266A, Harlingen, TX 78550.

Virginia

WRITING FOR PUBLICATION WORKSHOP. Richmond, July. Write: Presbyterian School of Christian Education, 1205 Palmyra Avenue, Richmond, VA 23227.

Washington

SEATTLE PACIFIC CHRISTIAN WRITERS' CONFERENCE. Seattle, June. Write: Rose Reynoldson, Humanities Department, Seattle Pacific University, Seattle, WA 98119.

WARM BEACH WRITERS' CONFERENCE. Stanwood, October. Write: Rich Hay, Warm Beach Camp, 20800 Marine Drive N.W., Stanwood, WA 98292.

WASHINGTON CONFERENCE SEVENTH-DAY ADVENTIST WRITERS' WORKSHOP. Auburn, June. Write: Marian Forschler, 18115 116th Avenue, S.E., Renton, WA 98055.

Wisconsin

GREEN LAKE WRITER'S CONFERENCE. Green Lake, August. Write: Dr. Arlo Reichter, American Baptist Assembly, Green Lake, WI 54941.

THE WRITING ACADEMY SEMINAR. Madison (Yahara Center), August. Write: Olga Williams, Executive Director, The Writing Academy, 913 Terrace Acres, Auburn, AL 36830.

Canada

ONTARIO BIBLE COLLEGE CHRISTIAN WRITER'S CONFERENCE. Guelph, Ontario, October. Co-sponsored by Evangelical Fellowship of Canada. Write: Mrs. Frances Bain, 275 Victoria Road North, Guelph, Ontario N1E 5J2.

CHRISTIAN WRITER'S SCHOOL. Otterburne, Manitoba, July. Write: Mrs. Sara Pasiciel, Winnipeg Bible College, Otterburne, Manitoba R0A 1G0.

Barbados

CARIBBEAN CHRISTIAN WRITER'S GUILD. Bridgetown, November. Write: William H. Almack, Box 239, Bridgetown, Barbados, West Indies.

◄CORRESPONDENCE COURSES►

If you are unable to attend one of the writer's conferences listed above, or if there is no writer's group in your area, you may want to sharpen your editorial skills and learn more about religious writing by enrolling in one of the following correspondence courses. With this kind of training you can proceed at your own pace, tailoring the courses to your needs.

CHRISTIAN WRITERS' FELLOWSHIP, PERSONALIZED STUDY PROGRAM. Joan Unger, founder and director. Write: Christian Writers' Fellowship, 5247 Abagail Drive, Spring Hill, FL 33526.

CHRISTIAN WRITERS' GUILD, "DISCOVER YOUR POSSIBILITIES IN WRITING." 48-lesson home study course. Norman B. Rohrer, director/instructor. Write: Christian Writers' Guild, 260 Fern Lane, Hume, CA 93628.

CHRISTIAN WRITERS' INSTITUTE. Five courses in three divisions. Robert Walker, director. Write: Sharon Grada, CWI Registrar, 396 East St. Charles Road, Wheaton, IL 60188.

◄CASSETTE TAPE LEARNING PROGRAMS►

Like other human beings, writers have five senses and can learn more by using as many as possible. Tape-recorded learning programs give you the advantage of listening as well as reading as you absorb information and instruction about how to become a more effective religious writer. In addition, with the tape under your control, you can listen whenever and as many times as you want. The following resources are available to the religious writer:

Cassettes of Writers' Conferences

Several of the writers' conferences listed above record tapes of lectures and workshop sessions and make them available for further study by the participants. Some, like the conference sponsored by the Christian Writer's Institute in Illinois, also make these tapes available to persons who were not at the conference.

Christian Writers' Guild Tapes

Six cassettes by Richard Armour, Sherwood E. Wirt, Margaret J. Anderson, and Norman B. Rohrer are available for $4.25 each. All six can be purchased for $19. Instruction to writers from these experienced persons are featured on the tapes. Order from Christian Writers' Guild, 260 Fern Lane, Hume, CA 93628.

The Christian Writers' Seminar

This home-study course of 10 cassettes with workbook, produced by Charlie Shedd and Floyd Thatcher, will give you step-by-step instruction on how to become an effective and successful writer. Write for details to: The Christian Writers' Seminar, P.O. Box 8682, Waco, TX 76710.

◄NEWSLETTERS AND MAGAZINES►

Another excellent way to keep in touch with other writers, receive regular news about markets and writing possibilities, and learn new skills from the experts is to subscribe to a publication designed for religious writers. Every writer should subscribe to at least one of these. You will find them very helpful and a stimulus to your continued progress.

CHRISTIAN AUTHOR NEWSLETTER, 396 East St. Charles Road, Wheaton, IL 60188, June Eaton, Editor. Published bimonthly, $2 per copy, $10 per year. Official organ of the Christian Writers' Institute.

CHRISTIAN WRITERS' NEWSLETTER, 300 East 34th Street (9C), New York, NY 10016. William H. Gentz, Editor and Publisher. Published bimonthly, $2 per copy, $10 per year.

CROSS & QUILL, 5247 Abagail Drive, Spring Hill, FL 33526, Joan Unger, Editor. Official bimonthly newsletter of the Christian Writers' Fellowship. Annual dues $18.

CURRENTS, Route 3, Box 393, Longview, TX 75603. Lee Longenecker, Editor. Quarterly newsletter of the Christian Writers' League of America. Membership $7 per year. *Channels,* a magazine published by the League two or three times a year, is also included in membership.

QUILL-O'-THE-WISP, 260 Fern Place, Hume, CA 93628. Norman B. Rohrer, Editor. Published quarterly for members of the Christian Writers' Guild. Annual membership $15.

THE CHRISTIAN WRITER, P.O. Box 5650, Lakeland, FL 33807. Thomas A. Noton, Editor/Publisher. A monthly magazine. $18 per year.

THE INKLING, P.O. Box 128, Alexandria, MN 56308. Marilyn Bailey, Editor, 1207 Dwane Street, South St. Paul, MN 55075. Monthly: $14 per year. One issue each year devoted to religious and inspirational writing.

◄BOOKS FOR RELIGIOUS WRITERS►

Books are among a writer's best friends. There is a core of reference books about writing that every writer will want to have, but the list below is confined to those that are published with the religious writer in mind.

A few of the titles listed are out of print, but we think every religious writer should be aware of them and may even be able to find them in some bookstores or borrow them from a friend or library.

Anderson, Margaret J., *The Christian Writer's Handbook*. New York: Harper and Row, Revised edition, 1983. 322 pages, $8.95. An exhaustive treatment of the craft with special attention to religious writers' needs, this is perhaps *the* classic in the field of how-to books for Christian writers, now in a new revised and enlarged edition.

Austin, Charles M., *Let the People Know*. Minneapolis: Augsburg Publishing House, 1975. 92 pages, $2.95. This media handbook for the local church covers the publishing of parish papers, bulletins, and the reporting of news in the local press as well as radio and TV publicity.

Aycock, Don M. and Goss, Leonard George, *Writing Religiously: A Guide to Writing Non-fiction Religious Books*. Milford, MI: Mott Media, 1984. 260 pages, $13.95. A writer and religious book editor collaborate to give direction to potential book writers on how to successfully write, market, and help with the sale and distribution of a religiously-oriented volume.

Bell, A. Donald and Merrill, John C., *Dimensions of Christian Writing*. Grand Rapids, MI: Zondervan Publishing House, 1970. 96 pages, paper. An examination of the qualities of effective Christian writing, covering semantics, credibility, and other characteristics.

Berg, Viola, *Pathways for the Poet*. Milford, MI: Mott Media, 1978. 234 pages, $9.95. An accomplished poet with more than 1,600 published poems provides this resource tool for the poet with emphasis on religiously-oriented writing.

Cox, James H., *Confessions of a Moonlight Writer*. Brentwood, TN: JM Productions, 1981. 97 pages, paper, $4.95. A church paper editor's guide to writing for the Christian market.

Duke, Judith S., *Religious Publishing and Communications*. White Plains, NY: Knowledge and Industry Publications, 1981. 272 pages. Facts and figures about the religious market useful to both writers and editors.

Folprecht, William, *Write the Word*. Milford, MI: Mott Media, 1976. 212 pages, paper, $4.95. This is a creative writing textbook that will provide inspiration, information, and instruction for the young journalism student. A combination of practical suggestions, personal examples, and anecdotes.

Gentz, William H., and other inspirational writers, *Writing to Inspire*. Cincinnati: Writer's Digest Books, 1982. 319 pages, $14.95. A guide to writing and publishing for the expanding religious market. Constructive insights and valuable tips from 30 leading writers on all aspects of religiously-oriented writing.

Hastings, Robert J., *How I Write: A Manual for Beginning Writers*. Nashville: Broadman Press, 1973. 157 pages, $3.95. An informative how-to book for the religious writer, filled with personal experiences and quotes from the experts, as well as long-established rules of writing.

Hensley, Dennis E., *The Freelancer: The Writer's Guide to Success*. Indianapolis: Poetic Press, 1984. $6.95. A general guide to freelancing, but highlighting inspirational writing by this popular speaker and leader at Christian writers' conferences and workshops.

Herr, Ethel, *An Introduction to Christian Writing*. Wheaton, IL: Tyndale House, 1983.

318 pages, $8.95. Written in a textbook style, this book gives basic instruction on the whole gamut of things a Christian writer needs to know, from research to final publishing, plus detailed and practical directions on the step-by-step process necessary for becoming a successful and published writer.

Klug, Ron, *How to Keep a Spiritual Journal.* Nashville: Thomas Nelson, Inc. $4.95. Directions on journal keeping, a practice that many religious writers feel is a help to writing from experience.

Kraft, Charles H., *Communication Theory for Christian Writers.* Nashville: Abingdon Press, 1983. $12.95. Introduces the reader to modern communication theory through the use of examples from modern life as well as the Bible.

McCarthy, David S., *Practical Guide for the Christian Writer.* Valley Forge, PA: Judson Press, 1983. 112 pages, paper, $7.95. A how-to book covering the whole process of writing and publishing from a successful author of books and curriculum material.

Moore, John A., *Write for the Religion Market.* Palm Springs, CA: ETC Publishers, 1981. 127 pages, $9.95. A practical how-to manual for writers dealing with news, feature, and article-writing based largely on personal experience.

Noton, Thomas A., *Getting Your Foot in the Editorial Door.* Lakeland, FL: TCW Marketing Group. 144 pages, paper, $7.95. An attempt, by the editor of a Christian writer's magazine and author of several books and articles, to promote understanding and eventual compromise between authors and editors.

Osteyee, Edith Filler, *Writing for Christian Publications.* Westport, CT: Greenwood Press, revised edition, 1969. 206 pages, $10.50. A classic textbook on the techniques of writing for Protestant church publications. Used by both religious journalism classes and denominational writing courses.

Schell, Mildred, *Wanted: Writers for the Christian Market.* Valley Forge, PA: Judson Press, 1975. 160 pages, paper, $4.95. An experienced author and teacher of writers gives guidance to writers; tips, guidelines, illustrations, and checklists make this a practical book.

Shedd, Charlie, *If I Can Write, You Can Write.* Cincinnati: Writer's Digest Books, 1984. 144 pages plus index, $12.95. One of America's most popular religious writers (with some 30 bestselling books) chats with potential writers about what makes him tick and what gives inspiration to his writing; filled with practical tips for every writer.

Spencer, Sue Nichols, *Words on Target: For Better Christian Communication.* Richmond: John Knox Press, 1964. 90 pages, paper, $2.95. A brisk guide to achieving clarity, simplicity, and strength of style in your writing.

Vaughn, Ruth, *Write to Discover Yourself,* New York: Doubleday/Galilee, 1980. $6.95. A thorough guide dealing with self-expression in writing through poetry, journals, prayer poems, reading card verse, etc.

Williams, Barbara, *Public Relations Handbook for Your Church.* Valley Forge, PA: Judson Press, 1985. 112 pages, paper, $7.95. A guidebook to publicity and public relations for the local congregation.

Wirt, Sherwood E., *Getting Into Print.* Nashville: Thomas Nelson, Inc., 1977. 132 pages, $2.95. Basic insights will broaden your horizons about Christian writing; this book came out of 15 years of teaching at Decision School of Christian Writing which Dr. Wirt directed, as well as other schools around the world.

Wirt, Sherwood E., *You Can Tell the World.* Minneapolis: Augsburg Publishing House, 1975. 128 pages, $3.50. The dean of Christian writing trainers writes in this book about the motivation behind Christian writing—"the effective spreading of God's Word through literature."

Wolseley, Roland E., *Careers in Religious Communications.* Scottdale, PA: Herald Press, third edition, 1977. 243 pages, paper, $4.95. The professor emeritus of religious journalism classes at Syracuse University gives information and help to those interested in establishing a career in religious journalism.

Zondervan Publishing House, *Zondervan Manual of Style for Authors, Editors, and Proofreaders.* Grand Rapids, MI: Zondervan, 1980, second edition. $3.50. One of the best of style manuals for religious houses and the basic book for many others.

·SEVEN·

Records & Files: Keeping Track of It All

by Geri Hess Mitsch, freelance writer, Aurora, Oregon

It may surprise you that some writers spend almost as much time on records and keeping track of markets as they do on writing. If you are going to be published, you must know *where* to sell as well as *how* to write. And the more you sell, the more important it is to establish and maintain good records, particularly business records. The IRS doesn't let you go free just because you're a freelance writer.

So let's talk about keeping track of manuscripts on their way to and from markets, recording the money coming in and going out, and the various files to set up.

If you haven't done so already, establish a filing system immediately. I've discovered many writers arrive independently at similar systems, and what is right for one is frustration for another. So tailor your recordkeeping to fit your needs and personality. Adopt, adapt, modify—until you're comfortable. *Remember, a file is for finding things, not storing them.*

◄MARKETS►

Knowing your markets means constant updating. Browse in bookstores. Watch for trends so you can write the right article at the right time, for the right editor. It keeps you from getting rejection slips that say, "We recently ran an article on this." Or, worse, "We don't use this type of material."

The *Religious Writer's Marketplace* and *Writer's Market* are your two main sources. Marking your potential markets with a Hi-Liter pen may prove satisfactory for a while, but eventually you'll want to go to a card file, which has several advantages. It can be:

1. filed alphabetically,
2. easily corrected when editors or policies change,
3. color-coded for categories or treatments,
4. added to, and
5. deleted from. However, I retain "ceased publication" cards in my file, dating and drawing a line through them. It serves as a doublecheck.

Using the magazine entries in this book and the *Writer's Market,* make up 4" by 6" (or 5" by 8") cards for present or potential markets. Use the same format each time, such as placing "Replies in——" at the same location. Add affiliations to give tips on slant and contents. *Pencil* in information to allow for easy changing of editors or policies.

Color-coding your favorite categories helps you spot cards faster: e.g., teens—green; devotional—blue. If you can't buy the right color card, merely color the tops of several at one time by overlapping five or six cards, each one about ¼ inch below the other, and swishing away with a wide-tipped felt pen. You can carry this same color scheme into your 8½" by 11" file folders, as explained later.

As a tremendous time-saver, and for only pennies a card, you can buy printed Master Market Cards. Then you just fill in the blanks. For information, send an SASE to: Writers Market Cards, P.O. Box 156, Aurora, OR 97002.

Instead of cards, you can chart your markets in a notebook, using a two-page spread. Use several sets, putting all children's magazines together, all Christian education magazines on another set, and so forth.

◄MANUSCRIPT INVENTORY►

Keeping track of what you have and where it is at all times, regardless of how many times you send it out, is absolutely necessary.

A card and file folder system helps you maintain a quick check on all manuscripts from idea through publication(s). Here's how it works.

Idea File

Capture those will o' the wisp ideas in 8½" by 11" file folders labeled under broad subject headings, collecting all those jottings you've made on backs of envelopes, paper napkins, and elsewhere. I color-code mine to correspond with my market cards: devotional ideas go in a blue folder.

Set up a 3" by 5" (or Rolodex) card file with these dividers: Queries, Works-in-Process, Mss. Out, and Mss. Sold. As an idea expands sufficiently, title a color-coded file folder for it and also type the title at the top of a 3" by 5" card. When you send the first query, enter the date, the publication, and the editor's name on the first line, leaving room for response. You'll want to keep in touch with friendly editors should they move to another magazine. File the card in the:

Query File

If rejected, add date and comments. On the next line, repeat the process for the next publication. When you get the go-ahead, add the date due and move the card to:

Works-in-Process File

This file will also have cards for manuscripts not requiring queries. Complete the manuscript, mail it, date the card, add publication sent to and move the card to:

Mss. Out File

This file has cards for all manuscripts currently in the mail. (Some writers have as many as 200 out at one time!) When a manuscript is sold, add the date, and the amount paid to the card. Study any changes the editor made in your manuscript. It's a wonderful way to improve your writing.

Now either (1) submit it to another publication, again adding date and publication on the card, and refile the card in Mss. Out File; or (2) move the card to:

Mss. Sold File

Keep cards in alphabetical order. If you change a title, make a cross-reference from the old to the new title. If manuscripts are sold but not paid for, keep a list in a notebook or in a section of your card file.

Meanwhile, each titled 8½" by 11" file folder has been filled with its carbons of query letters, correspondence, rough drafts, research notes, carbon of manuscripts when mailed, list of possible markets, tearsheets when published, fan mail, and rejection slips—unless you want to paper your room with them.

Some writers include, in this same folder, a history of submissions—the when, where, and what resulted, plus expenses and income for each story or article. Some jot this on the outside of the folder, crossing off the publication when the manuscript is sold or returned. Expenses are kept on the back of the folder. Others keep records inside the folder, tracking the IN and OUT journeys for the manuscript. File folders are arranged in one alphabet or in broad categories: all adult fiction together, and so forth. Still others set up the four sections as outlined above, shifting the folder as the manuscript moves from Query to Mss. Sold.

◄FINANCIAL FILES◄

If balancing a checkbook is as difficult for you as scaling Mt. Everest, be willing to learn to keep financial records. They are imperative.

Keep them simple yet adequate. Be consistent and accurate. That takes self-discipline.

As your income increases, so will your problems of reporting to the IRS. Seek professional help. A financial adviser, such as an accountant, usually saves you more money than the fees charged. This expert, whose fee is deductible, will help you set up a proper bookkeeping ledger and journal; keep track of changing tax laws; advise you about such things as amortization, depreciation, and investment tax credits; expenses in connection with a legitimate home office; and filing Tax Form C for small businesses.

Your careful records, verified with the receipts and cancelled checks you've religiously saved, will reduce the aspirins come tax-filing time.

Until then, you can use a simple Cash Disbursements system for all checks and petty cash. Purchase an eight-columnar expenditure book (or sheets if you prefer notebooks) at a variety or office discount store. Assign headings appropriate to your needs, such as: Postage; Books and Magazines; Office Supplies; Typing/Copying; Dues and Workshop Fees; Telephone; Transportation; Miscellaneous. *Every day*—consistency is a must—enter all expenditures and income, distributing each item properly. Pay by check if possible. When your income justifies it, open a separate checking account. Until then, plainly mark all checks and check stubs with a code such as "W" for writing. Mark each invoice with the check number and date of payment.

For small petty cash, such as a few stamps, write a check to "Petty Cash," for example, $25.00. Cash this and keep the money *separate* from your personal money, in an envelope. Each time you spend money from it, fill out a cash slip, recording the date, the item purchased, and the amount. Or write this information on the envelope each time. Keep receipts in the envelope.

Track long-distance calls by recording them on the date made, along with the person's name and number. Fill in charges when the bill arrives.

At the end of each month, total each column in your Cash Disbursements Journal, using a colored pencil. Balance these against your checkbook and Petty Cash records. Skip a few lines and begin entries for the next month.

Every month, or at least every quarter, transfer monthly totals to a separate summary page. By sub-totaling each quarter, you have an up-to-date financial picture. At the end of the year, total annual expenditures and income for tax purposes.

◄ADDITIONAL FILES◄

As you advance in your writing profession, there are other files you will want to set up. Some, like the Up File and Tickler File, will increase your efficiency. Others chart your progress. Or make comparisons among similar markets. Or provide a lift for your spirits when you leaf through your published works.

Tickler or Up File

Tickle your memory to do what needs to be done when you need to do it.

You can use a calendar or a weekly reminder from a stationery store, but a more versatile system is a Tickler or Up File.

Label twelve (8½'' by 11'') file folders January through December. During the year, drop items into the proper folder. An announcement of a March writer's conference would go in the January file for future consideration. The carbon of a letter about a payment due would go in the following month's folder.

Near the end of each month, pull the next month's folder. Schedule the jobs to be done throughout that month, then rotate the file to the back, bringing the next month's file "UP" front. This system helps you keep track of such things as seasonal submission deadlines for seasonal articles and when to politely jog the memory of an editor who "Replies in two months."

Guidelines and Sample Copies

Guidelines of how manuscripts should be submitted need to be updated. Send for new guidelines when an editor changes or pick up fresh guidelines at writers' conferences. I like to date mine and file them alphabetically, turning 8½'' by 11'' sheets sideways and printing the magazine name in the upper right-hand corner. You can file guidelines by broad subject headings, color-coded to match your markets. It's helpful to write "Sample Copy" when you get one. Some writers file the sample copies and guidelines together.

Your Published Works File

Start this file with your first published manuscript. If it is in a portion of a book, make a copy, and file it together with the tearsheets taken from the magazines that the editors send you when your articles appear.

    1. Arrange chronologically between plastic sheets in a three-ring binder. (You've arrived when it takes a new binder each year!)

    2. File alphabetically in a folder, or file in its folder along with query letters, carbon of manuscript, and other materials as explained previously.

Seasonal Submissions File

Set up a color code for each holiday, such as green for Christmas and yellow for Easter. Counting back to the proper month, e.g., *September,* for "Submit seasonal material three months in advance," type a green card: "SEPTEMBER. CHRISTMAS (3 mo.)." Add the names of all "three months in advance" magazines as you come to them. Repeat for other time limits and holidays. Interfile by months.

Tally Records

You may want to keep a tally of the number of times you've sold to a particular magazine.

    Solo III

    The Upper Room ЛНТ I

Some writers put all titles submitted on the back of their Market File card. Others keep a separate file for this history of sales and submissions to a particular publication.

Permissions Record File

    1. File the terms, details, and payments for all permissions granted you to quote copyrighted material.

    2. File copies of permissions you have given, and the terms agreed upon.

Book Reviews

Maintain a clipping file of all reviews of your books. If a clipping is not available, make a photocopy, including the title of the publication, date, and page number in which the review appeared.

◄INDEXES►

I: *Periodicals and Publications*
II: *Publishers and Organizations*
III: *Denominations and Faith Groups*
IV: *Subjects*

The following four indexes are planned to help the user gain maximum benefit from the information contained in this book. Each of the indexes has its own plan and intended use in the search for the proper markets for religious writing.

Index I is an alphabetical list of all the periodicals and publications described in the seven chapters of this book. In it are to be found not only the periodicals described in Chapters Two and Four, but also other publications described in Chapter Five, "Branching Out," and Chapter Six, "Getting Help."

Index II does essentially the same service for the reader looking for publishers, organizations, and other groups, both religious and secular, engaged in publishing or in aiding writers of religious material.

Index III groups both publications and publishers by denominational or faith group sponsorship. Thus the reader is able to find any entry in the book under a particular religious group's name. An index of Jewish periodicals and publishers, though, would be largely redundant in this place, as these are contained almost exclusively in Chapter Four. The reader is advised to go straight to pages 130–40 (periodicals) and 141–51 (publishers) for an alphabetical listing of these names. Special-interest areas to writers for the Jewish market are, however, included under the cross-denominational subject headings in Index IV.

Index IV will perhaps be the one you use most. Both periodicals and publishers are listed in it, grouped under headings that describe the subject material or audience those publishers seek. In using this index, be aware that many publishers other than those listed under each heading use similar material on any subject. Entries under each heading are included because the publisher or editor made special mention of some subject or audience in the report received by the author and editors of this book.

INDEX I
◄PERIODICALS AND PUBLICATIONS◄

(See also additional periodicals listed under regional publications and other specialized periodicals in Chapter 5.)

INDEX II
◄PUBLISHERS AND ORGANIZATIONS►
(See also lists of publishers under specific kinds of writing in Chapter 5.)

INDEX III
◄DENOMINATIONS AND FAITH GROUPS◄
(National groups involved in publishing and groups at whom publications are aimed.)

Assemblies of God

PERIODICALS:

Advance, 16
At Ease, 20
HiCall, 51
High Adventure, 51
Live, 59
Men's Ministries, 65
Mountain Movers, 67
Pentecostal Evangel, 73
Sunday School Counselor, 85
Woman's Touch, 93
Youth Leader, 96

PUBLISHER:

Gospel Publishing, 111

Baptist, American

PERIODICALS:

Baptist Leader, 20
Baptist World, 20

PUBLISHER:

Judson Press, 113

Baptist, Southern

PERIODICALS:

Christian Single, 30
Church Media, 32
Church Musician, 33
Church Recreation, 33

Baptist, Other

Brethren Churches

Catholic

Christian Missionary Alliance

Christian Churches

PERIODICALS:

Advent Christian Witness, 17
Alive! for Young Teens, 17
Christian Standard, 30
Disciple, 40
Forerunner, 46
Vista, 91

PUBLISHER:

CBP Press, 105

Church of Christ

PERIODICALS:

Firm Foundations, 46
Quality Publications, 77

Churches of God

PERIODICALS:

Bible Advocate, 20
Christian Adventurer, 25
Christian Leadership, 28
Church Advocate, 31
Church of God Evangel, 33
Gem, 48
Gospel Carrier, 49
Lighted Pathway, 58
Vital Christianity, 92

PUBLISHER:

Warner, 126

Church of the Nazarene

PERIODICALS:

Discovery, 41
Enduring Word, 42
Herald of Holiness, 51
Listen, 59
One, 70
Preacher's Magazine, 74
Standard, 83
Teens Today, 86
Together Time, 88

PUBLISHER:

Beacon Hill Press, 103

Covenant Church

PERIODICAL:

Covenant Companion, 37

Episcopal/Anglican

PERIODICALS:

Anglican Theological Review, 19
Canadian Churchman, 23
Cathedral Age, 23
Christian Challenge, 26
Episcopalian, 43
Episcopal Recorder, 43
Living Church, 59
St. Luke's Journal, 79
Witness, 93

PUBLISHERS:

Morehouse–Barlow, 116
Winston/Seabury, 127

REGIONAL PAPERS: 158–62

Evangelical Free Church

PERIODICAL:

Evangelical Beacon, 44

Evangelical Orthodox Church

PERIODICAL:

Again, 17

Fellowship of Christian Assemblies

PERIODICAL:

Conviction, 36

Foursquare Gospel Church

PERIODICAL:

Foursquare World Advance, 47

Jewish

See Jewish periodicals lists on pages 130–40 and publishers of Judaica on pages 141–51 as well as Jewish subjects in Index IV.

Seventh-Day Adventist

PERIODICALS:

Guide, 50
Liberty, 57
Our Little Friend, 71
Primary Treasure, 75
Signs of the Times, 80

PUBLISHERS:

Pacific Press, 119
Review and Herald, 122

Spiritualist

PERIODICAL: *Metapsychology,* 66

United Church of Canada

PERIODICAL:

United Church Observer, 89

PUBLISHER:

Canec, 105

INDEX IV
◄SUBJECTS►

(Periodicals and publishers listed under the entries in this index publish material for a readership interested in that subject. See also entries under specific types of publishing in Chapter 5.)

Academic
    Abingdon, 100; Augsburg, 102; Eerdmans, 109; Fortress, 109; Harper and Row, 111; Intervarsity, 113; Libra, 114; Oxford, 118; Princeton, 121; Westminster, 126; Zondervan, 128. Jewish: *Jewish Quarterly Review,* 135; Harvard, 144. *See also* Scholars, Theology.
African Religions
    Branden Press, 105
Archeology
    Biblical Archeologist, 21
Athletics
    Athletes in Action, 20; *Campus Life,* 22; *Sharing the Victory,* 80; *Working for Boys,* 94
Biblical Studies
    Advent Christian Witness, 17; *Bible Newsletter,* 21; *Biblical Archeologist,* 21; *Brethren Evangelist,* 22; *Catholic Biblical Quarterly,* 23; *Discipleship Journal,* 41; *Foursquare Advance,* 47; *Glad,* 48; *His,* 51; *Interpretation,* 54; *Lutheran Woman's Quarterly,* 63; *New Wine,* 69; *One,* 70; *Our Sunday Visitor,* 71; *Pentecostal Evangel,* 73; *Preacher's Magazine,* 74; *Pulpit Helps,* 76; *Quality,* 77; *Quiet,* 77; *Scope,* 79; *Shining Star,* 80; *Signs of the Times,* 80; *Small Group Letter,* 81; *Today's Single,* 88. Aglow, 100; Augsburg, 102; Baker, 102; Bethany, 103; Brethren, 104; Christian Schools, 106; Cook, 107; Doubleday, 109; Eerdmans, 109; Franciscan, 110; Gospel, 111; Harvest House, 112; Intervarsity, 113; Lamb, 114; Liturgical, 115; Loizeaux, 115; Moody, 115; Morehouse–Barlow, 116; Mott Media, 116; Multnomah, 117; New Leaf, 118; Oxford, 118; Pelican, 119; Prentice–Hall, 120; Randall, 121; Shaw, 124; Tyndale, 125; Welch, 126; Word, 127. Jewish: Adama, 141; Behrman, 141; Bloch, 142; Cambridge, 142; Fortress, 144; Hebrew Union, 145; Prometheus, 147; Rossel, 147; Union of Congregations, 149
Biography
    Allnut, 101; Christian Classics, 106; Creation, 108; Crossroad, 108; Giniger, 110; Nelson–Hall, 117; Steiner, 125. *See also* several of the publishers of Judaica on pages 141-50.